CODE POLITICS

CODE POLITICS
Campaigns and Cultures on the Canadian Prairies

Jared J. Wesley

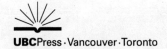
UBCPress · Vancouver · Toronto

21 20 19 18 17 16 15 14 13 12 11   5 4 3 2 1

Printed in Canada on FSC-certified ancient-forest-free paper
(100% post-consumer recycled) that is processed chlorine- and acid-free.

Library and Archives Canada Cataloguing in Publication

Wesley, Jared J., 1980-
    Code politics : campaigns and cultures on the Canadian Prairies / Jared J. Wesley.

Includes bibliographical references and index.
ISBN 978-0-7748-2074-5 (bound); ISBN 978-0-7748-2075-2 (pbk.)

    1. Political culture – Alberta. 2. Political culture – Saskatchewan. 3. Political culture – Manitoba. 4. Alberta – Politics and government. 5. Saskatchewan – Politics and government. 6. Manitoba – Politics and government. 7. Political culture – Prairie Provinces. 8. Prairie Provinces – Politics and government. I. Title.

FC3239.P6W48 2011   971.2   C2010-907871-3

e-book ISBNs: 978-0-7748-2076-9 (pdf); 978-0-7748-2077-6 (epub)

Canadä

UBC Press gratefully acknowledges the financial support for our publishing program of the Government of Canada (through the Canada Book Fund), the Canada Council for the Arts, and the British Columbia Arts Council.

This book has been published with the help of a grant from the Canadian Federation for the Humanities and Social Sciences, through the Aid to Scholarly Publications Program, using funds provided by the Social Sciences and Humanities Research Council of Canada.

Printed and bound in Canada by Friesens
Set in Futura Condensed and Warnock by Artegraphica Design Co. Ltd.
Text design: Irma Rodriguez
Copy editor: Lesley Erickson

UBC Press
The University of British Columbia
2029 West Mall
Vancouver, BC V6T 1Z2
www.ubcpress.ca

To my teachers

Contents

Foreword

NELSON WISEMAN

The commonalities and diversities of the Prairie provinces have intrigued historians, sociologists, and political scientists. Modernization theorists expected that technological revolutions in communications, advances in transportation networks, and an increasingly mobile populace would erode the significance of political borders, wear away regional identities, and undermine distinctive provincial discourses. Yet, the remarkably particularistic political cultures within the containerized vertical territorial lines of the Prairie provinces endure and resist corrosion. No unidirectional movement toward an unbounded, regionally integrated, consolidated prairie political ethos is evident. To be sure, horizontally crosscutting cleavages, such as social class, gender, age, and ethnicity exist on the Prairies – the poor in Alberta, Saskatchewan, and Manitoba face similar issues as do the First Nations, youth, women, and visible minorities of those provinces. However, the distinctive provincial milieus of those groups trump their shared concerns and conditions when one listens to the tone and temper of provincial politics in the three jurisdictions. Provincially idiosyncratic timbres are unmistakable and have become sharpened with time.

Sociologists and anthropologists usually gravitate to thinking about federal states and their sub-national units such as provinces as institutional manifestations of social diversity and cultural heterogeneity. Such a culture-centric orientation highlights social forces and underplays the power that a polity's formal, legally established structures exert in sculpting society. The causal arrow between institutions and society, of course, points both ways: governments and political parties reflect and shape their societies just as those societies inform the idiomatic language adopted by political parties, leaders, and governments in search of popularity. Ideally positioned for the task, political scientists appreciate how provincial governments and the parties and leaders who command them are not merely epiphenomena of their societies or echoes of their cultures. Once formed, governments use their jurisdictional supremacy and their institutional infrastructures – laws, bureaucracies, cabinets, budgets – to affirm their autonomy, assert their authority, and embed their status in the minds of their populace. At the same time, to be successful, political parties must advantageously lever the distinctive symbols and characteristic vocabularies of their provinces. In tracing the interconnected and interwoven circular relationship between agency – what people and parties say and do – and structure, Jared Wesley underscores agency as his central point.

The literatures on Manitoba, Saskatchewan, and Alberta suffer no dearth of treatment of their political personalities, social and economic forces, and the dynamics of election campaigns. Most of the available analyses are specific to a province. Wesley's salutary contribution is to disentangle in a comparative perspective the "Prairie paradox" of the three provinces whose partisan traditions differ so dramatically. He presents leaders and party manifestos as moulders of the "public mood," focusing on party platforms rather than on personalities, social forces, or campaign dynamics. Successful leaders and parties harness, direct, and redirect existing elements in the political culture. Wesley systematically searches out, identifies, and exposes the key values that have driven politics in each of the provinces. No simple enterprise; he brings a nuanced disposition and a sophisticated approach to the undertaking.

To decipher the differences among the structures of competition in the Prairie provincial party systems, Wesley grapples with the ideational environment of politics. His measured and rhythmic analysis coherently and cogently deploys the language of "codes" to highlight the individual provinces' contrasting partisan and ideological traditions. He demonstrates how the lexicon of Prairie politics varies among the three provinces to enrich our understanding of each province's distinctive political discourse. An example is the dissimilarity of the quite different utopian visions of the ideal society that have informed successful parties' campaigns in Alberta and Saskatchewan. Those visions, in turn, are contrasted with a political code that offers relative moderation and temperance – that conveyed by Manitoba's parties.

The broad terms and ideas Wesley spots, such as "freedom," "security," and "moderation," of course, are notoriously elastic, but he deftly traces their deployment over the decades.

Wesley's survey of the political codes of the Prairies since the 1930s covers substantial ground. It offers some potent comparative insights regarding, for example, the penchant of Alberta's dominant parties to locate their opposition as outsiders, the tendency of Saskatchewan's successful regimes to internalize within their province their community's conflicts, and the ability and preference of Manitoba's major parties to minimize their ideological tensions.

Wesley illustrates the sustained thrusts of the particular provincial political codes while dissecting the broad rhetorical themes of successful parties' platforms regardless of their temporal context. The adoption of these codes and their cross-generational transmission has not precluded their adaptation to changing conditions. Weaving together primary and secondary sources, Wesley buttresses his ideational framework with archival materials to explain why parties have won power and lost it. To his credit, he appreciates that alternative explanations are possible and many additional factors in addition to a community's political norms are at play. He offers readers a suggestive thesis and is not insistent about causality for he understands well that codes are flexible, contingent factors that are always at play, and that any mechanical, path-dependent analysis is limited. Skilfully organized, well-written, and demonstrating scholarly competence and intellectual agility, Wesley's account marshals the evidence of his research findings clearly, intelligibly, and logically to draw his conclusions.

This book contributes to demystifying the Prairie paradox of geographically adjacent provinces whose residents have such different subjective political proclivities. Those dispositions are yoked to particular worldviews of the nature of society and the proper role of government. The variety and persistence of ideologically distinctive Prairie political creeds has rendered the Prairies as a fertile region of the mind and the launch pad for so many political parties – the Progressives, the CCF, Social Credit, and Reform – that have burst forth from the region onto the broader national stage.

Acknowledgments

Having lived, studied, and travelled throughout the Canadian prairies, I am still amazed at how different political life is in Alberta, Saskatchewan, and Manitoba. There is a running joke in my family. If you fall asleep while making the drive from Edmonton to Winnipeg, there's one sure way of telling where you are when you wake up. If you look out the window and see an oil derrick or a cowboy, you're likely in Alberta. If you see a farmer at the wheel of a grain truck, stopped at a traffic light, you're probably in Regina. If you see a lonely person standing on a hill wearing a Winnipeg Jets cap, you know you've left Saskatchewan and entered Manitoba. There's truth in most humour. In the grand scheme of things, there is little to distinguish the three Prairie provinces – except when it comes to oil and cowboys, grain and farmers, hills and hockey fans, and politics. In my pursuit of explanations, I have accumulated many debts. To those I have missed and thanked previously, I ask for your forgiveness.

Some portions of this book were presented at the following meetings and conferences: the meeting of the Midwest Political Science Association and the Duff Roblin Fellowship Conference in 2008, the meetings of the Prairie Political Science Association and the Canadian Political Science Association in 2009, and the meeting of the Western Canadian Studies Association and the Umea Partnership Conference in 2010. This book benefitted greatly from those discussions.

Financial support for the Prairie Manifesto Project was provided by the Carl O. Nickel Fund for Western Canadian Studies (2005) and a doctoral scholarship from the Social Sciences and Humanities Research Council of Canada (SSHRC). Funding for research assistance was provided through University of Calgary Undergraduate Research Awards and the University of Manitoba Research Grants Program.

This book was written when I was in the Department of Political Science at the University of Calgary, and it was polished as I served on faculty at the Department of Political Studies, University of Manitoba. Both venues provide ideal, supportive environments for young scholars. Several people at the University of Calgary deserve much credit for ensuring that this study is both rich in content and methodologically rigorous. Special thanks are due to Keith Archer and Nelson Wiseman for their inspiration, advice, and encouragement and to Brenda O'Neill and Lisa Young for their patience and unwavering commitment to the pursuit of knowledge. I am also grateful for the friendship, support, and guidance of my colleagues Andrew Banfield, David Coletto, Gemma Collins, Catharine Dunlop, Scott Fitzsimmons, Steve Hobbs, Erika Ing, Michael Jensen, Kiera Ladner, Steve Lecce, Fiona Macdonald, George MacLean, Judi Powell, Andrea Rounce, David Smith, Kim Speers, David Stewart, Ella Wensel, Evan Wilson, and Mike Zekulin. This book is also the product of my mentorship under Diane Gray and Jim Eldridge and the camaraderie of Richard Neill.

Much thanks is also due to the many librarians, archivists, party members, and officials who helped me locate party platforms. This project would not have been possible without their enthusiasm and assistance. I am grateful to Emmett Scrimshaw for assistance with the Prairie Manifesto Project and to Emmet Collins for his diligence in copy-editing and preparing the index. Emily Andrew and Holly Keller, my editors; Lesley Erickson, my copy editor; and others at UBC Press made the publication process an enjoyable and efficient one. I also appreciated the guidance of the anonymous reviewers, whose intimate knowledge of Prairie politics helped to refine my own interpretations.

My greatest debts are owed to my family. To my aunts and cousins throughout the West, I owe many comfortable nights' sleep while on research trips. To my parents, I owe my passion for learning, my love of the Prairies, and my fortunate ability to combine both into a rewarding career. To my wife, Jamie, I owe my sanity, grounding, and sense of purpose. My life would be incomplete without her love and support. (This indulgence included moving to Winnipeg with a man who is "not a real doctor.")

No amount of writing, research, or thanks can repay these people and the many more to whom I owe so much. But I'll spend the rest of my life trying.

CODE POLITICS

Introduction
Cultures, Campaigns, and Codes

When it comes to their political cultures, residents of the Canadian prairies have long lived in remarkably separate political worlds. Throughout much of its history, Alberta has been considered the bastion of Canadian conservatism. Saskatchewan, to the east, is widely viewed as the cradle of Canadian social democracy, while Manitoba is home to the country's most temperate political climate. Alberta tilts right, Saskatchewan tilts left, and Manitoba maintains a relative balance between these forces. Perceptions of these cultural distinctions have persisted for over a century – despite decades of social, economic, and political change. The question is how? – for by most accounts the three Prairie provinces should not be that different. Random lines of latitude were chosen to divide them, making each province an entirely territorial and political creation (Archer 1980, 21). Across their borders, Alberta, Saskatchewan, and Manitoba rest on broadly similar geographical, social, economic, and institutional foundations. Stretching from Ontario's Canadian Shield in the east to the Rocky Mountains in the west, the economies of all three provinces are grounded firmly in export-based natural resource industries and, most recently, a burgeoning tertiary sector (Howlett 2006). Moreover, throughout most of their history, the three political systems have rested on common federal, Westminster parliamentary institutions and on plurality-based electoral systems. Considering these many parallels, the political diversity found on the Canadian prairies is vexing.

The persistence of this diversity is equally puzzling. Advances in technology suggest most communication or transportation barriers were lowered long ago. Migration has been made easier not only through enhanced air and ground travel but also through improvements to labour market mobility. All the while, the three provinces continue to draw newcomers from throughout Canada and around the globe. Ultimately, the three cultures are not as isolated, or insulated, as they once might have been.

This puzzle constitutes the Prairie paradox, to which the following chapters are addressed. Considering they were divided rather arbitrarily just over a century ago, and considering they share so many other socio-economic and institutional features in common, how could Manitoba, Saskatchewan, and Alberta develop into three worlds "thriving in the bosom of a single region?" (Smith 1976, 46). More specifically, given decades of development, how have the three distinct political cultures that emerged in the early twentieth century survived to this day?

Existing literature offers few solutions to this puzzle. This is not to say scholars have ignored political culture on the Prairies. Students of Canadian politics are indebted to W.L. Morton, Seymour Martin Lipset, C.B. Macpherson, Nelson Wiseman, Doug Francis, Gerald Friesen, and others whose research has revealed the impact of early immigration, historical economic developments, and critical events on the formative years of each province. Precisely *why* these different political cultures have survived – how century-old settlement patterns continue to influence the politics of each province – remains largely unexplained, however. We know how the three Prairie provinces started down separate cultural paths, but we know less about why these routes remained parallel, as opposed to crossing or converging. We know a lot about the origins and diversity of the three Prairie political cultures, but we know precious little about their continuity.

In this sense, *Code Politics* takes a modest, but significant, step toward solving the Prairie paradox. Specifically, this book explores the role that leading parties have played in perpetuating the differences between the political cultures of Alberta, Saskatchewan, and Manitoba. In this study, election campaigns are treated as rituals that offer dominant political actors the opportunity to renew their communities' core values every four years. By analyzing their campaign literature, the study asks, can an examination of dominant party rhetoric help us to understand how the three Prairie political cultures have persisted over time? That is, can we find evidence of Alberta's conservative ethos in the campaign themes developed by Social Credit and the Progressive Conservatives? Is the persistence of Saskatchewan's social democratic political culture attributable, in any sense, to the discourse cultivated by its natural governing party, the CCF-NDP (Co-operative Commonwealth Federation–New Democratic Party)? And have Manitoba's cultural traditions of temperance and modesty been sustained, in part, by the narrative constructed by the province's various Liberal-Progressive, Progressive Conservative, and New Democratic parties?

Grounded in a systematic analysis of hundreds of campaign artifacts from across the region and throughout the past seven decades, the answer is yes. Through their rhetoric, leading political parties have translated their respective political cultures into a series of unique and persistent campaign themes or codes. In Alberta, this has meant emphasizing notions of freedom, drawing on the American liberal concepts of individualism, populism, and autonomy. By contrast, Saskatchewan's dominant parties have played on the theme of security, including references to the collectivism, dirigisme, and polarization found in the British Labourite tradition. Meanwhile, Manitoba's leading parties have emphasized more moderate notions such as progressive centrism, pragmatism, and transpartisanship, harkening back to the values imported by the province's original Tory-touched liberal fragment. Each of these themes constitutes a unique code of political discourse that has transmitted and reinforced certain core values over time, thus helping to sustain the conservative nature of Alberta politics, Saskatchewan's social democratic ethos, and the mentalité of moderation in Manitoba.

While it is by no means a silver-bullet solution, any explanation of the evolution of political culture on the Canadian prairies must take into account the critical role of dominant political parties in sustaining the three different political worlds found within the region. Political cultures are not simply institutionalized into the formal apparatus of the state or automatically socialized into society at the grassroots level, although both of these components are also critical (see Chapter 2). Nor are political cultures mysteriously transmitted over time by some hidden hand. An examination of election platforms and manifestos reveals a primary carrier: political cultures are actively promoted, transmuted, and transmitted by dominant political parties.

Unravelling the evolution of the Prairie paradox requires a firm understanding of the terms *political culture* and *political codes*.

Political Culture

For decades, scholars have struggled to define *political culture*, a term that has been called popular, seductive, and controversial (Elkins and Simeon

1979, 127-28). The concept itself is by no means novel. In writing about the differences between the customs, mores, and habits of nineteenth-century Americans and Europeans, Alexis de Tocqueville was one of the first modern students of political culture. According to his account of democracy in America (1988 [1848], 434), "for society to exist, and even more, for society to prosper, it is essential that all the minds of the citizens should always be rallied and held together by some leading ideas; and that could never happen unless each of them sometimes came to draw his opinions from the same source and was ready to accept some belief ready made." Since that time, political culture has come to be associated with a wide range of topics, from political values and ideology to national character or "civic religion." Indeed, a survey of the literature in anthropology, sociology, history, and political science reveals a bewildering number of definitions (for reviews, see Chilton 1988; Harrison 2000; Formisano 2001; Johnson 2003).

Based on the core conceptualization of the term, however, the present study treats political culture as a set of common political values and assumptions that underpin a given political system.[1] Political culture is a collection of often unspoken assumptions and axioms that remain buried barely below the surface of political life in a given community (Bell and Tepperman 1979, 5). Defining political culture as a series of subjective propensities distinguishes it from the more explicit and contested *ideology* (Almond and Powell 1966, 24). What makes studying political culture so challenging is that there is no single book or tract, author or philosopher to which students may turn to find a definition of a community's culture. Indeed, a polity's guiding values are embodied in its shared rituals and symbols, entrenched in its institutions, echoed in the attitudes of its residents, reflected in the behaviour of its political actors, and illustrated in its general style of politics (Elazar 1994, 9; Hofstadter 1966). This fact has challenged analysts to discern ways of measuring a community's political culture.

To some, political culture is little more than a prevailing political ideology – one shared by, or at least one that governs, the political life of the community (see Kornberg, Mishler, and Clarke 1982, 53-58; Wilson 1992). The relationship between political culture and ideology is more complicated, however. Although there may be parallels between a particular ideology and a given political culture – for instance, Alberta's political culture is often labelled conservative, Saskatchewan's, socially democratic – the two concepts are not conceptually synonymous. As Bell suggests, "From the outset, political culture was intended as a broader concept with wider application than ideology. Political culture involves the study of all segments of society, including members of the general public whose ideas about politics are insufficiently coherent and programmatic to be called ideological. Moreover a single political culture could comprise several ideologies" (Bell 2000, 279). Along these lines, Wiseman (2007, 13-14) captures the primary distinction between cultures and ideologies: "Ideologies or political philosophies may be defined, dissected and debated at a metaphysical level without reference to a specific group, society, or nation. Culture is no less a mental construct than is ideology. It, however, cannot be explored solely on a theoretical plane, for it refers to real and specific groups, societies or nations."

In addition to being a prism through which outsiders view a given society, political culture is a lens through which a specific community views itself and the world around it (Laitin 1986, 12-17; Merelman 1991, 53). The culture helps to identify problems or challenges, and it defines the limits of acceptability in terms of their solutions (Edelman 1964, 31-41; Wilson 1992, 11). In other words, "If a person acts on the assumptions which are widely shared in his collectivity, he will 'pass' as a legitimate political actor. An 'outsider' who holds quite different views on the nature of the political game, on proper modes of conduct, and on goals and strategies will be identifiable as a deviant; he will not 'pass'" (Elkins and Simeon 1979, 127-28).

This holistic definition of political culture varies from several others in the discipline, most notably that of the psycho-cultural or Civic Culture school (for reviews of this distinction, see Stewart 2002; Bell 2000; Merelman 1991, 36-58). Headmasters Almond and Verba (1963, 1980) define a political culture in terms of its residents' cognitive, affective, and evaluative orientations toward the political system. To them, culture is an aggregation or average of individuals' beliefs and opinions (Verba 1980, 402). Because different patterns of orientations exist cross-nationally, a particular type of political culture does not coincide strictly with any single, given political system (Almond 1956, 396). (Civic, parochial, participant, and other types of culture exist throughout the world, for instance.)

Despite the popularity of the psycho-cultural understanding of political culture (Stewart 2002, 26), a different theoretical approach is presented in this study for several reasons. First, as Durkheim argues, culture is more than simply the sum of individual predispositions; rather, it lies in the broader social structure – what he terms the *conscience collectif* of a society or the "repository of common sentiments, a well-spring from which individual conscience draws its moral sustenance" (Durkheim 1965 [1897], 16). By the same token, a community's political culture – by definition, its shared values and norms – is more than a simple aggregation of individuals' beliefs or behaviours (Pye 1973, 72; Clark 1962, 214). Many feel Almond and Verba fall victim to false aggregation, reductionism, or the individualistic fallacy (Formisano 2001; Scheuch 1968). Just as researchers cannot use macro-level data (e.g., census statistics) to make valid inferences about micro-level actors (e.g., individual residents of a census district), they cannot do the reverse. In short, as Johnson (2003, 99) argues, analysts "gain little by treating the distribution of 'orientations' among a population as 'political culture' rather than, for example, simply as a 'mass belief system' or, more prosaically still, as 'public opinion.'"

Second, political culture is less transitory than public opinion (Bell and Tepperman 1979, 4-5). Just as descriptions of the weather offer us only limited glimpses into the climate of a particular community, one-off surveys of individual residents offer us only momentary glimpses of a community's beliefs and orientations. Wiseman (1986, 31) concurs, noting that the definition of *culture* as an aggregation of individual attitudes misconstrues the term's true meaning, which is fundamentally cross-generational.

For these reasons, the present study takes a more holistic approach to political culture. This is not to say that Almond and Verba's approach is entirely invalid. Although it may be misused as an indicator, their methodology is valuable in terms of measuring the reflection of political culture in individual attitudes (Rosenbaum 1975, 121-28). As it is defined in this book, however, political culture has less in common with the social psychology of individuals than the historical analysis of communities (Shiry 1978, 51).

The macroscopic approach used in this study carries with it some disadvantages. Critics have a valid point when they suggest it emphasizes cultural exceptionalism rather than true comparison. By analyzing the unique values and beliefs that distinguish Alberta from Saskatchewan and Manitoba, for instance, analysts may gloss over many important commonalities among its residents, not to mention diversity among them (Ellis and Coyle 1994, 2). Others are correct to note the tautology involved in many studies of political culture *cum* community character. If culture can be found in everything, it explains nothing (Harrison 2000, xv). Given these potential pitfalls, it is tempting to abandon the study of political culture altogether (Stewart 1994a, 5). Yet the persistence of obvious differences in the guiding value systems of different polities raises important questions for social scientific inquiry. "Accordingly," writes Stewart (ibid.), "interpretive caution and methodological pluralism would seem to be the most appropriate ways to cope with the complexities intrinsic to any political culture analysis."

A comprehensive, primary investigation of the political culture of each province is well beyond the scope of this study. Such a study would require in-depth field research into the symbols that underpin the various provincial communities. This research would likely involve a combination of focus groups, public interviews, direct observation, artifact analysis, examinations of popular culture, and other modes of ethnographic inquiry (Stewart 2002, 31-32; see also Chilton 1988; Merelman 1991). To be thorough, it would also require the examination of a wide variety of sources: "historical accounts, critical interpretations of literature and other creative arts, social scientists' quantitative analyses and qualitative studies of institutions such as religion, law, and government" (Lipset 1990, xiv; see also Putnam 2000, 26-27). Given the magnitude of this task, such investigations must await further resources. Instead, the present analysis draws on an extensive review of existing literature to define the content of each provincial political culture. Based on a strong consensus among Prairie scholars, it accepts the existence of three distinct cultures in the region as the basis of the research problem under investigation.

Admittedly, there are perils associated with this approach; chief among them, there may be a disjunction between what the three Prairie political cultures actually are and what prevailing academic wisdom reports them to be. If Stewart's (1994b; 2002, 33-34) examination of contemporary Maritime political culture offers any lessons for Prairie scholars, academic consensus does not necessarily equal truth, regardless of the number or credentials of the authorities involved. For instance, the three Prairie political cultures may be converging (whether into a common regional ethos, a Canadian variant, or a broader global culture) or subdividing into a series of territorially or non-territorially defined cultures (Friesen 1999; Henderson 2004). These trends may be masked by the often stolid nature of academic opinion, which tends to promote continuity over change. Without primary investigation, these arguments cannot be dismissed out of hand.

Nonetheless, the very nature of political culture suggests that prevailing academic wisdom remains a solid, if imperfect, measure of a community's time-honoured political norms. It is true: many contemporary descriptions of the three Prairie political cultures remain rooted in age-old assumptions about each community, and they are reinforced by generation after generation of scholarly writings (see Chapter 2). As a result, critics may suggest that these images constitute myths – fables or legends about Manitoba, Saskatchewan, and Alberta that bear little resemblance to contemporary affairs.

The arguments presented in this study do not dispute this view. In fact, it embraces the notion that political culture is, in many respects, an element of folklore. That Alberta's ethos remains conservative even though the province hosts the country's most expansive welfare state; that, despite the dramatic transformation of the provincial economy and society from its wheat-based heritage, Saskatchewan's style of politics remains rooted in what Lipset once called agrarian socialism; and that Manitoba's self-image of accommodation and conciliation persists in the face of dramatic social inequalities between its Aboriginal and non-Aboriginal communities – all of these are indisputable (and, in several respects, unfortunate) ironies of political life on the Canadian prairies. Yet they are ironies for a reason. They reveal the true nature of political culture as an abstraction of reality, not a direct reflection.

Thus, to the extent that prevailing academic wisdom reflects (or even reinforces) the dominant conception of a community's ethos, it is actually a useful measure of political culture. Argument by authority may be an imprudent means of establishing empirical facts, but when it comes to defining norms and values, that authority often conveys the very essence of the culture we seek to identify. In the strictest sense, then, the following analysis aims to explain the persistence of the conventionally accepted diversity among the three Prairie political cultures over time. The legitimacy of this prevailing wisdom awaits further study.

Political Codes

Understanding the nature of code politics requires an appreciation of the complex relationship between elite-level codes, mass-level cultures, and party ideologies. As Friesen (1984a, 32) suggests, "there are tendencies – patterns of thought and behaviour in any political system." At the mass societal level, the tendencies are embodied in the community's political culture – its overall psyche. At the elite level, these tendencies form codes of discourse among parties and their leaders.[2]

Although the term *code politics* may be new to some, the concept is by no means novel.[3] Richard Hofstadter (1957 [1947], viii, ix) refers to the notion as a community's political tradition – "a kind of mute organic consistency" in terms of a society's elite discourse (see also Friesen 2009; Blair and McLeod 1987, 1993; Wilson 1992; Verney 1978). To him, political systems

do not foster ideas that are hostile to their fundamental working arrangements. Such ideas may appear, but they are slowly and persistently insulated, as an oyster deposits nacre around an irritant. They are confined to small groups of dissenters and alienated intellectuals, and except in revolutionary times they do not circulate among practical politicians. The range of ideas, therefore, which practical politicians can conveniently believe in is normally limited by the climate of opinion that sustains their culture. They differ, sometimes bitterly, over current issues, but they also share a general framework of ideas which makes it possible for them to co-operate when the campaigns are over. (Hofstadter 1957 [1947], viii-ix)[4]

Samuel Huntington (1981) concurs with Hofstadter, suggesting that most, if not all, political systems feature a distinctive creed – a set of prevailing political values that constitute consensus among political leaders.

Like students of political culture, students of political codes cannot turn to a single source or authority for the ethos guiding a society's elites. This is especially true in Canada, where politicians have often "negotiated their collective identity in a non-declaratory manner. Canada's history is littered with the messy and inarticulate but functional compromises of its elites rather than with ringing proclamations, as in the American Declaration of Independence" (Wiseman 2007, 65). Yet an examination of these functional compromises is long overdue north of the forty-ninth parallel, where "no systematic attempt has been made to study the language and symbols used by Canadian leaders or their operating codes and styles to see whether there is a distinct political creed that is innately a part of Canadian politics" (Taras and Weyant 1988, 11; but also see Verney 1978).

By its very nature, each code is an elite-level interpretation or projection of the society's overarching values. A code, therefore, often resembles its community's mass-level political culture; the two are "bound together in a mutually reinforcing equilibrium" (Putnam 1993, 104). However, there is a critical distinction between codes ("formal, explicit, and relatively consistent definitions of political community" among political elites) and cultures ("the informal, implicit, and relatively inconsistent understandings of political community held by people within a given institutional setting") (Friesen 1999, 135). Codes emerge from a supply-side examination of elite politics, whereas political culture is revealed in a demand-side examination of society in general. The correspondence between the two concepts is not guaranteed; rather, it is an empirical question – indeed, one posed by *Code Politics*.

According to the code politics model, one of the main tasks of political elites is manipulating political discourse to enhance and maintain their authority. In this sense, political culture is a valuable resource for elites, for it provides them with a set of shared symbols around which to build social cohesion and popular allegiance (Laitin 1986, 15; Cohen 1974). From the demand side of the equation, then, the code politics model holds

> that mass publics respond to currently conspicuous political symbols: not to "facts," and not to moral codes embedded in the character or soul, but to the gestures and speeches that make up the drama of the state. The mass public does not study and analyze detailed data about secondary boycotts, provisions for stock ownership and control in a proposed space communi-cations corporation, or missile installations in Cuba. It ignores these things until political actions and speeches make them symbolically threatening or reassuring, and it then responds to the cues furnished by the actions and the speeches, not to direct knowledge of the facts. (Edelman 1964, 172)

Like cultures, codes are community-specific, meaning that the nature of elite discourse often differs starkly from polity to polity. It is true: the indi-vidual components of a given code may exist in other communities. For in-stance, Huntington (1981, 15) notes that notions of "constitutionalism, individualism, liberalism, democracy, and egalitarianism are no monopoly of Americans. In some societies, some people subscribe to many of these ideas and in other societies many people subscribe to some of these ideas. In no other society, however, are all of these ideas so widely adhered to by so many people as they are in the United States." The same is true of notions such as progress, alienation, collectivism, and pragmatism on the Canadian plains; all of these currents run through each of the three Prairie provinces. Yet their specific combination and salience help to distinguish the dominant discourses they comprise. Ultimately, each code contains a unique core theme that focuses elite-level competition on a different set of expectations about the state's function in society and the economy, and on its role in rela-tion to other states.

If Hofstadter, Myrdal, Huntington, and other students of so-called polit-ical traditions are correct, codes exist in nearly every democratic system. To these scholars, elites in any stable democracy must share a common set of core values to maintain political stability. Polities without at least some measure of elite-level consensus would be wrought with such intense con-flict and volatility as to paralyze their political affairs. By functional neces-sity, then, Hofstadter and his followers suggest that core sets of values lie at the heart of every stable democracy; the researcher's task is merely to un-cover them.

The present analysis turns these assumptions into a series of hypotheses and tests to see if provincial democracies on the Canadian prairies feature consistent modes of elite discourse (modes that correspond with their underlying political cultures). The results confirm the existence of such codes in Alberta, Saskatchewan, and Manitoba, yet these case studies fall short of establishing these codes as intrinsic elements of all democratic systems. An examination of dominant party platforms in other Canadian provinces may bear less fruit, for instance. Hence, without further investigation, the code politics model must remain confined to the Prairie provinces. For the time being, the methodology and findings provided by this study may serve to generate further hypotheses for testing in other contexts.

To summarize, a code is a unique discursive paradigm that persists among dominant elites in a given community over time. By virtue of the nature of representative democracy in Canada, codes are typically associated closely with the values embedded in the broader political culture; elites who propagate ideas that are incongruent with mass beliefs are unlikely to retain power (Bell 1993b, 153). Moreover, these codes outlive the conditions that contributed to their rise. Once established, codes persist despite exogenous events and endogenous developments and, because they are more than simply party ideologies or individuals' visions, these themes remain relatively constant despite changes in government and party leadership. Lastly, codes are community-specific – each polity has its own exclusive, dominant narrative. Thus, to conclude that a code exists in a given community, we must find evidence that a relatively unique, cohesive, and consistent set of culturally rooted values has been expressed by dominant elites over time (despite possible changes in party leadership, government, and the external environment). By contrast, a code does not exist if research reveals that no consistent, distinct theme has guided political discourse over time. If we found vast differences in rhetoric – from dominant party to dominant party, leader to leader, or decade to decade – or if we found overwhelming similarities between provinces in terms of their political discourses, then we must acknowledge that no code exists.

Where they do exist, codes form the foundation of dominant party rhetoric, which is most widely disseminated during election campaigns. For this reason, the present study makes extensive use of party platforms as its primary source of data. As the Appendix reveals in greater detail, over eight hundred separate pieces of campaign literature have been collected and consulted in this analysis. Summarizing the principal themes identified in dominant parties' platforms from each province, the following section offers brief introductory synopses of the three codes that have existed on the Canadian prairies over the past seven decades. The parallels between these codes and their underlying political cultures are obvious.

The Three Prairie Codes

Since the Great Depression, Alberta's dominant parties have crafted a freedom-based narrative that contains three core elements, each of which has figured more or less prominently at different points in the province's history. The first component of the Alberta code, populism, emphasizes freedom from government overreach, be it from Ottawa, Rome, or Edmonton. Through their campaign rhetoric, prominent parties have railed against all forms of external control – from government (and taxation), banks, monopolies, traditional political parties, mainline churches, or other sources of authority.

This anti-establishment sentiment is closely related to the second major facet of the Alberta code: individualism. Throughout much of the past seven decades, Social Credit and Conservative Party rhetoric has stressed the primacy of the individual as the core unit of society. In their platforms, we find constant reference to individual initiative, free enterprise, hard work, and a general go-it-alone philosophy – all of which correspond to the conservatism embedded in the province's political culture.

A third and final aspect of the province's code stresses the alienation of Alberta from important centres of decision making, specifically those in central Canada. In response, prominent Alberta parties have promoted the autonomy of the provincial state. In this sense, many argue that "since 1921 and regardless of party, Alberta has been governed by the 'Provincial Liberation Front'" (Engelmann 1989, 111). More disparagingly, Lisac (2004a, 2) suggests Albertans are "people whose leaders and image makers cast them as the downtrodden galley slaves of Confederation – and repeat the story so often that some of their listeners believe them." This mood of parochial boosterism (Leadbeater 1984, xi) has a certain sectarian element to it, one that corresponds with the strong sense of western alienation embodied in the province's broader political ethos.

Together, these three pillars – populism, individualism, and provincial autonomy – have helped structure Alberta politics around a freedom-based narrative that, itself, draws on the major aspects of the province's political culture.

If Alberta's dominant parties have advocated freedom in the face of oppression, Saskatchewan's have promoted protection in the face of vulnerability.

Drawing on elements of the province's political culture, leading politicians have portrayed Saskatchewan as a land of unrealized opportunity, one susceptible to threats from both inside and outside its borders. In this sense, the dominant narrative in Saskatchewan centres on the concept of security, three core elements of which constitute the province's political code.

First and foremost, dominant elites have stressed the importance of collectivism in preserving security in Saskatchewan. Matching the communitarian spirit found in the provincial political culture, dominant party platforms are replete with references to community, co-operation, partnerships, and togetherness. Second, while valuing collectivism at the societal level, the province's narrative also contains a heavy dose of dirigisme – the belief that the state should play a guiding role in both society and the economy. To a greater extent than their Prairie neighbours, Saskatchewan elites have consistently promoted government as a positive instrument in political, social, and economic life. Again, this sentiment finds support in the province's broader political culture.

Lastly, while the collectivist vision predominates, the Saskatchewan code also contains an element of polarization. Through their rhetoric, provincial elites have consistently highlighted the conflict between the prevailing force of social democracy and a traditionally weaker element of free-market liberalism. Leaders on the Left depict the latter as a menace, while those on the Right champion their cause in the face of an oppressive socialist majority. This same sense of polarization is present neither in the Alberta code, in which conservatism dominates to the virtual exclusion of left-wing influence, nor in Manitoba, where ideological moderation prevails.

Combined, these three elements – collectivism, dirigisme, and polarization – constitute the Saskatchewan code of security. Like Alberta's, Saskatchewan's code is a narrative with strong ties to the province's own unique political culture.

Whereas party dialogues in Alberta and Saskatchewan have pivoted on questions of Right versus Left, politics in Manitoba have been decidedly more moderate, divided instead between proponents of change and defenders of the status quo. Rather than accepting dramatic change as a necessary function of politics and debating its direction, most conflict in Manitoba has revolved around the need for, or speed of, change – one side has argued in favor of improvement and the other for the preservation of the existing order. This tension lies at the heart of the concept of progress – a concept over which Manitoba parties have struggled for ownership over the past century.

Indeed, progressive centrism constitutes the foremost element of Manitoba campaign discourse. More than in any other Prairie province, elites in Manitoba have consistently stressed the importance of avoiding extreme ideological positions in favour of middle-of-the-road incremental policies and programs. Thus, Manitoba elites have tended to be paradigmatically pragmatic, and the progressive centre itself has been defined both endogenously (from Manitoba's own political history) and exogenously (by global trends). This is not to say that Manitoba parties have been unprincipled or devoid of ideological commitment. As is recounted in Chapter 5 and elsewhere, Manitoba parties have taken distinct left-wing and right-wing positions throughout history (Wesley 2006, 2009d). Yet the differences between them have been much subtler than those found in Saskatchewan and Alberta. The overwhelming majority of Manitoba election campaigns have featured a "straightforward competition between those disposed toward reform and equalization and those who expressed the need for restraint and stability" (Peterson 1972, 115).

In this sense, the search for the progressive centre is related to the second component of the Manitoba code: pragmatism. In the province's dominant political narrative, there is little trace of the utopian visions of an ideal society embedded in the other two Prairie codes. This sense of reality underlies the incrementalism that pervades major party platforms in Manitoba, both in terms of their policy pledges and their rhetoric. With few notable exceptions, the focus of party elites has been on convincing voters that they offer a better administration of government rather than a fundamentally better way of doing politics. This is not to say Manitoba parties are pessimistic or defeatist, as some have suggested (see Friesen 1999, 127). Far from it. The pragmatism found in the Manitoba code merely reflects a belief that, because it has a stable and diversified economy and society, a better Manitoba is more attainable and desirable than an unrealistically ideal one.

A final related element of the Manitoba code is transpartisanship. In their campaign rhetoric, Manitoba elites have tended to promote a more fluid or flexible notion of party interaction than their counterparts in Saskatchewan or Alberta. At times, the Manitoba narrative has defined politics as a non-partisan affair (as the efforts to create broad, formal coalitions in the early twentieth century attest) or as multi-partisan (as seen during periods of negotiation over Manitoba's constitutional position in later decades). Together with progressive centrism and pragmatism, this transpartisanship helps to differentiate the Manitoba code from the more ideological and conflictual discourses that prevail in Alberta and Saskatchewan.

Thus, the values embedded in each Prairie province's political culture are reflected in the dominant discourse of its elites. Alberta's conservative political culture has lived on, in part, through the right-wing rhetoric of the Socreds and Progressive Conservatives, just as Saskatchewan's social democratic ethos persists in the elite code created by the CCF-NDP. By the same token, the modesty and temperance found in Manitoba's political culture resonates in the tenets of moderation promoted by its dominant parties. The theoretical, methodological, and empirical foundations of these findings are explored in greater detail in the following chapters, as are their broader implications for Prairie democracy.

Toward Decoding the Prairie Paradox

As a comparative examination of three provinces over a period of seven decades, the following analysis necessarily takes broad strokes. An entire book could have been written on the role of Social Credit in developing Alberta's political culture, for instance. Indeed, individual leaders, elections, parties, governments, and provinces have received book-length treatments. However, in the interests of comparison – a core element of any study of political culture – the decision was made to examine Prairie politics from a broader perspective. Extensive citations offer more depth than the comparative analysis affords.

For reasons of historical context and data availability, the present study begins in 1932. That year marked the midpoint of the Great Depression and came just months before the publication of the *Regina Manifesto* (Co-operative Commonwealth Federation [CCF] 1933). A landmark document in the history of Canadian party politics – and Prairie politics, in particular – the manifesto launched the country's first competitive socialist-minded party (the Co-operative Commonwealth Federation) and changed the nature and structure of politics across Canada (Whitehorn 1992; Praud and McQuarrie 2001). An even earlier starting point would have been ideal. As Morton (1967b), Engelmann (1989, 111), Courtney and Smith (1972, 311-16), and others convincingly argue, the roots of diversity in Prairie politics stretch back to the pre-war, Progressive era. Unfortunately, reliable data, including party platforms, are available only for the post-Depression period (DeLong 1988).

It bears notice: what follows is not a detailed history of each province, each election, each party, or each leader. Biographies and other accounts exist on these topics, and the following analysis does not restate them. Nor is this a revisionist history. With the benefit of a comparative vantage point and a century's worth of hindsight, many of the researchers noted would have reached similar conclusions. Hence, I have cited liberally from their work, which offers significant validation of my findings. The main task in preparing this book has been finding the proper frame in which to cast the intersecting and diverging histories of the three Prairie political cultures. With the aid of hundreds of pieces of campaign literature, the search produced a series of stories that, together, help to explain the diversity of politics in the region.

Above all, *Code Politics* is an analysis of so-called high politics on the Prairies, of how dominant political parties have struggled to meld primitive principles with the changing demands of their societies and economies, of how cultures, economies, institutions, and ideologies have interacted to produce three unique political worlds. In the portraits that emerge, there is not one realm of Prairie politics, but three.

1

The Prairie Paradox
Explaining Cultural Difference

By almost any measure, the three Prairie provinces should be more similar than their cultural distinctions suggest. They are separated not by topographic, racial, or other "natural" boundaries, but by artificial borders, drawn arbitrarily along lines of longitude (Archer 1980, 21). Although different in some important respects, the provinces' economies have historically shared a common reliance on natural resource exports. Moreover, throughout most of their history, Alberta, Saskatchewan, and Manitoba have all featured Westminster parliamentary traditions, plurality-based electoral systems, and other institutional factors commonly used to explain differences between political communities. Yet, according to common wisdom, Alberta remains Canada's most conservative political culture, Saskatchewan its most socially democratic, and Manitoba its most temperate.

Any account of political culture on the Canadian prairies must begin with the words of its resident authority, Gerald Friesen. In his classic account of the topic, Friesen uses a series of metaphors to capture the three main images of western Canadian culture: the cowboy hat, the jellied salad, and the eagle feather. Although he applies these descriptions to the region as a whole, they serve as powerful illustrations of the core differences between the three provincial political cultures. For instance, Alberta's political culture corresponds most closely with what Friesen (1999, 185) has labelled a ten-gallon-hat view of Prairie society – one imbued with notions of liberty and nonconformity often associated with the cowboy culture of the West (see also Barrie 2006; Denis 1995, 91). As Friesen (1999, 185) puts it, "The ten-gallon hat still represents the freedom of the frontier. Now, however, freedom is defined by its bearers as the absence of government, reduced taxes, fewer regulations and survival of the fittest on the open (both continental and global) range."

In contrast to Alberta's cowboy individualism, Saskatchewan's political culture may be likened to Friesen's jellied salad, a staple at the potluck dinners and fowl suppers that have characterized rural Prairie life for generations:

> The brightly-coloured salads may represent the left. They are not unique to the West but, as the singer Connie Kaldor reminds us, they did travel from thousands of western kitchens to decorate the tables of thousands of community fundraising dinners undertaken by church, school and political party. If the ten-gallon hat speaks of competition and the individual, this humble near-vegetable speaks of co-operation, community and equality. It will never occupy the centre of a national flag, but the jellied salad in church basement and community hall also contributed to the national medicare plan. (Friesen 1999, 185)

In one sense, the dish represents the collectivist ethic that pervades community events at which it is served. In another sense, the recipe for the jellied salad – pieces of fruit and vegetables suspended in a gelatin mould – symbolizes the gelling together of diverse groups and individuals within the broader provincial community.

Finally, Friesen's (1999, 184) third Prairie image, that of the eagle feather, symbolizes (as it does for some First Nations cultures) the elements of honour, friendship, and diversity that are sometimes associated with the settler societies of the Canadian west. Discussed below, Manitoba's political culture draws on this same spirit of conciliation and accommodation that characterizes normal periods in the province's politics. Periodic interruptions have occurred, but the prevailing norms of temperance and tolerance mitigate their intensity and duration.

Explaining Political Culture

Political Culture in Alberta
According to most observers, Alberta's political culture contains three closely related strains: populism, conservatism, and western alienation (Dyck 1996, 510; see also Harrison and Laxer 1995a, 5-7; Stewart and Archer 2000,

13-15; Pickup et al. 2004, 634; Mann 1955, 3-4; Rennie 2004, xi; Roome 2004, 6; Leadbeater 1984, xi; Pal 1992, 2; Denis 1995, 91; Morton 1967b, 37). On the first measure, Alberta is said to feature a climate of distrust toward elites, a penchant for nonconformity, an aversion to pitched partisanship, and an affinity for the tools of direct democracy (Mann 1955, 3-4; Rennie 2004, xi; Roome 2004, 6; Stewart and Archer 2000, 15). More pejoratively, some consider these characteristics symptomatic of the province's "high-strung, volatile character" (Morton 1967b, 37), or a sign of its redneck (Pal 1992, 2), or roughneck (Denis 1995, 91) heritage. Second, as a community, Albertans are said to favour rugged, right-wing individualism; laissez-faire liberalism; entrepreneurship; and fiscal orthodoxy – all qualities that have contributed to the province's image as the bastion of Canadian conservatism. Third, a deep-seated sense of western alienation remains a defining feature of Alberta's political culture. Nearly all accounts of the province's political culture refer to the Alberta government as a guardian of the provincial state and to the premier as "the societal spokesperson for his province" (Wiseman 2007, 240; see also Gibbins 1998). Macpherson (1977) and Elton and Goddard (1979) refer to this as a quasi-colonial mentality that disparages outside control over Alberta's economy and society, particularly by commercial interests in Ontario and Quebec and the federal government in Ottawa. All told, according to Mansell (1997, 61-62), "these factors have tended to produce a population with values more disposed towards self-reliance, with experience at adjusting to major shifts in external factors, and a perception that the main threats come from the outside than from within the province."

Those familiar with Alberta politics might find inconsistencies between these cultural traits and the realities of political life in the province (Tupper and Gibbins 1992, xv; Pickup et al. 2004; Laxer 1995; Stewart and Archer 2000, 44). Yet the common perception of Alberta's populist, conservative, alienated political culture endures. Chapter 3 explores one source of this persistence: dominant party rhetoric has helped to sustain these values in the face of such dissonance.

Political Culture in Saskatchewan

As Marchildon (2005a, 4) puts it, Alberta and Saskatchewan are "like Siamese twins, separated at birth ... In the typical stereotypes of these contrasting identities, Saskatchewanians are depicted as collectivist-inclined social democrats who emphasize security and egalitarian social development, while Albertans are portrayed as entrepreneurial 'small c' conservatives who are dedicated to the individualistic pursuit of liberty and prosperity." This characterization of Saskatchewan as featuring a social democratic political culture figures prominently, if not exclusively, in the existing literature (Mc-Grane 2006, 10; Rasmussen 2001; Wiseman 2007; but see Smith 2009). A closer review suggests this label is supported by four interrelated themes: (1) a spirit of communitarianism and civic engagement, (2) deep ideological and partisan division, (3) a sense of political and geographic isolation, and (4) a positive approach toward government.[1]

Most accounts of Saskatchewan's political culture make reference to "an ethic of co-operation and collective public action" (Dyck 1996, 441), although some authors suggest this ethos is shifting gradually from a populist mode of agrarian collectivism to a more conservative form of individualism (Leeson 2001; Smith 2009, 40). Either way, the political community in Saskatchewan is often described as the most engaged and active in Canada (Lipset 1968a, chap. 10; Friesen 1999, 110).

The division of the province between the Left and the Right is also a time-honoured tradition of Saskatchewan politics (Wishlow 2001, 170; Dunn and Laycock 1992, 225). Since the early twentieth century, heated debates have pitted "moderate democratic socialism versus a peculiar variety of liberalism" (Courtney and Smith 1972, 314), with democratic socialism and free enterprise constituting the political touchstones of the province (Andrews 1982, 58). This element of polarization has included an acceptance of the party as a legitimate vehicle for political debate and the party system as an ideal venue for conflict. As a result, "party politics in Saskatchewan has been active, intense, and for a good part of the province's history, highly competitive ... This is especially striking if one compares the political system of Saskatchewan with the Alberta and Manitoba systems. Partisan politics impregnates, with few exceptions, every issue faced by Saskatchewanians, whether it be the marketing of a particular agricultural commodity or the proposed establishment of a government-operated medical care insurance program" (Courtney and Smith 1972, 317).

Many authors also cite a sense of vulnerability and isolation as a third element of Saskatchewan's political culture (Eisler 2006). Dunn and Laycock (1992, 208) label this sentiment alienation because "the geographic and economic conditions in the province since the beginning of its white settlement history virtually guaranteed that the early numerical majority – farmers – would feel dominated by, and alienated from, distant economic and political elites." Although some observers agree (e.g., Courtney and Smith 1972, 290; Eisler 2004, 260), the inclusion of western alienation in a definition of Saskatchewan political culture remains disputed. Others suggest the province's ethos has lacked the same sense of sectarianism found elsewhere in western Canada. In contrast to the charged atmosphere found in Alberta, for instance, the Saskatchewan community tends to consider federalism as a "bureaucratic process instead of an emotionally and historically contested concept" (McGrane 2005, 26). In other words, political culture in Saskatchewan "has exploited the potential of federalism, benefiting from and contributing to national politics on the one hand and experimenting and innovating within its invisible boundaries on the other. In this respect no better example can be cited than Saskatchewan for the creative power of provincial politics" (Smith 2009, 53). This approach has a lot to do with Saskatchewan's historical position as a have-less province in Confederation; under these circumstances, being critical of the federal government has been a luxury few Saskatchewanians have been able to afford. Although the province has certainly not been immune to province-first sentiments – notable episodes include Blakeney's combative approach toward Trudeau's federal government in the late 1970s (Dyck 1996, 475; Dunn and Laycock 1992) and Brad Wall's recent defence of Saskatchewan's potash industry in the face of foreign investment – McGrane (2005, 26) adds much to our understanding when he asserts that "if western alienation in Saskatchewan is not dead, it clearly is on its deathbed." In either case, the notion of being isolated (if not alienated) remains an important element of Saskatchewan's political culture. This distinction is best captured by the common perception that whereas Alberta is a heartland of Confederation, Saskatchewan suffers a hinterland status (Baron and Jackson 1991, 313-24).

This sense of isolation is closely related to a fourth element of Saskatchewan political culture – an emphasis on the importance of the provincial government in both the economy and society (Dyck 1996, 439-40). First and foremost, "the susceptibility of the province to international price fluctuations and to shifts and changes in federal trade policies has resulted in an overriding sense of ... vulnerability on the part of Saskatchewan residents. These feelings, in turn, have led to political demands for a strong provincial government capable of effectively protecting and promoting the welfare of the provincial populace" (Dunn and Laycock 1992, 237). Thus, according to most observers, communitarianism (with oddly deep ideological and partisan divisions) and notions of isolation, vulnerability, and a positive view of the role of the state constitute core elements of Saskatchewan's political culture.

Political Culture in Manitoba

Compared with the popular impression of other Canadian provinces, Manitoba's political culture remains undeveloped in the minds of most observers.[2] Even to the most trained eyes, Manitoba enjoys no comparable political ethos to that of Alberta or Saskatchewan. In the words of Rand Dyck (1996, 381), the author of a leading undergraduate textbook on Canadian provincial politics, "Manitoba is a province without a distinctive political culture. If Manitobans have a self-image, it is probably one of a moderate, medium, diversified, and fairly prosperous but unspectacular province. Many value its ethnic heterogeneity; others, its intermediary position on federal-provincial affairs, interpreting east to east and vice versa."

Dyck is not alone. Many define Manitoba by its ambiguous mediocrity rather than by any unique political personality. This conclusion is drawn quite easily. Manitoba is the "keystone province," after all; it is the geographic centre of North America, the "heart of the continent," and the buffer between the "old" country of the east and Canada's "New West." Its population and economy are among the country's most diverse, and both are of average size. Relative to other major Canadian centres, even Manitoba's capital city, Winnipeg, is viewed as a "balance between exotic and obscure" (Read 2008). In short, Manitoba is Canada's middling province, positioned between prosperous and poor, east and west, old and new, exciting and bland.

Yet this view distorts the notion of political culture and misconceives the precise nature of Manitoba politics. Indeed, the province "is more than a fuzzy middle ground where the East ends and the West begins" (Marshall 1970). It has its own distinctive political ethos, which is grounded in the very concepts of modesty and temperance that make up its popular middleman image.

Manitoba has always been "a land of steady ways" in which "the simple, sturdy virtues of hard work, thrift and neighbourliness have been cherished and transmitted" (Morton 1967a, viii). As Morton (ibid., viii-ix) wrote four decades ago, "if it is too much to assert that a Manitoban can be recognized abroad, it is still true that life in Manitoba forces a common manner, not to say character on all its people. It is the manner, or mannerism of instant understanding and agreeableness at meeting, and rises from the need for harmony in a society of many diverse elements. This superficial friendliness is common to all North Americans, of course, but in Manitoba, a truly plural society, it is a definite and highly conscious art." Reflecting these tendencies, Manitobans, "though driven to strike out in new ways in politics, [have] remained fast wedded to the old ways in manners and morals" (ibid., 382). In this sense, Manitoba politics have featured a stronger strain of traditionalism than Canada's other two Prairie provinces (Dyck 1996, 382).

This tendency toward traditionalism is embodied in the province's political culture of modesty and temperance – a shared sense of identity that has both reflected and shaped the community's political evolution. Since the province lost its status as the commercial and transportation gateway to the Canadian west with the opening of the Panama Canal at the turn of the last century, Manitobans have adopted a decidedly realistic view of their economic and political future. Some regard this political culture as a form of prudent pragmatism – an unpretentious, unassuming, conciliatory approach to politics that holds as its principal goal the accommodation of diversity, the preservation of order and tradition, and the protection of Manitoba's median position in Confederation. Others view the province's culture as a brand of prudish pessimism – a sign of Manitobans' quiescence on divisive issues or reticence on the national stage. Where some see humility and realism in Manitoba's political culture, others see meekness and resignation.

The notion of temperance has also extended to the realm of federalism, where links between Winnipeg and Ottawa have been far friendlier than in other western Canadian capitals (Dyck 1996, 381). Even prior to achieving provincehood, Manitoba had held a central place in Canadian nation building, and its founding settlers, elites, and institutions were drawn predominantly from Ontario. As a result of these factors and its historical position as a have-not province, Manitoba has been more closely tied to central Canada than Alberta or Saskatchewan (Morton 1967b, 420-21). It has lacked the oppositional reflex found in the former (Friesen 1999, 9) and, compared with either of its western neighbours, exhibits the lowest level of provincial boosterism (see Thomas 1989, 2008).

In sum, Manitoba's political culture is characterized by two major themes: modesty and temperance. This conclusion is supported by a recent survey of prominent Manitoba political, governmental, and economic elites. When asked to define Manitoba's political culture, "the interviewees suggested that Manitoba was a society of conscious conciliation, driven by a keen sense of what was fair and unfair. They saw the community as remarkable and its citizens as committed to collective well-being" (Friesen 2010, 33).

One further caveat is necessary before the differences between these three political cultures can be explored. As in Wilson (1974, 440), this book is based on the assumption "that each province constitutes, in effect, an independent political system and has on that account a political culture of its own." By presuming the boundaries of a particular society, however, there is a tendency to gloss over the many sub- or supracultures that exist within or transcend the borders of that community (see Stewart 2002, 29-31). After all, there are two ways of defining a culture: from the top down (identifying the polity a priori, calling it a culture, and uncovering its values) or from the bottom up (searching for commonalities before drawing boundaries around a culture) (Chilton 1988, 428). Given the nature of the present study, a focus on the three Prairie political cultures implies a top-down approach. Yet readers should be mindful of the many subcultures within the Prairie region (e.g., farmers, northerners, women, First Nations, Metis, urbanites, seniors, and others) and that each province is part of broader national, continental, and global cultures (see Henderson 2004; O'Neill 2002). As Stewart (1994a, 75) puts it, "Canada has a political culture, as does Manitoba, as does Winnipeg, as does any neighbourhood in Winnipeg, and even does any particular household in Winnipeg."

Moreover, not all Manitobans, Saskatchewanians, or Albertans will feel part of their province's political culture (see Eager 1980; Barrie 2006; Ornstein 1986). In this sense, there are certain provincial countercultures to which many of the groups above subscribe. Deep-rooted feelings of disaffection and discrimination may lie beneath the veneer of commonality, for the very nature of political culture masks these divisions under the guise of uniformity (Verba 1965, 525-26; Rosenbaum 1975, 37-52, 151-59). For instance, the aura of conciliation and accommodation surrounding Manitoba's political culture tends toward complacency when it comes to the decades of inequality that continue to plague its society (Wesley 2010a; Friesen 2010). The same is true of the multicultural veneer that covers Saskatchewan's collectivist ethos; decades of racial tension and discrimination belie this sense of commonality (Waiser 2009). This is the dark side of political culture, one that should not be overlooked (see Myrdal 1969; Pateman 1980).

Yet, as Chilton (1988, 429-30) tells us, the "existence of a political culture is not defined by all people liking the culture, or regarding it as legitimate. Rather, it is defined by the ways of relating that people actually use to coordinate their dealings with one another. Culture is what is publicly expected and subscribed to, not what is individually preferred." Culture endures regardless of – and, in many instances, in spite of – its conformity with reality. One reason, as explored in this study, is the persistence of strong themes embedded in dominant political party rhetoric.

FIGURE 1

Wiseman's "Pattern of Prairie Politics"

	Alberta	Saskatchewan	Manitoba
Formative event	"Last best West" (1896)	Riel rebellions and the CPR (1880s)	Riel Rebellion and the CPR (1870s)
Major quake	Leduc oil discovery (1947)	Depression (1930s)	Winnipeg General Strike (1919)
Economic staple(s)	Agriculture (early twentieth century), oil (late twentieth century)	Agriculture, natural resources (late twentieth century)	Agriculture (early twentieth century), diversified economy
Dominant settler group	Great Plains American Liberals	British Labourites	Ontario Tory-touched Liberals

Source: Adapted from Wiseman (2007, Tables 1.2, 1.3, 1.4).

Wiseman's "Pattern of Prairie Politics"

An extensive review of the literature reveals only one in-depth, comparative analysis of the diversity of political culture on the Canadian prairies. In this research, Nelson Wiseman (2001; 2006; 2007, 211-62) attributes the distinct pattern of Prairie politics to a combination of structural factors, including formative events, economic staples, and early settlement patterns (see Figure 1).[3] This explanation, although valid, remains incomplete for reasons outlined in the following review. Specifically, by narrowing its focus to the origins of each province's political culture, Wiseman's account downplays the importance of explaining the persistence of these different sets of core values. That is a challenge taken up in this study.

Although by far the most comprehensive and coherent, Wiseman's account is certainly not the only one to make use of these structural variables to explain politics on the Prairies. Although extensive attention has been paid to particular elements of political life in the region – including the emergence of protest parties such as Social Credit and the Co-operative Commonwealth Federation (CCF) (Melnyk 1992; Naylor and Teeple 1972; Morton 1967b; Smith 1969) or the decline of the once-dominant Liberal Party (Wilson 1980; Fischer 1986; Smith 1981) – most of these studies have been case-specific. That is, they have tended to focus on individual provinces, elections, or parties, dividing Prairie politics into a series of separate "silos" (Wiseman 2007, 237). Thus, its scope and seminal nature make Wiseman's research the focal point of this literature review. As cited, other analyses have offered many of the same findings and encountered many of the same challenges.

On one level, Wiseman (2006) argues that each Prairie community has experienced its own unique series of formative events and quakes. He borrows this model from Lipset (1968a, 1990), who has compared the political cultures of Canada and the United States and traced their origins to the American Revolutionary War. Like Lipset, Almond and Powell (1966, 65) capture the essence of this approach when they note that "certain events and experiences may leave their mark on a whole society. A great war or a depression can constitute a severe political trauma for millions of individuals who may be involved ... [As a consequence, they may] acquire new conceptions of the role of politics in their lives and new goals for which they may strive."

Along these lines, Wiseman suggests that whereas both Manitoba and Saskatchewan were born out of the expansion of the Canadian Pacific Railway (CPR) and the resulting conflicts between the federal government and Metis peoples led by Louis Riel, Alberta's founding moment came amid the land rush of the late nineteenth century. Just as Manitoba once represented Canada's western frontier during the period of British and Ontario immigration, Alberta became the continent's "Last Best West," welcoming settlers from across North America (Wiseman 2007, 214). Decades later, each of the Prairie provinces underwent a series of cultural quakes. In Manitoba, the violent suppression of the Winnipeg General Strike of 1919 constituted a major turning point. The event helped to polarize yet mute the radical elements of the province's business and labour movements, thus setting the stage for the success of more moderate parties such as the Liberal-Progressives, the Progressive Conservatives, and the New Democratic Party (NDP) (Wiseman 1983, 8-9; Wiseman and Taylor 1979, 62; see also Morton 1967b, 362-72; McAllister 1984, 89-90). For Saskatchewan, the Great Depression provided the impetus for the further development of the continent's most extensive network of co-operatives, which, in turn, established the ideological and organizational foundation for the success of the CCF-NDP (see also Courtney and Smith 1972, 308-9; Marchildon 2005b; Bilson 2004, 140; Waiser 2009, 68). Wiseman attributes Alberta's recent development to the discovery of major oil reserves at Leduc in 1947; thereafter, politics in the province assumed their current air of free-enterprise liberalism (see also Barr 1984).

Historical explanations that hinge on formative events are prone to several weaknesses, many of which are shared with the staples and fragment approaches. Aside from those discussed below, the path-dependent nature of formative-events theory invites questions of contingency and infinite regress. How far in the past need we search to find a community's founding moment, and how do we determine when such an episode is truly determinative of future events? For instance, Peterson (1972, 69) suggests the roots of Prairie politics can be traced back to the last ice age, when glaciers blessed certain areas with better soil conditions than others. (As a result, he argues, ethnic settlement patterns were determined as much by geological factors as immigration.) In a similar vein, Stewart (2007) grounds the beginning of politics in Canada in early Aboriginal societies and the first contact between First Nations and Europeans (see also Saul 2008). Should we date the origins of the Prairie paradox to these early events? In short, the subjective, post hoc, and deterministic nature of formative-events explanations leaves the Prairie paradox largely unsolved. Recognizing this, Wiseman supplements this approach with two others.

In his second level of analysis, Wiseman (2006) notes that the economies of the Prairie provinces have also helped determine their separate political cultural trajectories. According to this view, although Manitoba, Saskatchewan, and Alberta "once shared a common and dominant agricultural base ... in recent decades, the politics of the three provinces have become increasingly diversified and distinct from each other as new staples have emerged" (Wiseman 1988, 181).

In a loose adaptation of staples theory (see Innis 1956), Wiseman argues that the nature of Alberta's agricultural and petroleum industries have both contributed to the province's right-leaning political climate. The province's farmers and ranchers have been commercially oriented, independent commodity producers whose position within the Canadian economy and global markets has made them as supportive of free markets as their counterparts in the natural resource sector (Thomas 1980, 28).

Conversely, the pre-eminence of wheat in Saskatchewan has tended to isolate its farmers by creating a sense of uncertainty amid unpredictable climatic and international economic forces. Despite diversification in recent decades, Saskatchewan's continued reliance on natural resources has perpetuated the boom-and-bust nature of its political economy (Dunn and Laycock 1992, 212-16; Rasmussen 2001, 241). For these reasons, Saskatchewan's economic environment has been most conducive to the collectivist thinking and co-operative endeavours at the heart of social democracy (see also Courtney and Smith 1972, 311-13; Fowke 1946; Dunn and Laycock 1992, 208-12; Friesen 1999, 101-5; but see Rasmussen 2001, 257; Eager 1980, 2; Fairbairn 2009).

Lastly, Manitoba's distinctiveness might be attributed to the fact that, in avoiding the boom-and-bust cycles experienced by its western neighbours, the province has not been given to the same type of "utopian sorties," including those led by Social Credit and the CCF (Wiseman 2007, 217). In this sense, Manitoba's stable, diversified economy has contributed to its ideologically balanced political culture (Morton 1967a, 392-96; Dyck 1996, 374; Hum and Simpson 2009).

Wiseman qualifies his use of staples theory, noting its many shortcomings in terms of explaining political diversity on the Prairies. For one, the common predominance of agriculture in each of the three provinces during their formative periods casts serious doubt on the usefulness of the approach (see Smith 1991, 434). For this reason, Wiseman's use of staples theory is almost begrudging. For example, the prominence of left-wing thought in Manitoba and Saskatchewan "seems counterintuitive" to him: "[Why] would social democracy take hold in an agrarian hinterland region where self-employed, independent small farmers dominated? In such a setting, individualist values, petit bourgeois entrepreneurial instincts, and right-wing ideas may be expected to prevail, as they have in Alberta. In contrast, social democracy, with its emphasis on collectivist values, government planning, and the welfare state, is traditionally the clarion of urban groups – industrial wage labourers and those without property" (Wiseman 2007, 212). Because neither Manitoba nor Saskatchewan can be considered especially urban or industrial societies, particularly in the formative years of each province, the paradox remains largely unsolved.

Johnson (1979, 91) approaches the paradox from the opposite angle, noting that Depression-era Saskatchewan and Alberta, "while different in some respects, were similar in terms of the presence of social and economic conditions which would support a *socialist* movement ... Alberta's social conditions were volatile enough, and the depression was severe enough that socialism could have succeeded *if the political circumstances were different*" (emphasis added). These political circumstances are the main focus of the present study.

Furthermore, according to Wiseman, "a closer examination of the past reveals that the politics of the three provinces have *always* been different from one another, and that economic factors do not appear to explain the difference. The Depression, for example, has been cited to explain the success of Manitoba's Bracken in maintaining power, the success of Alberta's Aberhart in gaining it, and the failure of the Saskatchewan CCF to come by it at all in the 1930s" (Wiseman 1988, 181, emphasis added; see also Morton 1967b, 460-62; Morton 1992b).

Another flaw exists in staples theory: Precisely how different do the economies of the various communities need to be? Up to the Second World War, each Prairie province's economy was heavily reliant on agriculture. Subtle differences existed, of course. Alberta's ranching industry was the most extensive, while Saskatchewan's dependency on wheat ran deepest. Beginning in the late 1940s in Alberta, and two decades later in Saskatchewan, the provinces developed their natural resource sectors. Again, there were disparities: the former was dominated by oil and gas, the latter by potash and uranium. Their neighbour's development of cleaner energy – through Manitoba Hydro – stands apart somewhat (see Hardwick 1984).

Yet whether in agriculture or natural resource development, the differences between the Prairie provinces' economies have always been a matter of degree rather than kind. Throughout much of the region's history, the economies of all three provinces have been primarily export-based, reliant on Canadian, continental, and global markets (Gibbins 2008). More recently, like most developed states, all three provinces have experienced the relative decline and radical transformation of agriculture (Gibbins 1984, 223; Norrie 1984, 63; Friesen 1999, 120), the challenges of economic diversification (Rasmussen 2001), and the concurrent expansion of the new middle class following the exponential growth of the service sector (Howlett 2006).

Thus, even if their economies differed at one point in time (a debatable proposition), the convergence and broad comparability of the three western economies suggests that their political cultures should be (growing) quite similar, according to staples theory. Considering all of these factors, the staples approach offers, at best, only a partial solution to the Prairie paradox.

Synthesizing these formative events and staples approaches, Wiseman rests the bulk of his argument on a third level of analysis. In it, he suggests the political diversity among the three Prairie provinces can be traced to their early immigration patterns. Based loosely on Hartzian fragment theory (see Chapter 2), Wiseman's rich account may be summarized as follows. Beginning with the opening of the West in the late nineteenth century, Manitoba drew the vast majority of its settlers from the Province of Ontario (Wiseman 1983, 3-5). These pioneers brought with them a Tory-touched liberalism (and a corresponding aversion to populist radicalism) not found in other parts of the Prairies (see also Young 1978, 5; Morton 1967a, viii; Dyck 1996, 381-82; Rea 1970). In partisan terms, this Tory-touched fragment not only helps to explain the long-term survival of the Conservative Party in Manitoba, it also suggests why socialism found a toehold in Manitoba in the form of the Independent Labour Party, the CCF, and, most recently, the NDP: the organic sense of community embodied in Toryism combined with the reform-minded philosophy of liberalism to produce an environment conducive to a moderate, democratic brand of socialism (see Hartz 1964; Horowitz 1966; McAllister 1984, 90-93).[4] British Labourites, whose brand of Fabian socialism found a sympathetic ear among the province's working-class population, seized this opportunity to establish the partisan foundations for the modern NDP (Wiseman 1983, 4-9). All told, this balance between Tory conservatism, liberalism, and social democracy formed the foundation of Manitoba's temperate political culture.

By contrast, Wiseman attributes the dominance of social democracy in Saskatchewan to the direct immigration of Fabian-influenced British settlers in the first decades of the twentieth century (see also Archer 1980, 11; Lipset 1968a, 43-44; Dyck 1996, 440). These immigrants settled largely in rural areas, providing the basis for what Lipset (1968a) termed agrarian socialism. Thus, while both Manitoba and Saskatchewan share a common social democratic impulse – distinguishing the Midwest from the parvenu political culture of the Far West – each owes its ideological heritage to a unique set of fragments (Wiseman 2007).

Meanwhile, with a larger proportion of American settlers than Manitoba and Saskatchewan, Alberta developed a greater penchant for laissez-faire liberalism (see also Flanagan and Lee 1992; Pickup et al. 2004, 634; Swann 1971, 57). "In 1911, American-born Albertans (22 percent of the population) outnumbered the British-born, Ontario-born, and European-born. Almost certainly, this was the largest concentration of Americans in any jurisdiction outside the U.S. Canadian-born Albertans were a minority in their own province" (Wiseman 2007, 244). By contrast, Americans made up 3 percent of the Manitoba population at the time, and 13 percent of Saskatchewan's (ibid., 226). As a result of its American roots, Alberta has proven to be fertile ground for right-wing populism and relatively inhospitable to Tory-touched liberalism and socialism.

In the end, Wiseman argues, these unique immigration patterns have contributed to the development of Manitoba, which features a more moderate mode of competition between the forces of Left and Right, into the Ontario of the Prairies. Saskatchewan, with its proclivity toward social democracy, has become the Britain of the Prairies, and Alberta, the most conservative of Canada's provinces, is "the Prairies' Great Plains America." Wiseman (2002, 218) asserts that "there is no single overriding political tradition on the prairies": there are three.

Like the formative events and staples approaches discussed above, the foundations of fragment theory have cracked over time. Space does not permit a detailed appraisal of fragment theory, only those critiques most pertinent to the present study, for critical reviews abound elsewhere (Stewart 1994b, 79-85; Forbes 1987; Ajzenstat and Smith 1998; Preece 1977; Wilton 2000). Wiseman (2007, 10) recognizes these criticisms, qualifying his research as an attempt to "extend but also swerve from the Hartz-Horowitz approach by contextualizing some of its features regionally." Nonetheless, several shortcomings remain in his analysis.

First, as with their economies, questions arise as to how different the settlement patterns of the three provinces really were. Consider Courtney and Smith's (1972, 304) description of Saskatchewan political culture as being "influenced by a British colonial heritage, an ethnically diversified population, an agricultural economic base, and a numerically preponderant rural electorate." To a greater or lesser extent, their account could be used to apply to early-twentieth-century Manitoba or Alberta (see Eager 1980, 65-67). As Friesen (1999, 5-6) suggests,

> The years from 1867 to 1940 saw the creation of the Prairies, a distinctive region built on wheat. The society was everywhere mixed in race and religion. Because each district seemed to offer a different combination of nationalities, the Prairies could be described as uniform in their diversity ... Whatever the leading ethnic group in a local district, the towns were mainly British Canadian. Some observers thought Manitoba was more Ontario, Saskatchewan more British, Alberta more American. Nonetheless, the cultural tone of the region was a distinctly Prairie version of English-speaking Canada, one expressed in the imperial views of the history texts, in the Protestant "non-denominational" notes of the schoolroom's daily Bible reading and in the parliamentary rules governing every official local meeting.

Second, although it provides an attractive description of the origins of political culture on the Prairies, Wiseman's work lacks a concrete explanation of the *persistence* of these differences. Wiseman (2007, 221) concedes this point, noting in passing that certain ideas became "rooted, institutionalized and cross-generationally transmitted in the provincial political culture."

Whereas Wiseman's analysis sidesteps this transmission process, this book focuses on it. Specifically, how have liberalism, socialism, and the Tory touch (as well as formative events and staples) been transmitted from these early periods to today's societies?

In response, fragment theory offers only "congealment" – a vague and often unspecified point at which a province's political culture freezes following decisive waves of immigration (see Chapter 2). In Wiseman's analysis, this congealment occurred almost a full century ago; in other words, subsequent decades were relatively uneventful when it comes to explaining the patterns of Prairie politics. For instance, Wiseman's account suggests that a group of liberal, early-nineteenth-century settlers from the American midwest had a more significant impact on Alberta than the original eastern Canadian pioneers, socialist-inspired Progressives, or the thousands of migrants that moved to the province over the last five decades (Sampert 2008).

At the same time, the effects of the formative events in each province – the Winnipeg General Strike, the Depression, and Leduc – are fading from the collective memory; they are limited in direct terms to the personal experiences of the generation exposed to them (Courtney and Smith 1972; Inglehart 1990). And economic paradigms have shifted from neomercantilism, to Keynesianism, to the present neoliberal consensus (Smith 1992). As Friesen (1999, 26) suggests, "the alternations in western circumstances during the present generation are so profound that Canadians living outside the region might be surprised by the scale of the changes" (see also Friesen 1996, 39-41). Indeed, according to Gibbins, "As the prairie lifestyle comes more and more to resemble that of other metropolitan regions in Canada and indeed North America, the distinguishing features of prairie society are becoming steadily erased. Attitudinal features, however, remain, and we are left with *a region of the mind,* nostalgic image of the beliefs and values of an earlier agrarian society that has been transformed almost beyond recognition" (Gibbins 1979, 164, emphasis added; see also Allen 1973; Friesen 1984a, 2; Gibbins 1984; Smith 1984; Friesen 1999, 27-31; Andrew et al. 2008).

Amid these transformations and convergences, the persistent differences among the three Prairie political cultures remain unexplained by fragment theory. As Stewart (1994a, 156) tells us, "even though political cultures tend to be relatively stable over time, they are certainly not *indefinitely* determined by the attitudinal attributes of the founding fragment." If cultural differences are somehow linked to settlement patterns, the persistence of the three "worlds" on the Prairies needs to be explained in terms of how values are transmitted not only from generation to generation but also from natives to newcomers. In the end, as Bell and Tepperman (1979, 23) argue, fragment theory "fails to explain how fragment cultures keep themselves alive, by acculturating *new* immigrants and children, thereby surviving, passing the culture form one generation to the next. In this respect, it resembles the theory of genetic transmission before the structure of DNA was discovered. Now we need a theory that explains the learning and modification of culture in simple, unmysterious terms. The ideology of the founding groups may indeed contain the genetic code of political culture, as Hartz suggests. But this insight alone is not enough."

Borrowing from this approach, Wiseman's use of fragment theory does not explain why or how each province's formative events, staples, and settlement patterns continued to hold influence despite these tremendous transformations. In short, although he may well be accurate in his *description*, Wiseman does not explain *how or why* the realities of the "old prairies" continue to shape the "new prairies" (Gibbins 1980, 1-2). He is not wrong in describing the present diversity among the three Prairie provinces as byproducts of their original political cultures. He is merely half-right. His account is not inaccurate: it begs supplementation.

Moving beyond Structure

Wiseman underestimates the role of agency in the development of Prairie politics. He is not alone in this: by their very definition, political parties and their leaders are assigned passive roles in traditional structural accounts. Wiseman finds company in downplaying the role of parties and leaders in Prairie historiography. As he notes, Friesen makes no reference to Tommy Douglas in his seminal history *The Canadian Prairies* (Wiseman 2007, 11; see also 1988, 178-79). When they are mentioned, political actors are often portrayed as products of social or economic forces.

To be clear, Wiseman does not dismiss the role of agency entirely. He merely reserves it for a secondary, limited role in explaining political outcomes. *Code Politics* turns this assumption on its head, emphasizing the primary role that agents (political parties) play in structuring their environment (political cultures). Just as Wiseman's recognizes the influence of agency, the following analysis acknowledges the effect of structure. However, rather than presenting them as largely byproducts of their political cultures, this book portrays parties as actively interpreting and propagating those same values.

This difference in emphasis is captured best in the following series of counterfactuals. Whereas Wiseman argues that there would have been no Tommy Douglas without a collectivist political culture, the pages that follow reveal that the persistence of Saskatchewan's social democratic impulse owes as much to Douglas's leadership as vice versa. The same is true of Aberhart, Manning, and Klein in conservative Alberta or Bracken, Roblin, and Doer in Progressive Manitoba. Wiseman (1988, 180) suggests that there can be no ideological leadership without a supportive political culture – that these leaders' successes were "based on their ability to understand and express the sentiments of their followers." Recognizing the reciprocal relationship between structure and agency, this book grounds political success in the leaders' abilities to define, shape, and cultivate those very same sentiments. For instance, William Aberhart's success among independent commodity producers in Alberta required that he first convince them of their petit bourgeois status (Pal 1992, 3). In other words, structural factors may make a particular province more receptive to a certain set of ideological influences, but this susceptibility must be exploited by a set of active agents. Demand must be met by supply.

In short, although he provides a valuable account of the origins of Prairie politics, Wiseman (2007, 221) leaves his readers without a clear understanding of the mechanism through which events, economic ethoses, and cultures are transmitted from one generation to the next or from established residents to new arrivals. One such mechanism lies in the power of rhetoric and, in particular, the development of party ideologies and provincial codes by political elites. As Huntington (1981, 10) argues, "structural paradigms ... are not totally wrong, but they are limited. They omit almost entirely the role [played by] political ideas and idealism, moral causes, and creedal passions." In these ways, the present analysis is intended less to correct than to supplement Wiseman's "rumination on Canadian politics" (Wiseman 2007, 1).

2

Politics over Time
Explaining Cultural Persistence

An entire century has passed since the first major influx of Anglo-Americans to the Canadian prairies. Yet, as witnessed by the persistence of three distinct political cultures they helped to establish, these early settlers continue to influence the region's politics to this day. The earliest of these immigrant groups settled the Red River Valley, in what would become the Province of Manitoba. By the turn of the twentieth century, Tory-touched, Ontario-bred British pioneers had come to dominate the province's political life, outnumbering and overpowering its First Nations, Metis, and French inhabitants. Decades later, immigration shifted westward, and different charter groups emerged in each of the two new, twin provinces. Over time, British-born Labourites rose to political prominence in Saskatchewan, and American frontier liberals gained authority in Alberta. Three separate political communities emerged in a single region.

In the mid-1930s, the Prairie provinces were as politically distinct as ever. Manitoba dominated by a moderate brand of progressivism, Saskatchewan by an agrarian variant of social democracy, and Alberta by a populist strain of conservatism (Laycock 1990; Morton 1992a, 1992b; Lipset 1968a; Macpherson 1977). These differences persisted as each province matured during the Second World War, the province-building period from the 1950s to the 1970s, and the onset of neoliberalism in the 1980s and 1990s. According to most observers, the distinctions endure to this day. Whether reflected in political party systems, institutions, or popular perceptions, Alberta's conservative political culture continues to be at odds with the social democratic ethos of Saskatchewan and the tenor of temperance embedded in Manitoba politics. What explains this persistence?

In search of solutions to the Prairie paradox, this chapter reviews three prominent explanations of cultural transmission. The first approach suggests that, once established during a community's formative years, a political culture simply freezes. In this perspective, the persistence of a political culture is an automatic and natural, albeit mysterious, routine of every society. Although popular in the earlier part of the twentieth century, these and other functionalist theories have since fallen into disrepute among social scientists. Strangely, however, variants of the so-called freezing thesis persist as explanations for cultural diversity on the Canadian prairies (see Chapter 1).

Breaking open the black box of cultural transmission, scholars have suggested two alternatives to the freezing hypothesis known broadly as socialization and institutionalization. Drawn from fields as disparate as sociology, history, anthropology, linguistics, psychology, economics, and political science, neither of these solutions is comprehensive in and of itself. A common thread unites them, however. Cultures are not diffused passively from generation to generation or from natives to newcomers: they are taught and learned, entrenched and interpreted. Thus, cultural transmission is an active process, one that requires analysts to examine the role of agency.

As the focal point of this book, dominant political parties are key agents in this context. Yet they are by no means the only agents responsible for cultivating political culture on the Canadian prairies. This chapter examines parties alongside other important actors, including families, churches, schools, peer groups, artists, civil society, academia, the bureaucracy, and the media. This broader perspective on cultural transmission then narrows to a discussion of precisely how dominant political parties use prevailing modes of discourse – or codes – to transmit political culture over time.

The Freezing Hypothesis

The approach to cultural transmission pioneered by political historian Louis Hartz (1955, 1964) holds that, once formed, political cultures undergo a form of congealment.[1] Hartz's theory of fragmentation posits that, when settling a new society, dominant immigrant groups entrench certain values drawn from their parent cultures. Feudal tories bring with them notions of collectivist conservatism, for instance, whereas liberals import a penchant for laissez-faire politics. By virtue of the new society's virgin ideological soil, these ideas achieve almost universal authority, "sinking beneath the surface of thought to the level of an assumption" (Hartz 1964, 5). Because the set of values depends on the time of the group's departure, settlers will only transplant a fragment of their original political culture. (The fragment is determined by both the dominant values present among the group's members and the point in the ideological evolution of the parent culture.) Thereafter, the fragment is severed from its parent society and the ideological competition therein, effectively freezing it in its stage of ideological development and spawning the new society's political culture.

This freezing process – the conversion of a fragment's ideology into a society's political culture – is not instantaneous, of course. It takes at least a generation, for the original settlers may still identify with the contentious ideological undercurrents of their homeland. "But their children are not in the same position," according to Hartz. "Their children do not remember the 'old country.' They have lived inside the fragment all their lives, their battles have been the battles of its unfolding, and to them it is a true land ... The new generations of the fragment have lived inside this culture, not outside of it" (Hartz 1964, 12). Thereafter, through the organic process of generational replacement, the fragment "renews itself from within" (ibid., 14).

For Hartz (1964, 14), the strength of the fragment's grip on a new society's political culture is demonstrated by its ability to meet "the *immigrant challenge*" – that is, the continual influx of newcomers. "By consciously articulating the fragment ethic, it [the political culture] provides an instrument for absorbing the immigrant into it" (ibid.). New belief systems may arrive or arise within the society, but they do not take hold once the original political culture is established. "This is not a question of the citizens of the fragment 'rejecting' later ideologies," Hartz notes. "Rejection implies precisely the kind of freedom they do not have. Because the very seeds of the later ideas are contained in parts of the Old World that have been left behind, the experience of choice cannot be said to exist, even though, as I have said, the fragment nationalisms are forever crusading against the 'alien' principles" (ibid., 25). Although it may appear to involve "all sorts of magic," Hartz describes this freezing process as "purely mechanistic" (ibid., 5, 6): "A part detaches itself from the whole, the whole fails to renew itself, and the part develops without inhibition. The process is simple, as intelligible as any historical process we normally take for granted" (ibid., 9).

Fragment theory has, nonetheless, been the subject of much criticism, particularly for being overly teleological and deterministic. These labels are easily affixed, considering Hartz's (1964, 25) own words:

> There is an obvious chain of cause and effect in the stages out of which the fragment tradition arises: the extrication from Europe, the atrophy of the future, and the unfolding of the fragment potential. Once the voyage is underway and the [old country's] shore has begun to fade, processes are set in motion which only the forcible return of the revolutionary context can alter ... Nor is it easy to see, given the original voyage, how one could prevent the potential of the fragment from flowering. Where men [sic] are not stifled by competition, they not only do what they please, but they do not know that they might be expected to behave otherwise.

More than this, Hartz's account lacks detailed consideration of *how* the fragment's values are articulated or transmitted from old to new constituents (Dawson and Prewitt 1969, 27). The process is left ambiguous, implying, on some occasions, some sort of conscious indoctrination or assimilation, at others, a more passive form of absorption or osmosis. Either way, Hartz left others to study the precise mechanism of cultural transmission, and two additional schools of thought have since emerged.

Socialization

According to a pioneer of one approach, Sidney Verba (1965, 515), "The study of political culture leads invariably to the study of political socialization, to the learning experiences by which a political culture is passed from generation to generation."

Given this study's macroscopic definition of political culture – as a set of common political values and assumptions that underpin a given political system – the following discussion draws more from the anthropological literature on cultural transmission than from the psychological or sociological (see Merelman 1991).[2] As Pammett and Whittington (1976, 3) note, "Socialization is seen by the anthropologist as enculturation, a process through which all aspects of a culture are acquired and internalized by successive generations" and various waves of immigrants. The psychologist, in contrast, focuses more on the cognitive development of individuals, while the sociologist's attention often turns to the development of roles within a society (ibid., 3-5). One important theme runs through most definitions of socialization, however: political culture is handed down not only from parents to children but also from natives to newcomers. The former requires analysts to study the passing of collective memories over time, the latter, the contemporaneous diffusion of values from one group to another. In this sense, socialization entails both reproduction and assimilation (Torney-Purta 2000, 88) – two separate but related "means by which people get tied to the social order and are persuaded to think a certain way" (Bell and Tepperman 1979, 3).

In this context, understanding the socialization process requires an appreciation of the multiplicity of ways in which values are diffused throughout societies and over time. Individuals are acculturated through direct contact with the political system, for instance, through formal participation or exposure to certain events (Rosenbaum 1975, 16-19; Dawson and Prewitt 1969, 191-94; Sears and Valentino 1997). At the same time, culture may be acquired indirectly through contact with various "interpreters and conductors" of political culture (Whittington 1978, 28). These agents may have a primary relationship with the individual (as a parent, peer, teacher, or other acquaintance), or their interaction may be secondary (as a celebrity, artist, or other more distanced figure). The socialization process may take place in public, as in schools or on billboards, or in private, as in the home or through the earbuds of an iPod. The content may be explicitly political and the ideological message clearly and purposefully manifest, or the political implications may be latent and unintended.

Given this scope, a number of different agents are involved in the socialization process. From early studies of parents, peers, and the media, students of political socialization have expanded their scope to include other sources, ranging from religious and political elites to artists and academics. Although a comprehensive examination of these agents is beyond the means and purposes of this study, a brief review will contextualize the examination of Prairie political cultures that follows. Considering the dearth of recent studies of socialization in the region, and given the lack of specific scholarly attention to the transmission of political culture-cum-community ethos, the following discussion is more speculative than definitive. As an exploratory review, it poses more research questions than answers, offering several hypotheses for further study.

Most models of political socialization presume that learning is cumulative. That is, although socialization takes place throughout one's life cycle, "early learning – all prior learning – is regarded as a sort of filter for later learning" (Eckstein 1988, 791). Proceeding from this assumption, many students of socialization continue to place heavy emphasis on the role of families, schools, and peer groups in the inculcation of political values among children and adolescents. Granted, some recent research suggests that these relationships are not as unidirectional as was once thought (McDevitt 2005; McDevitt and Chaffee 2002), and some studies challenge the strictness of the correlation between parents' predispositions and those of their children (Sears and Valentino 1997). Yet the overall impression is clear: children learn a community's core values through a combination of parental upbringing, formal education, and informal interaction with their peers. Many of these studies focus on the transmission of political attitudes, orientations, and partisanship, but their lessons may also be applied to political culture in the holistic sense. A community's ethos is as likely to be transmitted through dinner table conversation, classroom instruction, or friendly banter as any other set of political beliefs.

There is no reason to believe that these findings and theories cannot be applied to the Canadian prairies. Familial conversations about politics – when and if they occur – are likely to shape a young Albertan's assumptions about the political world. Through these processes, Albertan children may develop a lower level of appreciation for the role of the state in society compared to children in Saskatchewan, for instance. As McDevitt (2005, 69) describes, "In contemporary approaches, the transfer of political attitudes from parents to children is often described as a two-step process. The child comprehends the orientations of parents, creating an image of what parents are like, and subsequently adapts his or her beliefs to that image." In this sense, parents in Alberta may model the conservative ethos for their children, either explicitly or subconsciously, thus passing political culture from generation to generation.

Other acquaintances may have a similar impact on individuals. Beyond childhood and adolescence, the effects of peer pressure are just as noticeable. Being conservative may be viewed as un-Saskatchewanian in most social circles, for instance, just as being utopian may be seen as un-Manitoban. In some instances, individuals choose their peers. Such is the case with (im)migrants who decide to move to a particular province in search of a particular lifestyle (e.g., entrepreneurial-spirited people may move to Alberta). By the same token, residents may choose to stay in a community to maintain their milieu (e.g., realists may elect to remain in Manitoba). Both decisions illustrate the process of cultural self-selection – another key element of socialization on the Prairies. Further examination of these peer effects – through direct observation, public interviews, focus groups, surveys, or other methods – may help to shed light on this element of cultural transmission on the Prairies.

Presented in school, so-called textbook accounts of a society's culture are also widely viewed as a source of socialization. This should hardly come as a surprise, for "schools are the socialization agency most easily controlled by the political system" (Almond and Powell 1966, 71). In this vein, "All school systems carry on some form of political indoctrination. The myths and legends from the past, the policies and programs of the present, and the goals and aspirations of the future are taught selectively. Consciously or not, textbooks and other teaching materials justify and rationalize political practices" (Dawson and Prewitt 1969, 152).

Jones (1980) reports, for example, how history lessons in early-twentieth-century Prairie schools reinforced the zeitgeist of western settlement by romanticizing the work of the pioneers and their frontier spirit. Specific elements of each province's political culture, such as the collectivist spirit in Saskatchewan, may have been cultivated in the same way. An examination of the Saskatchewan Co-operative Commonwealth Federation's (CCF's) 1944 election platform reveals how much emphasis individual parties place on curriculums (for both pedagogical and political reasons):

> The present courses of study, particularly the high school courses, do not prepare children adequately for the world into which they will go and try to make a living. Young people leave high school now, after apparently having been engaged in learning for twelve years, and discover that they know practically nothing about how the world is run. They do not know the conditions under which the means of life are made and distributed; they do not know how our main industries are organized, managed, and controlled; they do not know how the national income is divided or why it is so divided; they do not know the life of the people beyond their own community. Their knowledge of current affairs both in their own country and abroad is equally deplorable. Their schooling has not prepared them for the social and economic realities of their life, and consequently has given them little or no encouragement to become intelligent citizens. (Co-operative Commonwealth Federation [Sask. Section] 1944d)

In the future, a study of contemporary curriculums in each provincial school system may reveal differences in the way Prairie history is framed. Does the National Energy Policy figure more prominently in Alberta social studies courses than in Manitoba's, for example? Is the socialist movement cast differently – that is, more positively – in Saskatchewan schools, as critics on the Right have suggested for decades? Does the inclusion of extra-curricular programs sponsored by credit unions in Manitoba have an influence on the province's political culture? Has the recent inclusion of Aboriginal-based curriculums affected youths' perceptions of their province's political ethos? These and other education-based questions are important avenues for future inquiry.

Closely connected to the school system, scholars must also focus on the academic roots of political socialization. The work of historians is of particular interest in this regard, for – as Bell and Tepperman (1979, 4) remind us – what a society "remembers about itself, its history, is a major source of its political culture. History as tradition literally 'gives across' or hands down institutions, practices, symbols and slogans from one generation to the next. History offers us 'myths' that make our values, beliefs, and assumptions clear, concrete" (see also Sapiro 2004, 10-11). In this sense, Cooper's (2002) observations regarding the impact of the Laurentian myth on the collective psyche of western Canadians are particularly insightful. Along similar lines, Barrie (2006) and Lisac (2004a) note how the writing of history in Alberta has glossed over its more progressive roots (see also Leadbeater 1984; Harrison and Laxer 1995a). Images of rugged individualists and the triumphs of free-enterprise capitalists whose hard work took the province from rags to riches are mythologized; meanwhile, images of the province's collectivist roots are marginalized. Similar critiques have been levelled at the collectivist mystique that surrounds Saskatchewan politics (Eager 1980; Baron and Jackson 1991; Waiser 2009; Fairbairn 2009). The result of these mythologies, themselves the product of romanticism and parochial boosterism, has been the development of an insular, almost dogmatic, historiography of each province (Leadbeater 1984, ix-xv).

Uncovering the genesis of Prairie historiography is a challenging exercise – one better left to professional historians such as Francis (1992, 1989), Friesen (1984a), and others. Nonetheless, "tracing footnotes back from the present day," as Stewart (2002, 33-34) did in the Maritime context, one finds the intellectual foundation of Prairie political cultures in the writings of three prominent scholars, all of whom wrote at around the same period in the mid-twentieth century. Planted in the soil of previous historical accounts, an explanation of the roots of Alberta's political culture was established by C.B. Macpherson in his landmark study *Democracy in Alberta* (1953). In it, he describes the province as a petit bourgeois society whose culture corresponds more closely with the American plains than eastern Canada, a theme that persists to this day in most accounts of the province's political culture (Bell 1992). Similarly, Saskatchewan's image as the bastion of agrarian socialism owes as much to Seymour Martin Lipset (1968) as any other academic figure. His book remains required reading for any student of politics in Saskatchewan and has shaped generations of scholars in their own writings on social democratic political culture (Smith 2007). W.L. Morton is to Manitoba as Macpherson is to Alberta and Lipset to Saskatchewan. His book *Manitoba: A History* (1957) remains the anchor of every major study on Manitoba's political evolution. It tells the story of Manitoba's formative years, the story of a society torn between the traditional politics of its Ontarian forebears and the progressive impulse of its western environment. This perspective is reflected clearly, if not cited explicitly, in most accounts of Manitoba's so-called middling political culture (Wesley 2010a).

This list of the "big three" scholars of Prairie political culture is not intended as a slight to other historians. Friesen, Francis, Owram, Archer, and others have contributed much to our understanding of politics in the region. When it comes to the three Prairie political cultures, however, the works of Macpherson, Lipset, and Morton serve as touchstones. Whether by authority or convenience, subsequent authors have drawn upon their writings, almost as gospel, to detail the content of each province's political culture. Considering this, one cannot rule out that *Code Politics* may have a limited effect on conventional wisdom. Some have challenged their interpretations, both in terms of their historical and contemporary accuracy (Smith 2009; Pal 1992; Bell 1993a), yet, overall, the conventional interpretation of political culture in Alberta, Saskatchewan, and Manitoba remains grounded in the interpretations of Macpherson, Lipset, and Morton, respectively.

This persistence suggests one of two possibilities: either the political cultures themselves have remained unchanged since these men wrote in the mid-twentieth century or political scientists have relied too heavily on outdated conceptions. On the latter, Bell's (1993a, 6-7) warning about academic authority is prescient: "It often happens that ideas gain considerable prominence in the social sciences without ever having been examined empirically ... The situation is rather like a group of early cartographers agreeing that a particular river drains into the Great Lakes without anyone's having taken a voyage to the river's end." In either case, however, the persistence of the Macpherson-Lipset-Morton interpretation of Prairie political culture suggests that accepted academic wisdom is an important element of the socialization process.

Just as many students and scholars of political culture have focused predominantly on the formative years of society, so too have scholars of political socialization focused primarily on the formative years of individuals by examining the role of families, schools, and peer groups in transmitting political culture from one generation to the next. This perspective has broadened in recent years as scholars have recognized that socialization takes place throughout the life cycle of individuals and societies (Pammett and Whittington 1976, 17). The shift has meant the inclusion of a whole host of other agents, including, most notably, artists, churches, and the media.

The idea that culture is communicated through the arts seems obvious. In examinations of the transmission of political culture, the influence of literature is of particular interest (Anderson 1983, 30; Lipset 1990, chap. 4). For instance, Francis (1989) notes how the cultivation of the West as a region of the mind owed as much to the fictional works of Margaret Laurence, Peter Stevens, Edward McCourt, Henry Kreisel, Dorothy Livesay, and others as it did to any explicitly academic or political writings. The romantic legends of the western frontier; the early pioneers' lifestyle of isolation, alienation, and deprivation; the positive and negative sides of ethnic diversity; the trials and tribulations of early economic development; tales of small-town gas stations and mosques – all have received treatment by some of Canada's most gifted artists. Future study might reveal that, over time, these and other elements of popular culture developed alongside the tenets of each province's political culture, often with reinforcing effects (see Street 1997).[3]

The role of the church – or, more accurately, organized religion – is often overlooked in the context of political socialization. Nonetheless, acknowledging the region's religious diversity is indispensable to understanding political culture on the Prairies, particularly in the early twentieth century. At that time, the three provinces featured unique combinations of religious forces, each of which corresponded with the nature of its political culture. Manitoba featured what Lipset (1990, chap. 5) termed coexistence in reference to the broader Canadian context. Periodic but highly charged struggles between Catholics and Protestants helped to set the province apart from its western neighbours, in which Protestantism generally held sway. The compromises reached between Manitoba's religious communities mirrored, and in many ways overlapped with, the process of conciliation in Manitoba's political realm. Elites such as Thomas Greenway and others drew upon this shared ethos to craft their political messages and cultivate the province's political culture.

Further west, there were also key divisions between Alberta and Saskatchewan. As Groh (1970, 26-27) points out, the Alberta brand of evangelical Social Gospel diverged considerably from the newer model adopted by the Anglican, Methodist, and Presbyterian churches that dominated Saskatchewan. Following a doctrinal shift in the late 1920s, the latter advocated a collectivist philosophy, whereas Alberta's religious community "being ... strict[ly] fundamentalist, maintained an individualist stance." On another level, the nonconformism embodied in Alberta's sectarian religious heritage appears to be linked to its populist political character (Mann 1955). An appreciation of this religious context is key to understanding why Tommy Douglas succeeded in Saskatchewan, while William Aberhart and Ernest Manning dominated Alberta. Given these parallels, it is difficult to deny the interdependent nature of the relationship between the religious and political cultures in each province. Religion appears to be responsible, at least in part, for helping to transmit political cultures over time.

The media is also considered a key component of most models of political socialization (Merelman 1991, 381; Hackett 2001). During the height of socialization studies in the 1970s, journalists, reporters, and broadcasters were cast as "the primary agents for transferring to young people a feeling of their political history and the common feelings and symbols which bind them to others within the same culture. They [created] a national pride, a belief in the country that form[ed] a basic attachment upon which the more specific attitudinal components of political culture [could be] built" (Whittington 1978, 28). The applicability of these lessons to the transmission of political culture at the provincial level remains to be studied. Yet there is little reason to believe that local newspapers and broadcasters should behave any differently than national ones. The influence of the *Winnipeg Free Press,* which has cultivated an air of traditionalism and aversion to ideological extremes through its editorial policies, on Manitoba politics is particularly noteworthy in this regard (Russell 2010). The effect of the long-term decline of local news media is certainly deserving of study, however.

Thus, a host of agents have helped to sustain the three Prairie political cultures, for journalists, novelists, artists, academics, and others often romanticize (or demonize) a particular definition of each political community (Bell 1993b, 6-7, 147; Ward 1975, 303). This brief discussion could have included any number of other cultural transmitters. Civil society organizations, from the Orange Order and the Ku Klux Klan to the Red Cross and Kinsmen Club, have all had an influence on political culture on the Prairies. So, too, have government public relations firms (Kiss 2009). This book, however, focuses on the importance of leading political parties as some of the most crucial of all value carriers on the Canadian prairies.

Institutionalization

A second somewhat related school of thought holds that political culture is transmitted through a formal process of institutionalization, by which certain values become embedded in the policies, laws, programs, agencies, organizations, and other brick-and-mortar structures of the state (Netherton 2001, 203). Populism may become institutionalized through the passage of referendum or recall legislation, for instance, or a spirit of collectivism could be embedded through the implementation of universal social programs or a steeply progressive taxation system (Rasmussen 2001). In such cases, the functioning of the institution itself often reinforces the original ideological impulses that produced it. By strengthening, legitimizing, and rendering routine the cause of direct democracy, plebiscites may fortify the populist elements of a given political culture. The same is true of public health care programs in societies of a collectivist bent. For these reasons, Berman (2001, 26-27) cites institutionalization as one of the "most important factors determining whether ideas are able to influence politics over the long term ... Once institutionalized, ideas take on a life of their own, changing the motivation and perception of political actors, affecting their decision making over the long term."

When they examine institutions for ideological content, analysts must study the reasoning and motivation behind them, rather than making tautological inferences from their existence (Christian and Campbell 1990, 116; Blyth 1997, 236; Goldstein and Keohane 1993a, 25-29). As Wiseman (1998, 59-60) argues, this requires attention to "the *rationale* for policy [as] policy by itself does not necessarily reveal a specific ideological impulse." In fact, "policies may be, and often are, dressed in different ideological clothing, but the outcomes are very similar" (ibid., 189). He cites public health care as a prime example of how adherents to different ideologies can be supportive of a policy for different reasons: conservatives out of a sense of community, liberals in the interests of equal opportunity, and socialists for reasons of universality. Wiseman (2007, 17) therefore warns, "when a policy is cited as evidence of an ideological inclination ... be skeptical. Apply the litmus test. Did the governing party nationalize an industry to redistribute wealth (socialism), or to help other industries, private ones, to grow and profit (liberalism), or for the purpose of nation building (possible toryism)?"

In the Prairie context, Wiseman draws similar conclusions about the various ideological impulses behind the co-operative movement. "To [Saskatchewan CCF premier Tommy] Douglas, co-operatives were paving stones on the road to a socialist society. To [Manitoba Progressive premier John] Bracken and [Alberta Social Credit premier William] Aberhart, in contrast, co-operatives were merely an efficient and responsive form of capitalism for small business entrepreneurs" (Wiseman 1988, 188-89). Therefore analysts should "not confuse or mechanistically link the ideological and policy realms ... What is vital at the ideological level is not a specific policy or program, but the *rationale* for it" (Wiseman 2007, 16).

With these warnings in mind, there are several institutional features that appear conducive to the transmission of political cultural values on the Prairies over time. In Saskatchewan, the government developed a family of Crown corporations in the utility, energy, resource, and service sectors, for instance. Once established, these agencies reinforced the communitarian and strong state values imbued in the province's political culture. Beyond legal institutions, the selection of provincial symbols can also help to sustain a political code. The decision to emblazon the Union Jack on its provincial flag or inscribe its licence plates with the word *friendly*, while trite to some, has both reflected and nourished the values of traditionalism and accommodation found in Manitoba's political culture (Wesley 2010a). Just as important, the absence of certain institutions can affect a province's political culture. As is discussed in Chapter 3, Ernest Manning's decision to hold an electrification plebiscite in 1948 had lasting effects on Alberta party politics. The electorate's decision to maintain a private system of electricity distribution, as opposed to a public utility such as SaskPower or Manitoba Hydro, proved to be a pivotal moment in the evolution of the provincial culture because it helped to sustain a value system based on free enterprise. (That the outcome was determined by fewer than one thousand votes in a 1948 plebiscite reveals the contingent nature of Prairie politics.)

These are just a few examples of how the values embedded in the three Prairie political cultures have come to be institutionalized into the structures of each state. A comprehensive study would also examine the cultural content of provincial constitutions, house rules, Cabinet structures, judicial opinions, emblems, slogans, brands, and other institutional features – full treatment of which is well beyond the scope of this study. All told, these policies, laws, symbols, and other institutions have helped to lock in the political cultures of each Prairie province. Street (1997, 146) is right:

"Culture does not just 'exist', it depends upon institutions and industries ... for it to be produced and reproduced."

Code Politics and Cultural Transmission

Isolating factors that help to sustain a political culture requires identifying specific agents of socialization and institutionalization. Researchers must determine precisely who is responsible for propagating the values embedded in the community's broader political ethos, for ideas only influence politics when they are carried by particular political actors. Given the durable nature of political culture, these values must be expressed repeatedly and with relative consistency over a long period of time so that the ideas involved in the genesis of the community's ethos are transmitted with little distortion across several generations. Thus, to be convinced that a specific agent (or set of agents) is at least partly responsible for nourishing a political culture, analysts must establish that it has persistently advocated the values entrenched therein. This does not imply intent on behalf of the agent (the propagation of cultural norms is often unplanned and subconscious); rather, it requires that the agent meet two conditions: (1) that the values it promotes correspond with those of the broader political culture and (2) that these values are expressed consistently over time.

All of the agents mentioned above – citizens, religious leaders, teachers, artists, academics, bureaucrats, journalists, and others – play important roles through socialization and institutionalization. This study explores one additional group of actors, whose contribution to the adaptation and revivification of a community's ethos is of prime importance: dominant political parties. In their campaign rhetoric, leading political parties have tended to emphasize the values entrenched in their political cultures. They have done so steadily throughout the past seven decades to such a degree that – regardless of the party label or leader – leading political elites in each province have been guided in their campaigns by a similar code of discourse. At least every four years, dominant parties have acted as carriers of their political cultures, transmitting unique sets of ideas and norms from generation to generation and from natives to newcomers during election campaigns.

The findings presented in the following chapters parallel Laitin's research in *Hegemony and Culture* (1986, 171), in which he observes:

> Political elites in any society will act strategically and ideologically in the
> hope of defining and delimiting which strands of their society's culture

should become dominant ... The dominant cultural subsystem, once chosen, spins political life into a "web of significance" which grasps elites and masses alike. Since [the political elites are] more concerned with the efficiency of control than the secondary consequence of having altered the cultural framework for action, the new elites will themselves become (often unwilling) subjects of their own past cultural choices. In this way, cultural subsystems have an impact on the subsequent choices of both elites and masses. Consequently, social science needs to develop theories capable of isolating this power of culture to influence politics.

This is the very essence of code politics, as it is discussed throughout this study. Dominant political parties craft their rhetoric to correspond with the political culture of their respective communities. Repeated frequently and reinforced by the success of the parties that emphasize them, these values form distinct campaign themes that, over the course of several electoral cycles, appear to "take on a life of their own." In the process, these dominant modes of discourse act as vehicles for the values embedded in the broader political culture. In short, dominant political parties act as carriers of political culture, transmitting it to both new generations and new arrivals during election campaigns. Their campaign messages and the broader codes in which they crystallize serve as periodic but consistent reminders of the community's core political values.

Descriptions such as Laitin's often attribute hegemonic tendencies or Machiavellian motives to political elites, treating their platforms as tools of propaganda designed to indoctrinate the electorate. This is not implied by the proposed "code politics" model. Like Edelman's, this study "concentrates on the mechanisms through which politics influences what [people] want, what they fear, what they regard as possible, and even who they are. There is no implication here that elites consciously mold political myths and rituals to serve their own ends. Attempts at such manipulation usually become known for what they are and fail" (Edelman 1964, 131). Political elites do, nonetheless, play a leading role in propagating and perpetuating political cultures. Precisely how these values are translated into party rhetoric is challenging to study, given the often secretive nature of platform development. During the course of this study, for instance, requests for literature (let alone interviews) from lead campaign officials were denied on many occasions. Moreover, the authors of most platforms are unknown because they are published under the authority of the respective provincial party association.

In the absence of direct observation or insider commentary, analysts are left with two sources of information on platform development on the Canadian prairies. The location of primary documents in various archives offers clues as to their genesis and authorship. Several collections contain sequential drafts of a given platform, for instance. Although their circulation varied from party to party, these documents were, in general, penned by high-ranking party officials – central campaign managers, party presidents, chiefs of staff, and (in several instances) the leaders themselves – and then distributed to members of the campaign team, key candidates, and the party executive for review before formal publication. Archival evidence shows that such practices took place in all major political parties dating back to at least the Second World War, revealing the existence and extent of party professionalization in the early stages of Prairie party politics (see Kirchheimer 1966; Farrell and Webb 2000; Panebianco 1988).

Scholars may also apply lessons from secondary literature on platform development to the Prairie context. Unfortunately, relative to most other aspects of party politics, political scientists know precious little about how manifestos are designed (DeLong 1988; see Budge and Bara 2001, 3; Walters 1990). This is especially true when it comes to the rhetorical elements of campaign platforms, as opposed to their specific policy content. Indeed, one of the most recent Canadian studies of the subject was published almost fifty years ago (Meisel 1960). Eerily, however, its conclusions appear readily applicable to Prairie politics, past and present. Foremost among them, as supported by the archival evidence cited above, it is clear that major parties in Alberta, Saskatchewan, and Manitoba have long employed a top-down approach to platform development. Despite hosting (semi-)annual policy conventions, engaging the grassroots in periodic consultation exercises, and consulting with expert policy advisers, the leader and his or her coterie of campaign strategists retain ultimate control over the party's election platform (Cross 2004, 34-45, 108-14; Carty 2002, 346, 372; Pelletier 1996, 143-44, 156; Scarrow, Webb, and Farrell 2000, 136-38). This is particularly true of its rhetorical content, which has become the subject of extensive focus-group testing prior to publication.

If anything, the centralization of control over the party platform has increased over time, particularly with the growth in importance of the media in campaign politics (Carty, Cross, and Young 2000, 178-210; Meisel and Mendelsohn 2001, 170; Hackett 2001; Paltiel 1996, 405-6). In this context, the party platform is a key tool of party communications (the so-called air war) (Flanagan 2007, 283; Blais et al. 2002, 18-25). Indeed, because they are "designed to pre-empt and direct media discussion" of the campaign (Bara and Budge 2001, 591), platforms serve as a key "reference point for television and press discussion of party policies" (Budge 1994, 455; see also Kinsella 2007; Flanagan 2007; Barney 2007). Given the centrality of the platform in the campaign, party leaders and their advisers place great emphasis on developing the proper message (Farrell 2006, 129-30).

For this reason, throughout this book, references are made to the influence of specific leaders on the course of Prairie political history. These assertions are based on the assumption that party platforms embody the rhetoric of the leaders themselves. This makes sense, considering that platforms are the only authoritative vision issued on behalf of the party – as endorsed by the party leadership.[4] Moreover, as Sayers (2002, 305) suggests, "Canadian parties have long been considered leader dominated," a trend that has only strengthened over time. Today, party leaders possess "enhanced autonomy and authority: they now control the far more centralized campaign organizations needed to fight modern elections" and thus exert considerable influence over the party's image and message (Carty, Erickson, and Blake 1992, 3). Although such observations are based on the Canadian experience in general, there is little reason to believe Prairie parties are any less leader-focused (see Bell 1993a, 472; Wiseman 1988; LeDuc 1994; Taras and Weyant 1988). For these reasons, leaders (and their entourages) are assumed to be interchangeable with the campaign face of each party (Noel 2007). This should not be taken as an argument that each leader *is* the party. As discussed, parties have many other faces (in the electorate, in government, and as organizations, for example) (Key 1964). Yet, when we examine political party platforms, we are on solid ground in describing parties in campaigns as Lougheed Conservatives, Schreyer New Democrats, and the like.

To determine how the values embedded in each province's political culture come to be translated into campaign rhetoric, one must therefore examine the role and calculations of party leaders and their campaign advisers. To them, political culture represents both a set of ideational constraints and a potential wellspring of power. Among other factors, the former derives from the nature of representative democracy in Canada, which ensures that "if the values of our political elites are incompatible with the values of the mass, then the elites will ultimately face electoral defeat" (Whittington 1978, 150). Related to this, "political culture provides a range of acceptable values and standards upon which leaders can draw in attempting to justify their policies ... Thus political culture shapes the perception of politically relevant problems, thereby affecting both the recognition of these problems as issues requiring some sort of governmental action and the diagnosis of what sort of action is appropriate. Political culture influences beliefs about who should be assigned responsibility for solving problems and what kind of solutions are likely to work" (Bell 2000, 277; see also Jenson 1987). Hartz (1964, 14) concurs with this logic, noting that political culture provides "a set of symbols for the conquering hero to use."

Thus, the relationship between dominant party rhetoric and political culture is quite complex. From one angle, the nature of campaign discourse appears to be the product of a community's heritage. Party leaders are really followers from this perspective, crafting their messages according to what fits best with the enduring political culture. Given the embeddedness of these values, party leaders must take into account the cultural characteristics of their communities and cope with "the trappings of traditional assumptions, institutions and political practices" (Tupper and Gibbins 1992, xvii). According to this view, for instance, William Aberhart invoked the image of Alberta as an oppressed society of independent pioneers not because that was necessarily his own vision of the province, but because he recognized that the society was steeped in rugged individualism. He had little choice but to shape his rhetoric around these norms if he wanted to attain (and retain) power. By the same token, Tommy Douglas's success is often attributed to the collectivist foundations of Saskatchewan society, which not only allowed but also persuaded the CCF leader to maintain a moderate brand of social democracy in his rhetoric. And John Bracken's decades in power had more to do with his appreciation for Manitoba's cautious, accommodative traditions than his own personal ideological leanings and leadership. In short, according to this first school of thought, dominant elites effectively inherit their ideas from the pre-existing political order (Berman 2001, 235). Successful party leaders – and the codes they help establish – are those that espouse values that correspond most closely with the prevailing norms of their society.

Wiseman's description of the pattern of Prairie leadership (1988) conforms to this model. In his most recent treatment of the subject, Wiseman is explicit in treating leaders as devices of their communities' political cultures: "Ideas and ideologies first appeared on the Prairies as imports from older societies. Their leading spokesmen and standard-bearers must be appreciated in terms that transcend quirks of personality and circumstance. Rather, the ideas and behaviour of Prairie political leaders – like those of leaders everywhere – are better understood as reflecting the popular and ideological-cultural bases of their support" (Wiseman 2007, 203). Wiseman does not rule out the role of agency entirely, of course. To him, "The question remains: are leaders unique actors and historical forces in themselves, or just products of their times and of their societies? ... They are both. They make and define their political times and they are made and defined by them" (Wiseman 1988, 179). Nonetheless, to Wiseman (ibid., 191, emphasis added), *"social context has been primary* and personalities have been secondary in explaining the electoral success and policy initiatives of Prairie premiers."

Although accurate, this perspective sheds light on only one side of the research problem. Ideas cannot be treated as givens in a political system: they do not rise to prominence of their own accord, nor are they sustained indefinitely. Rather, values must be defined, defended, and continually propagated in order to achieve prolonged prominence within a particular community. As is revealed in later chapters, this role is fulfilled, in part, by political parties. This point is best conveyed through a series of counterfactuals. Wiseman and others are correct: no social democratic culture would have developed in Saskatchewan without an amenable demographic and economic environment. Yet the dominant values themselves would be unlikely to persist unless they were promoted continually by leaders such as Tommy Douglas, Allan Blakeney, Roy Romanow, and Lorne Calvert. Temperance in Manitoba would not have retained its salience without a conducive attitudinal base; just as conservative populism would have lacked staying power without a receptive audience in Alberta. Yet the demands of the public had to be both articulated and met – functions fulfilled ably by dominant political parties. From this perspective, dominant parties are not simply products of their societal milieu: they are protectors, and crafters, of it. To a significant extent, then, political cultures owe much of their durability to the constant reiteration performed by dominant political parties. The three political cultures we see on the Prairies today are as much the products of over a century of campaign rhetoric as they are the products of socialization and institutionalization.

As Elazar (1994, 5) puts it, "To study the sources is not to study the political culture itself." As with any political phenomenon, change and persistence in political culture often spring from different sources (Pierson 2004). The forces that led to the adoption of a particular set of core values are seldom the same as those that contribute to their survival. In other words, "How an idea rises to political prominence does not necessarily reveal anything about how it might entrench itself as a durable factor in political life" (Berman 2001, 238). Like any prominent set of ideas, political culture requires periodic reaffirmation or restatement, just as a fire requires stoking (Hofstadter 1957 [1947], vii). The question becomes, who stokes the cultural fire? To answer, focus must be placed on the entire history of a community, not simply its formative period. In the context of the Canadian prairies, attention must be paid to a whole host of important actors and factors, not simply those in the early twentieth century. With this in mind, *Code Politics* disputes the notion that political cultures ever really freeze, as adaptations of fragment, staples, and formative theory suggest. Rather, cultures require (and receive) constant maintenance from a number of different political actors to persist in the face of intergenerational replacement, future waves of immigration, and other societal changes (Pal 1992, 97-98). Political cultures are actively socialized and institutionalized – two processes that, while discussed in this chapter, await further empirical study. As is examined in this book, cultures are also carried by leading political elites – notably by dominant political parties. As agents, parties have translated the values embedded in their communities' broader ethoses into powerful campaign messages. Through repetition, they have transformed these messages into dominant themes and, in the process, helped to transmit the three Prairie political cultures to new generations and new arrivals during election campaigns.

3 Campaigns in Alberta
A Code of Freedom

Most accounts trace the roots of Alberta's political culture to various events in the province's formative years. In particular, many attribute Alberta's distinctly conservative character to its unique early-settlement patterns. Immigrating northward to the western outreaches of the Canadian prairies at the turn of the last century, an influential group of American pioneers brought with them three interrelated values, each of which remains entrenched in the province's political ethos:

1. a laissez-faire brand of frontier liberalism that, over time, has become the foundation of Albertan conservatism
2. a penchant for radicalism – a distinct lack of deference – that has manifested itself in a persistent populist impulse
3. a synthetic form of anticolonialism vis-à-vis central Canada, through which a strong sense of western alienation has been expressed for several generations.

Questions remain as to how these values have survived so long after members of the founding fragment first arrived in Alberta. As this chapter shows, one answer lies in the rhetoric of dominant political parties, specifically Social Credit (1935-71) and the Progressive Conservative Party (1971-). A qualitative content analysis of their platforms and campaign literature reveals that the same concept of freedom that characterizes Alberta's political culture also animates its elite political discourse. This suggests that the values imported by American-born settlers several generations ago have lived on through the rhetoric of the province's dominant party elites.

Since the Great Depression, from William Aberhart and Ernest Manning to Peter Lougheed and Ralph Klein, Alberta's most successful party leaders have drawn on similar principles in crafting their campaign messages. In the process, each has acted as an important carrier of his province's political culture, emphasizing the same values found in Alberta's broader political ethos. They have preached individualism, stressing the importance of personal responsibility, free enterprise, private-sector development, entrepreneurship, a strong work ethic, the evils of socialism, and the protection of individual rights and liberties. Each leader has also praised the virtues of populism, highlighting the importance of keeping political and economic power in the people's hands. And all dominant party leaders have emphasized "Alberta-first" during campaigns, promoting the autonomy of the provincial government in the face of external threats and constraints. At first blush, this rhetoric appears to be little more than parochial braggadocio. There is plenty of that in Alberta party platforms, especially compared to those found in the eastern Prairies. If Saskatchewan and Manitoba leaders portray their visions as the best of all possible worlds, Alberta premiers are considerably less modest. To them, Alberta has the potential to be the best of all worlds. Boosterism aside, however, a much deeper sense of provincial pride and a desire to protect the province's self-determination lie below the surface of Alberta's dominant discourse.

Various premiers have placed unique emphases and interpretations on the terms *individualism, populism,* and *autonomy* (see Figure 2). On individualism, Aberhart's brand of civic republicanism set him apart from his laissez-faire successor, for instance. And Manning's plebiscitarian version of populism was distinct from Lougheed's "open government" rhetoric. What is more, alternative readings of these texts have produced varied conclusions among scholars. Some have interpreted Aberhart's message as socialist, for instance. Others see some elements of collectivism in Manning's emphasis on security, or a lack of individualism altogether, in Lougheed's red tory vision for Alberta. Yet, with the noticeable exceptions of Don Getty and Ed Stelmach, all long-serving Alberta premiers have spoken with the same accent on freedom throughout their combined seventy-plus years of campaigning. The persistence of this shared code of discourse helps to explain how the values imported by the province's early American pioneers continue to resonate in Alberta politics to this day.

FIGURE 2

Major iterations of the Alberta code

	Individualism	Populism	Autonomy
Aberhart	Civic republicanism	The people vs. the Big Shots	Alberta citizenship
Manning	Laissez-faire liberalism	Plebiscitarian populism	Isolationism
Lougheed	"Free enterprise that cares"	Open government	Contestation
Klein	Bootstrap individualism	"Ralph's team"	"The Alberta advantage"

William Aberhart, 1935-40

The origins of the modern Alberta code correspond with the genesis of Social Credit, the first of Alberta's two right-wing dynasties. The code's core values were developed under both William Aberhart and Ernest Manning, each of whom promoted the Socreds as the party of freedom – the champion of the individual, the wellspring of Alberta populism, and the defender of provincial rights.

As is recounted elsewhere, Aberhart's vision of Depression-era Alberta society was a thorough mixture of religious, economic, and political beliefs. His Social Credit gospel was promoted as an answer to the spiritual void left by traditional religions, the economic crisis created by a distorted form of capitalism, and the political vacuum left by conventional parties (Caldarola 1979, 37-39; Irving 1959). Aberhart's widespread popularity as an unorthodox radio preacher lent credibility to his nonconformist economic and political views, all of which were encapsulated by his attacks on the backward, "traditional type of mind" embodied by Canadian elites of the time: "that peculiar attitude which fears to try anything that has not been proven by actual experience to be well founded. It hinders all progress. The engineering type of mind is that attitude which tests by all the principles of scientific research and then goes ahead to try out in practice what it has decided in theory. We need this type of mind today" (Aberhart 1935, 61).

The crisis brought on by years of drought, low wheat prices, and the collapse of global markets offered Aberhart the opportunity to combine his teachings into a coherent ideology that would become the basis of a new political party and a powerful political narrative. As Bell (1993b, 150-64) and Irving (1959, 340-45) suggest, the deep economic, spiritual, social, and political crises brought on by the Great Depression provided the threat against which Aberhart provided a simple yet well-grounded defence. The core of Aberhart's message lay in his belief that the suffering of Albertans during the Great Depression was not due to a lack of hard work or faith. Rather, the economic crisis was the result of special interests perverting God's plan to reward the diligent (Groh 1970, 49). As is revealed in his election platforms and campaign literature, the path to prosperity (and salvation) led through freedom – of the individual, of the people, and of the provincial state.

An Association of Individuals

Although Aberhart made constant reference to the Alberta community writ large, the freedom and well-being of the individual stood at the core of his political message. His campaign rhetoric blended the principles of individual autonomy and capitalism as he promised to restore purchasing power to each Alberta citizen, bolster the province's system of free enterprise, and protect individual freedoms from the dangers of regimentation.

In his campaign literature, Aberhart (1935, 59, emphasis added) frequently defined his movement as follows: "Social Credit is that form of credit which arises from the *association of individuals* together which enables them to make use of the goods and services as, when and where delivered, before they are destroyed, disintegrated, or seized by others." In many ways, Aberhart's view of the citizen's relationship to the polity corresponds with what Ajzenstat and Smith (1998) have termed civic republicanism – a communal form of liberalism in which the individual is the primary unit of a society but feels a strong sense of communion with his or her fellow citizens. Some scholars have interpreted this sense of community as evidence of Aberhart's collectivist tendency, drawing parallels between the Alberta premier and his Co-operative Commonwealth Federation (CCF) counterparts in other parts of the Prairies (Elliott 1980, 11). Such readings misinterpret the core of his message, however.

Indeed, the communitarian elements of Aberhart's rhetoric – including his basic premise that "it is the duty of the State through its Government to organize its economic structure in such a way that no bona fide citizen, man, woman, or child, shall be allowed to suffer for lack of the bare necessities of food, clothing, and shelter, in the midst of plenty or abundance" (Aberhart 1935, 5) – have led many to interpret his ideology as leftist or even socialist (see Elliott 2004; Smith 2001; Stokes 1993).[1] These alternative, left-leaning interpretations are misguided for three reasons. First, much of the perceived collectivist character of Aberhart's Socred ideology is derived primarily from the philosophy and actions of the Social Credit League (in convention) and not the party (in government and in campaigns). As happened with the United Farmers of Alberta, the parliamentary and extra-parliamentary wings of Social Credit diverged significantly, and the grassroots advocated a much more utopian-Left program than the party establishment was willing to pursue (Stokes 1993, 105-8). The following discussion reveals that – as a party in campaigns – Social Credit was a predominantly individualist-conservative political actor, particularly once it reached office.

Second, we find in Aberhart's writings constant reference to the difference between Social Credit and socialism. Granted, up to the mid-1940s, the relationship between the two forces had been one of ambivalence, if not outright alliance. Although it distinguished him from his socialist opponents, Aberhart's opposition to public ownership appeared to rest as much on fiscal grounds as ideological ones (Bell 1993b, 71). In fact, in its infancy in the late 1930s, Social Credit openly collaborated with the CCF and the Communist Party (Bell 2004, 158-60; Finkel 1989, 50-51; Lipset 1968a, 153-58). Moreover, as his references to the oppression of the masses at the hands of an established elite suggest, there are obvious rhetorical parallels between Aberhart's message and the one promulgated by socialists at the time. Nonetheless, the Social Credit leader was careful to point out one crucial difference between his vision and that of his opponents: whereas socialism (he used the term interchangeably with *communism*) was grounded in collectivism, for Social Credit, "individual enterprise must be encouraged in every way possible" (Aberhart 1935, 14). Above all, this meant breaking monopolies (both public and private) and decentralizing power to maximize individual freedoms (ibid., 62).

Consider the following excerpt from the party's famous *Social Credit Manual.* In it, there are several overt references to the primacy of the individual:

> *Question:* Does Social Credit involve socialization, nationalization, confiscation or expropriation?
>
> *Answer:* No. Social Credit stands for controlled individual ownership. It holds to the decentralization of power and supports the rewarding of individual effort to the full possible enjoyment of the good things of life.

Question: What is the difference between Social Credit and Communism,
    Fascism, or Nazi-ism?

Answer: Social Credit makes the individual supreme. The State bends all its
    efforts to protect his rights. Under Communism, Fascism and Nazi-ism
    the State is supreme and the individual must sacrifice all his rights or
    privileges for the welfare of the State as a whole. (Aberhart 1935, 57)

Aberhart was adamant in his opposition to the confiscation of private
property and the thwarting of individual freedoms:

> It is plainly evident that we could feed, and clothe and shelter our people
> and still have many million dollars' worth for those who are capable of earn-
> ing through individual enterprise. This should convince our readers that
> Social Credit is not based on any confiscation scheme by which we take the
> wealth of the rich or well-to-do to give to the poor. Social Credit recognizes
> individual enterprise and individual ownership, but it prevents the wildcat
> exploitation of the consumer through the medium of enormously excessive
> spreads in price of the purpose of giving exorbitant profits or paying high
> dividends on pyramids of watered stock. (Aberhart 1935, 7)

Moreover, with his emphasis on providing credit to entrepreneurs, Aberhart's staunch defence of free enterprise – a key element of Alberta individualism – was evident throughout his campaign literature: "Credit is the life
blood of the State or community. Under no circumstances must it be allowed to stop its flow ... To encourage individual enterprise and to enable
the individual to provide more adequately for the future ... In order that
credit may be adequate to provide and distribute goods, the state must be
prepared to issue credit without interest to bona fide producers and dis-
tributors" (ibid., 22-23).

If readers of the *Social Credit Manual* harboured lingering doubts, the
solicitation of the private sector's financial support for the 1935 campaign
– and the placement of small business advertisements on half of the campaign book's sixty-four pages – confirmed the party's endorsement of free
enterprise.[2] In the end, for Aberhart, the source of the Depression was not
capitalism: it was the distortion and manipulation of capitalism by certain
powerful interests. Power, he argued, had to be returned to individual consumers in order to restore economic prosperity to Alberta.

Given these guiding assumptions, monetary reform was central to Aberhart's plan to reinvigorate the Alberta economy. Although it drew ostensibly

on the economic doctrine of British engineer Major C.H. Douglas, Aberhart's approach built conscientiously on a tradition inherited from the Greenback populists of the American Great Plains, some of whom had immigrated to Alberta as part of the first wave of white settlers. A 1963 Social Credit pamphlet noted, "It should be noted here that a much larger proportion of United States' citizens immigrated into Alberta – among them several senators – than into the neighbouring province of Saskatchewan. These immigrants had experienced the severe depression of the nineties in their own country; and had been deeply impressed with [then American Populist Party leader William Jennings] Bryan's famous speech, 'Shall Humanity be Crucified on a Cross of Gold?'" (Nichols 1963, 6)

Aberhart sought to restore personal autonomy and purchasing power to the Alberta consumer by first and foremost wresting control over the supply of currency from powerful eastern banks. His peculiar version of Social Credit monetary theory would have seen the Alberta government issue dividends to each citizen, which would then be used to purchase goods and services within the province. Aberhart's invention of the "A + B theorem" was, therefore, not only an attempt to adapt Douglas's economic model to the provincial context but also a concerted effort to package the theory in a more attractive format, one designed to appeal to the individual needs of average Albertans (Caldarola 1979; Long and Quo 1972, 4-5).[3] As is explained in the *Social Credit Manual* (Aberhart 1935, 14):

> It is wholly unreasonable to expect any person or group of persons in a province as wealthy as Alberta to exist without the bare necessities of food, clothing and shelter. To enable each citizen to secure these bare necessities, each of them will receive a pass-book in which at the beginning of each month will be entered the basic dividend for that month, say $25.00. This is supposed to provide for the bare necessities of food, clothing and shelter for every bona fide citizen, whether he works or does not work, and he shall not be required to pay it back or work it out. The only stipulation will be that the recipient must co-operate in every way possible. Those who work will be given their salaries, wages, or commissions over and above the basic dividends. This would at once remove all relief and dole from our land and recover the morale of our people.

Aberhart's plan was not without its critics, including those from the province's libertarian Right who feared that the establishment of Social Credit would amount to socialism by a different name. Indeed, as stated above, his doctrine has been interpreted as more collectivist than the present reading suggests. Aberhart's defence did, however, invoke the free-enterprise spirit that underpinned the capitalist system. In response to the self-posed question, "Will the issuance of basic dividends not make the citizen lazy?" Aberhart (1935, 61-62) spoke with a decidedly right-wing accent: "Paying a man that which is his right does not tend to make him careless or indifferent. It can easily be proven that once a man begins to get money he gets an urge to get more." He continued,

> *Question:* What if a citizen squandered his dividends and was hungry or improperly clothed?
>
> *Answer:* The Credit House Inspector would warn the citizen that he was abusing his rights and privileges and that it must be stopped or he would lose his dividends. If necessary, he could be put on an Indian list.
>
> *Question:* What would be done if a citizen would not cooperate or refused to work when opportunity called for it?
>
> *Answer:* Immediately after such conduct was called to the attention of the State Credit House Inspector, the offender would be warned that if he persisted in refusing work, his dividends would be cut off or temporarily suspended. Then, as there is no relief or dole, he would be compelled to work. (Ibid., 33-34)

All told, Aberhart held individual and personal responsibility as the central components of his Social Credit ideology.

The People versus the Big Shots

Aberhart's brand of civic republicanism and antisocialist rhetoric also played to the populist component of the Alberta code. Individuals in association constituted a community that, in turn, was responsible for its own governance. Accordingly, "the people" were at the heart of Aberhart's political vision. The result was a distinctly republican definition of democracy – a theme that, once again, drew inspiration from Alberta's American roots. In Aberhart's words, "First, in a democracy the people must be the decisive authority; and secondly, the State and all its institutions must exist primarily to enable the people to obtain the results they desire. From these we must conclude that there should be a minimum of interference with the people by the State, by a Bureaucracy, or by any Private Monopoly. The more regimentation to which people are subjected by State bureaucracies and private institutions, the less democracy it will be possible for the people to have"

(Nichols 1963, 49). In this spirit, Aberhart implored Albertans throughout his two campaigns to help him achieve "victory over the reactionary forces of financial orthodoxy and the champions of bureaucracy and state dictatorship" (Social Credit League of Alberta 1940).

Somewhat ironically, however, Aberhart's vision of democracy included the use of so-called scientific methods and experts to administer the complex inner workings of the state. According to detractors, this technocratic approach, by distancing decision making from the grassroots, raises serious doubts as to the authenticity of Aberhart's populist rhetoric. Consider the following description of how Aberhart planned to implement his Social Credit Plan:

> This is not a detailed plan containing exact specifications of every feature. Such a plan can only be prepared when the operation of its establishment is about ready to begin and the facts and figures are well-known. Our people must not be confused in this matter. A man may have in mind the general outline of the character of the house he intends to build. He may know the number of rooms that he intends to have and their relation and connection one with the other, but he does not ask the architect to draw the plan until he knows the size of the lot, the position in which the house will be placed, the materials available and so forth. So it is with a detailed plan for Social Credit in the Province of Alberta. It is surely evident that the Plan for Scotland, for example, will not do for Alberta. The circumstances, the resources, and the people are so different. (Aberhart 1935, 3)

Later he added, "It is the business of our experts to formulate and devise our own particular plan for this Province" (ibid., 59).

To critics, Aberhart's approach to policy making had the paradoxical effect of reducing the citizen's role to one of passive observer. From this perspective, the Socred's references to populism may be interpreted as a guise for a more authoritarian ideology. To others, they were a means of freeing the public and politicians from the administrative drudgery of bureaucracy, for which neither had much taste or talent. The latter interpretation is adhered to in this study. In rhetoric, if not necessarily in practice, Aberhart viewed the people as the sovereign authority in Alberta. Their will was to be expressed through elections, and their mandate was to be implemented – in a technocratic fashion – by a skilled but subservient group of experts.

This interpretation is supported by Aberhart's repeated attacks on monopolies, both political and economic. The link between the two domains was unbreakable; achieving political democracy and economic democracy were two sides of the same coin. Just as restoring autonomy to the citizen was connected to the empowerment of the consumer, so too was the fate of Alberta politics tied to the fortunes of its economy. Control over both spheres needed to be wrested from outside forces and returned to the people. As Aberhart explained:

> You will recall that I pointed out ... first, the fact that all our money is issued by a private monopoly composed of a few powerful banking corporations, and for every dollar they issue, one dollar of debt is created. In other words, they lend all our money into circulation, and we owe them every cent in existence plus the interest they charge. Second: the total amount of money which is issued to the people as purchasing power is never sufficient to buy the total production. So there is always a lag. These two facts make it impossible for governments to carry on without going deeper and deeper into debt under the present system. The reason is obvious. If the people have not enough purchasing power to buy the goods produced, governments cannot obtain sufficient revenue through taxation to meet their expenditures. They are forced to borrow the difference. And as the private money monopoly holds the purse strings, we have the humiliating spectacle of democratically elected governments being obligated to cringe before the money lords and acquiesce in their haughty demands, in order to obtain the money with which to carry on. Thus, we see there is a controlling power behind our government – the Hidden Iron Hand of Finance! (Nichols 1963, 52-53)

Aberhart's view of the relationship between political and economic monopolization is best captured in his assault on Canada's fifty Big Shots, an alleged cabal of financiers, federal government officials, and other members of the central Canadian establishment, whom he charged with distorting the capitalist system and impinging on the freedoms of Alberta's citizens and their government. In particular, according to Aberhart, this group had robbed Alberta of its cultural heritage – that is,

> the inheritance that falls to the right of the individual citizen living within the bounds of the province. The pioneering work of our forefathers [has brought the] great wealth of our natural resources ... to the very door of the individual consumer. Social Credit claims that each of these consumers has a right to share in the production from the natural resources of the province. At the present time this great wealth is being selfishly manipulated

and controlled by one or more men known as the "Fifty Big Shots of Canada." Social Credit claims that this cultural heritage is the property of the individuals who are bona fide citizens of our province, and should never be allowed to go entirely to the control of any small group of men. We call this heritage cultural because it gives the individual an opportunity to develop his individuality. (Aberhart 1935, 13-14)

Aberhart's populist attack on monopolies – economic and political on the one hand and public and private on the other – helped to distinguish his approach from that of those on the Left. The latter, he argued, were opposed to private monopolies in the economic realm but in fact endorsed public monopolization in both politics and the economy.

Alberta Citizenship

Aberhart's individualist and populist impulses were inextricably linked to his defence of Alberta's autonomy. To be clear, Aberhart did not advocate Alberta's separation from the rest of Canada. Like subsequent premiers, his emphasis was on protecting (what he portrayed as) Alberta's constitutional authority. At the same time, Aberhart layered his rhetoric with overt references to Alberta's independence as a sovereign community, defining the province as an autonomous society akin to a nation-state. Unlike any other party leader reviewed in this study, Aberhart conscientiously invoked terminology such as *our people* and *bona fide citizens* when he described the Alberta community. Such vocabulary is foreign to most provincial contexts. For instance, inhabitants are more likely to be called residents or, colloquially, Manitobans or Saskatchewanians. When asked how he intended to "prevent an enormous influx of the unemployed" into the province, Aberhart (1935, 61) was unequivocal: "Merely coming into the Province of Alberta gives one no claim on the basic dividends issued. *The qualifications of citizenship will be rigidly enforced.* The unemployed would think twice before they came to a province where no dole or relief was issued." "These dividends," he argued, "are not to be given on a basis of so much work done, but as a bare support of *citizenship, loyalty to the state and the best interests of the country*" (ibid., 21, emphasis added).

Aberhart's conceptualization of the individual's place in the broader community translated into a staunch defence of the provincial state's responsibility for protecting both the individual and the community. This sense of self-reliance – not only at the individual level but also at the state level – contributed to the autonomist elements of the Alberta code. At the height of the Great Depression, Aberhart (1935, 5) argued that "if Alberta cannot provide for the bare necessities of her people, what can the other provinces, especially Nova Scotia, do? Alberta cannot ask Ontario or Saskatchewan or Quebec to provide for her people. That would be unreasonable. They have all they can do to provide for their own. So the claim must be admitted, Alberta can and must feed, clothe, and shelter her own people, or they must suffer. No one else can be expected to do that which she must accomplish for herself."

Once in office, Aberhart began promoting autonomy as the primary element of his re-election campaign. This shift in emphasis was understandable from a strategic perspective. Notwithstanding a long list of legislative achievements in his first term, the public was growing restless with the pace of Aberhart's reforms (Elliott 2004, 133; Caldarola 1979, 40-41; Long and Quo 1972, 6). Most importantly, a short-lived prosperity certificate program was not enough to placate an electorate still awaiting twenty-five-dollar dividend cheques from the government. The dissent coalesced into a caucus revolt in 1937, which forced the premier to accede to his party's grassroots and appoint a Social Credit Board to implement the long-anticipated monetary reforms (Elliott 2004, 136-41; Caldarola 1979, 41-42).

The subsequent constitutional wrangling between the Alberta and federal governments, fought in the media and in the courts on both sides of the Atlantic, is one of the most-studied episodes in Canadian political history, and the precise details do not bear repeating here (see Mallory 1954; Macpherson 1977; Irving 1959; Saywell 2002, 187-203). Ultimately, the fight itself was of greater importance to the evolution of Alberta's political culture than its technicalities. Long after Aberhart's death, the courts ruled that the Alberta government lacked the constitutional authority to implement Social Credit monetary reforms; jurisdiction over banking and currency fell solely to the federal government. Yet the theme of Alberta's subjugation to Ottawa's authority remains a well-established element of party discourse to this day. What began primarily as an economic struggle to cope with the Depression morphed into a battle between a province's people and an oppressive federal government. Aberhart's successor, Ernest Manning, would serve as the main protagonist in this struggle, emphasizing Alberta's autonomy in the face of encroachments from Ottawa.

In the meantime, Aberhart's efforts to promote Alberta's autonomy took the form of provincial boosterism as Aberhart urged Albertans to "Pull Together and Keep Alberta in the Lead." According to the party's literature,

Alberta's Social Credit Government *leads* all Canada in preparation for Post-War Re-construction, Rehabilitation and Re-Establishment ... Alberta *always* leads!

Social Crediters were *first* in Canada to urge the full utilization of money, materials and manpower for the all-out prosecution of the war ...

Recognized as the best in Canada, Alberta's public health program includes free polio, tuberculosis and cancer treatment and care; free maternity hospitalization; expanded District Nursing and Health Unit services.

All Canadians praise the Alberta Education System, created by the Social Credit Government. The results speak for themselves ...

Alberta leads in Old Age Pension reform ...

Labor authorities recognize Alberta's Labor Legislation as the best in Canada. Your Social Credit Government introduced these laws, and will administer and amend them to labor's advantage. (Social Credit League of Alberta 1940)

Aberhart's rhetoric contained all three elements of the Alberta code – individualism (especially freedom of the consumer and free enterprise), populism (or freedom from economic and political monopolization), and autonomy (freedom of the provincial state from external control).

In his final years, Aberhart's attention turned toward federal politics, numerology and, increasingly, conspiracy theories (Bell 2004, 155; Elliott 2004, 143-44).[4] A tempered version of Aberhart's perceptions of a worldwide socialist plot to destroy capitalism would provide the basis for his party's reinvention following his departure. In the meantime, Aberhart's promotion of the three pillars of the Alberta code – populism, individualism, and provincial autonomy – served as the foundations of provincial discourse for decades to come.

Ernest Manning, 1944-67

Even prior to Aberhart's death in 1943, Alberta Social Credit had reached an ideological crossroads. Ernest Manning inherited a government adrift amid constitutional setbacks, robbed of its primary policy emphasis (monetary reform), and facing stiff challenges from the political Left (the CCF). The onset of the Second World War provided a brief respite from domestic political tensions and allowed Manning time to contemplate a new course. His response – a bold shift to the Right to establish Social Credit as Alberta's true conservative party – proved to be masterful. In particular, Manning's decision to pit Social Credit in a mortal struggle against socialism gave his party a new raison d'être – an ideological lease on life that would last the better part of two decades (Bell 2004, 159; Dyck 1996, 536). Manning put many of Aberhart's ideas to new ends and adapted the province's code to great effect.

Three interrelated events served as catalysts for Social Credit's ideological transformation under Manning. First, the onset of the Cold War resulted in anticommunist sentiment throughout North America in general and Alberta in particular. In an ironic twist, Soviet socialism became for postwar Socreds what unfettered capitalism had been for Aberhart. Second, the rise of Tommy Douglas's Co-operative Commonwealth Federation in Saskatchewan also played a crucial role in Manning's decision to push the Alberta Socreds to the Right (Bell 2004, 159; Smith 2001, 281-82). What had been a reformist approach to bank-dominated capitalism under Aberhart morphed into a reactionary defence of free enterprise in the face of an immediate regional and provincial socialist threat from the CCF (Long and Quo 1972, 6; Dyck 1996, 536; Groh 1970). And third, the discovery of oil at Leduc in 1947 ushered in a new era of economic and social prosperity in Alberta (Barr 1984). In general, this new-found "affluence blunted the early radicalism that had spawned political experimentation," including Social Credit monetary reform (Barrie 2004, 256; see also Smith 1992, 249; Flanagan and Lee 1992). The economic boom – framed by the government as a triumph of free enterprise – removed much of the left-wing, anti-capitalist impulse in the province (Stokes 1993, 124). Together, these factors prompted Manning to redefine Social Credit as a conventional, conservative party. Layer upon layer, Social Credit party ideology evolved to become one that pitted an alienated, exploited, free-enterprise, provincial society against a perceived socialist menace. It was a message that, while differing in subtle ways, built upon the three pillars of the political code laid by Aberhart.

Laissez-Faire Individualism

Manning's decision to shift Social Credit to the Right was most noticeable in the area of individualism. A steadily increasing stream of resource revenues tested the premier's mettle in this regard. A pay-as-you-go policy ensured that the province maintained its purported lead in social services, infrastructure, and other areas. Yet, amid the province-building period of the mid-twentieth century, Manning's promotion of individual liberties, self-reliance, and free enterprise was more forceful than any of his Prairie counterparts.

FIGURE 3

Social Credit, freedom and security

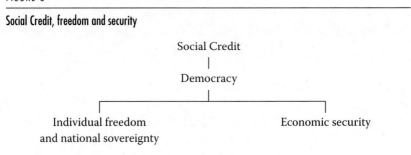

Source: Alberta Social Credit Board (1945, 7).

Early in his tenure, doubts persisted as to the balance between collectivism and individualism in Socred ideology. Under Aberhart, the concept of individual freedom had been counterbalanced, at least somewhat, by the communitarian notion of economic security. This is most clearly expressed in Figure 3, which is drawn from a Social Credit circular published in 1945, shortly after Aberhart's death. In his early campaigns, Manning maintained this message by committing his party "to strive by every lawful means to remove the constitutional barriers and financial restrictions which stand in the way of the people's best interests and hinder the establishment of a true economic democracy affording to all citizens an opportunity to enjoy a full measure of social justice, *economic security and individual freedom*" (Alberta 1948a, emphasis added). This dual emphasis was also reflected in slogans such as "Progress-Freedom-Security" (Social Credit League of Alberta 1948). The stress was always on the middle term, however.

Indeed, if titles and cover-page material offer any indication, freedom received top billing in most Social Credit literature. Various party pamphlets were titled "Alberta, Bastion of Freedom," "Let Us Establish Every Man in His Own Rights," "Battle for Freedom," and "Alberta's Fight for Freedom," for instance (see Alberta Social Credit Board 1945, 25). Over time, the balance tipped steadily in favour of freedom over security to the point that – by the time oil was discovered at Leduc – the former had established itself as the dominant theme.

Individualism (not collectivism) had always underpinned Social Credit's definition of both *security* and *freedom*. Manning defined the former in very narrow terms, while giving the latter substantial latitude. Consider the following passage from the party's 1945 *Questions and Answers* booklet:

What is meant by economic security? A person has economic security if he has reasonable assurance of obtaining the adequate material needs and comforts of life, such as food, clothing, shelter, fuel and health services, in order to live decently. If he cannot buy the things he needs, either through scarcity of goods or scarcity of money, he is denied the means of life, and therefore has no economic security.

What is personal freedom? It is the right of every person to determine the course of his actions, whether it be the choice of work, in acquiring the ownership of whatever property he can buy, or in moving about, as long as in so doing he does not interfere with or take away the same right from others. In other words, an individual has personal freedom when he is free to act, to choose or to refuse, without being dominated by others.

What do people want? Most people, irrespective of colour, race or creed, have expressed desire for a social system which will ensure them security with the greatest possible measure of freedom. They want their fair share of luxuries and a reasonable amount of leisure time so that they may enjoy cultural pursuits of their own choice. All in all, the people wish to attain a social system in which every citizen may have the right to an abundant life, liberty and the pursuit of happiness. (Alberta Social Credit Board 1945, 6-7)

In the first instance, *security* is defined in minimalist terms – along the lines of an equality of right versus an equality of opportunity or condition. This definition contrasted with the rhetoric of leading Saskatchewan parties, whose code revolved around a more collectivist notion of security (see Chapter 4). Second, Alberta Social Credit gave personal freedom very broad limits; borrowing from the American Declaration of Independence, the party suggested that "the right to an abundant life, liberty, and the pursuit of happiness" was the ultimate desire of all Albertans.

The shift of Social Credit away from freedom for security toward freedom and prosperity culminated with Manning's redrafting of the party's principles in 1963. The four basic principles were as follows:

1 The *individual* is the most important of all God's Creation on this earth.
2 The major function of any government is to bring to *people* the results which they (the people) want in the management of their affairs.
3 Security alone is not enough. We must have *freedom* with security.
4 That which is physically possible and desirable *can* and *must* be made *financially* possible. (Alberta Social Credit League 1963)

These four principles represented a recommitment to the values of Aberhart's original movement, a synthesis of those values cultivated during Manning's tenure, and a clear indication of the party's allegiance to individualism and populism. These principles were used verbatim in Social Credit literature over the next three decades (see Alberta Social Credit League 1971a, 1971b) and continue to influence the party to this day (see Alberta Social Credit Party 1993, 2008).

The party's commitment to these principles was both facilitated and tested by the onset of the province's oil boom. Under Manning, Social Credit staunchly opposed government intervention in the economy. Unlike his Tory successors, Manning's philosophy did not include plans for forced growth. In terms of both domestic policy and its opposition to regional economic development by the federal government, the Socreds remained committed to the principle that business subsidies interfered with the market as much as welfare state spending. Following the discovery of oil at Leduc, Manning's rhetoric shifted toward promoting Alberta as a bastion of free enterprise and highlighting the link between his government's laissez-faire approach and economic prosperity (Social Credit League of Alberta 1948).

The struggle for free enterprise was not always easy. As is recounted below, the private-sector side won the 1948 electrification plebiscite by just 151 votes. The alternative result might have changed the course of Alberta history by establishing a Crown corporation similar to SaskEnergy or Manitoba Hydro. As it was, the vote sustained the province's rightward course, allowing for the further "orderly development of Alberta's vast natural resources, through individual and competitive enterprise" (Social Credit League of Alberta 1952; Alberta Social Credit League 1955a).

As is reflected in his campaign rhetoric, Manning had a rising-tide-raises-all-boats approach to economic development rather than a supply-side or trickle-down approach. Because economic advancements would lead to social prosperity, "We shall put forth every effort and exert our whole energy to have the economic system adjusted so as to raise the standard of living of all our people" (Social Credit League of Alberta 1944). This, in turn, would draw more investment, which is why the government would pursue "a comprehensive program of practical measures designed to assist and encourage industrial economic and cultural development on a province-wide scale. New industry is attracted to Alberta by the development of our resources and the Government's unqualified stand for individual enterprise and a square deal for all" (Social Credit League of Alberta 1952). According to Manning, "There are those who give all the credit to the fact that oil was discovered, but ask any oil producer and he will tell you that the oil development policies of your Social Credit Government were among the biggest factors in encouraging and bringing about the tremendous development that has taken place" (Alberta Social Credit League 1955, 7).

As a result of these policies and a booming oil industry, the Socred government recorded a series of surpluses, which – according to Manning's laissez-faire rhetoric – were used to pay down the provincial debt rather than fund economic development or the massive expansion of social services. Manning maintained his pay-as-you-go mantra as he shifted from Aberhart's Treasury Office to the premier's chair, promising to provide social services and "administer relief according to the limit of our financial ability" (Social Credit League of Alberta 1944). As he put it, "Debt enslaves governments as well as individuals. Until 1935, Alberta was sinking into debt at the rate of more than $5,000,000 per year. This had to stop. In March 1936, the Social Credit Government put the province on a *pay-as-you-go* plan. It involved drastic measures. It took courage, but it was done" (ibid.). Thus, invoking Aberhart's commitment to do the same, Manning remained "determined that the debt of the Province must not increase as it did under the previous [United Farmers] administration and that the present debt shall be refunded at a rate of interest within the ability of our people to pay" (ibid.). In the premier's words, "No nation or community can borrow its way into prosperity" (Women's Auxiliaries of the Social Credit League 1968). This conviction – which persisted throughout their time in government – was as much a reflection of the Socreds' fiscal conservatism as it was a reflection of their fear that debt and deficit would force Alberta into a position of relying on banking interests in central Canada. The latter concern, in particular, matched the provincial creed of autonomy.

For all of these reasons, Manning staunchly opposed the implementation of Keynesian-inspired policy in Alberta. The premier contested the virtues of the social democratic welfare state for the following reasons:

- its universal, compulsory nature, which impinged on individual liberties
- its prescription of deficit spending, which offended both his sense of fiscal responsibility and his populist distrust of banking interests
- the imposition of premiums and service fees, which only served to reduce citizens' purchasing power
- its potential to concentrate authority in the hands of the federal government

- its encouragement of idleness on the part of welfare recipients
- above all, it was anathema to a system of true Social Credit. (Bell 2004, 155-56; Caldarola 1979, 44; Groh 1970, 48-52; Dyck 1996, 517-18)

Hence, according to Bell (2004, 158), Manning's state-building strategy was straightforward and consistent: "prudent (albeit high by the standards of the day) levels of spending on social services and infrastructure; entente with the business community; and alarmist anti-socialism."

When public health care appeared on the national agenda following the Second World War, Manning's position drew on these same principles. Indeed, of all the public policy issues, the medicare debate ended all questions as to whether Alberta Social Credit was a freedom-based, right-wing party. During the debate, Manning abandoned the rhetoric of collective security (which, to that point, had been a regressive strain in Alberta's political code) in favour of a discourse based on individual responsibility (the dominant strain). The health care debate also revealed the extent to which Manning viewed his party's mission as protecting an individualistic provincial political culture against an "insidious barrage of socialist propaganda" (Manning 1965, 5). To Manning, this barrage not only represented the encroachment of the federal government and a foreign philosophy on Albertan soil, it also represented a clash of political cultures.

Consider the following extended excerpts from his nationally distributed pamphlet, *National Medicare: Let's Look before We Leap* (Manning 1965).[5] In them, we find clear reference to the individualism embedded in the Alberta code, as opposed to the collectivist impulse found elsewhere in Canada:

> I am 100% in support of the proposition that high quality comprehensive medical services should be available to every citizen whether his income be large or small. I agree the Federal and Provincial Governments should bring such services within the financial reach of every family. Too many are willing to imply that anyone who opposes the welfare state method of meeting human needs is indifferent to such needs and satisfied with the status quo. Nothing could be further from the truth. I am unalterably opposed to turning Canada into a bureaucratic welfare state but I am as anxious as any socialist to see that every family is able to obtain complete medical care at a price they can afford to pay. My concern over the federal proposal is not, therefore, with its objective, but with the method by which it is proposed to attain that objective. (Ibid., 2)

Indeed, Manning took no issue with the comprehensiveness and portability of the federal government's plan (see ibid., 3-4). His main objection concerned the threat medicare, and collectivism in general, posed to individual liberties. Manning questioned

> the implications hidden behind the innocuous term "universal." At first this might be thought to mean that the benefits of the scheme will be available to anyone who wants to participate. This isn't what it means at all. What is meant by "universal" is that the plan arbitrarily includes everybody, whether they need the benefits and whether they wish to be included or not. It is a compulsory program in which participation is compelled by the state and not left to the voluntary choice of the citizen himself.
>
> This feature of the plan violates a fundamental principle of free society, namely, the right of each citizen to exercise freedom of choice in matters relating to his own and his family's welfare. Welfare state advocates will scream that this is not so but no man can truthfully say he has freedom of choice if he is forced to participate in a compulsory state scheme for his medical services, whether he wishes it or not.

As for his alternative, Manning preferred the use of deterrent fees and the establishment of a means-based system meant to help low-income Albertans pay private insurance premiums. Its voluntary nature would respect individual choice, promote self-reliance, and provide protection for the less fortunate through government assistance.

> What I am advocating as a superior alternative to the federal proposal is a voluntary state-subsidized medical insurance program, based on two sound fundamental principles:
>
> 1 That the individual has a responsibility to provide for his medical needs just as he has a responsibility to provide for his own needs in other areas affecting his welfare.
> 2 That society as a whole has a responsibility to ensure that such services are available at a cost to the individual within his ability to pay.
>
> The alternative plan I have proposed does not require any element of compulsion and therefore does not do violence to the basic principles of a free society ... In short, such a voluntary prepaid state-subsidized medical insurance program can, and will, achieve every legitimate objective of a

compulsory state medicare plan at a fraction of the cost to the public treasury and without any of its objectionable features. (Manning 1965, 12-13, 14)

Ross Thatcher's Liberal government in Saskatchewan and Duff Roblin's Conservative government in Manitoba offered similar arguments against universal health care. Eventually, all three premiers relented to federal government pressure as they realized their citizens would be paying into the national system regardless of their province's participation (Bell 2004, 167). Thus, in no small part, their grudging acceptance of the Keynesian welfare state was based on a conservative concern for taxpayers (Stokes 1993).

In the end, the importance of the health care debate to our understanding of Ernest Manning's individualistic vision for Alberta society lies beyond the narrower policy considerations. His spirited defence of individualism revealed the extent to which the Alberta premier viewed his role as one of protecting his province's political culture against an external – ideological and governmental – threat. This was clearly stated in his closing argument:

Canada is dangerously close to setting her feet on a path that can lead to but one ultimate end. That end will be a nation turned into a regimented socialistic welfare state. There are those who say this is inevitable and that Canadians who cherish individual responsibility and enterprise and freedom of choice are trying to hold back an irresistible tide. I do not believe that this is so.

I have a deep conviction that the majority of Canadian people want to stand on their own feet and do their own thinking and make their own decisions, shoulder their own responsibilities, and be free to challenge the limitless opportunities this nation affords to men of imagination, enterprise and the will to achieve ...

To those who want to see a free society preserved in Canada, the proposed compulsory federal medical care program is a direct challenge to individual liberty and responsibility. The time has come to let your governments know beyond all shadow of doubt that socialists and collectivists are not the only inhabitants of the field. (Manning 1965, 16-18)

Manning's defence of individualistic conservatism did not end there. Given that the economy was in working order in the late 1960s and that the province had "horizons unlimited," Manning shifted his attention to putting a human face on the Socred government (Alberta Social Credit League

1967). With the aid of his son, Preston, the premier released *A White Paper on Human Resources Development* just prior to the 1967 Alberta election (Alberta 1967; see Barr 1974, chaps. 11-13). More than a statement of policy, "this most significant document" represented a complete "reorientation of thinking" for the party: a principled, right-wing, postmaterialist response to the Canadian Left's calls for a just society (Alberta Social Credit League 1967; see Manning 1992, 44). In the White Paper – and subsequent book, *Political Realignment* (Manning 1967) – the Mannings laid the blueprint for a new right-wing party ideology that they termed social conservatism. True to the populist, individualist, and autonomist tenets of the provincial code, the party continued to support a free-enterprise economy, attack affirmative action programs and compulsory bilingualism, and promote a so-called mosaic approach to Canadian "unity through diversity" and "the separation of race and state" (Alberta 1967, 51-52). Manning retired before entrenching this brand of social conservatism in Alberta, and two decades passed before his son and Ralph Klein built their respective political parties around its general principles. In the interim, Peter Lougheed's Conservatives rose to power in Alberta.

One further note is required with regard to Manning's individualistic outlook. Like Aberhart's, Manning's worldview was implicitly grounded in the theological foundations of evangelism. Although religion was widely associated with Social Credit and its leadership (both Aberhart and Manning headed the Calgary Prophetic Bible Institute), religious references were surprisingly absent from most Social Credit literature uncovered by the Prairie Manifestos Project. On occasion, brief hymns were printed as part of some pamphlets (see Social Credit League of Alberta 1944), and beginning in 1963 the party began to incorporate the Wheel Cross logo into its publications (see Alberta Social Credit League 1963).

Yet, beyond these examples – and one publication in which the author refers to the competition between Social Credit and other political parties as a "war between philosophies" ("on the one hand ... the growing philosophy of the jungle, manifest in stateism [sic], centralization and a militant materialism, [on the other] individuality, personality, a militant Christianity" (Nichols 1963, 3) – overt religious references are scarce in Social Credit campaign literature. The conceptual connections between political individualism and the religious notion of individual salvation are obvious, and they were drawn explicitly by both Aberhart and Manning in their weekly radio broadcasts and study-group directives. Perhaps because of this clarity, Social Credit pamphleteers felt little need to include religious references in their campaign materials. Further investigation is necessary to answer these questions (see Groh 1970; Irving 1959; Flanagan and Lee 1992; Naylor and Teeple 1972; Mann 1955; Caldarola 1979, 39-40; Elliott 2004, 132-34).

Plebiscitarian Populism

In addition to his individualism, Manning also drew inspiration from Aberhart's plebiscitarian definition of Alberta democracy. Theirs was a brand of populism that demanded active (though not often direct) participation by "the people" in the governance of the state, while leaving representatives a free hand to pursue the directives conferred upon them during elections (see Laycock 1990, 203-66). Again, an alternative interpretation stresses the authoritarian tendencies involved in distancing the grassroots from policy making. Yet, as with Aberhart, Manning continued to emphasize the importance of the people in the grand scheme of politics and democracy. This view is conveyed in a 1944 informational booklet distributed by Manning's Bureau of Information and News:

> The political machine should be used by democracy to demand results, results dealing with their relationship with their fellow men and women. This can be achieved by The People electing more representatives whom they instruct as to the results in these respects required. These representatives should then use their authority to see that those qualified to devise proper methods are charged with giving The People what they want.
>
> The matter can be put in a sentence: In democracy all matters of policy, i.e., deciding results required, should be controlled by The People and all matters of administration, i.e., methods, should be centrally controlled, subject to such administration yielding the results demanded by democracy. (Alberta 1944a)

An important aspect of this plebiscitarian perspective is its unique conceptualization of electoral mandates. Rather than presenting a specific plan of action, plebiscitarian parties ask for a mandate to devise programs and policies while in office. As part of the bargain, the party commits to providing the electorate with status reports so that it might monitor the government's progress and render judgment at the next election. Alberta Social Credit proceeded along these lines; through its Publicity Bureau, the Manning government released annual reports to the public (Social Credit League of Alberta 1955, 1957, 1958, 1959, 1960; Alberta 1944b, 1948a, 1952). This policy turns a plebiscitarian party's election campaign into a statement of its record rather than a prescription for the future. Pledges typically offer "more of the same."

At times, Manning's vision of democracy in Alberta was at odds with Canadian constitutional conventions. Consider the following excerpt from a 1944 Social Credit brochure:

> As a citizen of Alberta, you, together with your fellow citizens, are the constitutional sovereign authority. Your government and your representatives have been elected by you to carry out the will of the people. That is the basis of democracy and in these days when our democratic ideals are being assailed it is important that the people and their governments bear this in mind.
>
> As the sovereign authority in Provincial affairs, the people of Alberta are entitled to receive from their Government a report on the progress which has been made under its stewardship. For this reason the information in this booklet is being made available to the citizens of Alberta. Any citizen of the Province wishing to receive a copy, may obtain one on request from the Bureau of Publicity, Legislation Building, Edmonton.
>
> Your Obedient Servant, Ernest C. Manning, Premier
> (Social Credit League of Alberta 1944)

This overtly republican definition of democracy – one that draws implicitly, if not explicitly, on the province's Americanized political culture – was repeated throughout much of the early Social Credit election literature (see Alberta Social Credit Board 1945, 5). Regardless of its technical accuracy (the Crown is sovereign in Canada), the rhetoric sustained a peculiar view of the provincial political system, one that placed the citizen at the centre of a populist democracy.

Manning's populism also included a willingness to use the tools of direct democracy. Following in the tradition of the Liberals and the United Farmers of Alberta – who had held plebiscites on prohibition in 1916 and 1923, respectively – the Alberta government conducted four separate plebiscites during Manning's tenure in office: one on electricity generation and distribution (1948), one on liquor sales (1957), and two on the adoption of daylight savings time (1967 and 1971). Of these, the 1948 vote is particularly important to understanding Manning's adherence to populism. According to official government (not party) literature:

The time has arrived when a definite decision must be made as to whether the requirements of the people can best be met by the generation and distribution of electricity being continued and extended by the Power Companies as at present or by generation and distribution of electricity being taken over and extended by the Alberta Government Power Commission as a publicly-owned utility.

Inasmuch as the decision made in this important matter will directly concern every citizen of the Province, the Government believes that the people themselves should be consulted and given an opportunity to express their preference. This procedure is in full accord with the highest concept of truly democratic government. Once the people have declared which of the two alternative policies they prefer, the Government will regard the implementation of that policy as an inescapable obligation and responsibility. A plebiscite on this important question will be furnished for each elector in conjunction with the provincial general election on August 17th [1948]. The plebiscite is reproduced below. All citizens are encouraged to exercise their democratic right to choose which of the two alternative policies they prefer. It will be the people's decision and their decision will be respected.

Electrification Plebiscite

Do you favor the generation and distribution of electricity being continued by the Power Companies as at present?

OR

Do you favour the generation and distribution of electricity being made a publicly-owned utility administered by the Alberta Government Power Commission? (Alberta 1948a)

That Manning, an otherwise ardent position-taker, did not offer a response to the plebiscite question is intriguing. (A review of government-issued and party literature from the 1948 campaign demonstrates the lengths to which Social Credit went to avoid taking sides on the issue.) From the perspective of his views on populism, however, the premier's strategy demonstrated a commitment to using the tools of direct democracy. Whether for reasons of principle or political expediency, Manning's use of the plebiscite to settle contentious public policy debates helped to reinforce (institutionalize) his populist rhetoric.[6]

Diverging somewhat from his mentor's definition of populism, Manning turned Aberhart's emphasis on private monopolies into an assault on state control (Caldarola 1979, 43-44). In 1948, for instance, Social Credit pledged to "fight unceasingly for the democratic rights of all citizens to exercise freedom of choice and action and individual initiative and enterprise, free from bureaucratic state interference or domination by any form of monopoly control" (Social Credit League of Alberta 1948). This meant pitting Social Credit's brand of true democracy against the allegedly authoritarian nature of socialism. According to the party's 1944 platform, by *true democracy* "we maintain that true representative government must be directed and guided by the will of the people, either outlined in an election platform or later formulated by petition or general request" (Social Credit League of Alberta 1944).

Manning turned both individualism and populism into vehicles for his antisocialist message. The following excerpt from a Social Credit pamphlet exemplifies the virulent tenor of Social Credit's rhetoric under Manning:

> Alberta's struggle for freedom and security has been a struggle for the rights of all humanity. In pressing for the reforms embodied in what is known as Social Credit, Albertans have challenged the menace of world domination by a supra-national monetary authority. Because Social Credit and a real democracy are integrated as one, the struggle in Alberta has been against all forms of totalitarian tyranny, whether communist, fascist, national socialist, bureaucratic or any other. Albertans have fought every attempt to centralize power, and have defended the personality of man, his dignity, his culture and his freedom. Alberta seeks to decentralize power; to make governments and institutions the servants of the people, and not their masters. Social Credit aims to elevate man to the highest pinnacle of economic, cultural, individual and social achievement. It will lead the way to personal security with a maximum of personal freedom. Social Credit aims to establish every man in his own right. No other human philosophy in the world today offers anything but ultimate slavery. (Nichols 1963, 105)

Although this style of rhetoric was certainly more forceful and salient, it did draw on themes raised during Aberhart's campaigns. In fact, lending further support to Wiseman's thesis, Manning's Social Credit party in certain instances made explicit reference to the connection between its own brand of frontier democracy and the values imported by the province's pioneers: "In common with others who migrated to the frontiers of Canada, Alberta's first citizens were imbued with a strong democratic spirit. In choosing Canada's West as their home, they sought in this new and undeveloped country the democratic freedoms and economic security denied them in the social environment they left behind. In short, they came West to create a social organization which would give them the political and economic democracy they desired" (ibid., 4).

Manning also built on Aberhart's notion of economic populism, even though Social Credit under his leadership abandoned all but token reference to monetary reform and actively sought to distance itself from the radical nature of the concept and those that continued to espouse it (Dyck 1996, 536). Arguing that "prosperity had replaced the need for dividends," for instance, Manning expelled the Douglassites from the party and disbanded the Social Credit Board (Stokes 1993, 124). Nonetheless, strains of Aberhart's economic populism resonated in Manning's rhetoric throughout his two decades of campaigning. Echoing his mentor's emphasis on the link between economic and political oppression, Manning argued, "In the economic sphere the money mechanism should function so that The People can use money as a voting system to demand the results they want, in the way of goods and services, from the economic organization. Therefore these money votes should be made available to The People so that they have full access to their economic resources to the extent that they desire to use them" (Alberta 1944a). Moreover, under his leadership, Social Credit continued to define "democracy [as] an ideal social system, which has never been fully realized by this or any other nation. Our people have political and religious freedom to a certain extent, which enables them to exercise the right of free speech and the right to worship. But complete economic security with a full measure of personal freedom has never been attained since all of our activities are still directly or indirectly controlled by those who manipulate our monetary system" (Nichols 1963).

All told, Manning continued Aberhart's tradition in both political and economic terms and helped to entrench populism in Alberta's elite-based code. Doing so also helped to sustain the province's populist political culture.

Isolationism

Manning's approach to Alberta's autonomy can best be described as a form of isolationist boosterism. When it came to defending Alberta's interests against federal encroachment, his campaign rhetoric was less confrontational than that of Aberhart or Lougheed because much of this conflict took place out-side election periods in Ottawa courtrooms and backrooms. Instead, Man-ning called on voters to help him "keep Alberta in the lead" – a message that, on a deeper level, involved a protectionist approach to policy develop-ment and federal-provincial relations. Less frequently but noticeably, he en-gaged in a war of words with the federal government and other "outside interests" over Alberta's autonomy in her own affairs.

Like all Alberta premiers since, Manning maintained a clear commit-ment to Canadian unity. This was especially true during the Second World War. Even then, however, Manning's support for Confederation was tem-pered by a concern for provincial rights. Consider the following excerpt from his wartime platform: "We stand pledged in support of Canadian Unity in all matters of National Interest and maintain that the strongest form of unity can only be secured in the British way, i.e., by giving the prov-inces the greatest possible amount of self-governing autonomy consistent with the rights of the other provinces and with the external affairs of the Dominion" (Social Credit League of Alberta 1944). In other words, if Al-berta as a province relied on the country's health as a whole, a strong Can-ada required a strong Alberta.

Regardless of this co-operation, however, it was clear throughout Man-ning's election literature that he considered Alberta to be a "first among equals" when it came to the interprovincial community. In every campaign, he invited Albertans to compare their lot with those of other Canadians and attributed the higher level of prosperity in his province to Social Credit's stewardship. There was an air of protectionism in this rhetoric, for Manning sought to insulate his government from ideological and partisan forces from outside the province, particularly the collectivism of the CCF and the creep-ing socialism of the Keynesian movement. In 1948, for instance, the Socred platform proclaimed, "Alberta today has the brightest outlook of any Can-adian Province. The vastness of her natural resources, the enterprise of her progressive people and the sound administration of her public affairs have brought Alberta to the threshold of a great era of economic and industrial development ... Insure your future and the future of Canada's leading Prov-ince by re-electing the government under whose progressive administration Alberta has attained the advanced position she enjoys today" (Social Credit League of Alberta 1948).

Manning suggested that he had to overcome numerous external ob-stacles to attain these standards:

This outstanding progress has been achieved despite the financial restrictions imposed by an antiquated and monopolistic national monetary system and by the constitutional limitations in the financial field imposed on the Provinces by the British North America Act.

Freed from these handicaps Alberta's progress and development could readily be such as to speedily ensure to all her citizens a full measure of social and economic security and a standard of living commensurate with her vast productive capacity. (Alberta 1948b, 3-4)

This type of protectionist, Alberta-first rhetoric persisted throughout each of Manning's seven election campaigns. In 1955, for example, he warned voters not to listen to the outside voices of Keynesianism and invited them to instead "compare Alberta with the rest of Canada then vote Social Credit. Let's carry on together. From the verge of bankruptcy to her present enviable position, Alberta's progress under Social Credit Government stands unequalled in Canada ... Don't be misled by false propaganda. Let's stay with Premier Manning. Vote Social Credit. Keep Alberta in the lead" (Alberta Social Credit League 1955b).

It was on the topic of natural resources that Manning's position shifted from a more passive form of parochialism to a more active defence of the province's interests. In much the same way as Tommy Douglas tilted province-building discourse in Saskatchewan to the Left (see Chapter 4), Manning used promises of rapid private development of the oil and gas industry to steer Alberta to the political Right. Of course, the Leduc discovery had lured investors and settlers from the United States, reinforcing earlier immigration patterns and strengthening the province's small-*l* liberal political culture (Caldarola 1979, 44; Flanagan and Lee 1992; Wiseman 2007, 247). More than this, however, because the discovery of oil eventually made Alberta a "have" province in 1964, Manning was able to frame the debate over natural resource development as an issue of federal-provincial jurisdiction, rather than simply an internal debate between the province's Left and Right. His rhetoric harkened back to Aberhart's preservation of Alberta's cultural heritage against the encroachments of the fifty Big Shots.

Lastly, Manning's push for Alberta's autonomy was embodied in his feigned support for monetary reform. In this sense, his attempt to institute a final, watered-down version of Social Credit monetary legislation seems purposefully designed to fail a constitutional challenge; it did just that following a reference to the Alberta Supreme Court in 1947 (Bell 2004, 160-61;

Swann 1971, 257). Thus, as Swann (1971, 257) contends, Manning continued to pursue monetary reforms that he knew would fail in order to maintain his grassroots Social Credit base and to cultivate a victim mentality vis-à-vis the federal government.

In sum, Manning's adherence to all three pillars of the Alberta code helped to sustain the conservative, populist, and alienated elements of the province's political culture through a global war and Keynesian revolution. In the end, having revamped the party's ideology twice during his tenure as premier – first as a champion of freedom in the face of Cold War communism and second as a free-enterprise defender against creeping social democracy and postmaterialism – Manning left the office to his successor, Harry Strom. The latter inherited both a political code steeped in the principles of individualism, populism, and autonomy and a government under threat from Peter Lougheed's surging Progressive Conservative Party.

Harry Strom, 1971

Strom was a moderate, reform-focused – if spectacularly uncharismatic – choice to lead the Social Credit party. Although well-suited ideologically to advancing Manning's plans to reshape the party, he inherited much of the ideological tension that attempts at realignment had created (Palmer and Palmer 1976, 128). In particular, Strom's emphasis on continuity – a cornerstone of his 1971 campaign – proved contentious among Social Crediters who felt the party needed to reinvent itself for a new decade and voters who were drawn to a new voice espousing the values of individualism, populism, and autonomy.

Conventional accounts of the 1971 election drastically understate the ideological dissonance between Strom's Social Credit and Lougheed's Progressive Conservative Party (see Palmer and Palmer 1976, 129; Tupper 2004, 209). An examination of their platforms suggests that, although both parties spoke in code, each did so in a unique fashion. There were real, if subtle, differences in their interpretations of the concepts of individualism, populism, and autonomy. Whereas Strom's approach was staunchly laissez-faire, plebiscitarian, and isolationist, Lougheed's was more activist, liberal-democratic, and interventionist.

It is true: Strom's only election platform lacked a focused theme and the "one big issue" that had characterized Manning's campaigns (Barr 2004, 195). Instead, the Socred's strategy involved labelling Lougheed and his red tory followers as socialists in disguise (Bell 1993a, 474), heralding his own party as the defenders of "the rugged independence of the individual"

(Alberta Social Credit League 1971a), and committing himself to "a new era of provincial development built on the firm foundation inherited from the past" (ibid.). Strom's choice of the campaign "Thirty-Six Years of Growth" illustrates the extent to which he ran on the strength of Manning's record and approach to governance. According to Strom:

> Over the past 36 years your Alberta Social Credit Government has gained an enviable reputation for honest, responsible administration of the affairs of this province. We intend to continue giving the people of Alberta that kind of government. I don't think Albertans can be fooled by glib promises of government give-away programs hastily hatched up at election time. It is already evident that the people of this province have recognized the shallow thinking behind some of the grandiose promises made during this election campaign. I would like to emphasize that the programs I am about to outline to you are the result of a great deal of careful study. They are responsible plans by a responsible government. They are based on progressive ideas. They are in keeping with Social Credit principles. They are within the bounds of our financial capabilities. Many of these programs are simply extensions of existing programs which have proven successful. (Ibid.)

Above all, according to Strom, "Your Social Credit government ... will meet the challenges of the future, as it met those of the past, with the ability to adjust to change and constant concern for the individual" (ibid.).

If election results offer any indication, the Alberta public preferred Lougheed's brand of new, active government to Strom's more cautious approach. Outlined below, Lougheed's active pursuit of freedom proved more appealing than the incrementalist version offered by Strom. Indeed, the Socreds' loss and subsequent decline suggest that, although speaking in code is a necessary condition for long-term political success in a given community, it is by no means sufficient to guarantee victory. Leadership and the ability to translate and transmit the ideas embodied in the provincial code are equally crucial to a party's success. Peter Lougheed possessed these talents to a degree that Harry Strom and his Social Credit successors did not. As a result, in the early 1970s, progressive conservatism became the ideological vehicle for the Alberta code.

Peter Lougheed, 1967-82

The Progressive Conservatives (PCs) did not exactly come out of nowhere to win the 1971 Alberta election, but the observation is not far from the truth. Despite a brief resurgence in the late 1950s, at the height of Social Credit's dominance, the Conservatives were in dire straits. In the party's own words, for half a century, "the Conservative voice had never been more than a squeak of protest in the Legislature ... The Progressive Conservative Party in Alberta in 1965 had no leader and no seats in the Alberta Legislature. What little active support it held was more apparent during Federal elections than during Provincial campaigns" (Progressive Conservative Association of Alberta 1971). Enter Peter Lougheed.

More than any other factor, the ideological struggle between the Conservatives and Social Credit was masked, and won, by virtue of Lougheed's public praise of the Socreds' principles, leadership, and record of achievement (Tupper 2004, 206; Palmer and Palmer 1976, 130). Indeed, the PCs rose to prominence in Alberta by speaking in the code that the Socreds had cultivated for nearly two generations. Doing so created the sense that the PCs were a safe alternative. In a 1967 campaign promise, for instance, Lougheed committed his party "to support the government in legislation and programs that were sound and beneficial to Albertans, and to provide constructive alternatives rather than opposition for the sake of opposition" (Progressive Conservative Association of Alberta 1980, 6). Four years later, the party stated:

> There is always the tendency when presenting an alternative and new government platform, to place such an emphasis upon "New Directions" that the public misunderstands the intention to continue – and not upset those existing government policies which have proved through time to be in the best interests of Albertans, and should not be altered.
>
> Such is our position with regard to the exploration and production side of the petroleum industry – i.e. the finding and the gathering of oil and gas. We give credit to the Manning Administration of the early 1950's for developing a system which provides a fair balance between the incentives for large investment by private industry and reasonable return to the owner of the oil and gas properties – the people of Alberta – through royalties, Crown lease sales and other factors of Provincial Government natural resource revenues.
>
> This is not to say that a Progressive Conservative Government will not make changes – but they will be changes in relation to current developments – reforms in relation to new circumstances – we publicly commit ourselves to maintaining the basic system.

We are not unmindful of the story of killing the goose that laid the golden egg. (Alberta Progressive Conservative Party 1971, emphasis added)

With this style of rhetoric, Lougheed positioned himself as a harbinger of safe change in Alberta. This strategy differed from the virulent attacks of previous leaders of the opposition and, by deferring to the tenets of the provincial code, helped establish the Conservatives as a trustworthy, realistic alternative for many voters (Scown 1973, 95). Respect should not be confused with complete ideological affinity, however, for Lougheed drew clear distinctions between his definitions of individualism, populism, and autonomy and those of his Social Credit opponents.

These differences were outlined early in Lougheed's political career. Soon after assuming the leadership in 1965, he issued what became a founding document for his party: *Guideposts for the Progressive Conservative Party of Alberta* (Progressive Conservative Association of Alberta 1967). The publication of these twelve guideposts represented a defining moment for conservatism and the political code in Alberta. Emphasizing local communities, market assistance, and a revitalized welfare state, the guideposts represented a clear definition of modern (red and blue) toryism (see Patten 2001; Dyck 1996; Harrison 1995). Lougheed confronted the social conservatism embedded in the Mannings' calls for realignment, setting the stage for one of many clashes for control of the political Right – and the definition of freedom – in Alberta. This type of competition over the interpretation of a community's creed – as opposed to its contents – forms the basis of the concluding chapter.

Free Enterprise That Cares
Lougheed's emphasis on individualism is evident throughout his 1967 guideposts. Like Aberhart, who attempted to balance individual liberties with collective security, Lougheed sought to protect individual rights and free enterprise while engaging in Alberta's most prolific period of province building. In his fourth guidepost, for example, Lougheed insists that a more active provincial government must not interfere with citizens' personal independence. "The rights and liberty of the individual citizen, such as the right of privacy or freedom to pursue one's own destiny, should never be trampled by legislation in the guise of public benefit" (Progressive Conservative Association of Alberta 1967). These principles were supported in his party's 1971 platform, in which Lougheed pledged to "ensure that an

individual citizen is entitled to live a private life, free from: (a) intrusion upon his seclusion or solitude or into his private affairs; (b) public disclosure of private facts; (c) publicity which places an individual in a false light in the public eye; (d) appropriation for advantage of a person's name or license" (Alberta Progressive Conservative Party 1971).

By way of protection, as is recounted repeatedly in later promotional literature, "The first piece of legislation introduced by Premier Lougheed was a Bill of Rights. It demonstrated his concern for the interests of individual Albertans and his intention to run a progressive but responsible administration" (Progressive Conservative Association of Alberta 1980). Moreover, in starkly American terms, "Section 1 of the Alberta Bill of Rights expressly recognizes, 'The right of the individual to liberty, security of person and enjoyment of property, and the right not to be deprived thereof except by due process of law'" (Progressive Conservative Association of Alberta 1982a).

Lougheed's promotion of free enterprise, particularly in the natural resource sector, was also especially forceful. In the tenth and eleventh guideposts, for instance, he insists that the

> provincial government should constantly struggle with the task of full development of our natural resources by private economic means, but in such a way as to also provide adequate returns to our own citizens ... We believe that a provincial government should not just preach free enterprise but should also promote this system by creating an atmosphere consistently favourable to it. This requires an acceptance that the free enterprise system may have defects but that it is by far the best economic system for the people of this province. (Progressive Conservative Association of Alberta 1967)

To this end, while recognizing "that a provincial government has a major role to protect consumers in today's free enterprise economy which has developed some unfavourable monopolistic tendencies," his rhetorical support of the private sector extended to virtually every area of the Alberta economy and society (Alberta Progressive Conservative Party 1971). For instance, whereas governments in Saskatchewan and Manitoba were experimenting with public ownership models, the 1971 Conservative platform promised "to develop a system of automobile insurance with the following objectives: (a) operation by free enterprise – independent of the Provincial Government – rejection of a Government-operated insurance system;

(b) requirement that all licensed automobiles in Alberta have mandatory third-party insurance coverage; (c) a premium rate structure that is fair and equitable for all concerned" (ibid.).

Moreover, in addition to a commitment to "develop a small business arm of the Provincial Department of Industry, along the lines of the United States 'Small Business Administration,'" Lougheed also extended the principles of free enterprise to the agricultural sector. There, he promised "to strike a fair balance between desirable government programs of help to farmers and the desire of the farmers themselves to control their own industry as free enterprisers without undue government interference ... To support Marketing Boards provided they are truly representative and run by producers and individual farmers; monopoly control will not be acceptable since such market power is in conflict with our free enterprise system" (Alberta Progressive Conservative Party 1971).

Lougheed's approach to social services, while avowedly more "compassionate" than Social Credit's, nonetheless reflected the importance of self-reliance (see Guidepost 8; see also Dyck 1996, 518; Tupper 2004, 220). Among other allusions to the support of free enterprise in the social realm, the platform also included a prospective "analysis of the possibility of leasing school buildings from private industry" (Alberta Progressive Conservative Party 1971).

Granted, although it supported free enterprise, Lougheed's blue tory approach to the Alberta economy posited a far more active role for the government than did Manning's. In times of prosperity, the Tories pursued government investment in the petrochemical industry through direct business subsidies, the creation of several new Crown corporations (including the purchase of Pacific Western Airlines), and experiments with Alberta's first quasi-private-public partnerships, such as the Alberta Energy Company. And when the provincial economy faced a downturn in the early 1980s, Lougheed's Economic Resurgence Plan remained true to blue tory principles (Progressive Conservative Association of Alberta 1982b): "He established programs to shield Albertans and Alberta businesses from rapidly rising interest rates. He maintained provincial government expenditures. In his view, abrupt cutbacks would exacerbate the downturn. Lougheed was prepared to run budget deficits if necessary. He saw no point in reducing public expenditures as the economy weakened" (Tupper 2004, 226). However, in his campaign rhetoric, if not in his actions in government, Lougheed was careful to emphasize free enterprise over dirigisme. To repeat an apt phrase from Gibbins (1979, 143), Lougheed's approach mirrored Alberta's political culture more generally because each demonstrated "a strong belief in the spirit if not necessarily the practice of free enterprise."

Liberal-Democratic Populism

Lougheed's guideposts were also replete with references to populism, notably a more liberal-democratic, open-government type of populism than the plebiscitarian version offered by Aberhart, Manning, and Strom (see Laycock 1990). For instance, his second guidepost stated that "the most democratic form of government is that which is closest to the people" (Progressive Conservative Association of Alberta 1967). Guideposts 1, 5, 6, 7, and 9 also committed the Conservatives to providing increased transparency in government planning, for "the public has the right to know" and hold its representatives accountable. In short, Lougheed promised more openness in government, attacking the technocratic philosophy applied by Social Credit.

This notion was echoed in the party's 1971 platform, in which the Conservatives pledged the following:

- To provide the individual citizen with protection against the unjustified actions of the provincial government.
- To give the citizen a fair chance to have his case adequately heard and presented before the Boards and Tribunals of Government.
- To assure [sic] the citizen a right of appeal from the decisions of the Provincial Government and avenues to permit his grievances to be presented to elected representatives.
- To narrow the gap between government and the people.
- To make government more responsive to the needs of the people.
- To assure that the M.L.A. is more responsive to the wishes of his constituents.
- To involve the individual citizen in the formation of our laws and programs.
- To expand the concept of representative democracy within the parliamentary system through the frequent use of free vote – i.e., a vote where the confidence of the government is not at issue.
- To increase the use of public hearings by the Legislative Assembly and major items of legislation so that individual citizens – not merely organizations – have an opportunity to appear before the Assembly to directly express their view.

- To encourage the use of petitions to the Legislative Assembly. To provide individual M.L.A.s with sufficient resources to improve the channels of two-way communication with the voters of the various constituencies.
- To allow television and radio broadcasts of the proceedings of the Legislative Assembly to improve public awareness of provincial matters.
- To institute a regular Fall Session of the Legislative Assembly of specific duration to assure that Cabinet Ministers are publicly answerable for their actions on at least two periods throughout the year. (Alberta Progressive Conservative Party 1971)

This list was expanded in 1979 to include the following:

- A more Open and Responsive Government.
- Greater financial accountability to the public through the new office of Auditor-General.
- Cabinet tours to every area of the province.
- Full television coverage and *Hansard* to bring citizens closer to the Legislature.
- Annual audited reports of the Alberta Heritage Savings Trust Fund made available to the public.
- Increased public participation in decision making through membership on government and advisory boards. (Progressive Conservative Association of Alberta 1979b)

Contestation

Lastly, Lougheed's consistent commitment to providing national leadership reflected his desire to promote the province as a strong, autonomous society. This emphasis marked a noticeable re-engagement of the Alberta state in federal-provincial relations after decades of isolationism under Ernest Manning. Granted, as with his Socred predecessors, there was a considerable amount of jingoism in Lougheed's rhetoric. In the twelfth guidepost, for instance, Lougheed insists: "We sincerely believe that God's endowment of this province with such abundant natural resources complemented by the skills and talents of our own people permit us realistically to set as our objective a society that is not inferior to that in any province or state in North America." Yet, rather than disengaging from the rest of the country, Lougheed sought a leadership role in Confederation. In this vein, he promoted "an Alberta government which recognizes the important role of leadership which can be performed by this wealthy and strategically located province in fed-eral provincial relations in the next decade" (Progressive Conservative As-sociation of Alberta 1967, Guideposts 12 and 3).

This shift was fuelled, in part, by federal-provincial tensions that began to escalate two years into Lougheed's premiership. In 1973, Prime Minister Trudeau's decision to tax oil exports pre-empted Lougheed's own plans to raise resource royalties. Although both policies were eventually imple-mented, the incident was a precursor of federal-provincial resource battles to come (see Elton and Goddard 1979, 61; Dyck 1996, 545-46). With these conflicts as a backdrop, Lougheed used his various election campaigns to generate a popular mandate to negotiate with Ottawa on behalf of the prov-ince and to signal to the federal government (and the rest of Canada) his intention to protect provincial rights. This dual strategy is evident in his election promises.

Consider the Progressive Conservatives' 1971 election campaign plat-form, which makes explicit reference to the need to "alter the present isola-tionist attitude of the outgoing Alberta Government and bring Albertans into the mainstream of Canadian life, performing a role of national leader-ship not provincial reactionism; [and in] conjunction with such a challenge – to also, communicate to Central Canadians, the aspirations of Western Canada and to hence assure equity and fairness in arrangements between both levels of government" (Alberta Progressive Conservative Party 1971).

Throughout various disputes with the federal government, which cli-maxed with the Trudeau government's announcement of the National Ener-gy Program (NEP) in 1980, the primary bone of contention between Lougheed and Ottawa was one of ideas, not simply interests. In particular, the two sides had conflicting conceptions of the proper balance of Canadian federalism (Tupper 2004, 215). Federal Liberals believed the risks and rewards of the Canadian economy should be borne by the entire country. Lougheed Con-servatives believed the provinces – while contributing to a strong, united, and economically stable Canada – should have autonomy in areas such as natural resources.

Lougheed stated his party's stance as early as 1971, when he pledged "to secure a firm policy declaration by the Federal Government that the Na-tional Oil Policy is not subject to the whims of Eastern Canadian political interests" (Alberta Progressive Conservative Party 1971). At times, this au-tonomist impulse manifested itself in pro-West rhetoric, promoting Al-berta's leadership within a broader regional context. Lougheed stated in 1979, "It is the feeling of western Canadians that we are coming into a new era, one of maturity and strength – with a deep desire to be a very important part of Canada, to reach our potential, to be part of the mainstream of Canadian life" (Progressive Conservative Association of Alberta 1979a). At others times, Lougheed alluded to Alberta's "quasi-colonial" relationship vis-à-vis the federal government (Smith 2001, 285-86; Elton and Goddard 1979, 68). In either context, Lougheed's push for more autonomy, particularly in the natural resource sector, was more like that of a sovereign national government than that of a Canadian province. His 1971 platform, for instance, included the following pledges:

- To have the Alberta Government play a much more vigorous role than in the past in promoting and preserving markets for Alberta crude, natural gas and other petroleum products – to refuse to accept a position that in this vital Alberta industry the Federal Government can negotiate agreements without consultation and concurrence by the elected representatives of the people of Alberta and the Alberta Government.
- To open a Washington, D.C., office of the Alberta Department of Mines & Minerals in order to assure [sic] that the Alberta Government is much better informed as to United States and World petroleum developments.
- To strive to secure a firm policy declaration by the Federal Government that the National Oil Policy is not subject to the whims of Eastern Canadian political interests.
- To continue to maintain a climate of attraction to foreign investment recognizing the large capital investment needs for further development of the oil industry – but at the same time to expect a social balance sheet from our corporate citizens reflecting recognition of their social responsibilities to the people of Alberta. (Alberta Progressive Conservative Party 1971)

Overall, Lougheed's 1982 provincial election slogan, "For Alberta," symbolized his campaigns' emphasis on autonomy. In addition, his decision to incorporate the provincial map into the Conservative Party's logo demonstrated a concerted effort to associate the party's brand with the province itself (see Progressive Conservative Association of Alberta 1982a). Notwithstanding its aggressive tone, the message contained in Lougheed's third guidepost bears repeating, however. According to Lougheed's definition of autonomy, "a strong Alberta means an even stronger Canada" (Elton and Goddard 1979, 68). "We believe in an Alberta government which considers themselves Canadian before Albertan," he wrote 1967, "and hence promotes

the cause of national unity and economic sovereignty as well as the determination of national purpose" (Progressive Conservative Association of Alberta 1967).

Thus, collectively, Lougheed's twelve guideposts formed the ideological
foundation of his five immensely successful election campaigns (see Alberta
Progressive Conservative Association 1971; Alberta Progressive Conservative Party 1971). By promoting individualism, populism, and autonomy,
Lougheed helped sustain values embedded in Alberta's political code and
broader political culture while – at the same time – conveying his unique
interpretations of these principles.

As the embodiment of Lougheed's devotion to these three values, the
Heritage Fund was a clear reflection of – and arguably his greatest contribution to – Alberta's political ethos. Faced with the decision of how best to
spend Alberta's growing oil and gas revenues, the premier resisted calls to
reduce taxes or dramatically increase social spending; either option, he believed, would lead to inflation and unsustainable population growth. Instead,
he opted to create a "safety valve of sorts" that allowed the Alberta government to invest revenues responsibly (Tupper 2004, 222). The resulting fund
was established in 1976 as a rainy day reserve that would, at the same time,
generate enough revenue through accrued interest to finance increased
spending in infrastructure, diversification, research, education, and loans to
other provincial governments.

Although Lougheed's use of the reserve to fuel economic and social development was unique, the Heritage Fund itself was not a particularly novel
idea. In 1955, Manning's Social Credit had pledged to "retire the debt in-
curred by former governments [and] create a reserve for future emergen-
cies" (Alberta Social Credit League 1955a). Yet Lougheed's promotion of
the fund as the centrepiece of his government's agenda combined all three
elements of the Alberta code into a single policy package. First, it embodied
the principles of fiscal responsibility and restraint, core elements of the pay-
as-you-go individualist approach to government financing established by
Manning. Second, by establishing Albertans' common claim to their natural
resources (invoked earlier by Aberhart's concept of the province's cultural
heritage), the fund promoted a populist sense of community in which the
people of the province received the benefits of their collective birthright.
Third, and perhaps most importantly, the Heritage Fund was sold as a means
of maintaining Alberta's economic and political independence. Whereas
Manning had focused on economic development in general as a means of
fuelling social progress and establishing Alberta's autonomy and supremacy,

Lougheed's focus was on local development as a way out of dependence on national and international markets and diversification as a means of protecting the province against the solvency challenges that faced many other territories reliant on natural resource exports, particularly oil and gas. The fund, therefore, not only became a vital instrument for government expansion, it also became a symbol of the province's autonomy and long-term self-sufficiency (Smith 2001, 286).

All told, beyond changes in emphasis, Lougheed's plans changed little between 1965 and his retirement following the 1982 election. The similarities between his original guideposts and the ten principles published as part of a party history in 1980 illustrate this continuity (Progressive Conservative Association of Alberta 1980). By following these principles, Peter Lougheed became "Alberta's most determined, innovative, and successful province builder" and "the principal architect of modern Alberta" (Tupper 2004, 204, 227). Ultimately, his positive definition of freedom earned him admiration from centrists, who saw him as a true red tory; admonition from the Right, which lampooned him as "Red Peter" and "Pinko Pete"; and the resentment of the Left, which had seen its share of the policy spectrum absorbed by Lougheed's redefinition of progressive conservatism. In sum, by promoting what he called "free enterprise that cares" (Progressive Conservative Association of Alberta 1982c), Lougheed outflanked critics on both ends of Alberta's political spectrum, dominated political discourse with his own version of freedom, and virtually extinguished opposition parties in the process (Archer 1992, 120). As Taras and Tupper (1994, 63) put it, "Peter Lougheed was politically dominant and his ideas, with the muted dissent of Alberta's social democrats, were Alberta's public philosophy." With seventy-five of seventy-nine seats in the legislature, Lougheed retired at the height of his party's popularity, having reshaped Alberta's political code and transmitted its political culture through the province-building period of the 1970s.

Don Getty, 1986-89

Not unlike Manning's rise to power in 1943, Don Getty's assumption of the premiership in 1985 marked an ideological turning point for his party. The forces impinging upon him were fourfold. First, despite Lougheed's best efforts, his successor inherited a provincial government unprepared for the economic downturn that commenced in Getty's first week of office (Lisac 2004b, 234). Rising unemployment rates, a real estate crash, an agriculture crisis, and bank closures left Getty little room to manoeuvre and, for the first time since 1935, forced the governing party to debate how (and, in some areas, whether) to fund the welfare state (Smith 1992, 2001). Second, Getty entered the premiership amid intense federal-provincial negotiations. Debates over Alberta's place in Confederation had subsided somewhat as he assumed office, but their resumption during discussions of the Meech Lake and Charlottetown accords cost Getty and many of his fellow premiers significant political capital (if not their careers). Third, the new premier found himself in the midst of a redefinition of western Canadian conservatism – one aimed squarely at his own breed of red toryism. Lured back into professional politics by what he perceived as ideological shortcomings in the federal Tory government, Preston Manning was orchestrating the political realignment he and his father had proposed two decades earlier. And fourth, the Mulroney Conservatives had risen to power federally. Although their federal cousins were flagging in popularity, having a Conservative government in power hampered the ability of the Alberta Tories to rail against Ottawa as a campaign strategy. Combined, these four developments helped to "put politics back" into Alberta and challenged progressive conservatism's grip on the Alberta code. In the face of recession and a global neoliberal movement, the new premier struggled to prevent his party from ceding the three pillars to opposition forces on the Right. Thus began the internal transformation of the Progressive Conservatives under Don Getty – a process that culminated in the selection of neoliberal Ralph Klein as party leader in 1992.

In the beginning, Getty's rhetoric contained few references to the provincial code. By pitting continuity, strength, and experience against the "unsafe change" that would be ushered in by an untried opposition, the Tory's first campaign in 1986 came to resemble that of Harry Strom in 1971. Getty told voters, "Your Vote is Important for Alberta. Albertans need vital, experienced leadership and a strong team to meet the challenges and opportunities in all sectors of the economy. Together we can shape the future in Alberta. Your decision is important. Vote for your Progressive Conservative candidate" (Progressive Conservative Association of Alberta 1986). Short on both policy and rhetoric, Getty's one-page newspaper platform focused overwhelmingly on the economy, especially job creation and the growth of small business. In the midst of recession, Getty pledged to "help Albertans gain employment in all communities and in all sectors of our provincial community" (ibid.). With promises of royalty reductions, industry and farm subsidies, economic diversification, and public works projects, the plan had a distinct blue tory flavour. Yet it lacked any concerted rhetorical emphasis on any of the three elements of the Alberta code.

The results of the 1986 election revealed the public's dissatisfaction with Getty's vision and confirmed the new contours of the province's electoral map. With the Liberals and New Democrats competing for seats in Edmonton, the Conservatives were left to dominate Calgary, southern Alberta, and rural areas in the north (Dyck 1996, 520-21). Although they maintained a substantial majority in the legislature, Getty's Tories faced some of the stiffest challenges from opposition parties in the history of the province (Stewart and Archer 2000, 12; Tupper 1991; Archer 1992).

In his first full term as premier, Getty set his sights on broader economic concerns surrounding the petroleum sector. Once again, his pump-priming approach differed little from Lougheed's blue tory philosophy as he cut royalties, offered incentives, and floated interest-free loans to private companies in an effort to revive the provincial economy (Smith 1992, 243). Responding to the economic downturn of the late 1980s, Getty attempted to arrest the $3.3 billion provincial deficit through a combination of tax, premium, and fee increases (totalling $1 billion) and a 6.3 percent reduction in government spending (Lisac 2004b, 237; Dyck 1996). Although the latter was attributable to a concern over fiscal orthodoxy, the former – like the federal Conservatives' Goods and Services Tax (GST) – was contrary to the free-enterprise values embodied in the provincial code. It also offended the sensibilities of fiscal conservatives, whose adherence to supply-side economics was gaining influence throughout North America. From them, Getty faced increasing demands to reach out to would-be Alberta Reformers, despite assurances from Preston Manning that he did not intend to create provincial-level organizations (Harrison 1995, 53-55; Dyck 1996, 516, 549-53; see also Archer 1992, 132-33; Lisac 2004b, 240; Taras and Tupper 1994, 65; Stewart 1995, 37). Combined, these pressures triggered a major shift in Alberta Conservative ideology and appeared to have persuaded Getty to embrace code politics.

Getty's choice of campaign slogan in 1989 – "Right for Alberta" – signalled his party's new direction (Progressive Conservative Association of Alberta 1989b). His second platform emphasized individualism, populism, and autonomy. In particular, the premier promised Albertans "leadership with integrity," and the literature suggested that "Don Getty has the trust of Albertans, because he listens, he cares, and he's honest. He has national stature, and he stands for Alberta on issues that affect our province" (ibid.).

In the process, Getty sought to redefine the provincial community in distinctly neoconservative terms, referring to the society as "a family of Albertans" (ibid.). This style of rhetoric linked the personal lives of Albertans to their civic interests, stressing the common threads of individual responsibility and the common good: "Here in Alberta, traditional values have emphasized families and helping out our neighbours ... To Don Getty, 'strong families make strong communities, which make a strong Alberta.' Most families face occasional crises – some have deeply rooted problems. Family breakdowns, drug abuse, and family violence are all critical issues, and they are being addressed. Fortunately, when taken in total, it is still hard to imagine a better place for a family, than here in Alberta (ibid.)."

Getty's emphasis on individualism is reflected most clearly in his promotion of private-sector development. The premier's focus remained on gaining "new economic strength for Alberta" through new jobs, diversification, and energy, but his rhetoric expanded to include promises of free enterprise and Canada's lowest taxes:

> *Free Enterprise* – Alberta remains a place where people are proud of what they can accomplish on their own and with their families. In the coming years, the Getty government will seek opportunities to reduce government involvement in some enterprises and position Alberta to compete in the North American and world markets.
>
> *Lowest Taxes* – Responsible management, even through tough times, has allowed Alberta to keep the lowest level of personal taxes in Canada! We have done this while still implementing a deficit reduction program which is on target. Alberta has no provincial sales tax. (Ibid.)

The results of the 1989 provincial election offer mixed evidence of the success of this rhetorical strategy. The Conservatives' share of the popular vote dropped a further 7 percentage points but cost the government only two seats. At the same time, Getty became one of the few premiers in Canadian history to lose his own seat while retaining control of government. Foreshadowing his party's future direction, one of Getty's chief accomplishments in the 1989 campaign was to recruit prominent candidates from Alberta's New Right, including former Social Credit and Representative Party leader Ray Speaker and future premier Ralph Klein.

Just two weeks before the defeat of the Charlottetown Accord, Getty retired from the premiership. His government had supported the accord, at least tacitly, in the interests of national unity. Beyond demands for senate reform, this had left Getty little room for anti-Ottawa rhetoric or appeals to provincial autonomy. Alongside continued emphases on rural aid and government restraint, Getty's most prominent second-term achievement had been his privatization of Alberta Government Telephones in 1990 – one of the province's original Crown corporations. Having exacerbated deficits through failed forced-growth experiments and having introduced a series of unpopular tax increases and service cuts, Getty could not balance the budget, however, and left his party and government in a fiscal and electoral crisis (Dyck 1996, 553; Taras and Tupper 1994, 64).

Regardless of these shortcomings, Getty's premiership should be considered a crucial interlude in his party's ideological evolution. Although often dismissed as the denouement of the Lougheed era, the Tory leader's decision to steer his party to the New Right marked a turning point in the history of Alberta conservatism. In hindsight, Getty's adoption of the neoliberal/neoconservative definition of freedom constituted the first stages of the Klein revolution.

Ralph Klein, 1992-2004

If history offered any lessons, all of the elements were in place for a turnover in government in Alberta in 1993. When Ralph Klein entered the premier's office in November 1992, his party had the support of fewer than one in five Alberta voters (Stewart 1995, 34; Barrie 2004, 261). The Conservatives – like all three outgoing governing parties before them – faced an economic downturn that challenged their image as prudent managers of the provincial purse. Pushed back to their rural base by the established opposition parties, the Tories also encountered a potential populist, individualist, and autonomist political rival in the Reform Party. Moreover, the plummeting popularity of Mulroney's federal government was weighing down Tory parties across the country. All told, the Alberta Conservatives were poised to confirm the "three leader" pattern of Alberta political dynasties – every governing party in the province's history to that point had elevated three, and only three, leaders to the Premier's Office (Pal 1992, 25; Archer and Hunziker 1992, 83). That the Conservatives managed to avoid the fate suffered by the Liberals, United Farmers, and Socreds remains one of the great surprises of Canadian political history.[7] That they actually managed to increase their popularity while orchestrating the most drastic program of government retrenchment in Alberta history is even more remarkable. Although it is beyond the scope of this chapter, the question remains, how did the Tories do it?[8] Popular accounts such as Lisac's (2004a, 230) suggest "they won by choosing the astonishing strategy of running against themselves." The legend portrays Klein as the only politician in (Canadian) history able to convince the electorate that spending cuts were not only obligatory but necessary to curb deficits that *his own party* had created.

Although it captures the spirit of the campaign, the legend oversimplifies Klein's rhetorical strategy. It is true – Klein did "run against" his two predecessors in the Premier's Office. Yet, in doing so, he drew upon common conservative principles that had long formed the ideological backbone of Alberta party politics. That Klein's governing philosophy was closer to that of Ernest Manning than Peter Lougheed says as much about the complex ideological relationship between parties on Alberta's Right, and the power of the provincial code, as it does about Klein's antipathy toward the Conservative Party. Moreover, as part of the evolution of the Alberta PCs in the late 1980s, Klein's neoliberal vision was well grounded in "the ideological and demographic core of the party" (Stewart and Archer 2000, 64) and an increasingly receptive public (Archer and Gibbins 1997). Klein's contribution to Alberta politics was therefore hardly revolutionary. It was simply, and quintessentially, in code. Like Aberhart, Klein packaged personal accountability and fiscal orthodoxy together, selling deficit reduction in folksy language that linked the Alberta government to Alberta families in debt (Smith 2001, 294-95). He invoked a spirit of belt-tightening to encourage average Albertans to support his cuts to social services (Barrie 2004, 265). In short, Klein had a populist, "tough love" approach to governing that stressed individual responsibility, collective solidarity, and provincial autonomy as the best means of reviving Alberta's economy and society (ibid., 256).

Bootstrap Individualism

Klein's vision of Alberta as a community of individuals strongly resembled the vision of Aberhart and Manning, who both made constant references to the strength of "individuals in association." In addition to frequent allusions to the importance of individual liberties, self-reliance, and free enterprise, Klein, like his Social Credit forebears, also called attention to the maverick roots of Alberta's political culture. As Friesen (1999, 90) argues, "Premier Klein's 'revolution,' as it was styled by government press agents, consolidated the self-perception of Albertans as the frontiersmen and –women who dared to live differently and, by taking such risks, who dared to prosper."

All of these elements of individualism figured prominently in Klein's campaign rhetoric. Consider the following excerpt from a 2004 PC pamphlet:

Albertans are unique – we have an eternal pioneering and entrepreneurial spirit. We are proud of our freedoms, our accomplishments, and our willingness to try new things. Albertans dare to be different. When Albertans decided the province should be deficit and debt free, everyone tightened their belts and pulled together to get it done. When farmers were overwhelmed by drought and BSE, Albertans stood tall and came to their aid. Even in tough times, Albertans are proud of being independent and determined. We have a strong feeling of self-determination that is balanced with our commitment to our families and the greater community – it's this spirit that makes us Proud to be Albertan. (PC Alberta 2004)

In addition to such rhetoric, each of Klein's four platforms was replete with references to free enterprise and personal accountability, including the following:

- A justice system that promotes safe communities, individual responsibility, and punishments that are tough but fair
- An economic development strategy that attracts investment and an economic climate that produces quality, private sector jobs
- 150,000 new jobs within the private sector
- Continued responsible financial management with no new taxes, no tax increases and *no sales tax* and continued reduction of red tape. (Progressive Conservative Association of Alberta 1997)

Ultimately, according to Klein, "Maintaining and strengthening Alberta's economic advantage requires a commitment to our success principles – belief in free enterprise; willingness to take risks; ability to stand up for Alberta; and the discipline to maintain a positive fiscal regime without debt. These are guiding PC principles" (PC Alberta 2004).

This individualistic rhetoric helped Klein link personal and governmental responsibility, particularly as it concerned deficits and debt. According to his 1997 platform, "We are working to operate your government like a typical Alberta family tries to operate: to keep our expenditures under control, to pay off our mortgage, to invest in household needs and to save a little for the future. Because the next generation has to live in this house called Alberta, and we want to leave it to them in the best shape possible" (PC Alberta 1997). Eleven years after his first electoral victory, drawing on the same metaphor, Klein announced, "On July 12, Albertans officially burned the province's mortgage – the provincial debt. Every Albertan played a part in building a positive future for our children and our grandchildren. Over the past 11 years we paid $12.8 billion in interest on debt. Well, our mortgage and those interest payments are gone. Our home is paid for and will stay that way" (PC Alberta 2004).

The premier was, however, always careful to note that improvements to the province's finances were "not a license to return to the free-spending ways of the past" (Lieutenant-Governor 1997, 1). This was a not-so-veiled attack on Lougheed's activist approach to governance. In contrast to his predecessors' Keynesian vision of the province, Klein's Alberta was "a place where government lives within its means and limits its role to whatever is necessary" (Progressive Conservative Association of Alberta 1997). Indeed, throughout his time in office, Klein maintained his "unshakable commitment to fiscal responsibility and accountability" – core components of the province's conservative political culture (Lieutenant-Governor of Alberta 2001).

To this end, Klein believed business was "responsible for economic development – government is responsible for a positive environment that promotes job creation and investment" (Progressive Conservative Association of Alberta 1993). With rhetoric reminiscent of Manning's economy-first, pay-as-you-go mantra, Klein told voters, "We must not lose sight of the fact that energy revenues are part of what allows Alberta to reinvest in health care, schools, roads, justice programs, and other initiatives that Albertans support. They allow us to pay down debt. Energy revenues help keep our personal taxes the lowest in Canada and help us reduce business taxes. A vibrant energy sector is indeed a key to a strong Alberta" (Lieutenant-Governor of Alberta 2001). The Klein government was, therefore, but one among many world governments adopting the New Right consensus, but Klein did so on distinctly Albertan terms (Smith 2001, 278-79; Friesen 1999, 90; Harrison and Laxer 1995b).

This New Right philosophy extended beyond a neoliberal approach to the economy. Although less pronounced during campaigns, neoconservatism – with its emphasis on personal responsibility – was also a key element of Klein's rhetoric (see Taras and Tupper 1994, 71-75; Dyck 2006, 87). For example, drawing on principles developed during Getty's second term, Klein's PC Party retained its commitment to traditional values and "the importance of the family ... [as] paramount in the development of social responsibility and a sense of self-worth" (PC Alberta 2004). As Trimble (1997, 13) notes, for neoconservatives such as Klein, "the fact that there is a massive gap between the rich and the poor is of little concern to the government as those who work hard are well off, those who slack off or fail to 'make something of themselves' are poor, and it is silly and counterproductive for the state to intervene in this 'natural' process. Neoconservatives, therefore, are in favour of 'cracking down on welfare fraud' and dramatically cutting social assistance payments." To Klein, reducing the welfare budget meant providing "for those who cannot fend for themselves – our first priority must be on self-reliance, providing assistance will come second" (Progressive Conservative Association of Alberta 1993; see also Dyck 1996, 554). Furthermore, in 2001, Klein promised a "new aboriginal policy framework with the goal of increasing the well-being and self-reliance of the First Nations, Metis, Inuit, and other aboriginal peoples of the province" (Lieutenant-Governor of Alberta 2001). In his view, "the state's role is simply to provide 'basic services' – self-reliant citizens must assume the primary responsibility for their own well-being" (Taras and Tupper 1994, 82). In reference to individualism, then, Klein sought a "social safety net that provides a 'hand up' rather than a 'hand out' by assisting, retraining and re-introduction to the workforce" (Progressive Conservative Association of Alberta 1997; see also PC Alberta 2004). All told, Ralph Klein's approach to politics was thoroughly individualist, harkening back to the origins of the Alberta code and the rhetoric of early Social Credit premiers.

"Ralph's Team" and Everyman Politics

Klein's bootstrap individualism was closely tied to his populist appeal. Among his most oft-used expressions, for instance, Klein emphasized the importance of governments' "keeping their promises." For this reason, Klein kept his 1993 campaign platform straightforward:

- A sound financial management plan
- A balanced budget within four years
- A safe place to raise our families
- Quality education for our young people
- Responsible social programs that help people to help themselves
- A thriving business-driven economy that encourages investment, jobs and provides employment opportunities
- Sustainable development so that economic growth and environmental protection go hand-in-hand
- A smaller, more open government
- A government that listens and keeps its promises every day. (Progressive Conservative Association of Alberta 1993)

Recapitulating and building on theses pledges, Klein's 1997 platform featured lists of "promises made ... promises kept."

Also, Klein's first two campaigns touted the strength of "Ralph's team," which included his slate of Progressive Conservative candidates, and invited all Albertans to join in the common endeavour (see Progressive Conservative Association of Alberta 1997). In a populist, personal message to voters during his 1997 campaign, Ralph and his wife, Colleen, announced:

> Our team is especially proud to be Albertans. Perhaps the greatest thing we can say is that we kept our word. Many did not think we would or even could, but, thanks to you, your support and the sacrifices by all Albertans, we have all succeeded as an Alberta team. We know that it has been difficult for many, but we now look forward to a period of exceptional growth and opportunity. All Albertans can be proud. We are giving our children and grandchildren a chance to look to the future with optimism. You are as much a part of the team as us. Thank you. (Ibid.)

Finally, Klein's campaign literature included numerous quotations from constituents that highlighted his down-to-earth character:

> "I like Ralph Klein. He's an ordinary person just like the rest of us. Best of all, he understands people issues like jobs, education, and health care." Jill Thomson, Assistant Registrar Records, Grande Prairie Regional College, Grande Prairie

> "When Ralph Klein was in Barrhead, I talked to him about the problems facing agriculture. He asked questions and took time to listen to the answer. He has a genuine interest in people and wants to know what they think. He is someone we can believe in. Let's give him a chance." Greg Rentz, Farmer, Barmead

> (Progressive Conservative Association of Alberta 1993)

Party literature followed a similar, populist format in 1997, this time emphasizing praise from outside – notably American – observers:

> "By articulating common sense solutions to problems, he's become a hero to many average voters." *Wall Street Journal*, February 23, 1995

"I would not have written a word about Ralph Klein if I didn't think he had a lot of lessons for American politicians and policy makers." John Fund, Wall Street Journal writer in *Calgary Herald,* March 11, 1995

"Putting our interest savings into health care and education shows that Ralph both cares and listens." Donna Weitz, Edmonton parent, December 1996

"Ralph Klein is the best premier of Alberta in at least the past 25 years, and arguably the most courageous in our 90 year history." Lorne Gunter, *Edmonton Journal,* January 3, 1996

"Alberta is now the model for other provincial governments and the federal government, which also face budget problems." *New York Times,* January 1, 1995

"Mr. Klein was basically just giving his province back to ordinary people. How that could be remotely unpopular, I don't understand." Jim Luder, Director, Research of Americans for Tax Reform, March 11, 1995

"The economic revival that we are seeing will rival the 1970s and in many ways the thousands of new jobs and new businesses throughout Alberta is the direct result of the prudent efforts of the Klein government." Rick LeLacheur, President and CEO, Economic Development Edmonton, January 1997

Klein's approach to policy making also had a distinctly plebiscitarian tone. In his 2001 Throne Speech – which was "really the essence of an election platform" (Johnsrude 1997) – the premier promised to "convene a provincial future summit" on "Alberta's debt-free future" (Lieutenant-Governor of Alberta 2001). After doing so, his 2004 platform promised that "a PC government will be guided by the advice of Albertans, including what 290,000 Albertans told us in the 'It's Your Future' survey." As a result of the survey, the Klein government issued a series of prosperity bonuses – a natural-resource revenue-rebate scheme remarkably similar to the Socreds' dividend and prosperity-certificate programs. Through the plan, announced in September 2005, the government distributed 20 percent of the provincial surplus (or $1.4 billion of $6.8 billion) directly to all Alberta citizens in the form of prosperity cheques. Just like Manning's short-lived citizen participation dividends (1955-57), "Ralphbucks" were discontinued when polls suggested the public preferred the money be spent on infrastructure and social services. Some observers saw the rebates as a signal that Klein, having fulfilled his promise to retire the provincial debt, lacked the vision to deal with post-deficit Alberta (Bell, Jansen, and Young 2007, 32, 44). Regardless of the impetus, the prosperity bonus program demonstrated Klein's willingness to return money to taxpayers, rather than spending it on their behalf.

In the end, of all his rhetorical feats, the most significant were Klein's populist redefinition of the role of the state and the lowering of public expectations for government (Friesen 1999, 91; Bell, Jansen, and Young 2007, 31; Dyck 2006, 86; Harrison and Laxer 1995b, 1; Wishlow 2001, 169). According to this view, the state should never eclipse the people. As Smith (2001, 303) puts it, Klein's revolution "represented an attack not only upon the deficit ... [and] the debt, but also upon government itself – what it does, how it is organized, how it delivers its programs and services, what citizens should expect from government, and how they should relate to government, as citizens or consumers." If Peter Lougheed had convinced the public that it was time to expect more from the Alberta government in 1971, Klein's message was precisely the opposite: government should "get out of the way and let people do what they do best" (PC Alberta 2004).

The Alberta Advantage

Klein also drew upon the autonomist rhetoric that had served his predecessors well. Klein's confrontational stance vis-à-vis the Chrétien government in Ottawa – on law and order, the environment, judicial review, federal overreach, Quebec's place in Confederation, and a variety of other issues – evoked images of Aberhart's relationship with King or Lougheed's relationship with Trudeau. According to the 1997 Throne Speech, for example, Klein's government pledged "to integrate services and eliminate overlap at the federal-provincial level. It will do this by clarifying and rebalancing administrative roles and responsibilities, especially in the area of social policy reform, by harmonizing systems of environmental management and the promotion of sustainable development, and by reducing trade barriers at home and abroad" (Lieutenant-Governor of Alberta 1997).

Four years later, his rhetoric was more forceful, as Klein played on the "strong Alberta, strong Canada" theme established in decades past:

> Like Albertans, the government is fully committed to a strong Alberta within a strong Canada. It rejects the destructive vision of separation and

embraces the concept of a united, diverse nation in which each province has an important role. Alberta will do its part toward maintaining a united Canada. The government will continue to support the concept of equalization, recognizing Alberta's role as a have province. At the same time, the government asks that Ottawa not intrude into the areas of provincial responsibility set out in the Constitution. It seeks a genuine effort from Ottawa to deal with the concerns of Albertans to make sure their voices are heard and their priorities addressed fairly. (Lieutenant-Governor of Alberta 2001, 5)

These priorities included an end to the Canadian Wheat Board's marketing monopoly, the elimination of the Goods and Services Tax on electricity and natural gas bills, and resistance to the implementation of the Kyoto Protocol (see Bell, Jansen, and Young 2007, 31). On the latter, Klein pledged to "work with industry and communities to protect Alberta from the negative impacts of the Kyoto Protocol, while taking steps to reduce greenhouse gas emissions" under a made-in-Alberta plan (PC Alberta 2004). Indeed, since Lougheed first released the party's guideposts in 1967, the Alberta Progressive Conservatives had maintained their commitment to preserving the province's status "as an equal partner in Confederation. We must strive to maintain sovereignty over provincial matters, believing that a strong and vibrant Alberta is a cornerstone of a strong and united Canada" (PC Alberta 2004).

Like Ernest Manning's, Klein's provincial rights rhetoric crossed over into the realm of boosterism as it touted Alberta's superior performance on a variety of fronts as a product of the province's unique political culture:

Alberta is the envy of the nation. We do have challenges, but fortunately we are in a position to address them. We see Alberta as a debt-free province that provides opportunity for every citizen. It's a place where people can choose freely; pursue opportunities and excel. It's a place where people are healthy and supported by the country's best health care system. It's a place where people are well educated because of a superb education system. It's a place where people enjoy a high quality of life. We see a prosperous province that thrives on ingenuity and entrepreneurialism and one where every individual can say, "I am proud to be Albertan." That Alberta pride is due to your hard work. You've helped build quite a legacy leading into our province's 105th birthday. 2005 will be a remarkable year as Albertans enter the second century of our province. (PC Alberta 2004)

Ultimately, Klein's cunning ability to cultivate anti-politician, anti-government sentiment and leverage it into support for his revamped Conservative Party was responsible for the Tories' comeback. This, in turn, was due to Klein's capacity to reshape the Conservative Party's definition of freedom, reverting back, in many ways, to the ideology of the Socred movement. In these ways, Klein's reinvention of progressive conservatism paralleled Manning's redefinition of Social Credit in 1944. Both helped to sustain a distinctly laissez-faire version of individualism, a plebiscitarian brand of populism, and an autonomist view of Alberta's position in Confederation – key elements of the province's political code and culture.

Ed Stelmach, 2008-

Having led the province into its second century deficit and debt free, Ralph Klein's future as premier appeared secure. This situation changed suddenly in spring 2006. Following the province's centennial celebrations, Klein mused openly about leading the Conservatives into the next election. Many in the party disagreed, however, and on 31 March the premier barely survived a mandatory leadership review at the party's annual convention. With only 55.4 percent of delegates supporting Klein's leadership, many Conservatives were prepared to rejuvenate the party. Shortly thereafter, Klein announced his plans to retire.

Like Social Credit in the mid-1940s and late 1960s, the Alberta Conservatives lacked a raison d'être after Klein conquered the deficit (Bell, Jansen, and Young 2007, 45). The ensuing leadership race gave the party an opportunity to recraft its image. As is recounted elsewhere, the race to replace Klein narrowed to a contest between his former finance minister, Jim Dinning, and two other candidates: University of Calgary professor Ted Morton and Ed Stelmach, a member of the party's inner circle but a less than dynamic cabinet minister from northern Alberta (Wesley 2007b; Stewart and Sayers 2008). As the process drew to a close in November 2006, the divide between the progressive and conservative wings of the party was laid bare: "Ted Morton's platform – a self-styled 'conservative plan for conservatives' – stood in stark contrast with Jim Dinning's, whose image as a red tory placed him firmly in the left wing of the Alberta PCs. These differences were magnified throughout the campaign, both by media seeking to portray conflict and by the candidates themselves in advertisements" (Wesley 2007a, 10).

In this polarized climate, Ed Stelmach's image as a compromise candidate played a large role in his victory. Having eschewed direct ideological or policy confrontation with either Dinning or Morton, and having avoided attacks from both of the front-running candidates, "Steady Eddie" was able "to build alliances with other candidates and supporters, and to reach out to 'loose' ... voters in future rounds of balloting" (Wesley 2007a, 11). In particular, Stelmach's alliances with fellow leadership contenders Lyle Oberg, Dave Hancock, and Mark Norris were made more feasible by his decision to emphasize inclusive leadership and meaningful participation over ideological confrontation (Stelmach 2006). Indeed, Stelmach's platform – Doing What's Right for Albertans – offered a vague "vision to unite Albertans to achieve greater opportunities; a higher standard of living; and a better quality of life for all Albertans." His plan included promises to "tackle challenges related to growth; improve quality of life for all; provide inclusive leadership and honest government; and build a stronger Alberta." Overall, his broader message was one of "Building relationships, not walls," both within the province and his party (Stelmach 2006).

Stelmach's surprise third-ballot victory therefore represented defeat for neither the progressive nor the conservative wings of the PC Party. Progressives could take solace in Stelmach's commitment to universal social programs and pledges to preserve Alberta's multicultural heritage, while conservatives could support his promises of democratic reform and fiscal responsibility. Hence, if Alberta's voters are known for adopting safe change during general elections, provincial Conservatives followed the same mantra in selecting Ed Stelmach as Alberta's thirteenth premier.

From his leadership campaign to his first general election, Stelmach's brand of conservatism is far more difficult to label than that of his predecessors, and his adherence to the provincial code is far less prominent. His 2008 general election platform – Change That Works for Albertans (PC Alberta 2008) – was long on policy and short on principles. Having issued one of the most detailed policy statements in his party's history (certainly since Lougheed's *NOW: New Directions* in 1971), Stelmach's vision did not lack comprehensiveness. Missing, however, was any indication of the motives behind the premier's definition of change. There were no guideposts (as Lougheed provided), no obvious statements of purpose (as found in Getty's second platform), no trace of Klein's colourful rhetoric, and no concrete statements affirming Stelmach's allegiance to the values of individualism, populism, and autonomy. Complicating matters, most of the party's 2008 pledges centred on valence issues – that is, Stelmach focused his campaign on issues with which most parties (and, likely, voters) had no disagreement.[9] In short, aside from vague references to low taxes, "innovation, determination, and hard work," Stelmach's first general election platform offered little indication as to which side of the progressive-conservative divide he belonged, nor whether he intended to campaign "in code."

Observers have, accordingly, differed in their assessments of Stelmach's ideological identity. Critics on the Right, including the Wildrose Alliance and many in the oil industry, claim he leans too far to the centre and neglects the needs of taxpayers and industry (see Wildrose Alliance Party of Alberta 2008). Critics on the Left – including New Democrats, unions, and environmental groups – claim his policies do not go far enough in addressing the social and ecological consequences of the province's explosive growth (see Alberta NDP 2008). It appears that Stelmach has carved out a space in the Centre-Right, much like Peter Lougheed did in the 1970s. There is, however, a key difference: whereas Lougheed's modern Toryism provided his party with an ideological foundation grounded in the provincial code of individualism, populism, and autonomy, Stelmach's vision is cloudier from an ideological perspective.

There are several ways to interpret this ambiguity. One approach is to dismiss Stelmach's vision as entirely incoherent from an ideological perspective – that is, we can view his 2008 platform as the product of a concerted effort to avoid ideological commitments and, instead, appeal to a wide range of societal interests with vague appeals and a shopping bag of miscellaneous election promises. According to this view, the Stelmach Conservatives are motivated purely by the pursuit of power and are willing to cobble together whatever popular policies are necessary to maintain control of government. A second, and more convincing, interpretation attributes an element of strategy to Stelmach's ambiguity. As in his leadership platform, Stelmach might be motivated by his desire to build "relationships, not walls." In this sense, his 2008 election manifesto can be viewed as a principled attempt to strike an ideological balance between progressive Toryism and conservative neoliberalism. Rather than being non-ideological, Stelmach's platform may be a purposeful attempt at blending the two streams of the Alberta Right – the old and the new – into a single coherent party ideology.

Borrowing from the neoconservative Right, Stelmach promised "an aggressive plan to get tough on criminals, reduce crime and make our communities safer"; borrowing from the neoliberal Right, he pledged "to protect our business advantages, including low business and personal taxes" (PC Alberta 2008). On the other hand, there was also a blue tory streak in Stelmach's vision of the government's role in economic development and diversification and traces of red toryism in his plans to end homelessness in

Alberta within ten years and increase funding for child care and women's shelters. Further evidence of a more compassionate brand of conservatism may be found in Stelmach's plan for "building our quality of life":

> A sense of community is at the heart of Alberta. We want to feel safe, to have the services we need, and to know that there is a safety net for those who need it.
>
> Our economic boom means opportunity, but also means families feel the pressures of growth. We need to catch up, and we have a plan to do that. Our goal is to be the best place in the world to work, live, play and raise our families ...
>
> Quality of life is more than low taxes and good services. Our children must experience the cultural and recreational wonders of Alberta. (Ibid.)

From this second perspective, then, Stelmach's rise to the leadership of the PC Party of Alberta represents the marriage of Lougheed's Toryism with Klein's New Right conservatism. Compared to his predecessors, however, Stelmach appeals to the provincial code far less frequently.

How long this marriage of new and old conservatism will last remains to be seen. In particular, observers must wait to measure Stelmach's rhetorical response to the 2009 economic crisis. In today's economically volatile environment – not unlike the conditions faced by Aberhart in 1935 and Getty in 1989 – Stelmach can be expected to convert to speaking in code during the next campaign. Early indications suggest that anti-Ottawa rhetoric, particularly on the topic of environmental policy and equalization, will also figure prominently in the next provincial election. A decision to speak in code may, in part, help to determine the future of the Progressive Conservative Party in Alberta – "the paramount political dynasty in a province known for its dynasties" (Bell, Jansen, and Young 2007, 27).

Conclusion

The most recent campaign notwithstanding, throughout much of the past seven decades, Alberta's two most successful parties have spoken to the public with a common accent. Emphasizing three core elements of freedom – individualism, populism, and provincial autonomy – Social Credit and the Progressive Conservatives have cultivated a dominant narrative that has helped sustain their province's conservative political culture. Indeed, their campaign appeals have often involved explicit references to American values, sources, and texts imported by the province's founding fragment. Pal

(1992, 3-4) describes how the connection between elite discourse and political culture has helped to sustain the latter throughout much of the last century:

> Given Alberta's population growth from immigration over the last two generations, the cultural argument can only work if newcomers absorb a preexisting set of political assumptions and arguments. A political culture like this must have a source and must be transferred across generations. Unless we are willing to accept some "hidden hand," it should also be clear that the culture needs to be actively maintained and transferred; it has no automatic preeminence. The source of Alberta's distinctive political culture is its political system itself, or more precisely, its party system ... and the strategic intervention of such leaders as Aberhart, Manning and Lougheed, who reshaped the political culture to meet new circumstances. Albertans have to look somewhere for their cues about politics, they have to listen to arguments about the nature of the political, and they have to see evidence of principles turned into practice in order to believe and to act on that belief.

As is discussed in greater detail throughout this book, the dominant political parties are the key providers of these cues.

Of course, the dominant parties' messages have not remained entirely consistent or static over time. Beginning with William Aberhart's brand of civic republicanism, and continuing with Ernest Manning's version of antisocialism, the Socreds redefined the nature of freedom in Alberta on several occasions to match changing external and internal conditions. By the same token, Peter Lougheed's reformulation of progressive conservatism helped reshape the political code once more. While downplaying the populist and individualist strains of the provincial narrative, Lougheed's Toryism posited a positive role for the Alberta government as the defender of provincial autonomy. Decades later, when the party suffered from flagging support, the Progressive Conservatives took a page from the Social Credit Party's campaign manual. Reinventing itself under Don Getty and Ralph Klein, the party tied together all three elements of the Alberta code into a coherent – and popular – New Right ideology. All told, each dominant party leader has offered his own unique vision of freedom in Alberta. In the process, the province's dominant "discourse has both reproduced itself from earlier manifestations and been transformed" (Wiseman 2007, 249).

Nonetheless, throughout the last seventy years, political discourse has revolved around the same broad rhetorical theme – Alberta strong and free.

Measured by their popularity at the polls, the Socreds' and Tories' common vision of Alberta as a conservative society has dominated political discourse as much as the parties have dominated the legislature. This dominance is not only a testament to the persistent "drawing power of right-wing appeals in Alberta" (Wiseman 2007, 249), it also shows how values cultivated in the formative years of the province have been transmitted to newcomers and successive generations during the last twenty provincial election campaigns.

4

Campaigns in Saskatchewan
A Code of Security

Saskatchewan is Alberta's Siamese twin (Marchildon 2005a, 4). Born out of the North-West Territories in 1905, the two provinces were separated as they entered Confederation. The incision was a purely political one, drawn cleanly along the 110th meridian instead of along a natural, topographic, or demographic cleavage. Its scars remain, nonetheless. Despite broad similarities in terms of their populations and economies, the political cultures of the two provinces are as different as any pair in Canada. Saskatchewan is known as the birthplace of social democracy in Canada, while Alberta is its cradle of conservatism. These differences are so stark that, by the 1980s, they could be seen emblazoned on each province's coat of arms: Alberta's motto is *Fortis et liber* (strong and free), while Saskatchewan's is *Multis e gentibus vires* (from many peoples, strength).

Like Alberta, "Saskatchewan's political movements, leaders, economy, and history have been plumbed far out of proportion to what one might expect for a rather small rural population" (Dunn and Laycock 1992, 207). In particular, the province's political parties have received an inordinate amount of attention because they have "both generated and reflected the colour and the intensity of the province's politics" (Courtney and Smith 1972, 290). This tradition began with Saskatchewan's first political juggernaut, the Liberal Party, whose longevity in office help set the province apart from its Prairie neighbours. Since then, the New Democratic Party (NDP) and its forebear, the Co-operative Commonwealth Federation (CCF), have received much of the focus, whether by virtue of their prolonged dominance of Saskatchewan politics or their distinctiveness as North America's most successful socialist parties (Lipset 1968a).

Just as several books have been written to explain the decline of the Liberal Party, so too have numerous theories been advanced to explain the somewhat surprising success of the CCF-NDP in Saskatchewan. Many claim the party tapped the vein of the province's political culture, be it communitarianism, civic engagement, intense partisanship, isolationism, or a generally positive attitude toward the state. Although it does not dispute their accuracy, this chapter does reverse the causal arrow in these interpretations. An examination of its campaign rhetoric reveals that the CCF-NDP not only drew upon but actively promoted three key facets of political life in Saskatchewan: collectivism, dirigisme, and polarization.

The first facet of political life, collectivism, connotes a sense of solidarity among Saskatchewan residents – a spirit of togetherness, co-operation, neighbourliness, and organic community – in which the polity is seen as something more than a sum of its parts. Dominant party leaders did, of course, emphasize the importance of individual rights and freedoms, for Saskatchewan is, after all, a liberal democracy; however, unlike Alberta, such discussions took place against a distinctly collectivist backdrop.

Saskatchewan's collectivism is of the bridging (as opposed to bonding) type, a distinction that helps to separate the province's discourse from that of Alberta (see Putnam 2000, 350-63). As is discussed below, the lack of liberationist rhetoric in Saskatchewan has a lot to do with the definition of the province provided by dominant parties. Premiers from James Gardiner and Tommy Douglas to Roy Romanow and Lorne Calvert have portrayed Saskatchewan as an independent – but seldom virulently autonomous – province. Thus, when criticizing Ottawa, CCF-NDP leaders have tended to focus less on the federal government per se and more on the party in power. That is, rather than attacking the order of government as an institution, they have focused on the Liberal and Conservative parties as actors, linking their shortcomings to those of their provincial wings in Saskatchewan.

This is not to say that Saskatchewan joins Manitoba in lacking the province-first rhetoric found in Alberta. The rhetoric exists, but it tends to be of a different degree and kind. Whereas Alberta's provincial rights rhetoric has been more aggressive (treating the state as the guardian of society against external threats) and Manitoba's more moderate, Saskatchewan's rhetoric has been more proactive and constructive. The province's political elite has sought to provide Saskatchewan with its own sense of provincial security by working *with* other provinces and the federal government whenever feasible. Indeed, Saskatchewan elites have frequently proposed strengthening the powers of the federal government.

The second characteristic of the province's political culture, dirigisme, implies a deep faith in the capacity and responsibility of the Saskatchewan government to address the social and economic needs of its constituents. Various leaders have promoted nationalization, social ownership, public enterprise, forced growth, Crown corporations, the expansion of the welfare state, regulation, and other elements of government intervention. The growth of the state was not pursued at all cost; in fact, a substantial dose of fiscal responsibility exists in dominant party platforms from the Great Depression to the 1990s recession. However, CCF-NDP leaders from Tommy Douglas and Woodrow Lloyd to Roy Romanow and Lorne Calvert have shared an overwhelming belief in government as a positive force in society and the economy. As is discussed in Chapter 1, both collectivism and dirigisme are connected to a sense of vulnerability and isolation in Saskatchewan's political culture. Banding together at the societal level and using the levers of the state are two means of protecting the Saskatchewan people.

The third pillar of the Saskatchewan code, polarization, also relates to these underlying tensions. Dominant parties of the Left (CCF-NDP) and the Right (the early Liberal Party) have highlighted the dangers inherent in allowing their opponents to guide Saskatchewan's society, economy, and politics. Some have referred to this as the politics of hope and fear, and its prevalence distinguishes Saskatchewan from its Prairie neighbours (Rayner and Beaudry-Mellor 2009). Although Social Credit and Conservative leaders in Alberta have, from time to time, courted polarization of the ideological variety, they have seldom made reference to the partisan side of this conflict. Meanwhile, Manitoba's code of moderation mitigates against ideological and partisan conflict to a great extent. This makes the salience of polarization a unique feature of Saskatchewan's political code.

Under the broader concept of security, these three elements constitute Saskatchewan's political code – a tradition of elite-level rhetoric that extends back to the Liberal Party's dominance in the pre-war era. Each dominant party leader has defined these terms in a slightly different way (see Figure 4). But by drawing on the common core values – which themselves are rooted in the province's political culture – Saskatchewan's natural governing parties have cultivated a unique political discourse, one that sets the province apart from both Alberta and Manitoba.

FIGURE 4

Major iterations of the Saskatchewan code

	Collectivism	Dirigisme	Polarization
Patterson	Solidarity and co-operation	Social security	Experience vs. experimentation
Douglas	"Working together"	"Security for all"	Social democracy vs. liberalism
Blakeney	Optimism in "our potential"	"New Deals for people"	Social democracy vs. conservatism
Romanow	"The Saskatchewan Way"	The Third Way	"Turning Saskatchewan Around"

William Patterson, 1935-44

Contrary to common wisdom, the origins of the Saskatchewan code can be traced to the period before Tommy Douglas's rise to power. It was the Liberal Party that dominated early Saskatchewan politics by preaching, and in many ways providing, security in uncertain times. It was only when the party abandoned this message in favour of a more individualistic rhetoric in the early 1940s that it ceded valuable ground to a new collectivist champion in the form of the CCF-NDP.

In the meantime, however, the first forty years of Saskatchewan politics is a story of masterful political leadership by the Liberal Party (Haverstock 2001; Wilson 1980; Eager 1980, 47-53). Above all else, it was the party's ability and willingness to cater to farmers' interests – through the promotion of security in an uncertain political, economic, and environmental climate – that helped the Liberals win eight of the province's first nine elections (Regehr 2004, 64). The party depicted Saskatchewan as a land of adversity, vulnerable to a variety of national and global forces, and Liberals portrayed themselves – and, by extension, the provincial government – as the primary protectors of Saskatchewan society. Consider Liberal premier William Patterson's response to drought and depression, as reflected in his party's 1938 manifesto:

> [Our] term of office has been the most trying and difficult period in the history of Saskatchewan. The Government, nevertheless, has met the situation

and dealt with the problems arising therefrom in a manner which, it believes, merits and should receive the approval of the people.

The first responsibility of the Government during this troublesome period has been to see that all who required assistance were adequately cared for, provision made for the sustenance of their livestock, and the seeding of their crops. Coincident with this primary duty, the Government pursued a policy of maintaining the credit of the Province, a consideration essential to the securing of sufficient funds to provide for the enormous and extraordinary expenditures that the magnitude and widespread character of the assistance demanded ...

Because of conditions beyond the control of any government, the Province is passing through a very serious crisis. To successfully meet and solve the problems facing the people and the Government of the Province, it is necessary that there be stability of government in Saskatchewan ... Only by the return of a Liberal Administration can Saskatchewan be brought safely through its present difficulties, stability of government be assured, and a full measure of democratic freedom be maintained. (Saskatchewan Liberal Association 1938, 2, 12)

Patterson's message was clear: Saskatchewan was a pregnable society that required protection – security – that could only be provided through the co-operative, strong-state approach of his own Liberal Party. This rhetoric, combined with active antagonism from the province's Left, served to establish the early foundations of the province's collectivist, dirigiste, polarized political code.

The Saskatchewan Liberals championed the cause of solidarity, dedicating themselves to securing "the active co-operation of all the people, irrespective of racial origin, religion, creed, or the economic class to which they belonged, in the creation and promotion of a true Provincial spirit and outlook" (Saskatchewan Liberal Party 1933, 7). At the close of the Anderson Tories' term in office (1929-34), Patterson suggested that Saskatchewan had strayed from its collectivist roots:

The Liberal Government while in power laid sound foundations upon which to build a province inhabited by an intelligent, prosperous, contented, united, and loyal Canadian people, bent upon homebuilding. We regret that the last Provincial election campaign put on by our opponents tended to disrupt communities, disunite our people, and generally create dissension ... The Liberal Party when returned to power will do everything possible to overcome the bad fortune which has befallen the province during the past two years, and again establish that contentment among our people which comes through mutual trust and goodwill associated with a knowledge that we are enjoying the highest degree of intellectual opportunity and the comfort which the economic condition of the world will permit. (Ibid., 19-20)

This collectivist spirit was embodied in the Liberals' support for co-operation and the Progressive farmers movement that it spawned. During the 1944 campaign, for instance, Patterson argued that "Saskatchewan has made very great progress undoubtedly due to the fact that there has been unity of purpose among its people and also because the basic principle underlying Liberal administration has been *co-operation*" (Saskatchewan Liberal Association 1944c, 1).

At the same time, the Saskatchewan Liberals promoted the virtues of active government, particularly as it applied to a strong Parliament and provincial legislature (Saskatchewan Liberal Party 1933, 18). Early Liberal platforms promised "peace, progress and prosperity" through the expansion of the provincial state, for instance (Barnhart 2004, 11; Regehr 2004). As stated in the party's 1934 platform:

Assuming office upon the creation of the Province in 1905, the Liberal Party likewise assumed the great responsibility of laying the foundations of the Province, providing it with a code of laws establishing essential services for the development of Saskatchewan and to meet the economic, social and cultural requirements of its people.

During those twenty-four years the population of Saskatchewan was multiplied three times to become the third most populous province of the Dominion; its area was transformed from being largely unproductive territory into one of the greatest wealth producing provinces of Canada. With only a meagre railway mileage at the outset, Saskatchewan as a result of Liberal policy today boasts the second greatest railway mileage among the nine provinces and the largest mileage per capita; schools multiplied and re-multiplied; a satisfactory municipal system was created; starting with no public buildings, no publicly owned services, no good roads, none of those institutions essential to our modern needs, the Liberal Party provided the Provincial Parliament Buildings, a great University, three Normal Schools, three Sanatoria to combat tuberculosis, two Mental Hospitals, a Home for the Aged and Infirm, Court Houses and Land Titles Offices; a telephone system unexcelled anywhere for efficiency and low cost of service; a Farm

Loans scheme which has loaned millions to farmers at a low rate of interest; the commencement of a Provincial Power scheme; Maternity Grants, Mothers' Pensions, Old Age Pensions; assistance to various cooperative organizations designed to advance the welfare of our farming community; [and] a Provincial Highway and Main Market roads system with thousands of bridges, numerous ferries, and thousands of miles improved and built to standard and the work of graveling commenced. (Saskatchewan Liberal Party 1933, 7)

This early dirigiste approach was based on Patterson's contention that "the people of this Province are entitled, at all times, to receive and enjoy that measure of social services which present day standards require. It is the policy of the Government, therefore, to continue and expand all existing social services as may be practical and as soon as occasion may require" (Saskatchewan Liberal Association 1938, 8-9). His support of the state persisted amid volatile economic and political conditions. During the Second World War, Patterson argued, "Notwithstanding the difficult years through which the Province has recently passed, the Government of Saskatchewan is supplying social services on a wide and comprehensive scale, and its record in this respect will bear comparison with other parts of the Dominion" (Saskatchewan Liberal Association 1944b, 9).

In particular – and in code – Patterson promised advancements in what he referred to as "health security" (Saskatchewan Liberal Association 1944b, 8-9). As touted in its 1934 platform, "The Liberal party, which during its 24 years in office, was responsible for placing upon the statute books of Saskatchewan some of the most advanced health legislation in the world, and inaugurated many free health and social services, pledges itself to a continuation and extension of such policies and services" (Saskatchewan Liberal Party 1933). The party remained true to this objective in 1938, promising "to institute as soon as possible further provision of state aid in connection with medical, dental and hospital care," including the expansion of diagnostic and treatment facilities (Saskatchewan Liberal Association 1938). In 1944, Patterson pledged to increase the number of public health nurses, provide free cancer treatment, and follow Ottawa's lead in establishing a nation-wide system of public health insurance (Saskatchewan Liberal Association 1944b).

Patterson's Liberals were also prepared to use the levers of the state to provide security to farmers facing foreclosure during the drought conditions of the 1930s. To this end, the heaviest responsibility of the Department of Agriculture has been that of supplying feed and fodder for livestock, and seed and seeding supplies for the drought areas ...

The Government is hopeful that the period of drought in Saskatchewan has been broken, and that, as a result of future normal production, employment will again be available for the unemployed, and that producers, as formerly, will be able to take care of their own needs and requirements. Should these hopes not be fulfilled, the Government stands ready to render the same degree of aid and assistance as it has rendered in the past, and it will consider this to be its first duty and its first consideration, regardless of anything else. (Saskatchewan Liberal Association 1938, 9)

The close connection between the Liberal Party and farmers that resulted helped to sustain the party through internal scandals and the onset of the Progressive movement – two factors that had helped topple old-line party governments in Alberta and Manitoba (see Regehr 2004, 60-61; Eager 1980, 65).

Although distinctly dirigiste, the Liberal Party's tremendous outlay of public funds was not without fiscal restraint. "Prudence and economy in the administration of the public business" were cornerstones of the Liberal Party's approach to government (Saskatchewan Liberal Association 1944b, 3). Indeed, throughout the twentieth century, references to good government and efficient administration became a hallmark of dominant party rhetoric as it pertained to the growth of the Saskatchewan state. Some may find parallels between this emphasis on fiscal restraint and the brand of pay-as-you-go province building being undertaken in neighbouring Alberta. There is some truth to this comparison, but the Saskatchewan Liberals, despite the rhetoric, were far more supportive of state growth than was Social Credit. The Liberal Party's approach to state building was fiscally responsible, but it was dirigiste, nonetheless.

The Liberals' positive approach to government intervention also extended to the federal realm, as the party was generally supportive of Ottawa's role in providing security to Saskatchewan residents. This is not to say that Patterson abandoned the cause of province rights. Throughout his 1938 and 1944 campaigns, for instance, the Liberal premier made the following pledges:

- "To press upon the Federal Government the necessity of removing all tariff duties on farm implements." (Saskatchewan Liberal Association 1938, 4)

- "To follow an aggressive policy of insuring that, as far as possible, activities connected with the development of Northern Saskatchewan ... shall be directed into and through the Province of Saskatchewan." (Ibid., 8)
- "To advocate and press for the adoption by Canada of a policy which will provide the largest possible measure of unrestricted and unhampered trade between the nations of the world." (Saskatchewan Liberal Association 1944b, 3)

Yet Patterson's province-building program also involved a conciliatory approach toward federal-provincial relations. This tack no doubt reflected the fact that Mackenzie King's Liberals were in power in Ottawa as much as the party's own philosophical commitment to a strong central government. Patterson was quick to praise his federal counterparts for – and take credit for negotiating – any significant fiscal transfers to Saskatchewan (Saskatchewan Liberal Association 1938, 10; 1944b, 4). On other occasions, Patterson was openly supportive of centralization, suggesting "it is essential that, in a country such as Canada, there should be a strong central Government empowered to deal with all matters of national scope and concern":

> Under the scheme of Canadian Confederation, powers of legislation and governmental activities are divided between the Provincial Governments and the Dominion Government. Briefly, all matters (legislation and governmental activities) concerning all Canada and all the Canadian people are designated to be within the power of the Dominion Parliament, while all other matters concerning a Province and its people are designated to be within the powers of each Provincial Legislature. This division of power and responsibility is essential if Confederation is to be preserved and Canadian people are to remain a united nation.
>
> This Government deprecates the deliberate attempt made in certain provinces to usurp the powers now designated to the Parliament of Canada and to legislate upon matters known to be purely within the domain of the Parliament of Canada, all for the purpose of creating dissatisfaction among the Provinces. Undoubtedly, the persistent pursuit of such a policy will end, ultimately, in the disruption of Confederation. (Saskatchewan Liberal Association 1938, 11-12)

References like this were aimed squarely at Social Credit and the CCF – the Liberals' two major rivals. Thus, on both the provincial and federal fronts, the Saskatchewan Liberals helped to establish the dirigiste character of elite discourse in the province while cultivating the strong-state ethos that characterizes its broader political culture.

In addition to its emphasis on collectivism and dirigisme, the Liberal Party's greatest contribution to code politics in Saskatchewan was its polarization of campaign discourse through partisan and antisocialist rhetoric. This was particularly evident after the party's return to power in 1934.[1] Liberals charged that their socialist opponents in the Farmer-Labour Party (FLP) and its successor, the CCF, were atheist, antidemocratic, reckless, and bent on confiscating land from Saskatchewan farmers (Lipset 1968a, 136-40).[2] By contrast, according to its 1938 platform, "The Liberal Party is absolutely opposed to any form or system of Government which would establish a Dictatorship in Saskatchewan ... The Government believes in freedom of speech, a free press, the right of assembly, freedom in matters of religion, and the right of citizens to pursue their selected avocation in life" (Saskatchewan Liberal Association 1938, 12). In this sense, according to Patterson, "Liberalism is more than a political party. It is a way of thinking and stands for all the better things in life ... Why then, change it for a lot of untried theories which, if put into practice, would gradually regiment us all and finally, do away with the freedom we now enjoy? Think! Act! Vote Liberal. Keep Socialism out of Saskatchewan!" (Saskatchewan Liberal Association 1944a).

Patterson added volume to this antisocialist rhetoric in the 1944 election – one of the most ideologically charged campaigns in Saskatchewan history. That year, the Liberal leader drew a clear line between liberalism and socialism, the former representing democracy and progress, the latter oppression and regression. In this context, Patterson's shift to the individualist Right in the following passage is particularly noteworthy:

> The Government of Saskatchewan believes that the maximum standard of social and economic welfare is attainable under a system of government which gives the individual the largest measure of personal freedom and maximum opportunity for exercising his initiative and ability. Its policies have been, and will continue to be, based on this principle. During the war and in order to make possible a total war effort, the people of Canada have accepted a limited measure of regimentation. The object of the Government will be to have these restrictions removed as early as possible to the end that freedom of action, freedom of enterprise and freedom of opportunity will be restored, subject always to proper provision for the protection of the public interest.

Only by the return of a Liberal administration can Saskatchewan be assured of efficient administration, sound progress, practical development and the maintenance of the largest measure of democratic freedom. (Saskatchewan Liberal Association 1944b, 15-16; see also Regina Liberal Association 1944a)

In addition to their formal platform, the Liberals released reams of leaflets condemning the CCF as the harbinger of totalitarianism in Saskatchewan. The literature compared Tommy Douglas's plans with those of Nazi Germany, Soviet Russia, and Sweden (countries where recipients of state assistance were reportedly "put under State guardianship and are inmates of workhouses" [Regina Liberal Association 1944b]). The Liberals made reference to CCF speakers' handbooks and asked voters, "How would you feel if, tomorrow, you woke up to find that, by law, you would be told what to produce, how many hours you had to work, how much you were to produce, where to ship it and what form of payment you would receive for your labours?" (ibid.). Moreover, they asked,

Do you think that a party which promises to abolish the Democratic system of Government and impose in its place State Socialism and ultimately a Dictatorship can suddenly transform Canada into the Utopia they promise? ... Do you want planners and boards of so-called experts to experiment with your public and private business? Have you thought of the chaos which will exist while the wreckers are engaged in scrapping the Democracy? What has happened in other countries where they have been experimenting? The C.C.F. is not a factor in the political life anywhere in Canada. Our fellow Canadians have definitely shown that they will have nothing to do with the C.C.F. experiment. (Regina Liberal Association 1944a)

In the process of polarizing political debate in the 1930s, however, the Liberals transformed themselves from the party of co-operation and solidarity – promising to "provide the people with the highest possible standards of services and *security*" (Saskatchewan Liberal Association 1944a, 15, emphasis added) – into the party of individualism and freedom. They strayed from the code they had helped to establish. As is discussed in Chapter 3, a similar antisocialist shift to the Right proved profitable for Alberta's Social Credit Party in 1944. The strategy proved far less effective for the Saskatchewan Liberals, however. For decades, the party had succeeded by establishing a code based on collectivism and dirigisme by establishing itself as the champion of co-operative and public enterprise. When the Liberals shifted to classic liberalism amid challenges from Social Credit and the CCF, however, they vacated the very position – abandoned the very code and culture – that had helped them retain power for much of the pre- and interwar period. In terms of the provincial code, this left Patterson relying on polarization alone as he entered the landmark 1944 election (see Haverstock 2001, 204). If election results offer any indication, it was a fateful decision.

In the final platform of their dynasty, the Liberals quoted from British prime minister Winston Churchill, arguing that "our people would be the last to consent to be governed by a [socialist] bureaucracy" (Saskatchewan Liberal Association 1944b). Ironically, avowedly left-wing parties would oust both Churchill's Tories and the Saskatchewan Liberals in the coming months.

Tommy Douglas, 1944-61

In the waning years of their government, the Liberals argued that Tommy Douglas's dreams of socialist experimentation were made possible by virtue of their own policy legacy and prudent management of the public purse. There was some truth to this argument. The Liberals had made concepts such as progressive taxation, state-sponsored health care, collective bargaining, northern and rural development, co-operation, and public enterprise part of the province's political vernacular (Bilson 2004, 152-56). "Similarly, the acquiescence of early Liberal governments in the farmers' demands for public regulation of the economy accustomed the citizens to active government" (Courtney and Smith 1972, 305). From this perspective, when they abandoned these principles, the Liberals ceded valuable ground to their opponents. Thus, amid the political uncertainty that followed the Second World War, an opportunity emerged for a new natural governing party in Saskatchewan.

The CCF's vision for Saskatchewan, of course, took shape decades earlier. Hopes of Saskatchewan being an egalitarian, collectivist society had emerged out of the Depression. As the principal standard-bearer for the Left at the time, the FLP's first concern was to provide Saskatchewan residents with security for their farms and homes. For the FLP, this security would be achieved, above all else, through socialism. According to the *Regina Manifesto* (CCF 1933, 1), the CCF's founding statement of principle, "We aim to replace the present capitalist system with its inherent injustice and inhumanity by a social order from which the domination and exploitation of one class by another will be eliminated; in which economic planning will supercede unregulated private enterprise and competition; and in which genuine democratic self-government based on economic equality will be possible." As late as 1938, running officially under the CCF banner, the party advocated "social planning in the place of ruthless competition now practiced under Capitalism" – a change that would have resulted in nothing less than "a new economic system," a "cooperative Commonwealth in which the principle regulating the production, distribution and exchange will be the supplying of human needs" (Co-operative Commonwealth Federation [Sask. Section] 1938b).

The FLP-CCF's dirigisme also extended to the social realm. In 1934, the party asserted its belief "in the responsibility of the government to provide opportunities for work, adequate maintenance or unemployment insurance" (Regina CCF Council 1934). In addition, the party "advocated the socialization of all health services" – a pledge that was "not advanced for election purposes or made contingent upon Dominion participation or contribution" (ibid.). By 1938, the CCF was campaigning openly for what it called socialized medicine: "that system of medical practice which guarantees to every individual of the state, without regard to their economic condition, any and all necessary benefits of medical science, both preventative and curative" (Co-operative Commonwealth Federation [Sask. Section] 1938a).

Overall, the early FLP-CCF platforms were promoted as the "sure road to safety and real Democracy" for Saskatchewan and its people (Co-operative Commonwealth Federation [Sask. Section] 1938a). Yet, both provincially and nationally, the party failed to gain enough support to pry loose the Liberals' grip on government. It was only after provincial party leader George Williams joined the war effort in England in 1941 that the CCF began to seriously challenge for power. Only then did the CCF's "vision of a better world to follow the sacrifices endured during war time" seem to resonate in Saskatchewan (Dyck 1996, 465).

Under new leader Tommy Douglas, the CCF increasingly distanced itself from the socialist orthodoxy contained in the *Regina Manifesto*. Following disappointing results in the 1934 and 1938 elections, references to socialism were removed almost entirely from CCF literature.[3] Over time, the use of the term *social ownership* was replaced with promises of social planning and co-operation. Drawing on many of the themes already established in the Saskatchewan code, Douglas's message was as straightforward as it was familiar: a CCF government would not seek to own or control everything, but it would work toward establishing "security for the people" (Co-operative Commonwealth Federation [Sask. Section] 1944d; see also McLeod and

McLeod 2004, 177; Praud and McQuarrie 2001, 146; Lipset 1968a, 142-43; Eager 1980, 56).

Under the famous slogan "Humanity First," Douglas's original Program for Saskatchewan included four major commitments:

1 Provision of Security for the People in their Homes and Jobs
2 Provision of Social Services (Old Age Pensions, Health Services, etc.)
3 Provision of Educational Opportunities and Guarantee of Democratic Rights
4 Public Ownership, Planned Development of Natural Resources, and Finance. (Co-operative Commonwealth Federation [Sask. Section] 1944d)

The lead plank indicates the important place held by security in his vision of Saskatchewan's future (ibid.).[4] Indeed, this book's use of the term *security* as a label for the province's code is drawn *in vivo* from Douglas's early campaign literature; in leaflet after leaflet, Douglas promised the Saskatchewan people farm security, labour security, health security, and educational security, among other forms of protection and safety (CCF [Saskatchewan Section] 1949; CCF Provincial Office [Saskatchewan] 1952).

This emphasis on security was necessary, according to Douglas, given the vulnerability of Saskatchewan's population. Drawing on the isolationist elements of the province's political culture, the CCF leader made constant references to the notion that internal and external forces continuously threatened the province and that only a CCF government could provide the necessary protection to achieve prosperity and abundance. This was particularly evident in Douglas's description of the hazards of farming: "Farming is full of '*ifs.*' A Canadian farmer can make a good living *if* he has enough land to make an economical unit, *if* he gets enough rain to make his products grow, *if* insects or frost or hail or other hazards don't destroy his crop before it is harvested, *if* there is a market for his products, *if* the price is good, and *if* the cost of production and the cost of living are not too high" (CCF [Saskatchewan Section] 1952c).

Indeed, the contingent nature of life in Saskatchewan was a prominent theme in CCF campaign literature. Later, reflecting on the ten-year anniversary of his victory in 1944, Premier Douglas suggested that

Saskatchewan was once called the "hard luck" Province. However, in the last few years – years almost paralleling the period of CCF administration – she has grown until her robust condition has earned for her the name of

"Province of Opportunity" ... There are many who remember what an appalling financial situation this Province groaned under. In 1937, for instance, just seven years before the victory of the CCF, no less than 70 percent of the population was receiving some form of relief. There are few Saskatchewan people who think it is a mere coincidence that our great come-back and the constant widening of our economic frontiers date from the first years of the CCF Government. (CCF Provincial Office [Saskatchewan] 1954)

In response to this vulnerability, much like the early Saskatchewan Liberals, Douglas drew on the three interrelated elements of the provincial code. For him, security would be provided through collective action, solidarity, social ownership, and co-operation; it would be attained by strengthening the provincial state, particularly through the growth of Crown corporations and social services; and it would be preserved amid constant attacks from opposing forces and parties – particularly liberalism and Social Credit.

Better Together

Douglas's rhetoric contained a heavy dose of collectivism, for he attempted to connect the people to one another and to their government. Some observers may interpret the latter component as a form of populism, drawing parallels between Douglas's appeals and those of Social Credit premiers in Alberta. Although accurate, the label misconstrues the Saskatchewan leader's overall message. A social democratic brand of populism was certainly present in Douglas's rhetoric; indeed, it sat uneasily with the dirigisme found therein. Yet populism was framed in distinctly collectivist – not individualistic – terms. Moreover, as will be discussed, populism seldom stood alone from the overall sense of community Douglas was promoting. For these reasons, populism is included within the broader notion of collectivism.

Douglas's emphasis on community and government solidarity was evident in his descriptions of the CCF's origins: "Founded in 1932, elected first in 1944, it has proven to the world that ordinary people, acting together through their government, can secure for themselves and their families more of life's good things" (CCF [Saskatchewan Section] 1956a, 39; 1960a, 33). This emphasis turned the victories of the CCF into triumphs for society as a whole. Reflecting on his party's record at the end of his final term, Douglas referred to the achievements as "the success story of a people and their government. United, the people of Saskatchewan and their CCF government can face the future with confidence ... The people and their CCF government are going forward together, partners in the building of a province" (CCF [Saskatchewan Section] 1960a). Literature from his final campaign in 1960 proclaimed, *"There is still much to be done – but it has been successfully demonstrated that by working together under the CCF banner the people of Saskatchewan can solve their problems"* (CCF Saskatchewan Section 1960b, 8).

To this sense of solidarity, Douglas attached a spirit of collective responsibility – a choice that distinguished his approach from the personal-responsibility mantra of dominant party leaders in Alberta. In contrast to individualistic Alberta Social Credit premier Ernest Manning (see Chapter 3), Douglas argued in 1948 "that society as a whole should assume responsibility for the welfare of those who through misfortune, illness, age or physical or mental disability are unable to care for themselves; and that all people should have the best health services, regardless of their individual ability to pay" (CCF [Saskatchewan Section] 1948d). This approach is best illustrated in Douglas's support of universal health care. In contrast to Manning's opposition to national medicare (Manning 1965), Douglas stated during the 1960 Saskatchewan provincial election:

> Your future – the future of your family, your community, province and nation – depends upon good health. It is a primary need of every individual. Therefore, the highest standard of health care that medical science can provide must be recognized as a fundamental right of every person.
>
> But it is no longer possible for individuals – with limited financial resources – to pay the bills resulting from serious or prolonged illness. Medical science has made great advances. But most health services are costly and beyond the grasp of many of us.
>
> Because of this, it must become the responsibility of society, of all of us together, to organize health resources for the benefit of all and with barriers to none. (CCF [Saskatchewan Section] 1960b)

Whereas Manning had opposed the compulsory national medicare plan introduced in the mid-1960s on the grounds that it offended individual freedoms, Douglas invoked a spirit of collective responsibility in defence of mandatory participation. To the CCF premier, "Like the provincial hospital plan, a medical care plan must include everyone if it is to succeed. By spreading the risks over all people, and using provincial revenues to cover part of the costs, it is possible to keep premiums low and yet provide all necessary care. It is everyone's concern that all persons enjoy good health!" (ibid.).

Douglas's promotion of social planning and public ownership drew on similar collectivist values. According to his first platform, "Social Owner-ship is ownership by the people of the means whereby they live, that is, of the means of making, distributing, and exchanging the things which are ne-cessary to the health, strength, comfort, and dignity of human beings" (Co-operative Commonwealth Federation [Sask. Section] 1944a). In addition to promoting public insurance and liquor and electricity distribution, Douglas advocated provincial control – social ownership – over fossil fuels, min-erals, and lumber.

> The CCF has always taken the view that the natural resources of this prov-
> ince are the natural heritage of the people of Saskatchewan and ought to be
> developed for the benefit of all the people of Saskatchewan. At the present
> time these resources are being exploited by private companies and corpora-
> tions for their own gain. The CCF says that this must cease. Our natural
> resources must cease to be exploited in a hit-and-miss manner for the
> benefit of promoters, investors, and absentee capitalists; they must be de-
> veloped in the public interest and for the public benefit. The CCF stands for
> the social ownership of natural resources. (Ibid.)

Reference to natural resources as "the natural heritage of the people" may sound familiar: Alberta's first Social Credit premier, William Aberhart, used similar rhetoric to craft a discourse of provincial autonomy (Aberhart 1935, 13-14). Although he used similar terminology, Douglas's notion of western alienation was a decidedly regressive strain of thought in his promotion of social ownership. In comparison to Aberhart – who aimed to insulate his province from interference by central Canadian industrialists, politicians, and financiers – Douglas's promotion of social ownership was directed more at breaking down domestic monopolies, at returning power to the Saskatch-ewan *people* (versus the *Saskatchewan* people).

Douglas's collectivist rhetoric also contained support for the co-opera-tive movement. Particularly during his first campaign, Douglas made a con-certed effort to displace the Liberal Party as the champion of co-operation by drawing parallels between the aims of co-operators and the goals of so-cialists (a group to which he still belonged publicly in 1944):

> Above all, the moral driving-power of co-operation and socialism is the
> same. A successful co-operative is based on neighborliness, on the mutual
> trust and friendliness which exists among the co-operating members. In

the same way, comradeship is the moral dynamic of socialism. Only friends can make and maintain a socialist society. Only by the sinking of personal egoism, ambition, and love of power in a shoulder-to-shoulder working with our fellows for the common good can we ever reach and keep a society of wealth and strength and sweet content ...

That is the hope of the Co-operative Commonwealth Federation. A C.C.F. government in power in Saskatchewan will actively support the co-operative movement to that end; it will work for the day when the people of this province will co-operatively own all the means of supplying their every-day requirements. It will regard the co-operative movement not as a rival – that would be absurd – but as a partner, an independent but friendly partner, in the great work of bringing to the people of Saskatchewan an increasing measure of security for themselves and opportunity for their children. (Co-operative Commonwealth Federation [Sask. Section] 1944g)

Security for All
Douglas's collectivist impulse extended beyond the social and economic spheres. He was also willing to use the Saskatchewan state in his pursuit of solidarity, collective responsibility, social ownership, and co-operation. Indeed, government intervention was the central element of his promise to provide security to the Saskatchewan people. Douglas's plan rested on a combination of rural and urban policies – "that means security for the workers on their farms and security for the workers in towns and cities" – alongside enhancements to social services, democratic rights, and planned economic development (Co-operative Commonwealth Federation [Sask. Section] 1944d). Because all of these policies required a strong state, the dirigiste character of the Saskatchewan code was reinforced.

Douglas first and foremost promised security for the farmer – "greater security than is enjoyed in any other province" (Co-operative Commonwealth Federation [Sask. Section] 1944f, 1956). According to the premier, "Insecurity for farmers in Saskatchewan may be summed up in two words, debt and eviction" (Co-operative Commonwealth Federation [Sask. Section] 1944f). In turn, the farmer's "*protection* depends upon legislation to prevent exploitation of farmers by financial institutions" (CCF [Saskatchewan Section] 1948a). Specifically, Douglas promised to use the levers of the state to "protect the farmer from unjust foreclosure and eviction"; to "protect from seizure that part of a farmer's crop that is needed to provide for his family"; to "use, if necessary, the power of moratorium to compel the reduction of debts to a figure at which they can reasonably be paid"; and to "prevent the growth of debt by placing a crop failure clause in all mortgages and agreements of sale" (Co-operative Commonwealth Federation [Sask. Section] 1944h). In a collectivist tone, Douglas argued that these measures were designed to ensure that "both debtor and creditor will share in the burden" of bad economic times (ibid.).[5]

By appealing to the largest segment of the electorate, Douglas consistently emphasized the importance of agriculture to Saskatchewan society, insisting that "upon the welfare of the farmer depends the prosperity of the whole province" (Co-operative Commonwealth Federation [Sask. Section] 1948a). At the same time, the CCF leader drew parallels between the interests of farmers and workers. Douglas also pledged to provide security against "foreclosure and eviction of urban home owners, just as it will for the farmers" (Co-operative Commonwealth Federation [Sask. Section] 1944d, 1944e). Moreover, in 1944, Douglas suggested "the minimum wage is to urban workers what parity prices are to farmers," and he supported strengthening both areas as a means of providing security to all Saskatchewan residents (Co-operative Commonwealth Federation [Sask. Section] 1944d). In the remainder of his Urban Security platform, Douglas argued "that people who work in towns and cities should be provided with security in their homes; that they should be assured of steady employment with adequate wages, and that they should have a voice in determining the conditions under which they work" (Co-operative Commonwealth Federation [Sask. Section] 1944d). On behalf of workers, Douglas also asserted the "fundamental right of union organization" and the "right to bargain collectively" (Co-operative Commonwealth Federation [Sask. Section] 1944d). Each of his platforms included pledges to advance labour rights, minimum-wage rates, work standards and conditions, and workers' compensation benefits. As others have noted, the relationship between the CCF and labour was "uneven, and sometimes adversarial" (McLeod and McLeod 2004, 186). Douglas's position (relative to his opponents') was, however, strong enough to earn the party support from the Saskatchewan Federation of Labour, which issued numerous pamphlets on the party's behalf, particularly in the 1950s and 1960s (see, for example, Saskatchewan Federation of Labour 1956a, 1956b, 1960, 1964).

All the while, Douglas continued to argue that "under the present Capitalistic economy, public opinion has forced Governments to assume a degree of responsibility for those citizens who are unable to care for themselves" (Co-operative Commonwealth Federation [Sask. Section] 1944b). For this reason, *"Humanity does come first.* The welfare of the people must be the first concern of any government" (CCF [Saskatchewan Section] 1960a, 13). To this end, Douglas proposed a host of new social services and pledged to improve and expand many existing ones, including mothers' allowances, pensions for seniors and the disabled, job-training programs and work projects, health care, education programs, and child protection services (Cooperative Commonwealth Federation [Sask. Section] 1944b). So bold was this province-building program that, within four years of assuming office, Douglas could boast that his government's $52 million plan was "the largest budget in the history of Saskatchewan, because more services are being provided for the people than ever before" (CCF [Saskatchewan Section] 1948e). The 1948 CCF campaign, like the three that followed, was based on consolidating the many gains made in Douglas' first term.

As Saskatchewan's system of social services expanded, the CCF began comparing its record with those of neighbouring provinces, particularly laissez-faire governments led by Alberta's Social Credit Party and Manitoba's Liberal-Progressives. Douglas appealed to voters to "keep Saskatchewan in the lead!" on issues such as rural electrification, automobile insurance, health care, and other social services (see, for example, CCF Provincial Office [Saskatchewan] 1956b; CCF [Saskatchewan Section] 1956a, 1956b; CCF Saskatchewan Section 1960a, 1960c). Like that of the Alberta Socreds, this brand of braggadocio was motivated, at least in part, by a sense of protectionism against external partisan and ideological forces. Boosterism was considerably less salient in the Saskatchewan CCF's provincial platforms, however, and it was also of a different kind. Whereas the Socreds took an isolationist approach, Douglas promoted his government's dirigiste measures as worthy of export to the rest of Canada. If Manning's was more frequently a firewall approach (closing off Alberta from the rest of the country by touting its achievements to the province's citizens), Douglas employed more of a bridging strategy (promoting the Saskatchewan CCF as a national pioneer).

Douglas's strategy is evident in his push for "more abundant living" (CCF Saskatchewan Section 1960d), which included his famous pledge "to undertake a comprehensive prepaid medical care program." The CCF's medicare program – a Canadian first – was designed to ensure that "everyone in Saskatchewan, irrespective of ability to pay, has the right to good health" (ibid.). Douglas promoted Saskatchewan as an innovator in the provision of social services. In his final campaign, the premier boasted: "For almost 16 years the

progress of Saskatchewan has been under the guidance of your CCF government. For its bold approach to economic development, its pioneering of
health and welfare services, its sound management of the public purse –
and, above all, of its overriding concern for human values – *the* CCF's *record
can be matched by no other government in Canada*" (ibid., 1).

This boosterism also extended to the realm of federal-provincial relations. Douglas's 1948 platform, for instance, expressed his desire for a
mandate to deal with "the Liberal Government at Ottawa" on the establishment of a national welfare state. Promoting his province as a front-runner
in the sector, Douglas argued, "An overwhelming victory for the C.C.F. in
Saskatchewan will serve notice on Ottawa that the people are one with the
government in demanding immediate action in establishing an overall system of social security" (Co-operative Commonwealth Federation [Sask.
Section] 1948a). It is of note that, according to the CCF, this "provision of
security, for both rural and urban dwellers, [was] largely a matter of appropriate legislative action and [would] involve little in the way of governmental expenditure" (Co-operative Commonwealth Federation [Sask.
Section] 1944d). Premier Douglas was careful to note that the expansion of
social services was not being financed through tax increases but through
increased government revenue from economic growth. Thus, the main
task of his government was to balance economic development with social
progress – "to increase the wealth production of the province in order that
there may be more money available to provide a higher standard of living
for those who toil and a greater measure of social security for those who
are unable to work" (Co-operative Commonwealth Federation [Sask. Sec-
tion] 1948a). Indeed, throughout Douglas's premiership, the CCF remained
committed to balanced budgets and fiscal responsibility. As Marchildon
(2004, 367-68) explains, "Keynesian deficit financing was rejected as an
option given the province's open economy and Douglas's fear of being controlled by the banks. The price paid for the approach was the fact that programs were not initiated before the means to pay for them in full were
found."

Douglas's promise of security therefore required establishing Saskatchewan as a modern, economically developed province. Throughout his tenure, Douglas promoted what he called "a balanced economy," an economy
divided evenly among agriculture, natural resources, and industrial development (CCF Saskatchewan Section 1960b). Planned growth in each of
these sectors was "justified as a means of diversifying the economy, creating jobs, and generating revenue for expanded social services" (Dyck 1996,

466). As Douglas put it, "The slogan of the CCF is 'Humanity First.' We believe that a fair portion of our increased wealth should be used to provide increased security for our old age pensioners, recipients of mother's allowance, handicapped persons and other needy groups in our province. The whole aim of our expansion program of stimulating wealth production is to enable us to raise the standard of living of Saskatchewan citizens and particularly of those in greatest need" (CCF Provincial Office [Saskatchewan] 1952).

This belief that economic development should be harnessed to provide enhanced social services persisted throughout each of Douglas's campaigns, even as the discovery of natural resources began filling provincial coffers. According to the premier in 1956:

> In recent years Saskatchewan has progressed in a manner unequalled in our brief history. The discovery of oil, uranium and other minerals has made possible the establishment of new industries. Almost every month new manufacturing plants are being located in our province. Electric power and natural gas are bringing their benefits to communities which have never enjoyed them before.
>
> More important still is the fact that the increasing revenue from this expanding development has made possible improved educational, health and welfare services. New schools and hospitals are being built and a greater measure of social security is being enjoyed by our people. Better roads and telephone facilities are improving our way of living. (CCF [Saskatchewan Section] 1956b)

Summarizing his party's position on economic growth in 1960, Douglas noted: "The CCF places great emphasis on industrial development. The growth of industry means economic stability for the province as a whole. New factories provide employment and higher income for our people. Economic growth brings new sources of revenue for the province – money to pay for the CCF health, welfare, education and other services which mean better living for all" (CCF Saskatchewan Section 1960d).

Douglas relied heavily on the public sector to pursue economic development, particularly in the early years. This dirigiste approach drew on his collectivist belief in social ownership. It also drew heavy criticism from opponents on Saskatchewan's Right. Douglas's response, immortalized in his Mossbank debate with Ross Thatcher, was equally forceful in campaign literature:

The CCF is proud of the government's record in Crown corporations. As a matter of fact, the *Crown corporations have been an essential ingredient in Saskatchewan's postwar development.* The government has lost $1.8 million on six Crown corporations – six which are now closed down. At the same time, the government has made $12.5 million from the others ... *The remaining Crown corporations have served Saskatchewan's people well – by providing essential public utilities at lowest cost, by developing services available to the province as a whole, and by utilizing unused resources.* SASKATCHEWAN'S CROWN CORPORATIONS HAVE BEEN DESIGNED TO MEET NEEDS, NOT TO PILE UP PROFITS. (CCF Saskatchewan Section 1960b, 2-3)

This rhetoric notwithstanding, Douglas gradually responded to public opinion and opposition from free enterprise by shifting his party's economic strategy from its focus on public ownership and local manufacturing to a mixed economy based on resource extraction. From the beginning, Douglas was opposed to full nationalization of all industries. By 1944, promises of a completely state-run economy had been removed entirely from the party platform and replaced by calls for planned, collective, or co-operative ownership of select industries (see Co-operative Commonwealth Federation [Sask. Section] 1944a, 1944d). Furthermore, in his party's 1948 platform – Plan for Plenty! – Douglas

envisage[d] the development of our economy by the close and harmonious activities of private enterprise, the co-operatives and public utilities. The CCF government has encouraged and will continue to encourage development by private enterprise wherever it is not monopolistic in character. The C.C.F. believes that there are certain undertakings which people can do for themselves on a co-operative basis rather than in any other way. The C.C.F. believes that provincially and municipally-owned enterprises can and do render a service to the people at a minimum cost and without exploitation. (Co-operative Commonwealth Federation [Sask. Section] 1948a)

In particular, he pledged "intense exploration and development" of oil, natural gas, petrochemicals, and minerals (ibid.). To guide this development, Douglas promoted two "principles of industrial expansion": (1) "the government has a responsibility to give leadership in securing the greatest possible development of our natural resources to increase the wealth production of our province," and (2) "the government will see that these resources are developed in order that the benefit shall come back to the people to whom the resources rightly belong" (ibid.).

In its promise to provide security for the farmer and for the worker, to establish social security through economic development, and to secure public ownership of key industries and services, Douglas's vision was distinctly dirigiste. It was not without its ideological and fiscal limits, however. Douglas would not push for complete nationalization; nor would he proceed with state expansion without the requisite economic development to finance it. Nonetheless, his promotion of government as a positive element in Saskatchewan's society and economy was a major contribution to the development of the provincial code and the persistence of the strong-state component of the province's political culture.

Culture War

Douglas's polarizing approach to party politics was also very much in keeping with the dominant mode of elite discourse established by his Liberal predecessors. Whereas many accounts portray the Saskatchewan CCF as a defensive-minded party when it came to campaign strategy, a review of its literature reveals otherwise. Douglas's most virulent attacks were reserved for the Liberals and Socreds, whom he accused of being in bed with privileged interests and out of touch with the needs of the Saskatchewan people. By contrast, Douglas portrayed his party (and government) as defenders of Saskatchewan's nascent social democratic culture against assaults from the province's Right:

> In constant opposition to the C.C.F. stand the business monopolies and their followers, the same groups which have always worked against the farm organizations. Through their servants, the capitalist press and the reactionary politicians, they flood the country with repeated warnings that the people will lose their freedom under the C.C.F. But the only freedom the monopolies have ever been really interested in is their freedom to exploit the public ...
>
> So the battle goes on, with the farmers and workers on one side, and the owners of finance and industry and the people who are fooled by their propaganda on the other. It is the same struggle over the same issues which has been going on for fifty years. But now, at last, the farmers and wage earners have their own political party, financed and controlled by themselves, and ready to challenge the monopolists for the political leadership of Canada. (CCF [Saskatchewan Section] 1952c, 6-7)

Douglas's criticisms were wide-reaching. He attacked partisan rivals within and outside the province and linked his domestic foes to their counterparts in Ottawa and Alberta, in particular. As the Saskatchewan premier described in a 1956 campaign leaflet, the CCF and its partisan opponents were "as different as night and day" (Co-operative Commonwealth Federation [Sask. Section] 1956). On the topic of agriculture, for instance: "*Liberal, Conservative* and *Social Credit* Governments in other provinces could all have passed farm security legislation. But none of them did, because they all believe in giving preference to Big Business. The *Liberals* in the Saskatchewan Legislature voted unanimously against the Farm Security Act, and the *Liberals* at Ottawa have tried to have it destroyed in the courts" (ibid.).

Douglas's most powerful provincial foe was the Liberal Party, which he portrayed in 1944 as "the tool of the Mortgage Companies and vested interests. It's time we elected a people's Government rather than a Mortgage Companies' Government. To free yourself from the bondage of interest – To give your family security in their home – Vote CCF!" (Co-operative Commonwealth Federation [Sask. Section] 1944c). Douglas released reams of pamphlets with titles such as *What the Liberals Have Not Told You!* that condemned the then-governing party for harbouring a secret, corporate agenda (Co-operative Commonwealth Federation [Sask. Section] 1944h).

Once in office, Douglas continued his offensive, employing a number of different techniques of negative campaigning. First, he compared his own government's record of progress to that of his opponents, inviting the people of Saskatchewan to "Remember! A vote for anyone but the CCF is indirectly a vote to return to do-nothing Liberalism" (CCF [Saskatchewan Section] 1952a). Second, he was fond of listing long strings of unfulfilled campaign pledges, arguing that "unlike the Liberals, the CCF makes no promises that cannot be kept! Instead of rash, irresponsible statements, the CCF *plans,* then promises, and more important, the CCF *performs.* The record proves that conclusively ... For *performance* and not promises alone, *vote* CCF" (CCF Provincial Office [Saskatchewan] 1956a), see also 1956b, 1956c; also CCF [Saskatchewan Section] 1952b).

Third, Douglas touted his own government's superior record of balanced budgets and debt repayment and blamed the Liberals for poor fiscal management during their three decades in office (see, for example, CCF Saskatchewan Section 1960b, 8; Fines 1960). "If a Liberal government were elected in Saskatchewan, and if they attempted to keep the promises they have made," he suggested during the 1956 campaign, "it would cost the province $99,500,000 in their first year of administration in addition to the regular budget! ... It is to be noted that [Liberal leader Hammy McDonald] is glibly promising the expenditure of many extra millions of dollars of prov-incial funds but makes no attempt to suggest how those additional millions are to be raised. Since the Liberals have always criticized the CCF budgets for being too large, the Liberal promises to spend vast additional sums be-come ridiculous" (CCF Provincial Office [Saskatchewan] 1956a). Douglas's concerted strikes against Liberal leaders – including Hammy McDonald (Co-operative Commonwealth Federation [Sask. Section] 1948c) and Walter Tucker (CCF Provincial Office [Saskatchewan] 1956a) – clearly illustrated his belief in attack advertising.

Douglas's most effective strategy involved linking the provincial Liberal Party to its unpopular federal cousin – "the Liberal Government at Ottawa" – which he repeatedly accused of betraying Saskatchewan workers and farmers on a whole host of issues (from freight rates and tariffs to natural resources and social security) (CCF [Saskatchewan Section] 1948e; Co-operative Commonwealth Federation [Sask. Section] 1948a, 1956). In 1948, Douglas argued:

> Four years ago the C.C.F. pledged itself to fight unceasingly against those economic forces which exploit you and against those vested interests which undermine your security. In carrying out its promise, the C.C.F. has in-curred the wrath of the financial clique that has been allowed too long to prey upon our people. The only real opposition to the C.C.F. has come from the mortgage interests, the lending institutions, and the spokesmen of big business. Throughout this prolonged struggle, in every contest of the Sas-katchewan government against the few with special privilege, the Liberal government at Ottawa has championed the cause of those who seek to keep the farmers, the workers and the small business men in a permanent state of economic servitude. (Co-operative Commonwealth Federation [Sask. Section] 1948a; see also CCF [Saskatchewan Section] 1948b)

Indeed, like his successors, Douglas was unafraid of reaching beyond his provincial boundaries to pick a partisan fight. For a period in the 1950s and 1960s, as governments in both Alberta and Saskatchewan were building their social security systems, these partisan attacks morphed into nothing less than a cross-border culture war over the definition of the terms *freedom* and *security*. Under attack by what he called "Social Credit carpetbaggers" from Alberta, Douglas mounted a spirited defence of his province's social democratic ethos (CCF Saskatchewan Section 1960c).[6]

For Alberta Premier Ernest Manning – the nominal leader of Social Credit's campaign operations in Saskatchewan – freedom meant being free from government intervention, be it in the market or in society (see Chapter 3). Tommy Douglas conceptualized the term quite differently. The CCF did promote itself as staunchly democratic, reiterating its commitment to "Freedom of Speech, Freedom of Elections, Freedom of Religion, because these are the essence of democratic liberty" (Co-operative Commonwealth Federation [Sask. Section] 1944d). This list of inalienable rights was gradually expanded to include freedom of assembly and expression of opinion, the right to health and education, the right to hold property without fear of confiscation by creditors, the right to due process and collective bargaining, and freedom from racial and ethnic discrimination (Co-operative Commonwealth Federation [Sask. Section] 1948a).

Yet, invoking Franklin Delano Roosevelt's rhetoric, Douglas expanded his definition of liberty to include both freedom from fear and freedom from want. In no uncertain terms, the Social Credit premier of Alberta told voters, "Security alone is not enough. We must have *Freedom* with Security" (Alberta Social Credit League 1963). Douglas reversed the emphasis, arguing that one could not have (political) freedom without (economic) security. The resulting debate was a battle between competing worldviews – conflicting codes and cultures – that Douglas used to help polarize political debate in his province. A 1948 pamphlet titled *This Thing Called Freedom* epitomizes the Saskatchewan premier's approach (Co-operative Commonwealth Federation [Sask. Section] 1948b). In it, Douglas defines liberty in broader terms than the individualist approach taken by Social Credit. To Douglas,

> freedom means much more than the right to vote and speak as we like and the right to a fair trial in the courts. These are freedoms which we have already won, and while we must preserve them, we must not stop there. There is still another freedom to be won, and that is economic freedom, or as President Roosevelt defined it, "freedom from fear and freedom from want." Political freedom by itself can mean being free to go hungry and without a job; it can mean being free to produce farm commodities below the cost of production. Until we add economic freedom to the political freedom we already have, we will never be entirely free men and women. (Ibid.)

Douglas's assault on Social Credit only intensified over time, particularly as the Socreds gained a stronger grip on government in Alberta. In 1948, for instance, the Saskatchewan CCF published a particularly scathing pamphlet titled *The Social Credit Hoax* in which the party warned provincial residents: "When the Social Credit party was first elected to power in Alberta in 1935 it appeared to be a progressive party. But it was based upon an impossible theory which was never put into effect. The pretense at attempting to do this was by means of legislation that everyone knew was unconstitutional. Since the death of William Aberhart, Social Credit has constantly and rapidly moved to the right, until today it has replaced the Conservative party as the most reactionary group in Canada" (CCF [Saskatchewan Section] 1948c). The pamphlet accused the Socreds of being "in league with Big Business," of having "fascist tendencies," of "double talk," and of committing various other misdeeds – ultimately leading the reader to the conclusion that "Alberta lags behind Saskatchewan" (ibid.).

If election returns in either province are any indication, Douglas's fight with Manning and his Alberta Socreds was more theatre than reality – more shadow boxing than an actual duel at the ballot box. Just as the CCF failed to make a breakthrough in Alberta, Social Credit was never a real threat in Saskatchewan. It won only a handful of seats in the 1950s and 1960s (mostly along the Alberta border, where Aberhart's and Manning's radio broadcasts reached the ears of avid listeners). One might, however, attribute the Socreds' weakness in Saskatchewan to Douglas's active attempt to inoculate the provincial electorate against their brand of freedom-based discourse.

The 1960 campaign was Douglas's last before he left provincial politics to head the federal CCF. In that election, voters found him as virulent as ever in attacking his partisan opponents and as staunch as ever in defence of his collectivist and dirigiste approach to government. In an apt statement of his approach and philosophy, Douglas argued prior to his departure that "Saskatchewan's greatest resource will always be her people. The happiness and *security* of men, women and children is the ultimate objective of all CCF programs" (CCF Saskatchewan Section 1960d, emphasis added). While recognizing the "dignity of the individual [and] the undeniable right of every person to health, opportunity and freedom," Douglas emphasized his party's belief "in a family's right to an adequate income, in a man's right to work in the job of his choice, in a woman's right to security for herself and her children, in a child's right to security and education" (ibid.). As discussed previously, *security* involved cultivating a spirit of *collectivism* and *dirigisme* while polarizing Saskatchewan politics into a struggle between the forces of the Left and the Right. It was under Douglas that the three terms received renewed emphasis as the core of the Saskatchewan code, thus helping to sustain the values embedded in the province's political culture through a crucial phase of its province building.

Woodrow Lloyd, 1961-70

As Eisler argues (2006), subsequent CCF-NDP leaders have played relatively minor roles in reshaping Douglas's vision of Saskatchewan politics and society. This was especially true of his immediate successor, Woodrow Lloyd, who drew on the familiar theme of "progress with purpose" during the 1964 election (CCF Saskatchewan Section 1964). Revealed in a confidential memo released in 1964, Lloyd's campaign strategy involved three main planks: (1) to contrast what the party viewed as Lloyd's superior record and leadership with that of the Liberals' Ross Thatcher, (2) to point out the negative nature of "American-style Hucksterism" being employed by the Liberals during the campaign, and (3) to stress the importance of protecting medicare from a Liberal Party bent on dismantling it (Benjamin 1964). All three planks drew on elements of the provincial code.

First, Lloyd's campaign literature played on the same themes of community responsibility and solidarity that had served Douglas so well in decades past. Highlighting the party's twenty-year record in office – including its so-called progress in the area of industrial development and social services – CCF pamphlets suggested that future achievements were "attainable as long as we have a government which is prepared, in partnership with the people of this province to innovate and to strive for an ever improving way of life. These things are the pride of the Province – the boldness, the optimism, the robustness of our people. Take these away and Saskatchewan becomes just another unimportant jurisdiction in Canada" (CCF Saskatchewan Section of the New Democratic Party 1964a). In other words, Lloyd argued, "This is your province. Keep it that way. Elect a government that respects you and has confidence in your province" (CCF Saskatchewan Section of the New Democratic Party 1964c).

Lloyd also played on the spirit of collective action and civic engagement in the province's political culture. According to a 1967 CCF pamphlet on education reform, for instance, "Good education for *all*, regardless of ability to pay, will make it possible for *everyone* to *contribute* to a better, more prosperous Province ... There's an old maxim that says: 'God helps those who help themselves.' In other words – no one is going to do it for us – we've got to roll up our sleeves and do it ourselves! Look around you. Think about it. Talk to your neighbours, your friends ... Vote for the people most likely to push for it. Fight for it! It's worth fighting for" (CCF Saskatchewan 1967a).

Second, Douglas's successor also built on his dirigiste legacy, particularly as it applied to the importance of public enterprise. Again citing his party's record in office, Lloyd suggested that "Crown corporations aid economic growth":

> Saskatchewan's growth in recent years has been supported by necessary public services. The Saskatchewan Power Corporation has increased its output of electrical energy five fold in the last ten years. Economical and reliable power has made it possible for industries to come to Saskatchewan and to produce in competitive markets. Economic supplies of natural gas help attract new industries such as steel, potash and petro-chemicals, heavy fuel consumers. A transportation and communication network is vital to industrial development. Government programs in highways, grid roads, telephones, transportation, have provided these arteries for industry. Basic studies of available resources are another ingredient for industrial development. Through efforts of the resources departments, the University, and the Saskatchewan Research Council, industries now have available a great deal of information on which to plan development. Services related to agriculture are assisting our basic industry to grow and adjust. Farm sewer and water opens new possibilities in livestock production. Community pasture development facilities increased cattle production and helps to stabilize farm income. Public investment in drainage and flood control makes more land available. (CCF Saskatchewan Section of the New Democratic Party 1964a)

Projecting into the future, Lloyd promised to develop "resources for Saskatchewan's benefit. Under the next CCF government development will continue – without sell-outs and giveaways – with real advantage to Saskatchewan people. Based on sound development will be new advances in health, educational opportunities, incomes, recreation and cultural life, consumer protection, and provision for the elderly" (ibid.).

Third, Lloyd had been groomed in the polarized environment of Saskatchewan party politics, having served as Douglas's health minister during the medicare debates of the early 1960s. As premier, he continued this part of his party's rhetorical tradition, pitting the CCF's brand of social democracy against the "survival-of-the-fittest," "quick-buck philosophy" of his chief rivals, the Liberals (CCF Saskatchewan 1967b, 1967c). The attack was as much partisan as it was philosophical. According to Lloyd, liberalism (or Thatcherism, as Lloyd termed it) was a primal approach to politics:

When man was primitive, and jungle law prevailed, only the strong survived – those who could claw and fight and win the meager resources available to keep people alive.

Animals still live that way.

Sadly, some people still live that way, and believe in it to boot.

Even some politicians subscribe to this philosophy. Just look around you
...

Isn't it amazing that in this day and age of plenty, and of scientific know-
how, when we have it in our power to let everyone share in the good life,
some people still believe in the laws of the jungle?

Amazing, and sad too – especially in Saskatchewan, which pioneered
civilized and humanitarian laws long before anyone else in all of North
America.

We can be proud of the medical and welfare facilities available in
Saskatchewan.

We are way ahead of the rest of Canada and most of the world.

But we would do well to remember that the price of progress is constant
vigilance ...

Our medical services should enter a dynamic new phase of improvement and expansion to meet the demands of the people.

Survival of the fittest? We have it in our power to make *everyone* fit.
That's the *civilized* way to do things. (CCF Saskatchewan 1967c)

Throughout his leadership, Lloyd remained focused on the issue of health
care as he charged the Liberals with threatening to abandon the universal
medical insurance plan developed under his watch as health minister. CCF
pamphlets from 1964 reflect this concern:

Libs Want Semicare – Not Medicare
As the election approaches, the leaders of the Liberal Party are redoubling
their efforts to project an image of whole-hearted support for Saskatchewan's Medicare Plan. 'Twas not always so.

As recently as October 28, 1963 ... Ross Thatcher ... said the Liberals
would have a plan but it "will be formulated by experts and will operate
with the co-operation of the medical profession." This statement came only
two weeks after the Saskatchewan College of Physicians and Surgeons had
again repudiated the Saskatchewan plan and called for an Alberta-type
"semicare" program. (CCF Saskatchewan Section of the New Democratic
Party 1964a)

"Let's face it," Lloyd argued, "*The greatest threat to medicare is the Liberal Party*" (ibid.).

These charges served two purposes. The first branded the Saskatch-ewan Liberal Party as a threat to the province's welfare state and left-wing traditions. The second drove a deeper wedge between Saskatchewan's so-cial democratic heritage and the conservative political culture of Alberta. Lloyd was as forceful in his attacks on the Manning government as Doug-las had been:

> In neighbouring Alberta, 1963 saw the introduction, with appropriate fan-fare, of a program dubbed Manningcare which had the full support of the medical profession. How well has it been received by Albertans, and how does it compare in cost with Saskatchewan medical care insurance?
>
> By mid-January 1964, less than 15 per cent of Alberta's population had registered under the plan. Even those families which qualify for the max-imum subsidy – families which earn so little they pay no income tax – must pay $72 per year out of their own pockets to get coverage in Alberta.
>
> For families not eligible for the subsidy, the cost of insurance in Alberta can range as high as $159 per year ...
>
> This same family in Saskatchewan would pay ... $46 – about one-third the cost of comparable coverage in Alberta. (CCF Saskatchewan Section of the New Democratic Party 1964a)

Lloyd turned the 1964 campaign into a contest between the CCF's brand of social democracy on the one hand and free-enterprise liberalism and Al-berta conservatism on the other. If election results serve as a measure, vot-ers preferred the latter, and the polarization of the electorate worked against the CCF as it lost power. The CCF remained on the opposition benches for the next seven years. In the end, Lloyd's premiership was defined by its con-tinuity and brevity.

Establishing a precedent for defeated CCF-NDP premiers, Lloyd bowed to party pressure and stayed on as leader for the next election. After casting a controversial vote in favour of the left-wing Waffle Manifesto at the 1969 federal NDP convention, Lloyd was pressured by moderates in the Sas-katchewan CCF to step down as leader in early 1970 (Praud and McQuarrie 2001, 150; Dyck 1996, 470-71; Norton 2004, 232-33). This early departure makes him the second shortest-serving CCF leader (next to Lorne Calvert) since the party first gained office. Nonetheless, over his nine years as leader, Lloyd played an important role in strengthening his party's commitment to

providing security to Saskatchewan. By sustaining Douglas's dirigiste definition of collective responsibility and polarizing the party system further,
Lloyd's campaign rhetoric in the 1960s helped entrench the province's political code and sustain its political culture.

Allan Blakeney, 1970-87

Drawing on the same themes as Lloyd, Allan Blakeney led the newly chris-
tened New Democratic Party to power in 1971.[7] The new leader's platforms
– dubbed the New Deal for People – played a pivotal role in his party's re-
covery. Not only did they reflect the three core elements of Saskatchewan's
dominant discourse but, in doing so, they also helped Blakeney perpetuate
the province's social democratic political culture through the boom times of
the 1970s and early 1980s.

"Our Potential"

To promote the ideal of collectivism, Blakeney made constant reference to
the importance of the Saskatchewan community. The NDP premier made a
concerted effort to focus on the human side of the province's massive economic growth. "The wealth of a province and its people flows not only from
its resources, its rich farm land, its minerals, its forests," he argued, "it flows
too from the way of life that these people build for themselves" (Saskatchewan NDP 1975c, 8). Rooted in the province's political culture, this way of
life was a combination of sacrifice, collective action, and cautious optimism.
These values were inscribed on a 1982 party brochure that called upon voters to imagine "what we can achieve together if we're all willing to work for
it and try new approaches" (Saskatchewan NDP 1982b).

This belief in the collective potential of the Saskatchewan people was
emphasized in each of Blakeney's five election campaigns. His efforts resembled a community self-esteem building exercise. Take the following excerpt from his 1971 platform:

> We, the people of Saskatchewan, have the vision and the courage to make
> our plans and dreams come true.
>
> We have done it before. We sweated to bring power to every farm when
> the defeatists said it was impossible. We saved farmers from the clutches of
> the mortgage companies – built a mighty power and gas utility – created a
> grid road system. And the first publicly-sponsored auto insurance, hospi-
> talization and medicare programs in North America.

All these and more the people of Saskatchewan did – even as the doom-sayers were claiming they were "too expensive" and "wouldn't work."

Today, our province is again desperately in need of leadership to revital-ize our economy and create a climate of confidence. And again the doom-sayers are talking the language of a defeatist government and a defeated party. They have no faith in the people of Saskatchewan.

The New Democratic Party has kept that faith. With the positive, dy-namic premiership of Allan Blakeney and a team of able, progressive candi-dates, we can build a brighter future.

They say it can't be done. But working together – we'll do it! (Saskatch-ewan New Democratic Party 1971, 15)

Having defeated Thatcher's Liberals in 1971, and having presided over the first few years of the province's new boom, Blakeney continued with his col-lectivist rhetoric in 1975. Once again, he emphasized the uniqueness of Sas-katchewan's political culture:

To me there is something special about Saskatchewan – something worth fighting for.

Today, we are enjoying good times; more jobs; record incomes; growing population. We are proving that we can control our own destinies ... right here.

But it has not always been this way. We have always had to battle against the seasons; against the whims of the marketplace; against those who would exploit us and undermine our distinctive way of life.

Yet we have created a province which is uniquely our own. Saskatch-ewan is a food basket for the world. We are leading the way in reforms and new ideas. And when I go to Ottawa to speak for Saskatchewan, I sense a growing new respect for our province and our people.

It has been my privilege to be a part of our struggles and our reforms. That is a heritage passed on to me.

It is my hope to keep Saskatchewan moving ahead. I invite you to join your neighbours in helping our NDP Government get on with the job. (Sas-katchewan NDP 1975a)

Blakeney's belief in the Saskatchewan community's ability – and respon-sibility – to control its own future formed a significant portion of his nat-ural resource strategy.

Three years later, Blakeney's emphasis on collectivism continued. The premier suggested, "As individuals, working together, progressive minded Saskatchewan people can take well-earned pride in the advances we've made and they will want to guard against losing them" (Saskatchewan NDP 1978). The theme persisted throughout his fourth and most trying campaign: "The 1980's will continue to be a decade of challenge," Blakeney insisted in 1982. "A Saskatchewan NDP government will meet this challenge, and ensure the contributions of all Saskatchewan citizens are recognized" (Saskatchewan NDP 1982c). Blakeney's appeals included a special emphasis on the role of women (Saskatchewan NDP 1982) and Aboriginal peoples (New Democratic Party of Saskatchewan 1982).

Yet Blakeney reserved his most powerful collectivist rhetoric for his fifth and final election. In 1986, for the first time in fifteen years, the NDP leader campaigned from the opposition benches against Grant Devine and his governing Progressive Conservatives. Under the slogan, "Together We Can Do It!" (Regina Elphinstone New Democrats 1986b), Blakeney remained resolute in his belief in the potential of the provincial community:

> Over the past months I've had the chance to talk with many of you and to hear your ideas for getting Saskatchewan working again. You've told me about the great potential of this province and its people ... We share your belief in Saskatchewan's exciting future. That's why we're committed to a government that's as honest and hard-working as the people of Saskatchewan ... Together we *can* get Saskatchewan working again!
>
> Saskatchewan is a province of great potential. Working together, we can meet the challenge of building a secure future. Allan Blakeney and the New Democrats will provide sound leadership for a new generation.
>
> I'm proud to be part of this team. It's an exciting combination of energy and experience – farmers, business people, professionals, clergymen and working people. They share a common belief that we can build a prosperous and secure future for Saskatchewan. They share a common determination to see that this province fulfills its potential. (Regina Elphinstone New Democrats 1986a)

The New Deal

Blakeney's faith in the Saskatchewan state was as deep as his belief in the potential of its people. "Government is one of the keys to building a promising future," he remarked during the 1982 campaign (Saskatchewan NDP

1982b). Based on this premise, Blakeney's various New Deal manifestos offered the clearest expression of Keynesianism ever expressed by a Saskatchewan political party (Wilson 1980, 21). One of the most widely circulated and influential platforms in Prairie history, the New Deal combined plans for increased government ownership, planning, and regulation with renewed support for the welfare state and labour (Rasmussen 2001, 240; Praud and McQuarrie 2001, 151; Saskatchewan NDP 1975c).

Given the ambitious nature of his development plans on the one hand and the economic and geographic realities facing his province in the early 1970s on the other, Blakeney recognized that his objectives might well require new approaches to industrial development. Notwithstanding his openness to joint ventures between government and the private sector (Saskatchewan NDP 1975c), however, Blakeney and his party remained firmly committed to public ownership as a primary development strategy. For example, Blakeney's 1971 New Deal pledged to "give first priority to public ownership through crown corporations. Co-operative ownership will be encouraged. Partnership arrangements between government and co-operatives or private developers will be undertaken when appropriate. Limits will be established with respect to foreign equity capital, and every effort will be made to limit foreign investment in resource development" (Saskatchewan NDP 1971a).

This approach was applied most clearly to the natural resource sector, where Blakeney's promotion of public enterprise was partly grounded in his belief that, "where feasible," the Saskatchewan state ought to "reclaim ownership and control of foreign-owned resources" (Saskatchewan NDP 1971a). This conviction is one reason why Blakeney offered to "consider the feasibility of bringing the potash industry under public ownership," for instance (ibid.). This belief, in turn, was based on "faith in Saskatchewan people. We believe them capable of developing their own resources for their own benefit. Outside help is sometimes necessary, but a sellout is not. Development must be aimed at maximizing benefits for people – not maximizing profits for big business and its promoters" (ibid.). In no uncertain terms, Blakeney proclaimed that the Saskatchewan NDP's natural resource strategy was "based on the belief that our resources belong to the people of Saskatchewan, [with] our government as the steward" (Saskatchewan NDP 1982b). In other words, "If Saskatchewan is to achieve economic stability, we must maintain control of our resource revenues. This Government is committed to that aim" (New Democratic Party of Saskatchewan 1980).

Based on these collectivist and dirigiste principles, Blakeney pledged to establish Crown corporations to explore and develop potash, oil, gas, coal, uranium, and hard minerals. According to Blakeney, "Crown corporations are a tested and proven way of making sure we all benefit from the economic growth in Saskatchewan ... They prove we don't have to rely on outside interests to build our economy. We can do the job ourselves" (Saskatchewan New Democratic Party 1982a, 12). Thus, public ownership meant "getting 'a piece of the action' for Saskatchewan people" (ibid., 14), for "citizens – not just the developers – should share in our resource revenue" (Saskatchewan New Democratic Party 1978).

Capitalizing on an upswing in commodity prices, Blakeney established significant government ownership in the potash, oil, and uranium industries – a move that put him to the left of his caucus (Gruending 1990, 82) and the more market-based approach of Peter Lougheed's Conservatives in Alberta (Dyck 1996, 448). Like Lougheed, Blakeney's 1975 election campaign emphasized the importance of maintaining provincial jurisdiction over the natural resource sector (see Chapter 4). Unlike his western neighbour, however, the Saskatchewan premier pushed forward with public development of his province's resources, once again emphasizing the collectivist and dirigiste elements of the provincial code (Eager 1980, 62).

Superficial similarities between Lougheed and Blakeney did not end there. Both Prairie premiers sought to increase their governments' resource revenue to secure social justice and further economic development. To facilitate this, Blakeney borrowed a policy measure from his Alberta counterpart and introduced his own version of the Heritage Fund. Although the instrument was similar, the motivations behind Blakeney's fund were different. Whereas Lougheed used his province's Heritage Fund primarily as a means to protect (and symbolize) Alberta's autonomy, Blakeney saw his province's Heritage Fund as a tool for securing Saskatchewan's unique political culture and traditions. In this sense, the NDP premier saw "in the revenues accruing from potash, uranium and other resources the foundations for his social democratic dream" (Gruending 2004, 300).

Rather than "stuff it in a mattress like Alberta," Blakeney argued that resource revenue ought to be invested directly in social programs (Saskatchewan NDP 1982b, 6). According to a 1982 pamphlet, "Sound management of resource revenues means a brighter promise ... for today, and tomorrow." For this reason,

> In 1976, resource revenues were placed in the Energy and Resource Development Fund ... Why was the Heritage Fund created? For two reasons.

So people could clearly see what was happening with the revenue from non-renewable resources, and secondly, to provide a way to meet present and future needs ...

The Heritage Fund works for us in three ways.

- It provides funds to enrich ongoing programs. And that's good because it means needed programs like Medicare are guaranteed.
- It makes money available for needed capital projects like the expansion of the College of Veterinary Medicine.
- It's a way of ensuring a sound economic future by investing in income-generating, job-creating assets like the Potash Corporation of Saskatchewan.

It's Common Sense. After all, if you won a million dollars in a lottery you wouldn't just blow it all in a poker game. And you wouldn't stuff it in a mattress. You'd spend some of it on things you needed. You'd invest some for your own security. And you'd invest the rest for your children. That's how the Heritage Fund works for you. (Ibid., 4-5)

Blakeney's dirigiste approach extended beyond the natural resource sector. On the agricultural front, his proposal to establish a Land Bank was the New Deal's most controversial plank (Praud and McQuarrie 2001, 151). According to Blakeney's 1971 platform, "To preserve the family farm, foreign and corporate involvement will be curbed. A Land Bank Commission will be set up to purchase land offered for sale by retiring farmers and others, and make it available to encourage more viable family farms" (Saskatchewan New Democratic Party 1971). Considering the intense criticism surrounding the FLP-CCF's earlier use-lease programs, Blakeney's Land Bank scheme was particularly bold and went further than Douglas had been willing to tread (Hoffman 1983, 51). In the end, the program never did purchase much land. The agricultural economy recovered in the mid-1970s, and most farmers avoided using the program. It remained on the books throughout Blakeney's premiership, but was cut by Devine in 1982 (Gruending 2004, 290-92). In the meantime, the Land Bank and Blakeney's resource development policies together served as a testament to his faith in dirigisme – a core element of the Saskatchewan code.

In sum, Blakeney's New Deal was a classic statement of his party's commitment to providing state-based security against unfettered markets and their laissez-faire champions. His faith in public enterprise as a positive force was illustrated in his final platform as premier, in which he argued,

"Working with Saskatchewan people, your NDP government has shown that a dollar spent by a government is as good as a dollar spent by anyone else and circulates just as well" (Saskatchewan NDP 1982b).

At the Crossroads

Like Patterson, Douglas, Lloyd, and other Saskatchewan leaders before him, Blakeney also made polarization a key component of his campaign rhetoric. His strategy was three-pronged. First, drive a wedge between the NDP on the Left and all other parties (chiefly the Liberals and Conservatives) on the Right. Second, charge these opponents with endangering Saskatchewan's way of life, particularly its roots in family farming and social democracy. And third, brand right-wing parties as defeatist – as all too willing to get in bed with external interests, such as multinational corporations or the federal government, and as all too quick to abandon the province's people in times of need. These labels could then be compared, unfavourably, with the NDP's own image as the party of homegrown optimism.

True to this script, in his first two campaigns, Blakeney positioned the NDP as the Saskatchewan community's defender against encroachments by big business, unforgiving markets and, above all, the Liberal Party. For instance, Blakeney contrasted his support of Saskatchewan's welfare state with cuts made by the Thatcher government. And he repeatedly promoted the NDP as "the people who brought you Medicare" (Saskatchewan NDP 1978; Saskatchewan New Democratic Party 1978).

In addition to his staunch defence of dirigisme, Blakeney offered an aggressive attack on free-enterprise liberalism, particularly as it applied to natural resource development and the family farm. Blakeney argued in 1971, "We must reverse the 'socialism for the rich, free enterprise for the poor' philosophy" (Saskatchewan NDP 1971a). Playing on the collectivist theme, Blakeney insisted that "Saskatchewan's natural resources are the rightful heritage of the people of our province – not the preserve of private interests. The New Democratic Party believes that the Liberal policy of selling out our birthright is both unwise and unnecessary" (ibid.). For this reason, according to Blakeney, "We totally reject the Liberal approach of give-aways and sell-outs to private and foreign promoters for the sake of a 'quick buck'" (Saskatchewan NDP 1971b).

Blakeney also accused the Liberals of abandoning the family farm – a distinctively Saskatchewanian way of life that was increasingly under threat during the 1970s. "Liberal policy makers, in the name of 'economic efficiency,' are doing everything in their power to promote even larger, corporately managed farms, and to hasten the depopulation of rural Saskatchewan," he wrote in 1971 (Saskatchewan NDP 1971a). For this reason, he argued that it was time for Saskatchewan people "to take a stand. The New Democratic Party rejects the capitalist economic doctrine that human values must be sacrificed if they stand in the way of technology and 'efficiency.' Technology and efficiency are means, not ends. We need to shape and control them to build, not destroy our rural communities" (ibid.). In other words, "A New Democratic Government will put farming first, because our provincial economy depends on our farm economy. But economics is only one measuring stick. Farming must also be considered in human terms" (Saskatchewan New Democratic Party 1971).

Drawing on the elements of vulnerability embedded in Saskatchewan's political culture, Blakeney's rhetoric bordered on alarmism when he insisted that the "values of rural life" were in serious jeopardy:

Saskatchewan is at the crossroads. Rural life is being threatened as never before by governments in Ottawa and Regina which are devoted to a cheap-food policy and unfettered operation of the market economy. Only a major effort by the government and people of this province will head off this threat.

The Ottawa Liberal government, with the help of its Regina counterpart, has set a deliberate course, based solely on short-sighted economics. That course will lead to the takeover of Saskatchewan by agribusiness. Instead of family farms, there will be huge corporate enterprises run by a few hired hands. Small communities – and consequently rural life – will vanish. Only giant "service centres" will dot the landscape – centres dominated by the same corporations that own the land ...

Provincially, the Liberal government has accepted or encouraged this erosion. It has shut down small hospitals without consultation; it has imposed stringent pupil-teacher ratios, thus forcing closure of classrooms; it has failed to mount any effective opposition to the federal Task Force Report.

The New Democratic Party believes the time has come for Saskatchewan citizens to unite in a common effort to fight the present trends. (Saskatchewan NDP 1971a)

Throughout the campaign rhetoric, Blakeney linked the Saskatchewan Liberals to their federal counterparts. In this vein, there were obvious parallels between Lougheed and Blakeney. Indeed, on the topic of natural resource development, Blakeney's campaign rhetoric was actually more assertive than Lougheed's.[8] In his New Deal '75, Blakeney announced: "Saskatchewan's legal right to control its own resources is under attack. Ottawa has imposed a heavy and unfair double tax on provincial royalties to try to force the province to give up revenue. They kept down the price of our oil in central Canada, while we continued to pay the full world price, or more, for the goods we buy from central Canada" (Saskatchewan NDP 1975b).

Yet a closer examination of each premier's campaign literature reveals that the target of the attacks was subtly different. For the Alberta premier, who drew on a code of autonomy and a political culture steeped in western alienation, the focus was squarely on the federal government as an institution (see Chapter 3). For Blakeney, like Douglas and Lloyd before him, the target was the federal Liberal Party (and, by extension, its provincial wing). Saskatchewan's political code and culture lacked the same sectarian impulse found in Alberta; instead, Blakeney's rhetoric drew more heavily upon the partisan elements of his dispute with Pierre Trudeau's Liberals. Consider the following passage from his 1975 platform:

> Resources: Oil. Potash. Owned by the people of Saskatchewan. But *the Liberals* want the lion's share of the benefits for Ottawa and their corporate friends. Our future depends on what we do with our depleting resources. We need the tough, independent, Blakeney NDP Government to defend those resources ...
>
> Now that the value of our resources has gone up, we have a chance to catch up ... Resource revenues are the key to Saskatchewan's success. But *other political parties* don't want the benefits of our resources to come to the people of Saskatchewan. They say the NDP Government is greedy.
>
> They say we shouldn't squabble with Ottawa – we should let Ottawa have its way. We should give the royalties from our resources to the multinational corporations and hope for the best.
>
> The NDP says that Saskatchewan resources belong to Saskatchewan people. (Saskatchewan NDP 1975b, emphasis added)

According to Blakeney, Saskatchewan remained at a crossroads in 1975. Concerns not only surrounded the agricultural sector but also natural resources, and the foe was not simply the Liberal Party but also the resurgent Conservatives. This shift in focus was a relatively seamless one for Blakeney. As he explained it, "Conservatives here at home are 'in bed' with the Liberals and the companies" (Saskatchewan NDP 1982b, 7). "Liberals and Conservatives would give those revenues away to the big corporations. And that would mean no money to improve hospitals, schools and our neighbour-hoods" (Regina and Area New Democrats 1978). In reference to the Liberals, he charged: "If you want to know who is calling the shots, look at who is paying the bills. In the last provincial election, banks, trust and insurance companies, along with resource developers and other assorted corporate connections, gave the Saskatchewan P.C.'s here over $120,000 to try and elect Dick Collver. Now they're trying the same thing with Grant Devine. What they want is your business" (Saskatchewan New Democratic Party 1982a, 13).

More broadly, in attacking the Tories, Blakeney borrowed Douglas's criticism of the defeatist, laissez-faire approach to development in Saskatchewan:

> Conservatives are always attacking Crown corporations. They just don't believe that Saskatchewan people are capable of doing a good job. They'd sell out Saskatchewan. Dick Collver tried to grab power by promising to sell out public oil, gas and potash holdings. Now Doctor Devine is peddling the "snake oil" ... Conservatives attack Crown corporations because they don't believe the people of Saskatchewan can do things for themselves. So they try to destroy public confidence in companies like the potash corporation as a first step in selling them back to their multinational friends.
>
> *Why are the Conservatives working to destroy our companies?* Why would any politician claiming to represent the interests of the people want to destroy companies that give us a stake in resource development, and provide utilities and other important services at rates among the lowest in Canada?
>
> The answer lies in Conservative economic policies which have changed little since they were hatched in Europe hundreds of years ago. They simply don't believe Saskatchewan people have the capacity to do things for themselves. They'd rather destroy public confidence in companies like the Potash Corporation of Saskatchewan, then sell them to their friends in the multinational resource companies. (Saskatchewan New Democratic Party 1982a, 15)

Like Douglas and Lloyd, Blakeney's attacks on the Saskatchewan Right extended beyond provincial boundaries. Writing in the early 1980s, he suggested, "Conservatives across the country are attacking public control of resources and the social and health programs which can be financed by resource revenues. The NDP government of Saskatchewan is the only government in Canada defending both provincial rights over resources and energy security for all Canadians. A strong New Democratic Party is our best hope for a strong Saskatchewan within a strong Canada" (New Democratic Party of Saskatchewan 1980).

Just as his predecessors had focused their attention on Alberta Social Credit, so too did Blakeney cast aspersions eastward on the Manitoba Tories:

> The Conservative Lyon government was elected in Manitoba in 1977. It adopted a policy of "acute and protracted restraint," and drastically reduced public investment in Manitoba's economy. The results are well known; Manitoba is now the only province in Canada with a declining population, the provincial economy is wavering between recession and depression, and Winnipeg is the new "boarded up capital of Canada."
>
> The Manitoba experience provides a good example of what happens when eighteenth-century Conservative economic policies are inflicted on a thriving economy. A comparison of economic performance during the NDP years from 1970-77 and the Conservative years from 1978-80 reveals clearly that the Conservative public investment slashing was a disaster for Manitoba and Lyon is still waiting for his masters from the private sector to "take up the slack." (Saskatchewan NDP 1982b, 21)

In short, "Instead of bowing once to Ottawa ... twice to Edmonton ... with a curtsy to Houston," Blakeney's resource development policies were distinctly homegrown (ibid., 7).

In addition to protecting Crown corporations from the neoliberal designs of the Saskatchewan Conservatives, Blakeney portrayed the NDP as the only party committed to preserving – and extending – the province's legacy in social services and health care: "In Saskatchewan, people trust the Blakeney Government to protect Medicare. But games played with Medicare in Conservative provinces have created mistrust and uncertainty. The NDP continues to: oppose health premiums and deterrent fees; make health services available regardless of cost; oppose extra billing; properly fund our hospitals and health services; [and] introduce new programs like prescription drugs, children's dental care and many more" (Saskatchewan New Democratic Party 1982b, 7). Blakeney carried this message forward to the 1982 campaign, in which his slogans – "We Care!" and "Keep a Good Thing Going" – were designed to polarize the party system by distinguishing his proven, dirigiste approach from the New Right alternative being offered by Devine's Tories. By the same token, the NDP's new slogan, "The People Who Care"

("... Instead of Not Caring at All"), was designed to juxtapose its social democratic roots against the neoconservative approach of the PC Party (ibid.).

Once again, these attacks extended beyond Saskatchewan's borders:

> Conservatives have sacrificed the principles and practices of medicare on the altar of greed. Tory Alberta threatens to withdraw from the medicare plan if the Federal Government initiates a ban on extra billing ... On March 10, 1982, the Liberal-Conservative coalition in B.C. increased premiums, hospital emergency care fees and ambulance fees ... The story is even worse in Conservative Ontario ... Conservatives here in Saskatchewan are "toeing the Party line" ... If a Conservative offers you a Certificate of Guarantee not to tamper with Medicare this time, ask him how much it cost to print ... and whether they had to pay in advance. (Saskatchewan New Democratic Party 1982b, 7)

Tearing a page from the Liberal Party's playbook in the early twentieth century, Blakeney warned Saskatchewan voters not to support the "experiments" proposed by right-wing Tories:

> It is clear Conservatives here want to experiment like Reagan has in the U.S. Like Reagan they would: cut pensions, medicare and help for the poor; cut education, social services and environmental protection; give tax breaks for oil companies, giant corporations and people earning over $50,000 a year; [and] de-regulate the railways.

> Conservatives won't learn from experience; but they want to experiment with you. They're determined to repeat the mistakes made elsewhere.

> People who vote Conservative expecting to get help with the cost of living are like turkeys who vote for an early Christmas. (Saskatchewan New Democratic Party 1982b, 8)

All told, this rhetoric was designed to further polarize Saskatchewan politics, this time into a contest between the social democratic NDP and New Right Conservatives. To accomplish this, Blakeney contrasted the NDP's reputation for providing "a secure future for everyone" (Saskatchewan NDP 1982a) – through togetherness and a strong state – with Devine's individualistic, small-government vision of Saskatchewan's future.

Poll numbers heading into the 1982 election suggested the strategy was well advised – Blakeney's New Democrats led Devine's Tories on a number of issues, including leadership (Dyck 1996, 475). In this context, the lopsided results of the 1982 election came as a surprise to most observers. The Devine Conservatives not only ousted Blakeney's three-term government, they also formed the largest majority in Saskatchewan history.

Blakeney's loss to Devine in 1982 can be attributed to a number of factors. In the end, however, Blakeney suffered the same fate as Woodrow Lloyd in 1964. Having presided over one of the most comprehensive province-building exercises in Canadian history, his message of security lacked the same sense of urgency it had in 1971. Devine's promises to make "Saskatchewan open for business" – like Thatcher's appeals in 1964 – appeared to capture a decennial mood for change in the Saskatchewan electorate. This tendency is not unique to Saskatchewan. As Pitsula and Rasmussen (1990, 24) note, "After many years in power, left-wing [parties] can become the status quo that they once fought to change, and lose touch with the concerns and opinions of ordinary citizens." To a large extent, this is what happened to Blakeney's New Democrats in 1982, when they surrendered power to the Conservatives.

Like Lloyd before him, Blakeney remained at the party's helm, serving as leader of the opposition and guiding the New Democrats into the 1986 election. The campaign, itself, proved to be the last great hurrah for Keynesianism in Saskatchewan. The bidding war between the Conservatives and New Democrats has been called "one of the sorriest episodes in Saskatchewan political history" (Pitsula 2004, 328); only Goodale's opposition Liberals stayed out of the fray, preaching fiscal responsibility instead of new government spending. Blakeney's Commitment to Saskatchewan continued to hold up jobs as the top priority, and the party continued to promise to secure a "fair share of resource revenue for Saskatchewan people" (Regina Elphinstone New Democrats 1986a). In addition, by opposing free trade, federal agricultural policy, and cuts to transfer payments, Blakeney called on voters to "stand up for Saskatchewan: send Mulroney a message" (ibid.).

In the end, running on many of the same principles and policies they had since 1978, Blakeney's New Democrats were "wrong losers" in 1986. Although it gained a larger number of votes province-wide, the NDP's support was concentrated in urban areas, which were substantially under-represented in the legislature (particularly following Devine's redistribution in 1986) (de Vlieger 2001). Blakeney retired soon thereafter, having sustained Saskatchewan's code and culture through one of the province's most remarkable periods of economic growth.

Roy Romanow, 1987-2001

Roy Romanow was chosen by acclamation as Blakeney's successor in 1987. A veteran New Democrat since his election to the legislature in 1967, Romanow made his first major mark as leader in 1989, when he led the New Democratic caucus out of the legislature to protest the Devine government's plan to privatize SaskEnergy. The ensuing seventeen-day boycott paralyzed the legislature, galvanized public opposition, and forced Devine to revoke the offer of sale (Pitsula 2004, 333-34; Marchildon 2004, 364-66). This episode was followed by the NDP's four-month filibuster of the debate over the privatization of the potash industry, which helped solidify Romanow's reputation as a guardian of Saskatchewan's dirigiste traditions (Baron and Jackson 1991, 243-51).

These events notwithstanding, since his failed bid for the leadership in 1970, Romanow had earned a reputation as the party's leading moderate, someone who leaned "to the right of the party's political spectrum" (Praud and McQuarrie 2001, 154). In this, Romanow's version of social democracy differed from his predecessors' in several notable ways. Keynesian orthodoxy was replaced by adherence to market-based solutions, and references to labour and class politics were curtailed significantly in each of his campaigns (Roberts 2001). Moreover, under Romanow, the Saskatchewan NDP focused on promoting itself less as the vanguard of an ideological (social democratic) movement and more as a competent government administrator (Rasmussen 2001, 259). Romanow's version of the "The Saskatchewan Way" was, in effect, an adaptation of the provincial code to the deficit crisis and the global neoliberal paradigm of the early 1990s. Indeed, in its kinship to Tony Blair's Third Way philosophy of economic pragmatism, Romanow's approach foreshadowed global developments on the political Left (Praud and McQuarrie 2001, 163; Rasmussen 2001, 259). All the while, the New Democratic leader continued to contrast his party with various opponents on the political Right. Thus – in the face of a global recession and the transformation of the Saskatchewan state and economy, not to mention party system – Romanow continued to speak in code and helped to carry elements of Saskatchewan's political culture into the twenty-first century.

"The Saskatchewan Way"
First and foremost, Romanow stressed the collectivist elements of his party's ideology over its ties to traditional social democracy. As Leeson (2001, 8)

puts it, Romanow's "conception of politics owed little to classical ideas about socialism and class conflict. For him prairie politics had been about cooperation and community, about coming together behind strong leadership to accomplish what outsiders would not do for the province."[9] According to Romanow, these principles constituted the Saskatchewan way – the traditional Saskatchewan values that underpinned the province's political ethos (Saskatchewan New Democratic Party 1991b, 8).[10]

Romanow rested the bulk of his 1991 campaign on this foundation and two familiar themes: co-operation and community (Dunn and Laycock 1992, 238). His party's 1991 platform stated,

> The Saskatchewan Way is community – people coming together to accomplish that which they cannot accomplish alone. It is the fundamental belief that everyone in our province has something to contribute to the good of the community overall. When an individual or family prospers, we all prosper. When an individual or family suffers, we are all the lesser for it. The community divisions of the last decade – fostered by a government determined to drive a wedge between people for the sake of politics – must be put behind us, and a new era of cooperation must be our goal.
>
> As a united community, Saskatchewan is unbeatable. Our history proves it. Against all odds we overcame harsh climate, long distances from markets and sparse population to build a province which has been home to some of North America's greatest accomplishments. On the threshold of a new decade, our renewal as a province demands a new era of community and cooperation. (Saskatchewan New Democratic Party 1991b, 1-2)

Romanow used this collectivist rhetoric to sell his broad, long-range plans for fiscal restraint and economic development. Emphasizing "first things first – common sense financial management" (Saskatchewan New Democratic Party 1991b, 2), Romanow's New Democrats aimed to "turn our economy around in the 1990s and ignite the spirit of community which built Saskatchewan. The values of co-operation, compassion, and fairness can help build a future of hope, opportunity, and prosperity for all Saskatchewan people" (Saskatchewan New Democratic Party 1991a). This style of rhetoric differed from the more individualist pull-up-your-bootstraps approach employed by Ralph Klein in Alberta.

Having conquered the deficit by the end of his first term, Romanow credited the accomplishment to Saskatchewan's collective spirit. His 1995 platform stated,

There's a new day dawning in Saskatchewan. A day which holds the promise of jobs and opportunities for all.

We stand at this new dawn of hope and opportunity because we have
come together as a community these last four years.

We have met enormous challenges threatening our province ...

Four years ago, your New Democratic government took office and found
Saskatchewan's finances and administration in chaos.

The people of Saskatchewan attacked the problem with determination ...

Government based on partnership, on co-operation, and on communities – we've made an exciting start in the last four years. It's the Saskatchewan way, and it's working.

Together we have laid a foundation for an expanding economy, effective
government, and strong communities. I invite you to join with us and help
build our future together. (Saskatchewan New Democratic Party 1995, 6-7)

Four years later, in 1999, Romanow pledged many of the same policies,
and they were framed in much of the same collectivist rhetoric. "People in
Saskatchewan share common dreams," he argued. "We all want the opportunity to build a better future for ourselves, our children and our neighbours.
We all want a province that is a community – a place where your neighbour
looks out for your children, where everyone pitches in to help when there is
a need and where people have the opportunity to achieve their dreams"
(Saskatchewan New Democratic Party 1999).

Thus, in each of his campaigns, Romanow's vision conscientiously drew
on the principles entrenched in the Saskatchewan code and political culture. His rhetoric built explicitly

on the fundamental values of our province – the values of caring, sharing,
cooperation and compassion. Saskatchewan people have always worked
together to do what cannot be done as individuals – providing health care,
educating our children and building our transportation system. We are also
innovative and enterprising as individuals – creating and building the farms
and businesses that underpin our economy.

The Saskatchewan way combines community values and cooperation
with individual initiative and enterprise. (Saskatchewan New Democratic
Party 1999)

The addition of this minor but noticeable strain of individualism reflected
Romanow's adherence to a new, liberalized form of social democracy. In this

sense, Roy Romanow can best be described as a Third Way social democrat, one whose continued emphasis on collectivism helped to preserve his province's code through its transition to a neoliberal world order.

The Third Way

The Third Way coalesced into a coherent ideology in the late twentieth century, just as Romanow rose to the leadership of the Saskatchewan NDP. Granted, many of its core principles had surfaced decades earlier (Broadbent 1999, 75; Green-Pedersen and van Kersbergen 2002). Yet, by shifting focus away from full employment and government largesse as its goal and comprehensive state planning as a means to that end, the Third Way movement marked a turning point in the history of social democracy, in Canada as elsewhere (Kitschelt 1994, xiii). Ultimately, the Third Way emerged out of opposition to the New Right and dissatisfaction with the Old Left. Giddens (2000, 2) calls it "a different framework, one that avoids both the bureaucratic, top-down government favored by the old left and the aspiration of the [new] right to dismantle government altogether." As its two most famous exponents, Tony Blair and Gerhard Schroder (1999), put it, the Third Way strives to meet old goals such as social justice through new means, including economic dynamism. To do so requires embracing a market economy without promoting a market society. The Third Way is an attempt to unite the two main forces of the Left – liberalism and socialism – under a shared ideological outlook and, in many instances, a common partisan banner (Wesley 2006).

Far from marking an end to the Saskatchewan code, Romanow's adoption of the Third Way offered a new vehicle for the collectivist, dirigiste elements of the provincial ethos. To be sure, he drew narrower limits on the scope of government intervention. Spiralling deficits and a global paradigm shift had brought an end to classic Keynesianism in Saskatchewan. Nonetheless, like his predecessors, Romanow continued to promote the value of government in Saskatchewan's society and economy.

Romanow's conversion of the Saskatchewan NDP to the post-Keynesian version of social democracy was facilitated (or encouraged) by a wide range of interrelated factors (see Rasmussen 2001; McGrane 2006, 9-10; Dyck 1996, 482-84; Praud and McQuarrie 2001, 160-65; Wishlow 2001, 178). "There are sweeping changes today in Canada and the world," he noted in 1995, "changes that put stress on families, communities and our way of life. It's the duty of government to find the right policies and programs for a changing world" (Saskatchewan New Democratic Party 1995, 7). In response to these stresses, Romanow's rhetoric not only harkened back to his party's roots in collectivism and fiscal responsibility, it also drew considerable policy inspiration from the New Right. He promised to hike several taxes, ranging from those on income and corporations to those related to consumption (fuel, goods, services, and tobacco). Romanow also pledged to abolish Devine's flat income tax, restore social programs (most notably health care), and review all privatization deals (Saskatchewan New Democratic Party 1991b). In this vein, Romanow's fiscal approach differed from that being pursued in Alberta. Whereas Premier Klein focused on shrinking the size of government by slashing state spending, Romanow preferred a mixture of supply- and demand-side solutions (de Clercy 2005; Denis 1995).

Borrowing from the Right, however, Romanow did pledge to cut government spending, slash Cabinet and civil servant salaries, issue back-to-work orders to end public service strikes, and pass balanced-budget legislation.[11] To eliminate the so-called Devine deficit by 2006, Romanow also promised to restore the province's fiscal house through comprehensive auditing, the creation of a Royal Commission to investigate the government's finances, and a balanced budget within four years (Saskatchewan New Democratic Party 1991b). Overall, Romanow remained "committed to the goal of financial management and fair taxation for the long-term economic security of our people and our province" (ibid., 5).

Romanow emerged from the 1991 campaign with a massive majority, but he inherited an equally massive budget deficit from the Tories. Under these constraints, the new premier "governed in a less interventionist and more fiscally conservative manner than the Conservatives" (Praud and McQuarrie 2001, 156). These measures, combined with an increase in resource revenues, allowed Romanow to post a $119 million surplus by 1995 (ibid.). Looking back on his premiership, Romanow considered balancing the budget as his government's proudest achievement (ibid., 162-63). Yet, true to his party's roots in fiscal responsibility, the premier also added a characteristic "word of caution about the challenges we still face":

We have a mountain of unpaid 1980s debt. The interest on it costs almost as much, every year, as we invest in education.

That's why New Democrats are committed to a long-term plan to retire Saskatchewan's debt. It's also why our plan must be prudent and affordable.

Don't be misled by politicians who make expensive promises. Saskatchewan followed that path in the 1980s, and we'll be paying for it for many years. (Saskatchewan New Democratic Party 1995, 7)

Under Romanow's guidance, the province's fiscal and economic gains failed to usher in a new era of government intervention. Writing in 1995, the premier boasted, "Saskatchewan has a balanced budget for the first time since 1982. We did it the Saskatchewan way – by living within our means. The challenge now: to begin paying down the debt, and to make sure Saskatchewan never gets into this kind of financial mess again" (Saskatchewan New Democratic Party 1995, 25). Like Klein, Romanow's objective was "to run the provincial government with the same frugal common sense that the people of Saskatchewan use to run their own households. That means putting away the provincial credit card, and paying as we go for what we really need" (ibid., 27). In short, Romanow insisted, "Thanks to the hard work and determination of the people of Saskatchewan, our province can now make plans for what to do with provincial budget surpluses over each of the next four years. Under our plan, projected surpluses will be invested as follows: approximately one-third for debt reduction; one-third for tax reduction; and one-third for jobs and health care" (ibid., 68). This tripartite approach to spending government surpluses – "lower taxes, less debt, better services" – drew its inspiration from the "balanced, realistic and achievable" ethos of the Third Way (Saskatchewan New Democratic Party 1999).

Although his fiscal approach married Tommy Douglas to Tony Blair, Romanow's economic strategy was distinct from his CCF-NDP forebears. "In contrast with his predecessors," Praud and McQuarrie (2001, 163) note that "Romanow assiduously courted the business community and favored less direct state intervention in the economy." Hence, he pledged to reinvigorate the economy by establishing a "Premier's Council on Economic Co-operation to renew the economic partnership among Saskatchewan's businesses, co-operatives, farmers, labour, and government" (Saskatchewan New Democratic Party 1991b, 6).

Despite obvious nods to the private sector and the New Right, Romanow's economic development plans did not include a complete abandonment of dirigisme, however. "Saskatchewan people want to work, and to contribute to the well-being of their families and the prosperity of our province," he argued in 1991 (Saskatchewan New Democratic Party 1991b, 6). Echoing Allan Blakeney, Romanow insisted that "we don't have to wait for big business or wealthy outside investors. *We need a provincial government that is able to provide sound economic management for our future.* Together, we can get Saskatchewan working, providing jobs and prosperity for all" (ibid., 6, emphasis added). Furthermore, Romanow suggested in 1999 that "our provincial government plays a key role in what kind of community our province will be. It delivers health care, educates our children, builds our highways and administers the justice system. Provincial government policies help determine whether the economy will grow and jobs are created" (Saskatchewan New Democratic Party 1999). Such rhetoric was aimed at opposition forces, whose calls for smaller government were once again gaining salience in Saskatchewan.

In contrast to his right-wing opponents (the Conservatives, Liberals, and nascent Saskatchewan Party), Romanow continued to value public enterprise as a means of providing essential services and economic growth. However, unlike Blakeney, Romanow's approach to the province's family of Crown corporations was not simply to protect them as Saskatchewan's birthright; Romanow believed they should be made competitive both within and outside Saskatchewan's borders (Marchildon 2004, 374-77; Dunn and Laycock 1992, 224).

Romanow's dirigisme also extended to the agriculture sector, where his security-based rhetoric once again resembled that of his CCF and NDP predecessors. "Agriculture is Saskatchewan's number one industry, and provides a unique way of life for thousands of farm families. The severe cost-price squeeze, high interest rates, and unfair taxes are causing financial hardship to farm families and driving hundreds of them off the land. We need a provincial government that is committed to the long-term economic security of farm families, and to the long-term prosperity of Saskatchewan agriculture" (Saskatchewan New Democratic Party 1991b, 7). To protect the "rural quality of life ... the heart of our Saskatchewan culture," Romanow made a commitment to redeveloping the farm safety net – a set of programs designed to shelter farmers from the risks associated with the transition to new farming techniques and products (Saskatchewan New Democratic Party 1995, 51, 57).

Overall, Romanow's "common sense approach to economic and social renewal" – one that was avowedly "within our means as a province" – was definitely of the Third Way variety (Saskatchewan New Democratic Party 1991b, 4). The NDP premier's rhetoric placed new limits on the scope of the Saskatchewan state, to be certain. This may lead some to conclude that government interventionism is a recessive strain in the Saskatchewan code. Yet, by helping to direct political discourse in the midst of the 1990s recession, Romanow's rhetoric did help sustain the dirigiste values embedded in the province's political culture. This is seen, quite clearly, when Romanow's message is compared to those of Conservative premiers in Alberta (Chapter 3) and Manitoba (Chapter 5). Romanow helped protect a prominent (if narrower) place for the government in Saskatchewan's economy and society.

"Turning Saskatchewan Around"

Romanow's attempt to protect the government's role was aided by his relentless maligning of the political Right. Throughout each of his three campaigns, the NDP leader continued to blame Saskatchewan's climate of economic unease and political distrust squarely on the Tories. For instance, Romanow framed the 1991 election as a referendum on the Devine government's performance. According to party literature, the New Democrats sought to restore the Saskatchewan economy and society to its traditional social democratic roots:

> This election is about the PC government's record – nearly ten years of disappointment, dishonesty and division.
>
> When Grant Devine was elected in 1982, Saskatchewan had balanced budgets, a strong economy, and a bright future.
>
> Now we are deep in debt, our economy is unable to generate enough jobs and opportunities, and the future is uncertain for thousands of farm families, working people, professionals and small business people.
>
> People have become cynical about government in Saskatchewan. Unfair tendering, widespread political patronage, and an arrogant disregard for public accountability have been trademarks of the Devine PC government.
>
> That's not the Saskatchewan way. (Saskatchewan New Democratic Party 1991c)

In each campaign, Romanow argued that the Devine Conservatives had abandoned the traditional values of Saskatchewan politics. "Saskatchewan has a proud tradition of making high quality health care accessible to all Saskatchewan people," he suggested in 1991 (Saskatchewan New Democratic Party 1991b, 11). Four years later, he added, "Comprehensive public health care was one of the core commitments of Tommy Douglas's 1944 election platform, and one of the proudest accomplishments of his and Woodrow Lloyd's governments. Implementing medicare was also one of the biggest political fights in our province's history. We fought tooth and nail for medicare then – and we have ever since" (Saskatchewan New Democratic Party 1995, 33): "But the PC government has undermined and threatened our health care system. The PC record has caused increasing concerns about rising costs, inadequate accessibility, and cutbacks in services ... Over the past ten years the Devine PC government has undermined Saskatchewan health care and betrayed Saskatchewan people" (Saskatchewan New Democratic Party 1991b, 11).

Although tempered considerably, these attacks continued in 1995. Among other anti-Conservative innuendos, Romanow's second platform included statements such as the following: "Instead of sky-high deficits and soaring debt, the Romanow government has balanced the budget and is working to shrink the debt. In place of hit-and-miss mega-projects, the NDP government is following a comprehensive development strategy" (Saskatchewan New Democratic Party 1995, 16). In short, "We just can't afford four more years of PC government" (Saskatchewan New Democratic Party 1991c). Moreover, Romanow reiterated, "Building good government had to start by ending the abuses of the past. The people of Saskatchewan had their faith in government sorely tested during the 1980s ... Elected to office in 1991, we rolled up our sleeves and got to work. We opened the books. We cleaned up the mess ... This was no small issue. The previous government was hiding what it was doing with public money ... The government's books obscured rather than detailed what was going on with public revenues and spending" (Saskatchewan New Democratic Party 1995, 61).

Romanow's 1999 platform marked a return to blunt criticism in its page-by-page evaluation of "the opposition record and plan." This time, Romanow was careful to spread his criticism to both opposition parties – the Liberals (whom he labelled indecisive) and the Saskatchewan Party (whom he continued to refer to as the Tories, despite the formation of the new party in 1997). Consider the following sample of statements, distributed throughout the document:

- The Tories will freeze the health budget for five years. This means no money for more doctors and nurses, no money to pay for new drugs ... and no money to improve services – or even to keep existing services when costs increase.
- The Liberals in Ottawa cut health care spending across Canada by $6 billion per year. Liberal Leader Jim Melenchuk has said that he wants American style, for-profit clinics in Saskatchewan.
- The last time the Tories were in power, people left rural Saskatchewan at record rates ... The Tory platform does not commit to investing one dime in agriculture or rural development.
- The Liberals in Ottawa have caused many of the problems in rural Saskatchewan with the unilateral elimination of long-term support programs, badly designed interim programs and terrible transportation policies. The provincial Liberals ... were unable to agree on what to say about rural Saskatchewan's future.

- The Tories never balanced a budget. They ran up a $15 billion debt – and then changed their name. The Tory plan still does not add up – a $1.8 billion tax and spend scheme will mean a return to deficits and more debt.

  The Liberal platform called for spending every nickel that the government has. Since losing three by-elections, they've started talking about cutting taxes as well. They are having trouble agreeing on what to do.

- The Tories' record on financial management is so bad that they've changed their name to hide from it ... Today, the Tory plan is simple. Do it again.

- Liberals in Ottawa introduced gun registration instead of working on the Young Offenders' Act. The Liberals have trouble agreeing on what to do about crime so their [provincial] platform does not mention the issue. (Saskatchewan New Democratic Party 1999).

Indeed, just as Douglas, Lloyd, and Blakeney had linked the federal and provincial wings of the Liberal Party, so too did Romanow suggest that there were organic links between Tories in Ottawa and Regina. For instance, on the topic of agriculture policy, the NDP leader argued that the "Mulroney and Devine governments have failed to provide adequate long-term stability and security for Saskatchewan farm families" (Saskatchewan New Democratic Party 1991b, 7).

As in 1986, the 1999 Saskatchewan election resulted in yet another "wrong winner," this time the New Democrats. Although it lost all of its rural seats to the upstart Saskatchewan Party – which capitalized on what it portrayed as the government's failure to respond to the farm crisis – the NDP was able to retain power by negotiating a coalition with Jim Melenchuk's Liberals (New Democratic Party of Saskatchewan and the Liberal Party of Saskatchewan 1999). It was the first hung parliament in Saskatchewan since 1929 and, in many ways, it served to reinforce opinion among Romanow's detractors that he was a closet Liberal. The coalition experience left Romanow disenchanted throughout his abbreviated third term (Marchildon 2004, 386; Dyck 2006, 84).

Romanow resigned from office in 2000, leaving behind a "pragmatist-compassionate" brand of politics that has revolutionized the NDP's approach to government (Praud and McQuarrie 2001, 162). Yet Romanow's constant references to the principles of security – most notably his championing of collectivism, his redefinition of dirigisme along Third Way lines, and his continued attempts to polarize the party system – helped foster some sense of familiarity in his program of government restructuring.

Romanow's stewardship of the Saskatchewan NDP helped renew and sustain the province's political ethos amid the turbid waters of yet another economic crisis.

Lorne Calvert, 2001-7

Romanow's successor, Lorne Calvert, represented the NDP's Centre-Left, and promised to return the province to its more orthodox social democratic traditions (Praud and McQuarrie 2001, 165). Making good on this promise not only meant promoting the province's communitarian culture and creating polarization in the system between the New Democrats and the right-wing Saskatchewan Party, it also meant once again defending the Saskatchewan state – most notably its Crown corporations and public health care system. All of these components of Calvert's strategy were in code, and each was encapsulated in his campaign slogan, "Forward, Not Backward."

Facing an increasingly formidable foe in the form of the Saskatchewan Party, Calvert criticized the opposition's plan for the province's future, asking Saskatchewan voters to move forward with the NDP, not backward with the Saskatchewan Party:

> We can go forward together, with strong and innovative Crown corporations that provide the lowest package of utility costs anywhere in Canada. Not backward, as the Sask Party proposes, with the privatization of these public assets to make some people rich while the rest of us pay more for privatized services.
>
> We can go forward together ... in publicly-funded and publicly-run health care facilities. Not backward, as the Sask Party would take us with their plans for reckless corporate tax breaks that will undermine our health care and education and open the door to privatized health services ...
>
> It's up to you. We have a clear choice in Saskatchewan ... We're stronger when we work together. Let's build the future for Saskatchewan families here, and now. (Saskatchewan New Democrats 2003)

It was a familiar rhetorical tactic. By blending a spirit of communitarianism with support for the Saskatchewan state, and by presenting the opposition as a major threat to Saskatchewan values, Calvert built on a code inherited from Douglas, Lloyd, Blakeney, and Romanow.

Drawing on the collectivist element of the provincial code, Calvert announced: "I'm proud of our province and what we've accomplished together. Now is not the time for reckless cuts and privatization. We're stronger when we work together" (Saskatchewan NDP 2003a). Four years later, in 2007, he added: "A strong community is also a safe community with an unbreakable social fabric, where neighbours care about neighbours and where everyone benefits from our shared prosperity. Lorne Calvert and the Saskatchewan New Democrats will build a strong and prosperous Saskatchewan, where everyone benefits from our shared prosperity" (Saskatchewan New Democrats 2007, 30). With collectivist and dirigiste rhetoric reminiscent of Allan Blakeney's optimism in the 1970s, Calvert argued,

> Saskatchewan's economy has been transformed. We have sharpened our competitive edge, and the results are all around us for everyone to see. Let there be no doubt: hard work and careful planning have paid off. Our economy is booming like never before.
>
> But with our economic strength comes a greater responsibility. How to make sure that everyone benefits from our shared prosperity? And how to ensure that our economic growth is both lasting and sustainable? ...
>
> New Democrats have a proud record of fulfilling our commitments. I invite you to read more about what we have achieved together – accomplishments that are truly making life better for Saskatchewan families and building even brighter futures here for young people.
>
> There has never been a better time to fulfill your dreams at home in Saskatchewan. With your support we will help lead the way to a bright and sustainable future for all Saskatchewan families. (Ibid.)

Calvert also combined these two elements of the Saskatchewan code (dirigisme and collectivism) with the third (polarization) to produce a scathing attack on his partisan rivals: Saskatchewan Party leaders Elwin Hermanson (in 2003) and Brad Wall (in 2007). In contrast to the NDP's brand of cautious optimism, Calvert characterized the Saskatchewan Party as defeatist and even menacing. In 2003, he suggested, "Hermanson and the Sask Party have an extreme agenda of radical change for Saskatchewan. Many will lose and few will win as they sell off Crown corporations to outside interests, and give $240 million in corporate tax breaks to banks and other businesses" (Saskatchewan NDP 2003a). Four years later, the NDP premier argued, "While Lorne Calvert and the NDP have been busy promoting Saskatchewan across Canada, the Sask Party never misses an opportunity to complain and to bad-mouth our province. It seems that the only people who don't know about our boom are in the Sask Party. Brad Wall even held a

Calgary fundraiser where he disrespectfully told the audience that Saskatchewan people and their voting habits are 'certifiable.' Good news for Saskatchewan is treated like bad news by the Sask Party" (Saskatchewan New Democrats 2007, 8).

Calvert reserved his strongest criticism for the Saskatchewan Party's health care policies and its alleged privatization plans for Saskatchewan's family of Crown corporations. He charged, "The Sask Party's plan to open the doors of health care to for-profit companies would take us dangerously close to U.S.-style two-tier care, where the care you get depends on how much you can afford to spend. New Democrats are committed to Saskatchewan values: quality health care for everyone" (Saskatchewan New Democrats 2003, 20). Furthermore, according to Calvert's 2007 platform:

> The Sask Party knows that they can no longer come right out and say they want to privatize our public health care system. Instead, they hide their agenda behind phrases like "efficiency review" and "health audit." But make no mistake, they cannot be trusted to protect public health care.
>
> Like right-wing governments in other provinces, we can expect the Sask Party's agenda of cuts and privatization to lead to private for-profit hospitals and privatization of hospital cleaning and food services. (Saskatchewan New Democrats 2007, 21)

In regard to the Saskatchewan Party's plans for privatization, Calvert asked voters to help him "keep our Crown corporations publicly-owned, strong and innovative" (Saskatchewan New Democrats 2003, 13). In 2003, he announced:

> Now it's time for Elwin Hermanson and the Sask Party to come clean on their agenda for Saskatchewan's Crown corporations.
>
> Some Sask Party MLAs have said they would sell our Saskatchewan owned-and-operated corporations when they can get "the best bang for the buck" ...
>
> A fire sale of Crown corporations would generate short-term cash to compensate for the Sask Party's unsustainable tax cut promises. But it would do long-term damage to the quality services, reasonable rates and jobs those corporations provide for Saskatchewan people. Elwin Hermanson and the Sask Party would put the future of our Crown corporations – and our economy – at risk. (Ibid., 13, see also 36)

Through this type of rhetoric, Calvert continued his party's tradition of associating its own policies and programs with the security-based values embedded in Saskatchewan society and contrasting his party's vision with that of its "backward" right-wing opponent. In doing so, Calvert adapted the strategy employed by Tommy Douglas and Woodrow Lloyd: he labelled his chief rivals as admirers of the Alberta government. In one 2003 pamphlet, for instance, Calvert suggested that "Elwin Hermanson and the Sask Party just can't stop complaining about our province. They'll criticize just about everything in their drive to make Saskatchewan more like Alberta. Sask Party, Alberta Envy" (Saskatchewan NDP 2003b).

Borrowing a page from Romanow's playbook, in 2007 Calvert also attempted to link the new leader of the Saskatchewan Party with his former colleagues in the Devine government: "Brad Wall is not up to the challenge of leading our province. The last time we had a conservative government, they recklessly sold off Saskatchewan's assets and nearly bankrupted the province. Brad Wall worked for that reckless government. Brad Wall and the Sask Party share the same values of right-wing governments of the past. They want to cut government spending on services you rely on and they want to privatize Crowns" (Saskatchewan New Democrats 2007, 35).

Lastly, like both Blakeney and Romanow, Calvert attempted to connect the Saskatchewan Party to its federal relative, the Conservative Party of Canada. This link was made on the issue of environmental protection, in particular:

> Like their federal Conservative friends in Ottawa, the Sask Party doesn't take environmental protection seriously at all. Only a few short years ago, their MLAs were warning us that there wasn't really a "trend to global warming." Sask Party MLA Don Toth even went so far as to say that it was "one big hoax," and that if global warming was even happening, it was "nice to have a nice winter." If it comes to deciding to protect the environment in the face of pressure from large corporations that want to make more money faster, whose side will they be on? (Saskatchewan New Democrats 2007, 27)

Lorne Calvert's two campaigns as premier illustrated the power and persistence of the Saskatchewan code, but given his loss in 2007, the NDP leader's strategy also served notice that speaking in code is no guarantee of political success. (As is discussed elsewhere in this book, Calvert finds company in leaders such as Harry Strom, Don Getty, Woodrow Lloyd, Allan Blakeney, and Sidney Spivak.) The rise to power of his opponent, Brad Wall, coincided with a softening of the Saskatchewan Party's right-wing image (Blake 2008). When he assumed the leadership of the party after the 2003 election, Wall was faced with the challenge of growing the party beyond its rural base. To do so, the new leader acknowledged that, while the party's platform appealed to its traditional core constituency, "there were a few areas that Saskatchewan voters weren't quite comfortable with in the last election" (Saskatchewan Party 2004). Chief among these was the party's ambiguous stance on the privatization of Crown corporations. As part of the Saskatchewan Party's 2007 platform – *Securing the Future: New Ideas for Saskatchewan* – Wall committed to maintaining this element of Saskatchewan's strong state: "Keeping Saskatchewan's Crown corporations public and working for Saskatchewan people is an important part of the Saskatchewan Party's plan for Securing the Future" (Saskatchewan Party 2007, 29). These references to security placed Wall's rhetoric within the bounds of the Saskatchewan code. In this sense, employing the dominant discourse appears to have paid dividends for the new premier.

Conclusion

With uncanny similarities to earlier NDP defeats, Lorne Calvert's party relinquished power to a surging right-wing force after spending a decade rebuilding the province's sense of security. If history provides any lessons, Saskatchewan voters seem eager to support the CCF-NDP in bad economic times and right-wing parties in good. Ironically, the natural governing party's ability to turn around the Saskatchewan economy sows the seeds of its own demise. Regardless of his lack of success at the polls, Calvert did keep alive an age-old rhetorical tradition and, in the process, helped to carry Saskatchewan's political culture into the province's second full century. It remains to be seen whether his successor, Dwain Lingenfelter, will adapt the code to his advantage and continue the electoral cycle by returning the NDP to government.

Considering their shared emphasis on providing security for the people of Saskatchewan, there are more similarities between Saskatchewan's two historical governing parties than appears at first glance. Responding to the demands of farmers and Progressives, early Liberal leaders such as William Patterson constructed a series of Crown corporations to deal with electrification, telephones, and other public utilities, and they were active supporters of the co-operative movement, including the Saskatchewan Wheat Pool. The CCF-NDP has built on these institutional and rhetorical foundations, proffering its own vision of Saskatchewan's security. These visions, in turn, have varied from leader to leader, ranging from Douglas's Fabian-inspired plans for prosperity and Lloyd's "Progress with Purpose" to Blakeney's New Deals, Romanow's "Saskatchewan Way," and Calvert's way "Forward." All, however, have emphasized the state's role in preserving the Saskatchewan community against the threat of free-market liberalism, be it in the guise of the Liberals, the Conservatives, or the Saskatchewan Party. And all have continued to stress these values regardless of economic boom or bust. Together, three elements of dominant party rhetoric – collectivism, dirigisme, and polarization – have formed Saskatchewan's unique political code. Reiterated roughly every four years, these campaign themes have helped nourish the social democratic ethos engrained in the province's century-old political culture.

5

Campaigns in Manitoba
A Code of Moderation

Despite its easternmost position, Manitoba is the Prairies' political middle ground. Ideologically, its politics span the spectrum between right-tilting Alberta and left-leaning Saskatchewan, and its political culture is grounded in the values of modesty, temperance, accommodation, and conciliation. This ethos has roots in the late nineteenth century, when a combination of western liberal-progressivism and eastern conservatism made Manitoba a sort of ideological melting pot of Confederation. As with Alberta and Saskatchewan, the question remains, how have the values cultivated by Manitoba's founding settlers survived to this day? Why does Manitoba's ethos of modesty and temperance persist?

While distinct settlement patterns and transformative events have contributed to the development of Manitoba's political culture (see Chapter 1), and while socialization and institutionalization have helped to sustain it (see Chapter 2), the campaign rhetoric of its dominant parties has also played an influential role. At the height of their influence, each of Manitoba's three post-Depression governing parties – the Liberal-Progressives, the Progressive Conservatives, and the New Democrats – have epitomized the province's penchant for moderation. In the process, each has contributed to the development of a political code based on three core pillars. First, various leaders from John Bracken to Gary Doer have cultivated a sense that Manitoba politics is best contested in the progressive centre: a haven from the extremism of the Left and the Right and a middle ground where the prevailing paradigms of the broader Canadian and Western democratic communities hold sway. There are relatively few references to touchstone concepts such as security and freedom in Manitoba campaign platforms, for example. Instead, most dominant party leaders have emphasized the importance of progress – of moving neither left nor right but forward. Progress in Manitoba has meant forging ahead and keeping pace with national and international trends rather than leading the way (as in Alberta and Saskatchewan). Reflecting the sense of modesty embedded in the province's political culture, Manitoba leaders have focused on building a better Manitoba and comparing themselves to their predecessors rather than being the best among their contemporaries in other provincial governments.

Manitoba's dominant parties have also stressed the importance of finding pragmatic – cautious, prudent, rational, measured, non-idealistic, well-tested, incrementalist, business-like, frugal – solutions to the challenges confronting the province. These values derive, in part, from the province's roots in Toryism, with its emphasis on stability and the preservation of order, and in part from progressivism, with its proclivity for simple truths and good government. Combining these values, Manitoba's most successful leaders have asked voters to judge them on the soundness of their proposals and the competence of their management, as opposed to their boldness or charisma.

Some liken the Manitoba code to a form of politicophobia – fear of debating controversial issues, dividing the province, or losing elections (Taylor and Wiseman 1977, 176). Rather than confront these challenges, they suggest, Manitoba politicians simply leave them in abeyance, "whistling past the graveyard" of historical grievances (see Thomas 1997). Others view the approach as placing provincial interests above partisan ones. Either way, this form of stewardship has been practised by Manitoba's most successful premiers, beginning with John Norquay, who "believed that the government should represent not a party but a province, both to conciliate groups within it, and also to strengthen the province in negotiations with Ottawa" (Morton 1967a, 197).[1]

Ultimately, this goes some way in explaining why – with the notable exceptions of Ed Schreyer and Sterling Lyon – most of Manitoba's party leaders have been praised for their congeniality, as opposed to their charisma (see Dyck 1996, 385-86). They have been viewed as both reformist (adopting change when necessary and where popular) and conservationist (standing by established ends and means and relying on compromise and patience).

As Morton puts it, Manitoba leaders have tended to be "hard-headed, practical men who took life as they found it, were skeptical of reform and ... indifferent to idealism" (Morton 1967a, 335). Again, this places Manitoba in sharp contrast with Alberta and Saskatchewan, where leaders have been lauded for their personal magnetism and boldness, and where politics is closer to theatre.

Manitoba elites have also practised a noticeably transpartisan brand of politics during campaigns. With few notable exceptions, leading Manitoba politicians have sought to blur, and in some cases reach across, party lines, provincial boundaries, and levels of government in search of broad electoral coalitions. Leaders of Manitoba's most dominant parties have prided themselves on being brokers on the provincial and national stage, on embodying the values of conciliation and accommodation at the heart of the province's political culture. For example, a relatively high number of Manitoba politicians have made careers at both the federal and provincial levels. Although the following list is by no means exhaustive, prominent examples of level jumping among Manitoba politicians include Conservatives Joy Smith, Rick Borotsik, Vic Toews, and Duff Roblin; Liberals T.C. Norris, Stuart Garson, Jon Gerrard, Gils Molgat, Lloyd Axworthy, Sharon Carstairs, and Reg Alcock; and New Democrat Bill Blaikie. Others have not only crossed levels but also blurred party lines, most notably Progressive Conservative leader John Bracken, Liberal-appointed governor general Ed Schreyer, and Conservative-appointed ambassador to the United States, Gary Doer. Thus, more than their counterparts in the western Prairies, Manitoba elites have adopted a more fluid concept of partisanship.

This concept of partisanship does not, however, entail a complete abandonment or aversion to party competition: such sentiments would be labelled non-partisanship or anti-partisanship, respectively. Rather, the nature of partisanship in Manitoba suggests that dominant leaders have approached the topic with more flexibility – maligning their opponents on occasion but more often than not, and more frequently than elsewhere, seeking to transcend party differences by placing the provincial good above narrower interests. Theirs has been a distinctly transpartisan approach to political competition.

Progressive centrism, pragmatism, and transpartisanship – these three themes constitute Manitoba's code of political discourse. Each dominant party leader has interpreted these concepts somewhat differently – and several have spoken off script. Yet, through constant repetition of these values

FIGURE 5

Major iterations of the Manitoba code

	Progressive centrism	Pragmatism	Transpartisanship
Bracken	Anchor: classic liberalism	Managerialism	Coalition before party
Roblin	Anchor: province-building paradigm	"Balanced" development	Progress before party
Schreyer	Anchor: Keynesianism	Government planning	The people before party
Doer	Anchor: neoliberalism	The Third Way	Progress before party

over several generations, the most successful politicians in Manitoba's history have helped to sustain the province's modest and temperate political culture.

This chapter focuses on the three main iterations of Manitoba's code of political moderation: liberal-progressivism (defined by John Bracken), progressive conservatism (formulated by Duff Roblin), and new democracy (crafted by Ed Schreyer) (see Figure 5). The analysis begins with Brackenism – the middle-of-the-road ideology promoted by Manitoba's longest-serving premier. Like William Aberhart in Alberta and Tommy Douglas in Saskatchewan, Bracken's vision served as one of the formative articulations of the Manitoba code. Whereas Aberhart staked out the Right and Douglas the Left, Bracken defined the progressive centre as the fertile middle ground of Manitoba politics. He also avoided the anti-partisan and hyper-partisan rhetoric of his Prairie counterparts, pursuing a pragmatic political course. Bracken's successors, Stuart Garson and Douglas Campbell, reinforced this vision before ceding power to Duff Roblin's Progressive Conservatives in the late 1950s.

Yet, as transformative as it was, Roblin's arrival did not represent a comprehensive reinvention of the provincial code. Just as Peter Lougheed and Roy Romanow adapted their parties' ideologies to fit within the broad boundaries of their provincial discourses, shifting their codes in the process, so too did Roblin reshape progressive conservatism and moderation in Manitoba. When his successors – particularly Walter Weir and Sterling Lyon – pulled the Conservatives back to the Right, joining the Liberal-

Progressives on that side of the spectrum, room was left for a second adaptation of the progressive centre.

Since Ed Schreyer's rise to power in 1969, his party's brand of new democracy has served as the primary vehicle for Manitoba's modest, temperate political culture. From 1969 onward, Manitoba politics has featured a two-party-plus system, with the Progressive Conservatives and New Democrats alternating in power to the exclusion of the Liberal Party. Theirs is a recipe for political success (and failure) that dates back to the Bracken era: when any major party strays too far from the principles of progressive centrism, pragmatism, and transpartisanship, its opponents sit poised to assume the mantle of government and ownership of the provincial code.

Thus, the constant repetition of moderate campaign messages – beginning with Bracken, Roblin, and Schreyer, and continuing most recently with Gary Doer – has helped transmit Manitoba's culture of modesty, tolerance, conciliation, and accommodation over several generations. If the concept of freedom is key to understanding how political culture has been sustained in Alberta, and if security is the foundation of the Saskatchewan code, a code of moderation lies at the heart of Manitoba politics.

John Bracken, 1922-43

The Liberal-Progressives dominated Manitoba politics to a degree that no party has ever duplicated. Born as the United Farmers of Manitoba (UFM) and rechristened the Progressives in 1928, the party fused with the provincial Liberals in 1932. Thrust into a leadership role in its formative years, the party came of age in government, having been baptized by fire during the turbulent times of the 1930s and 1940s. Within decades, the Liberal-Progressives came to symbolize more than a political party or even a government. Not unlike Social Credit in Alberta, the Lib-Progs came to be synonymous with Manitoba politics. As was the case further west, after thirty-six years in government, the Liberal-Progressives defined the code of Manitoba politics. The bounds of acceptability were set around a modest role for the state, a humble vision of Manitoba's future, and a loose conception of partisanship.

As the party's first leader, John Bracken used what he referred to as the harsh realities of drought, depression, and war to craft a political discourse grounded in the cultural values of modesty and temperance inherited from the province's founding settlers. Brackenism, as it came to be called, reflected a conscientious effort to find the moderate middle between (1) Left and Right, (2) novelty and stability, and (3) old-line and anti-party politics in

Manitoba. Progressive centrism, pragmatism, and transpartisanship, in turn, constituted key pillars of the Manitoba code.

Between Left and Right

Bracken positioned his party in the middle of Manitoba's political spectrum by promoting liberal-progressivism as a centrist solution to the challenges of the inter- and postwar world. Bracken positioned the Labour Party and the Co-operative Commonwealth Federation (CCF) to his left and the Conservatives and Social Credit to his right. On the topic of social services, for example, the party

> tried in its policies to meet essential needs at a minimum cost. It takes the position that while neither prodigality nor extravagance can be tolerated, a basic minimum of service must be provided. The public must reach its own conclusion as to the wisdom of the Government's policies. In reaching it, however, it is respectively suggested, that there be kept in mind the fact that the Labor-C.C.F. group would increase these expenditures, while apparently the Conservative group would decrease them. It would thus seem that a *middle course* such as we have been following is in accordance with the view of the great majority of people. (Manitoba Liberal and Progressive Provincial Committee 1936, emphasis added)

Throughout his campaign literature during the Depression and the Second World War, Bracken cultivated this centrist position, offering Manitobans tried and tested mainstream solutions while positioning the Left and the Right as extremist in their approaches to the economic downturn and postwar reconstruction (Netherton 1992, 180). Bracken strode the line between the CCF on the Left, which came to dominate Saskatchewan, and Social Credit on the Right, which gained prominence in Alberta.

Bracken likewise maintained a laissez-faire approach to economic and social development amid the rumblings of province building elsewhere in Canada. In the process, Bracken resisted calls from the Left (the CCF) for a greater redistribution of wealth in society and calls from the Right (the Conservatives and Social Credit) to further curtail government spending. During the difficult times of the Second World War, he argued,

> It is obvious that under these conditions the mere distribution of wealth within the confines of this province will not make an adequate programme

possible. The wealth which we would seek to redistribute originates as products of the farm, the forests, the mines, the lakes and the workshop. If these products continue to be worth less than they cost our society to produce, our society will continue to be poor; and no amount of attempted redistribution of a wealth thus restricted will make the society prosperous, indeed the very class of society whose supposed wealth we might seek to redistribute will itself be poor. (Bracken 1940)

In hindsight, Brackenism may seem backwards, even harsh, in its response to the various crises confronting Manitoba in the second quarter of the twentieth century. Yet, compared with many other Canadian and Western democratic governments at the time, the Liberal-Progressives fit well within the global norm. The party may have lasted longer in power than most, thus carrying its 1920s principles through the 1950s, but its approach was by no means unorthodox. It became out of date, perhaps, but it was never radical.

Between Novelty and Stability

Bracken also tread the middle ground between conventional politics and the more radical brand that had gained acceptance elsewhere in the Canadian west. In this sense, Bracken straddled the line between stability and novelty, leaning slightly toward the former in projecting a modest, pragmatic vision for Manitoba's future.

Indeed, there was a heavy dose of modesty and realism in Bracken's frank assessment of Manitoba's economic problems in the late 1930s, just as there was a noticeable element of pragmatism in his approach to solving them. "Today we meet under vastly different circumstances from those of ten years ago or of five years ago," he wrote with humility in his party's 1932 manifesto.

Today the economic picture is wholly different from that of even three years ago. To use the words of [prime minister, R.B.] Bennett: "We are living in the most abnormal conditions under which people have ever lived ... We are in the midst of one of the most serious crises the world has ever known ... We are living in the most difficult days this country has ever experienced." With these conditions facing our people, the Government deems it its duty and its responsibility to say frankly to the electorate that the changed economic conditions, regardless of their cause, demand an adjustment, not only as to the character and extent of Government activities carried on and the incidence of the burden of their cost, but also as to the question of wider markets and, in addition the difficult and perplexing problems of debt adjustment. (Manitoba Liberal and Progressive Provincial Committee 1932)

This realism, again embedded in the province's self-effacing political culture, was especially evident in Bracken's evaluation of Manitoba's agricultural industry. As he wrote in his 1936 manifesto: "Agriculture has been in the past and is today, the chief basis of our material wealth. This industry, through no fault of its own, has been forced to retrench in recent years ... The simple truth is that agriculture as a wealth producer in Manitoba has been going backward in recent years ... Agriculture must be aided to regain its economic health, otherwise grass will soon grow on the streets of Winnipeg and the long line of unemployed will soon stretch to lengths heretofore never contemplated" (Manitoba Liberal and Progressive Provincial Committee 1936).

Bracken envisaged a modest future for Manitoba's economy, given these circumstances. In this sense, the premier promoted his party's pragmatism – its ability to make due with fewer resources, effectively muddling through by balancing efficiency with compassion. Responding to the Depression, for instance, Bracken said of his government: "In its administration of relief, while it has received less assistance from Ottawa by way of loans and grants than any other Western Province, it has received general commendation on its businesslike yet sympathetic handling of this most perplexing problem" (Manitoba Liberal and Progressive Provincial Committee 1936). Rather than projecting an idealistic future, Bracken depicted an idyllic one in which his government would provide stability – rather than outright prosperity – for Manitoba society. As Netherton (2001, 231, emphasis added) suggests, built into Bracken's vision "was the idea that the primary role of government was to provide *stability* while navigating turbulence and crisis. Like the last of the great windjammers, the idea was that the ship of the state would trim sails and batten down hatches when times got tough."

This concept of government, in turn, explains Bracken's repeated pledges to provide Manitobans with "sound, businesslike and economical administration of public affairs" (Manitoba Liberal and Progressive Provincial Committee 1936). This attachment to the principles of thrift and utilitarianism also fit well under the category of pragmatism. In this vein, Bracken considered most social programs (including health care), justice measures (including crime prevention), and labour legislation (including workplace safety and anti-strike laws) in terms of their utility to the whole of society:

> The production of material wealth is an essential function of society. But it ought not be the only economic aim of the people. It is as important to save what is produced as it is to produce more; and it is to society's advantage that human waste and loss of life, as well as material waste, be kept at the lowest possible minimum.
>
> It is estimated that the economic waste each year due to illness, accidents, fire, strikes, unnecessary bankruptcies and crime exceeds the present annual value of Manitoba's crops ...
>
> It is now clearly recognized by every well-organized society that a well-planned programme of prevention, prosecuted with energy by the Government and accepted generously by the public, goes a long way toward lessening these losses. Such a program has been in the process of development in Manitoba for many years. It is being extended more and more by the Government for the reason that in all these lines, prevention of disease, and accidents, and fire and other casualties and crime is far more economical to society than the cost of attempts to cure them after they have occurred. (Ibid.)

This rational approach to the provision of public services extended beyond preventative measures. Again positioning his government in the centre of the province's political spectrum, Bracken suggested,

> The cost of health, education and other public services, such as Mothers' Allowances, Child Welfare, Hospitalization, the care of the aged and the care of the mentally afflicted is a heavy one for the community. The cost of neglecting these services would, in direct ways, be much heavier upon the community. The question for the Government to decide is, where, in the best interest of the public, is the line that most closely approximates the minimum needs of the community for these services and the minimum cost of them to the community?
>
> The Manitoba Government now contributes $5,600,000.00 a year out of its $8,000,000.00 of controllable expenditures for these services. The Labor-C.C.F. political group says this is far too little, and they have severely censured the Government's program on this ground in recent years. The present Conservative party hints that these services cost too much, but

dares not face the public with specific proposals for reductions. (Manitoba Liberal and Progressive Provincial Committee 1936)

At the same time, Bracken portrayed his government's program as the sanest (that is, practical or sound) of all competing approaches available to Manitoba voters. On the topic of reinvigorating the provincial economy, for example, the premier argued that "taxes must be kept down to the lowest possible point; social experiments of an unsound or costly nature must be avoided; contracts must not be lightly broken; and the threat of communistic teachings must be answered by such an expression of confidence in a sane programme as will encourage legitimate enterprise to again accept its rightful place as an employer" (Manitoba Liberal and Progressive Provincial Committee 1936). Bracken effectively opposed socialism by characterizing it as untested and idealistic.

To establish the practicality of his own programs, Bracken continually referred to the economic and fiscal paradigms of his time and portrayed his policies as mainstream. Indeed, true to the province's Tory roots, Bracken was skeptical of straying too far from established norms when it came to addressing the Depression and postwar development. Indeed, if he was boastful at all, the Manitoba premier took pride in being the leader of western Canada's quintessentially liberal province. Following the tight-fisted fiscal paradigm of his times, for instance, Bracken's vision included maintaining the lowest taxes and "the lowest annual expenditure of any Western province" during the Depression (Manitoba Liberal and Progressive Provincial Committee 1936). In 1932, Bracken boasted that "Manitoba was the only province in Canada that reduced expenditures from year to year" (Manitoba Liberal and Progressive Provincial Committee 1932), a claim that marked a clear distinction between his fiscally orthodox approach and that of the Keynesian Conservatives or the socialist CCF.

At the same time, Bracken pursued a mainstream program of austerity to mitigate the effects of the agricultural and market crises of the 1920s and 1930s. In addition to drastic cuts in government expenditures and reductions in government services, Bracken raised taxes. Thus, at the height of the Depression, reductions in government spending were carried out "with the lowest cost to the people and least disturbance to essential services" (Liberals and Progressives [Manitoba] 1932), and direct relief was provided "at the lowest possible cost consistent with the maintenance of health" (Manitoba Liberal and Progressive Provincial Committee 1936).

Bracken also pursued a conventional, laissez-faire approach toward economic matters. Again, his philosophy fit well within the "passive neo-classical rentier-redistributive paradigm" of his time, placing him well within the centre of the Canadian political spectrum (Netherton 2001, 231). Bracken's Liberal-Progressives viewed freer trade as the solution to many of Manitoba's economic challenges, for the fundamental remedy for economic malaise lay in "wider markets to the products of our primary industries (agriculture, fisheries, forests and mines)" (Liberals and Progressives [Manitoba] 1932). At the same time, like Aberhart in Alberta, Bracken railed against the evils of both public and private monopolies, intervening in the market, when necessary, to ensure fairer competition. Doing so, he believed, would restore confidence in the capitalist system and bring about renewed prosperity in Manitoba (Manitoba Liberal and Progressive Provincial Committee 1936). As traditional as Canada's other governing parties when it came to fiscal and economic policy, the Liberal-Progressives' reputation as a stolid, classic liberal party is well deserved.

In contrast to the prevailing view in the literature, the Liberal-Progressives faced significant, if often muted, opposition throughout their time in office. Criticism ranged from suggestions that the party was moving too quickly to suggestions that it was moving too slowly to address the economic and so-cial problems confronting Manitoba society. Bracken responded by point-ing to his pragmatic, incrementalist middle course. Answering his critics in 1932, for instance, Bracken acknowledged that "five years ago the general criticism of the Government was that, while it was honest and reasonably efficient, it had done nothing – it had been a 'do nothing' Government – and it was the prevalent view that the times demanded development. The Gov-ernment at that time went to the people on a programme of development, development of our resources, development of our agriculture, develop-ment of our industries, development of our transportation routes. That pro-gramme too was carried out both economically and satisfactorily to the non-partisan mind" (Liberals and Progressives [Manitoba] 1932). As Bracken said of his government's progress after fourteen years in power, "the meas-ures presented have been many, they have been progressive in character without being radical and they have been carefully designed to meet the best interests of the Province as a whole" (Manitoba Liberal and Progressive Provincial Committee 1936).

Although he denigrated "social experiments of an unsound or costly na-ture," Bracken's pragmatic approach did not lead him to dismiss government enterprises out of hand (Manitoba Liberal and Progressive Provincial Committee 1936). "In this connection," he argued, "public ownership has its place and is to be encouraged whether it can serve the community better than private or co-operative enterprise" (ibid.). According to W.L. Morton (1967a, 435), whose father once served in Liberal-Progressive cabinets, "It was not that the principle of private enterprise had been replaced by that of socialism; neither extreme of doctrine entered into the matter. It was rather that government and people had formed a working partnership to conserve and develop the wealth of Manitoba's rugged natural heritage. That partnership was the result of the easy and intimate union of a democratic people with a government they made their own in outlook and manner." This balanced approach reflected Bracken's search for the pragmatic, progressive centre.

In sum, when putting his manifestos before the electorate, Bracken emphasized his party's pragmatic approach to politics, asking Manitobans to demonstrate their willingness "to solve their problems, not by the reactionary unconcern accepted in days gone by, nor yet by the radical and untried experiments of more recent times; but rather by means of studied progress, and a middle of the road programme, aimed to bring us something more of equity, something more of social justice and something more of progress than has been our lot in recent years" (Manitoba Liberal and Progressive Provincial Committee 1936).

Between Old-Line and Anti-Party Politics

Bracken also struck a balance between old-line approaches to Canadian party politics and the virulent anti-partisanship of the early-twentieth-century farmers' movements. The Manitoba premier's early commitment to businesslike government and fairer treatment for western Canadian producers conformed to the latter. Yet the tamer tenor of Bracken's appeals to the federal government and his willingness to co-operate with established political parties set him apart from his counterparts further west. This moderate, transpartisan tack helped Bracken appeal across party lines, at both the elite and grassroots levels – a critical task given the traditional eastern Canadian foundations of the early Manitoba party system.

The premier repeatedly promised Manitobans a "non-partisan business administration rather than a political one" (Liberals and Progressives [Manitoba] 1932). Indeed, Bracken's slogan for the 1927 campaign – "A Business (Not a Party) Government" – embodied this approach. So too did his establishment of "a Civil Service that is efficiently officered, free from partisanship, not over-staffed, and embued [sic] with the spirit of faithful service to the Province" (Manitoba Liberal and Progressive Provincial Committee 1936). According to the premier's philosophy on governance, "We are not here to play politics or to represent a single class, but to get down to the serious business of giving this province an efficient government, and in that task we will welcome all the cooperation offered to us from the opposite side of the House" (Morton 1967a, 384).

In response to the Depression, for instance, Bracken maintained his "belief that the first step towards the realization of improved conditions in Manitoba ought to be the abandonment of party warfare and the establishment of a Government which will represent as far as possible the unprejudiced, non-partisan thought of the Province ... We believe that this will do much to increase confidence, not only in the future of the Province and its institutions, but also in the probable efficiency of the Government and the effectiveness of its policies" (Manitoba Liberal and Progressive Provincial Committee 1932).

In many ways, Bracken's monopoly of Manitoba's progressive centre was facilitated by his flexible approach to partisanship. Over his two decades as premier, Bracken managed to fuse his own party to the Liberals, co-opt much of the Conservative Party, and create crisis coalitions during the Depression and the Second World War. Such manoeuvring allowed the government to cut a wide ideological path throughout much of the 1930s and 1940s, while sheltering the Liberal-Progressives from partisan attack. (Indeed, throughout the Liberal-Progressives' term in office, and under all three leaders, the party's name seldom appeared in campaign advertising. Rather, the party issued platforms almost exclusively on behalf of "the Coalition" or "the Government.") In this sense, the term *non-partisan* is somewhat of a misnomer. Bracken's transpartisanship was as much tactical as it was populist, reflecting his strategy to maintain power in a multi-party system during periods of intense political and economic crisis.

His flexible approach to partisanship and coalition building is revealed in a letter to CCF leader S.J. Farmer in October 1940 (Bracken 1940). On behalf of the Liberal-Progressive government, he pledged to

> invite members of all the other groups to unite in a non-partisan administration – an administration that will have the support of all Manitobans of all political faiths to support and advance in this time of war a programme in which, we can surely all agree ... We do so with the confidence that you ... do not in times like these believe in party first and the country last. We are

not today only C.C.F.-Labor or Liberal-Progressive or Conservative or Social Credit, but rather Canadians and democrats and freemen. Our cause, even Manitoba's cause, is at this time greater than your party or our own. (Ibid.)

Through appeals such as these to both elites and voters, Bracken maintained his non-partisan coalition in the face of the Depression and in the midst of the Second World War – key turning points in the evolution of party systems in Alberta and Saskatchewan, respectively. (There, such appeals to transpartisanship were decidedly out of code.) Moreover, that Bracken was able to contain not only the old-line Tory and Liberal parties but also Social Credit and the CCF within his various coalitions – all in the *same* government from 1940 to 1943 – is as much a testament to the power of the transpartisan narrative he had designed as to his skills as a tactician. The latter two parties had enjoyed great success in the western Prairie provinces, both electorally and in cultivating such distinct political codes. Bracken's own manoeuvring and powerful rhetoric created an environment that was not conducive to the ideological and partisan appeals of these two rivals.

Bracken's transpartisan approach also extended to federal-provincial relations, where he "consistently urged collective action" among all Canadian governments – of all partisan persuasions – to address the challenges of the Depression and postwar reconstruction (Manitoba Liberal and Progressive Provincial Committee 1936). In contrast to the more assertive and combative stances often assumed by his counterparts in Saskatchewan and Alberta, the Manitoba premier was willing to reach across party lines and provincial borders to find solutions for his constituents and Canadians as a whole. Consider his collaborative approach to resolving the fiscal imbalance between the federal and provincial governments in the 1930s: "With a view to effecting the most equitable distribution of taxation and to preventing overlapping, we shall seek, in co-operation with the Dominion and the other provinces, to determine and put into effect a more satisfactory delimitation of the fields of taxation as between the provinces, the municipalities and the Dominion" (Manitoba Liberal and Progressive Provincial Committee 1932).

Four years later, Bracken retained his conciliatory tone, offering to broker a compromise between the federal government and the provinces over the issue of social program funding. As Bracken described it, "Because of the relatively low income returns of certain of the provincial units, this weakness in our constitutional set-up should be corrected, by the Dominion assuming the responsibilities for more of the public services, either directly or by additional money grants, in preference to giving the Provinces wider powers of taxation and leaving them with their present heavy responsibilities for these services" (Manitoba Liberal and Progressive Provincial Committee 1936). Bracken notably referred to the situation as a weakness – not a fundamental flaw or injustice. This less provocative tone again differentiated the Manitoba premier from his counterparts elsewhere in western Canada. Perhaps because of this, his solution was eventually implemented, not only improving the relationship between Ottawa and the provinces but also easing horizontal tensions between the wealthier and not-so-wealthy members of Confederation.

Liberal-Progressivism after Bracken

Bracken's departure for the federal scene – to lead the newly named Progressive Conservatives – spelled the end of his wartime super-coalition. His decision to join the federal Tories was ironic and awkward, given his association with the provincial Liberals, but understandable, given his fluid conception of partisanship. In Bracken, who served from 1922 to 1943, "Manitoba had one of the longest-serving premiers in Canadian history ... This term was, in one respect, even longer than 21 years in that he also set the leadership style for years after his departure ... He is remembered for little but his style, since his initiatives were deliberately few, and his immediate successors left even less of a mark on the province" (Dyck 1996, 385). Stuart Garson and Douglas Campbell ran campaigns that drew on the same core principles and record. As a result, by the late 1950s, the Liberal-Progressives had cast a "grey pall of pragmatism" over Manitoba politics (Morton 1967a, 466). Brackenism had laid the foundation for Manitoba's political code of moderation – with its emphasis on progressive centrism, pragmatism, and transpartisanship – thus helping to sustain Manitoba's modest and temperate political culture through the turmoil of depression and war.

Although it matched the tenor of the 1930s and 1940s, this vision appeared increasingly out of step with national and global trends. An era of depression, drought, war, and other hard times gave way to a new period of optimism in Manitoba. Meanwhile, a new Keynesian paradigm had replaced the classic liberal mindset of the interwar years. Together, these forces decreased the demand for the pragmatic, prudent, administrative brand of government provided by the Liberal-Progressives and raised new questions about how best to facilitate, manage, and harness potential postwar growth. In the process, the "progressive" mantle passed to another Manitoba party.

Duff Roblin, 1958-67

Since its eclipse of liberal-progressivism in the 1960s, progressive conservatism has served as a second, if inconsistent, vehicle for Manitoba's modest
and temperate political culture. Its founder in Manitoba, Duff Roblin, presented the ideology as an avowedly sensible alternative to the decidedly un-
progressive brand of laissez-faire, non-partisan politics being practised in
Manitoba at the time. In the process, the Tory leader restaked the progressive centre along Keynesian lines, using Canada's broader province-building
spirit for support. And while maintaining a commitment to business-like
government, he re-injected a sense of competitiveness into Manitoba's
transpartisan political climate. This revamping helped sustain Manitoba's
political code (and political culture) through the most expansive period of
growth in the province's history.

On the surface, there are many parallels between the resurgence of the
Manitoba Progressive Conservatives in the late 1950s and the rise of the
Lougheed Tories in Alberta a decade later (see Chapter 3). These similarities
are more than coincidental. In designing his approach, Lougheed literally
borrowed a page from Duff Roblin's playbook, having travelled to Winnipeg
to discuss strategy with the Manitoba premier in the summer of 1964 (Pal
1992, 19-59; Roblin 1999, 212-13). Just as Roblin had attacked the Liberal-
Progressives for being a staid political force, Lougheed portrayed Harry
Strom's Social Credit as old and tired, as laissez-faire conservatism in a
rapidly changing world (Elton and Goddard 1979, 52). Yet, beyond broad
strategic and policy similarities, the two Progressive Conservative leaders
pursued different goals and employed different rhetoric in their rise to
power. In particular, the success of each leader was due, in part, to his ability
to adapt progressive conservatism to fit his unique provincial code. Whereas Lougheed emphasized the importance of enhancing Alberta's freedom
(that is, adding transparency to government, providing power to individuals, and attaining supremacy and autonomy on the national stage), Roblin's
message was far more modest and moderate. The Manitoba PC leader focused on redefining the progressive centre in his province; in the process, he
aimed to have Manitoba catch up to national standards in terms of economic growth and social services. All the while, Roblin promoted the importance of placing progress before party, eschewing what he saw as
political jockeying by his opponents. In these three ways, Roblin helped to
revamp the Manitoba code and rekindle the values of modesty and accommodation at the core of the province's political culture.

Redefining the Progressive Centre

Given the level of dominance attained by the Liberal-Progressives, Roblin's primary task was straightforward if challenging: to win power, he would need to capture the province's moderate middle ground. Considering the Lib-Progs' ideological monopoly in Manitoba politics, which they defined in laissez-faire terms, this would require redefining the progressive centre along an entirely new set of mainstream values. Drawing inspiration from the Keynesian, province-building paradigm of the time, Roblin portrayed the Liberal-Progressives as out of touch with the new realities of the post-war world. The global centre had shifted, and the Lib-Progs had failed to keep pace.

At the same time, by drawing his party to the middle of the political spectrum, Roblin effectively outflanked the CCF as Manitoba's most moderate, progressive alternative. According to Roblin (1999, 86), this amounted to a two-front strategy, fighting "one campaign against the Liberals on the right ... and in the country, and another campaign against the CCF on the left and in the city. We made the progressive centre our own."

On the first front, Roblin criticized the Campbell government's laissez-faire approach to government, posing his own brand of progressive conservatism as the only truly progressive alternative – the only means of keeping Manitoba moving ahead, let alone catching up with the rest of the postwar world. "The progressivism of the Liberal Government is a carefully nurtured myth," Roblin suggested while in opposition. "This is a do-nothing cannot-get-off-the-spot government. It is old and tired. It lacks ideas and initiative. It is the very opposite of progressive" (Progressive Conservative Party of Manitoba 1960). In newspaper advertisements during the 1958 provincial election campaign, Roblin argued that "36 Years is *too long* for Any Government" (Progressive Conservative Party of Manitoba 1958a). According to one ad, "After 36 years this tired *old* Government has lost its initiative ... After 36 years this tired *old* Government has lost its prudence ... After 36 years this tired *old* Government has lost its efficiency ... After 36 years this tired *old* Government has lost the confidence of the people" (ibid.).

The PC leader's conscientious choice to exclude the term *progressive* when referring to Campbell's Liberal Party reflected this rhetorical strategy. By doing so, Roblin avoided debates between the Left and Right that were taking place in Alberta and Saskatchewan at the time. Instead, true to the progressive elements of the Manitoba code, he turned the election into a question of how much change should take place and how quickly the government should act. "For over a generation," Roblin contended in a 1962 campaign pamphlet,

> the attitude of the Government in Manitoba consisted basically of minding the store, of doing the essential minimum. The Manitoba Progressive Conservative Party, under my leadership, argued that this was not enough – that many people in Manitoba were not being given equality of opportunity: some were being denied the opportunity for education, some lacked needed medical and health care, some were being denied understanding treatment in detention institutions in the province, many were suffering indirectly through a lack of government initiative. In 1958 we promised a fuller measure of equality of social opportunity for the people in Manitoba. (Manitoba Progressive Conservative Association 1962)

In a separate advertisement, he asked voters,

> Could there be any greater difference or contrast between the Government's attitude and our program? Our program would encourage enterprise and initiative, not curb it. Our program calls for action, not inertia. I give you this solemn pledge – Manitobans need not wait one extra day for action should it elect a Conservative Government on Monday ... Why wait another day or another year? We will start now. We will establish our farm credit policy now – spell out in legislation our farm program so that we can stop this drift and indecision. Why wait for next year ... If we are to assess the true needs of a twentieth century roads program, we must begin now. We have no intentions of waiting ... I believe the rising generations of younger Manitobans want to see a government that reflects their own spirit of initiative and their own dissatisfaction with things the way they are. I look to them for support on Monday, just as I look to every Manitoban who is willing to admit that we cannot afford another five years of drift and inertia. Let this be the last week of the long-continuing reign of what Professor Morton called "negative democracy." Let Monday be the first day of the new beginning, the start of the great task of reconstruction and development.
>
> My hope is that our party today reflects the mood and spirit of Manitoba today. It is in that spirit that I ask for the support of everyone of you – at the polls and thereafter. A partnership of the people and their government in the noble task of building a greater, more prosperous province ...

The next step forward is a Roblin Government! (Progressive Conservative Party of Manitoba 1958b)

Moreover, according to Roblin, progressive conservatism was required to keep pace with the postwar growth taking place elsewhere in Canada. These sentiments were reflected in his "Open Letter to All Manitobans," published in the *Winnipeg Free Press* days before the 1958 vote: "I believe a clear majority of our people in the Country and City alike earnestly desire a new Provincial government. We are tired of a lack-lustre and do-nothing administration, 36 years old, clearly failing to keep up with Canadian progress. We urgently need to make up for lost time. Government and people must work together to build a better Manitoba. The Progressive Conservative Party has the means by which you can make the changes you desire, but your active co-operation is essential" (Progressive Conservative Party of Manitoba 1958c). Thus, like Douglas in Saskatchewan and Lougheed in Alberta, Roblin promoted a more active approach to governance than his predecessors. He did so for different reasons than the leaders of Saskatchewan and Alberta, however. While Douglas saw government intervention as a means to secure social justice and Lougheed viewed it as a means to strengthen Alberta's autonomy, Roblin saw the growth of the Manitoba state as a means of maintaining (or regaining) Manitoba's middling position in Confederation.

Roblin continued this progressive rhetoric once in government, repeatedly comparing his brief record of action to decades of procrastination by his predecessors. "We believe the achievements of the Special Session just six months ago – which your endorsement and support made possible – represent the kind of progressive and positive action that Manitobans want from their provincial government," he argued during the 1959 campaign (Progressive Conservative Party of Manitoba 1959a).

Three years later, Roblin contended,

Every corner of Manitoba has been affected by the new drive and growth in the province. Manitoba is no longer a let's-wait-and-see-and-then-do-nothing province. In northern development, education, medicare and social programmes, highways, farm policies, industrial activity and employment Manitoba is pacing the nation. *This clearly was not true when the Roblin Government was elected in 1958 but it's true today.*

Said Professor Murray Donnelly ... "Roblin has utterly altered the philosophy of Government in Manitoba. He is undoubtedly the most outstanding premier in the history of the province."

The reason he is outstanding is that he repudiated the do-nothing philosophy of Government in our province. With a Roblin Government it's *Manitoba on the march.* (Progressive Conservative Party of Manitoba 1962c)

Roblin's position on agriculture provides one illustration of his active approach to government. In 1959, the new premier contended,

> *The Roblin Government did more in ten months to deal with the real problems of farmers than the previous administration had done in ten years.*
>
> The Roblin Government accepted as a basic part of its farm philosophy that the pricing of farm products fell within the jurisdiction of the Government of Canada. No province can undertake such programs as price supports, deficiency payments and international commodity agreements.
>
> But, unlike the Campbell Government, the Roblin Government did *not* say, "There is nothing a provincial Government can do," and did not attempt to conceal a do-nothing program with a "Letter-to-Ottawa" campaign. The Roblin Government moved promptly and effectively to attack the cost side of the cost-price squeeze that is damaging farm income prospects ... *In ten months they set up the farm credit provisions that have been lacking in Manitoba for decades. THEY BELIEVE IN ACTION IN GOVERNMENT.* (Progressive Conservative Party of Manitoba 1959b)

Yet, as the Conservative premier argued, "Nothing could more sharply outline the difference in the approach of the Roblin and Campbell Governments to the problems confronting the administration in Manitoba than the records of the two Governments on the question of flood control":

> From the time of the flood in 1950 the Campbell Government had eight years in which to protect the people in the valleys of the Red and Assiniboine Rivers. The Roblin Government had had ten months. And yet by the end of those ten months of Roblin Governmentworks will be in under [sic] construction that will protect the homes and farms and industries in the Red River and Assiniboine River valleys against a flood *60% greater than the flood of 1950 ...*
>
> All the procrastination in the world will do nothing to reduce the threat that constantly hangs over those that live in the valleys of these rivers. The threat can only be reduced through *action.* (Progressive Conservative Party of Manitoba 1959b)

There were signs of immodesty in Roblin's rhetoric, to be certain. At times, his statements were far bolder and optimistic than Manitoba's code of moderation or culture of modesty prescribed. Take the following 1958 campaign advertisement:

Wake up Manitoba!

It's long past time for Manitoba to shake off its "poorer Province" complex. Backed by a vast storehouse of natural resources and a strong virile people ready and eager to share in its development, Manitoba needs the courageous, imaginative leadership and initiative of a new vigorous Government. With *your* help and support on June 16, Manitoba can acquire that type of Government. Regardless of your former political affiliations now is the time to Support – *Duff Roblin* and his *Progressive Conservative* Team. (Progressive Conservative Party of Manitoba 1958a)

On the topic of economic development, in particular, Roblin's "Talking Points" for PC candidates suggested that Manitoba had the potential to be one of Canada's strongest performers:

Manitoba people have the enterprise, the imagination, the vigor and the re-
sources to lead the nation in development. They require only government
leadership and co-operation.
    The Progressive Conservative Party spurns the implication that Manitoba must follow behind the other provinces of Canada in terms of growth. They believe that the province has the people and the resources for increased growth, development, expansion and to create a greater province ... The Progressive Conservative Party rejects the attitude of the Campbell Government that Manitoba must stand still while other provinces develop and expand. (Progressive Conservative Party of Manitoba 1958d)

Statements such as these suggest that Roblin's ground war against the Liberal-Progressives was far less conciliatory than the broader campaign he waged through public speeches, published pamphlets, and newspaper advertisements.

Even in these statements, however, Roblin did show signs of being more modest than first appearances suggest. Despite the bravado, for instance, Roblin's overall approach was motivated less by boosterism than it was by his desire to have Manitoba catch up to the rest of the postwar world. His immediate objective was to bring Manitoba's programs and infrastructure up to date, helping them to reach Canadian and twentieth-century standards after having fallen behind under the "penny wise dollar foolish" philosophy of Liberal-Progressive governance (Progressive Conservative Party of Manitoba 1958d). In reference to his economic development goals, for instance, Roblin aimed to ensure that "Manitoba continues to enjoy a sustained rate of economic growth *in keeping with the rest of the continent*" (Progressive Conservative Party of Manitoba 1966c, emphasis added).

This mantra is illustrated in the Preface of the party's 1962 platform:

> During the past four and a half years, substantial progress has been made in bringing Manitoba *up-to-date* in the fields of education, welfare and other social policies; great investments have been made in roads, hospitals, old folks' homes, parks and other needed facilities, while at the same time the economy of the province has been broadened and strengthened. In the four years ahead, emphasis should be placed on *continuing our progress* in building the economy of Manitoba. The challenge facing both the people and their government is the job of providing full employment in a free society, making the maximum use of both our human and natural resources, and of *improving Manitoba's position* in the increasingly competitive trading world now opening up before us. Progress along these lines will provide benefits in which all our people can share and will be the basis for new improvements in education, welfare and other important government services to the people. (Progressive Conservative Party of Manitoba 1962b, emphasis added)

Indeed, Roblin's statement that he hoped to create a "Greater Manitoba" was apt, for it avoided the superlatives that characterized campaigns in other parts of the Prairies. According to a confidential internal document dated November 1960, the Roblin government viewed its goal as bringing necessary change to the province to place Manitoba near – but not necessarily at – the top of Confederation:

> On June 16, 1958, the people of this Province voted for the Progressive Conservative Party led by Duff Roblin and the new Manitoba programme ...
>
> Duff Roblin's Progressive Conservatives promised the people of Manitoba that a Roblin Government would provide the leadership and policies necessary to give a *needed* thrust to the economic growth of this province,

to provide *good* education for our children, to provide *needed* social welfare programs, to "provide *20th century* roads in the 20th century."

Roblin promised that Manitoba would *aim to stand high among the provinces of Canada in terms of growth and pride*. He promised that the resources and talents of Government and people would join to build a *richer, prouder province* and a *wealthier* and *more vigorous* economy. (Progressive Conservative Party of Manitoba 1960, emphasis added)

Through rhetoric such as this, Roblin sought to ensure that Manitoba "compares *favourably* with other Canadian provinces" (Progressive Conservative Party of Manitoba 1966c, emphasis added). He considered it his role as premier to inspire "a new spirit of confidence in the people of Manitoba" (ibid.).

These were modest aims compared to appeals being made at the time by Ernest Manning and Tommy Douglas. To the west, these premiers were asking voters to keep their respective provinces in the lead (see Chapters 3 and 4). Reflecting the humility embedded in Manitoba's political culture and the moderation in its code, Roblin sought to provide Manitobans with a "prouder and richer province," "*a greater and more prosperous Manitoba*," while minimizing references to being the best of all worlds (Progressive Conservative Party of Manitoba 1962a; 1959b, emphasis in original). Indeed, compared to the relatively jingoistic rhetoric in Alberta and Saskatchewan, Roblin's message was focused on keeping Manitoba moving ahead on its own separate track. In this sense, Roblin was more likely to compare his own record with those of his predecessors than those of his contemporaries. There was some interprovincial comparison, to be certain, yet Roblin remained focused predominantly on building a better Manitoba. These tendencies are evident in a 1962 pamphlet:

> The last four years have seen more action in Manitoba than ever before in our history. Agriculture is at a new peak; industry is expanding; educational opportunities have been expanded; the sick and needy are better cared for; good roads stretch out to all parts of the province and electrical power is being increased. On all fronts there is movement forward.
>
> And still Manitoba has the lowest provincial tax structure in Canada, along with oil-rich Alberta.
>
> The Progressive Conservative Government under Duff Roblin's leadership has challenged the initiative, talents and industry of all Manitobans.

Our province is moving ahead more than ever before ... These results
can only be achieved by hard work. This is the secret to success ... the government and the people working as partners for progress. (Progressive
Conservative Party of Manitoba 1962a)

If Roblin's early campaigns were spent trying to pry loose Campbell's grip
on the term *progressive* by touting his record of "getting things done" (Progressive Conservative Party of Manitoba 1962a), he spent much of the 1960s
trying to retain his own grip on the term amid attacks from the CCF-NDP
on the Left. On this second campaign front, Roblin admits that his party's
red tory "Program for Progress" drew heavily on the philosophy and policies
of the province's Left (Roblin 1999, 77-79).[2] Netherton (1992, 184) sheds
light on this struggle as it unfolded between election campaigns: "Since the
Keynesian modernization paradigm of the Roblin government represented
the same patterns of state intervention advocated by the CCFNDP, there
appeared to be no fundamental paradigmatic divisions between them." Roblin's positioning helped the Tories outmanoeuvre the CCF in several ways.
By accepting many of their platform planks, including the introduction of
hospital insurance and old-age pensions, he stole much of their policy space.
At the same time, Roblin's posturing removed the ability of the CCF to
portray the Liberals and Conservatives as one and the same. Ultimately,
Roblin's rhetoric proved so popular among the electorate that, as opposition leader Gildas Molgat put it, the Liberals found it "difficult to be more
liberal than Roblin" (Lang 1991, 43). The CCF-NDP, meanwhile, could only
offer its tacit compliance.

Indeed, the PC and CCF's shared vision of a more active provincial government helped forge an informal arrangement that kept Roblin's minority
government in power from 1958 to 1959.[3] Thereafter, following the Tories
first majority government in forty-four years, this overlap helped keep the
CCF out of government until 1969, when Edward Schreyer's New Democrats drew on similar principles in their rise to power.

In the meantime, Roblin developed the modern Manitoba welfare state
on the maxim that "we are our brother's keeper," blending principles of collectivism and expansion with elements of paternalism and fiscal responsibility (Progressive Conservative Party of Manitoba 1959a). This balance
was a key part of his effort to redefine the province's progressive centre. In
this vein, Roblin grounded his government's policy on social security, *"not
only on the basis of humaneness, decency and social obligation ... but also on*

the basis that it's an investment in the economical way of helping people to help themselves" (ibid.) Furthermore, in 1966 Roblin suggested,

> While this Government believes that many positive steps through education, labour mobility and in many other ways must be taken to encourage and assist all members of society to participate actively in productive areas of endeavour it also recognizes that there are some, the widows, the disabled, the aged and the inadequate [sic] who require assistance.
>
> In the complex mid-twentieth century environment in which we live, this assistance must be provided by the state. (Progressive Conservative Party of Manitoba 1966c)

This philosophy guided Roblin's approach to the Manitoba health care system. "No modern and moral community can deny to those of its people who are ill the best of medical attention and the best of hospital accommodation," he stated in 1962. "The Roblin Government, when it took office in 1958, accepted this as a fundamental right of the people and undertook to provide the accommodation" (Manitoba Progressive Conservative Association 1962). In so doing, Roblin resisted Alberta premier Ernest Manning's calls for an entirely private health service and the Saskatchewan premier Tommy Douglas's implementation of a universal health care system. Instead, Roblin chose a middling course, preferring to implement a provincial model based on accessibility and need as opposed to means or entitlement. As late as the 1966 election, Roblin advocated a "voluntary, universally available ... medical services insurance plan" (Progressive Conservative Party of Manitoba 1966b). It was only after the federal government encouraged a nationwide program that Roblin relented to pressures for a compulsory plan. After adapting the Blue Cross system, by paying the premiums of those Manitobans unable to do so, Roblin reluctantly accepted Lester Pearson's health care plan in 1966. Like Manning in Alberta, Roblin was persuaded to join when faced with the prospect of sending Manitobans' tax dollars to Ottawa without receiving benefits (Roblin 1999, 150-73). Roblin portrayed himself as the champion of the progressive centre – defender of both social programs and fiscal responsibility.

Roblin continued to outflank parties on both the Left (the CCF) and the Right (the Liberal-Progressives) as "the appeal of his reform policies" continued to gather steam (Dyck 1996, 404). As Roblin said in an interview during the 1962 campaign, "We've made mistakes. That's part of getting things done. Liberals say we go too fast, the NDP say we go too slow. When you have criticism on both sides like that, it is likely the province is getting good government" (Shilliday 1962). John Bracken made an almost identical reference with regard to his party's placement between the Conservatives and the CCF. In this vein, the premier's agenda matched those of provincial governments across Canada. Roblin's province-building strategy had a distinctly Manitoban flavour, however. Built on the middle ground between the social democratic program pursued by the CCF in Saskatchewan and the free-enterprise approach of Alberta's Social Credit, Roblin's philosophy was uniquely progressive conservative. Indeed, Roblin's success relied more upon this political dexterity as on any other factor. Through it, he conveyed "an image of being pragmatic, competent, efficient, and 'non-ideological' in character. Composed of both reform and conservative elements, the Roblin government moved back and forth, from right to left and back again, as necessary, to outmaneuver its parliamentary opponents" (Wiseman 1983, 107).

Ultimately, Roblin's approach was the epitome of moderation, for he sought to balance the virtues of the Right and Left while focusing debate on incremental change rather than stolid inertia. In the PC leader's own words,

> As a conservative, I found it natural to accept and build on the goodly inheritance of the past. As a progressive, I found it natural to seek out the promising opportunities of the coming day and to align both old and new with the welfare of the community. There was no preconceived dogma to restrict us. Tradition was respected while practicality and pragmatism were guidelines to public utility, all within the bounds of a robust respect for civility and the human equation ... [We] could tell the electorate what we wanted to do and why we wanted to do it and how the public interest would be served. The vacuum was filled and the progressive-conservative centre was our own. (Roblin 1999, 78)

"Getting Things Done"

In addition to championing the progressive cause, Roblin also attempted to usurp the title of Manitoba's most pragmatic party. In this vein, he emphasized his government's capacity to provide better government than his opponents. Highlighting its sensibility and reliability, for instance, Roblin touted his 1959 platform as "a *sound,* progressive program to make the most of Manitoba's human and economic resources" (Progressive Conservative Party of Manitoba 1959a, emphasis added). "In the new Manitoba of today, with its growing, expanding economy," Roblin suggested, "this progressive program is well within the *means and competence of sound and business-like government"* (ibid., emphasis added).

This business-like method was applied to issues such as housing, health care, welfare, and child protection. Roblin once argued (through his minister of health and public welfare, George Johnson): "As a Government we decided that the basic social security of Manitobans had to be underlined and underpinned. We want to make sure that everyone in need has that need met and we want to see that our method of meeting needs is *business-like, efficient, well organized and coordinated"* (Progressive Conservative Party of Manitoba 1959b, emphasis added).

Roblin's health care strategy reflected this co-ordinated approach. Unlike Tommy Douglas, who viewed the issue in terms of social security (see Chapter 4), or Ernest Manning, who framed it in terms of personal freedoms (see Chapter 5), the PC premier saw medicare as fulfilling both social *and* economic goals. For this reason, in his various platforms, Roblin placed advancements in health care under "investment in human resources" (Progressive Conservative Party of Manitoba 1962c). Consider the following statement, from his 1962 "Talking Points":

Health is fundamental to the well being of the community. No prosperous and modern community such as Manitoba can justify policies that fail to guard the health of the public ...

Investment in health is paying off in the reduced sickness of Manitobans. Over the four years of Roblin Government, the province's investment in health has more than doubled. As a consequence of it many people are now engaged in productive work who otherwise would be in hospitals and institutions ...

For any community good health is good business. The Roblin Government, recognizing this as well as the human values involved, has invested heavily in the health of the people of the province. (Ibid.)

Like the Liberal-Progressives before him, Roblin's pragmatic, business-like approach involved a heavy emphasis on fiscal responsibility and prudence. As he stated in 1962,

Sound finance is essential to sound Government. Responsible and prudent financial management can contribute in a positive and active way to providing the climate for growth and for development.

Investment in economic growth and in human betterment and welfare are prime essentials to the building of a strong economy and a happy community. But this investment must be responsible, it must be prudent. In Manitoba, under the Roblin Government, it has been both prudent and responsible ...

[As evidence, the] Roblin Government has never presented an unbalanced budget. Every year the provincial treasurer has not only balanced the budget but has carried substantial surpluses forward. Each year has ended in Manitoba being in a financially sound position ...

[Moreover,] Manitoba shares with oil-rich Alberta the distinction of having the lowest provincial tax structure. Provincial government spending per person in Manitoba, at $147.50, compared with $170 in Saskatchewan, $175 in Ontario, $204 in Alberta and $212 in British Columbia, is the second lowest in the nation.

Those people who say that the Roblin Government is a big spending government are distorting the facts. It is a low tax level, business like government. (Progressive Conservative Party of Manitoba 1962c)

Roblin also took a pragmatic, balanced approach to what he called human betterment and economic growth. "While recognizing the development of human resource as the most important task of government," according to the party's 1966 platform, "Mr. Roblin and his team ... also recognized the need for economic development" (Progressive Conservative Party of Manitoba 1966c). To accomplish his economic aims, the premier promised "a government of action" – one "resolved to borrow against future development to meet present needs" (Morton 1967a, 485). *"The financial programmes of the Roblin Government have got Manitoba on the March,"* he claimed in 1962. *"They are using money as an instrument for growth, for expansion and for the creation of a richer, more prosperous and a greater Manitoba"* (Progressive Conservative Party of Manitoba 1962c).

Even though it involved high levels of public investment and government planning at each stage, Roblin's economic development strategy was measured and incrementalist. Recounting his party's achievements in 1966, for instance, the premier remarked, "The Roblin Government has built Manitoba into a strong industrial province. The Government has clearly stated policies to add to this growth and development and to assure [sic] that, year by year, Manitoba achieves new levels of industrial and commercial activity" (Progressive Conservative Party of Manitoba 1966c). Roblin's pragmatic economic vision also reflected the mantra of moderation in Manitoba's code and the spirit of conciliation entrenched in the province's political culture.

This sentiment was reflected in Roblin's promise to establish a "Manitoba Economic Consultative Board," which would be

> made up from representatives of labour, agriculture, industry, finance, university and government. This body will be charged with the task of establishing broad targets for *sound growth* and industrial productivity with the aim of securing the *voluntary co-operation and co-ordination* of the main sectors of our economy to the end that we achieve a high rate of economic growth from which all may benefit. This board will be based upon the experience of the Committee on Manitoba's Economic Future and will help bring about a *united and cohesive effort* involving all vital sectors of the community. (Progressive Conservative Party of Manitoba 1962b, emphasis added)

Similarly, Roblin took a pragmatic approach toward the issue of public versus private ownership, offering to pursue either route, depending on the context. As he stated in his 1959 campaign manual:

> The Roblin Government favours individual initiative in the general fields of industry and commerce, but believes that the provincial administration can co-operate with private business in the best interest of all the people of Manitoba and of the business community. While avoiding direct competition in areas that can be more effectively handled by private enterprise, a Roblin Government will always be alert for techniques by which it can be of positive assistance and can raise levels of productive output and standards of living to make a greater and more prosperous Manitoba. (Progressive Conservative Party of Manitoba 1959b)

Again, this pragmatism differed from those courses charted by Roblin's counterparts in Alberta and Saskatchewan.

Overall, throughout each of his campaigns, Roblin emphasized his party's "proud record of 'Getting Things Done'" (Progressive Conservative Party of Manitoba 1962a) and his personal ability to provide skilled stewardship. Referring to its platforms, "The Roblin government [was] proud to remind voters and opposition alike of the promises made. They were *sober, serious* promises designed to build a greater Manitoba. They have been kept" (Progressive Conservative Party of Manitoba 1960, emphasis added). As stated in his final campaign platform, in 1966:

Leadership is vital to good government. In Duff Roblin, Manitoba has one of Canada's most able and dynamic political leaders. At issue in this election is the issue of leadership.

With a record of unequalled achievement, with a clear, progressive plan for the future, and with a hard-working, harmonious team, Manitobans have good reason for their confidence in the leadership of Premier Duff Roblin. Good government gets things done – and there is more to come if Manitoba is to march with the times and realize the full promise of its future. (Progressive Conservative Party of Manitoba 1966a)

"Progress before Party"

Roblin also took a decidedly flexible approach to partisanship, highlighting the differences between his own Progressive Conservatives and their opponents while labelling the latter as overly zealous in their political attacks on his government. Like John Bracken, the PC premier portrayed himself as a man who placed the interests of his province ahead of the interests of his party. This sense of transpartisanship should not be confused with the nominally non-partisan approach of the Liberal-Progressives. Unlike Bracken and his successors, Roblin firmly believed in the value of party politics. Indeed, as the grandson of the Tories' most recent premier at the time, Rodmond Roblin, Duff's rise to power represented the "resurrection of the old party politics rejected between 1915 and 1922" (Morton 1967a, 483). "In our system of representative parliamentary government," the younger Roblin later wrote, "it is through political parties that the public is offered a choice of policies and personalities ... Parties are a necessary part of the mechanism in our style of political democracy" (Roblin 1999, 66). From this perspective, Roblin (ibid., 52) considered the Liberal-Progressive era to be a closed system in which Brackenites of all partisan stripes colluded to keep incumbents in office. As Roblin put it, "All the features of the traditional parliamentary system – the clash of ideas, debates about policy, vigorous criticism, sustained review of government record – were sadly curtailed. With the government's position so strong, the opposition was muted. Thus, there was a stately maintenance of things as they were, or at best a glacial response to changing times" (ibid.).

Yet, true to the Manitoba code, Roblin subscribed to a looser conception of partisanship than his words suggest. A supporter of party politics in general but averse to blind partisanship, he was not afraid to reach across party lines in search of support or policy. For instance, Roblin ran as an anti-coalition Independent in 1949, citing a desire to "return to a normal democratic party parliamentary system" (Roblin 1999, 77). In this, Roblin was equally critical of his own party, whose campaign message he characterized as "we're not the government. Vote for us" (ibid., 61). Early in his legislative career, Roblin seconded motions by Communist MLA Bill Kardash, not because he agreed with the Labour leader on policy, but because he wanted to air the debate (ibid., 56).

Bereft of his party's base after years in opposition and coalition, the Tory leader was, in many ways, forced to take a flexible approach to partisanship. When Roblin assumed control of the Progressive Conservatives following the 1954 leadership race, the party was moribund in many constituencies, had little to no campaign funds, and had a shaky policy apparatus (Roblin 1999, 67-68). Following almost a decade in coalition, Roblin found that "in some ridings, only the old-timers had ever had an opportunity to vote for a Progressive Conservative candidate. In one area, wiseacres advised me to visit the graveyard because there I would find the only known Progressive Conservative supporters" (ibid., 69). Fortunately for Roblin, the Liberal-Progressives were at the same level of organizational disarray. Years spent in coalition and decades in power had eroded much of the constituency-level apparatus that had helped carry the United Farmers to power three decades earlier (Lang 1991, 22). Roblin began rebuilding the Conservatives through a series of intensive visitations – tours of the province in which he not only reached out to known Conservative supporters but also "started looking for good people and worrying about their politics later" (Roblin 1999, 69). His success recruiting candidates and supporters was largely attributable to his transpartisan approach and his moderate, progressive message.

During campaigns, however, Roblin conveyed a more virulently partisan attitude. Certain statements – particularly those included in his party's confidential "Talking Points for PC Speakers and Workers" (Progressive Conservative Party of Manitoba 1958d, 1959b, 1962c, 1966c) – were far more partisan than the Manitoba code suggests. They include pointed criticisms of the Liberal-Progressives, including charges of "incompetence, waste, inefficiency, lack of imagination and lack of vitality. The Campbell Government should be retired. It is time for a change to a Progressive Conservative Government. *It is definitely time for a change!*" (Progressive Conservative Party of Manitoba 1958d).

What is more, a year later, Roblin's framing of the 1959 election call reflected a more aggressive approach than would be expected under the

Manitoba code. In response to the defeat of his minority government, Roblin argued that his opponents "refused to *let us get on with the business of
Manitoba.*" In a tone that lacked any sense of conciliation,

> Said Premier Roblin: "The Opposition does not approve of our program.
> We're going to find out if the people do."
>   *A minority government cannot effectively govern the province of Mani-
> toba. The Conservative Party recognizes that a vigorous opposition is essen-
> tial to democratic government but, equally, a government must have a
> majority to get on with the business of the province.* (Progressive Conserva-
> tive Party of Manitoba 1959b)

In short, citing the hyper-partisanship of his opponents, Roblin asked voters
for a "*working* majority in the Manitoba Legislature" (ibid.).

There is no disputing the partisan quality of this rhetoric. Dominant
leaders in Saskatchewan were levelling similar attacks on their opposition
parties (see Chapter 4). However, the *trans*partisan nature of Roblin's critiques – his reference to the importance of placing province before party –
helped to distinguish him from his counterparts elsewhere on the Prairies.
For instance, even in criticizing his opponents during the 1959 elections,
Roblin was careful to cite their unwillingness to co-operate with his government as their principal shortcoming. "We ask that you give your support to
our new program – the measures which were delayed with the defeat of
the government by both Opposition Parties in the spring session this year,"
he wrote in campaign literature in 1959. "We believe our program reflects
the progressive spirit of the people of Manitoba. We ask for your consideration and support of these measures ... Given a majority, you have our pledge
that these further measures shall be put into effect. We stand ready and willing to get on with the business of Manitoba" (Progressive Conservative
Party of Manitoba 1959a).

In particular, he chastised Campbell for introducing an amendment to
the 1959 budget speech, which he "could not and would not support," urging
voters to see his government's defeat from a victim's perspective:

> Obviously the gentlemen on the other side have no confidence in our good
> faith ... If that is the way they feel then I think they should vote for this
> amendment and no budget speech will be held and we can take the issue to
> the people ...

Premier Roblin made a definite pledge that the budget debate would proceed in the normal way.

The Liberals and the CCF insisted that Premier Roblin hand over control of the legislature to them, or they would not co-operate. This he could not do and this he would not do.

In their bid to seize effective control of the legislature – a parallel to Hon. L.B. Pearson's motion in the short parliament that Mr. Diefenbaker should resign and let him take over – the Opposition parties defeated the Government.

The defeat of the Government took place in four clearly defined steps:

1 Premier Roblin warned the leader of the Opposition, Mr. Campbell, that the amendment was a vote of confidence.
2 Premier Roblin urged the Liberals to withdraw their amendment.
3 Premier Roblin promised that, if the amendment was withdrawn, the budget debate would take place in the usual way.
4 The Liberals and the CCF assumed an intransigent pose and, knowing clearly the result of their actions, combined to vote for the resolution, defeat the Government, and force an election. (Progressive Conservative Party of Manitoba 1959b)

Roblin portrayed himself as the victim of an overly partisan opposition, whose politicking and political jockeying only served to slow the province's progress (ibid.).

Indeed, through to his very last campaign – eight full years after he had defeated Campbell's Liberal-Progressives – Roblin continued to insist that "the Liberal Party of Manitoba – the Gloomy Grits – are attempting to convince the people of Manitoba that their province is debt-ridden, tax-burdened and depressed – that the people and the Government of the Province are not providing that thrust of growth that will permit Manitoba to share in the boom of Canada" (Progressive Conservative Party of Manitoba 1966c). Accordingly, Roblin accused "the Gloomy Grits" of seeking

to prejudice the province for narrow partisan purposes. Their interest is not centred on growth and development in Manitoba. Their interest is in undermining confidence through "poor-mouth" postures and in attempting to so alarm the people of Manitoba that they will vote for the Liberal Party

...

Say the Gloomy Grits: *Things could hardly be worse in the economy of Manitoba, and it's all the fault of the Roblin Government. Put us in power, and we'll cry in sympathy with you* ... Gloom-mongers, poor-mouths, debt-depressives, Manitoba Liberals, professional poverty peddlers cannot and do not speak for Manitobans and do not alter the fundamental and clear fact that *Manitoba is on the march*. (Ibid., emphasis added)

Some may interpret this rhetoric as an attempt to polarize the Manitoba party system between liberal-progressivism and progressive conservatism. To some extent, this is true. Yet a closer examination reveals considerable nuance in Roblin's message. In keeping with the Manitoba code of transpartisanship and its political culture of accommodation, Roblin accused his opponents of being overly partisan as he labelled the PCs as the party of progress. When it came to flood protection, for instance, the premier argued, "While the Liberals *talk* about propaganda and 'poppycock'" – a reference to the opposition's charges that Roblin's plans were little more than hollow partisan promises designed to buy votes – "the machines roll, the plans are finalized, and the protection against flood moves forward" (Progressive Conservative Party of Manitoba 1959b). Roblin portrayed his party as the only one willing to rise above partisan politics to "get on with the business of Manitoba." Accurate or not, this rhetoric was in keeping with the code of moderation and the culture of accommodation embedded in Manitoba politics.

Having redefined the progressive centre through his brand of pragmatic, transpartisan politics, Roblin left the premiership after almost a decade in government. His approach was the epitome of moderation, for he sought to balance the virtues of the Right and the Left while focusing debate on incremental change rather than stolid inertia. So complete was his contribution to the province's political culture that the Tory leader was recently commemorated by the *Winnipeg Free Press* as "the greatest Manitoban" of all time (Goodhand 2008).

Roblin won the 1966 election before making an abortive bid for the leadership of the federal Progressive Conservative Party. To explain his departure, Roblin later wrote, "I had done what I set out to do, and the time had come for a new voice to be heard" (Roblin 1999, 181). These new voices would never replicate Roblin's success nor fully reclaim the progressive centre that he had dominated for over a decade.

Progressive Conservatism since Roblin

Since Roblin's retirement, the Manitoba Conservatives have swerved from the political code he helped to establish – swaying from centre to right, embracing pragmatism then dogma, engaging in partisanship then conciliation, and passing in and out of government in the process. Throughout this period, progressive conservatism in Manitoba could best be described as a constant struggle between the forces of traditional conservatism, cautious progressivism and, more recently, neoliberalism.

Traditional conservatism found its strongest proponent in Roblin's immediate successor, Walter Weir. Weir's premiership, which lasted just nineteen months, remains one of the shortest in Manitoba history.[4] This brevity was due, in large part, to Weir's inability to balance rural conservatism and urban progressivism – two forces that divided not only his party but also the province (Doern 1981, 32; Peterson 1972, 104). Granted, Weir did offer "mixtures of the older neoclassical fiscal paradigm with a Keynesian economic strategy" (Netherton 1992, 184). Yet his prioritization of the former was at odds with the new definition of the province's progressive centre. Weir was, in other words, speaking out of code.

Following Weir's retirement, urban progressives took control of the party under the leadership of Sidney Spivak. From the beginning of his leadership, Spivak attempted to reposition the Tories in the postwar progressive centre. In the mould of Bracken and Roblin, Spivak described himself as "a practical idealist without illusions": "I'm not interested in any kind of 'isms,' capitalism, socialism, left or right," he said in a 1973 Tory publication. "I'm only interested in what will work" (Progressive Conservative Association of Manitoba 1973). In these terms, Spivak attempted to place his party in the middle of the province's new political spectrum, between what he called "the excesses of a government which is dominant or the abdication of responsibility of a government which is merely passive" (Spivak 1973). He urged Manitoba voters to choose "freedom and opportunity" over the NDP's brand of social engineering on the Left and the "every man for himself and the devil take the hindmost" approach of the Liberals on the Right (ibid.). The strategy was unsuccessful at the ballot box, as Spivak's progressivism proved no match for Schreyer's. Moreover, confronted with an almost entirely rural caucus, Spivak encountered much resistance in steering the party back to the progressive centre (Swainson 1973, 6). As one commentator remarked at the time, Spivak's "occasional Roblinesque urges are more

than counterbalanced by a hopelessly right-wing caucus. A Spivak government would be simply the Roblin regime shorn of talent and progressivism"
(ibid.). Spivak's tenure at the helm of the Manitoba PCs demonstrates that
speaking in code may be a crucial component of political success, but it is by
no means sufficient to guarantee victory.

Sterling Lyon's rise to power illustrates the opposite extreme: although
being a moderate may be a political asset in Manitoba, campaigning in code
is by no means a necessary condition for short-term success at the polls.
Lyon successfully challenged Spivak for the leadership of the Conservatives
in 1975, steering the party back to the Right once more.[5] Lyon's vision of
Manitoba's future challenged the foundations of the postwar Keynesian
consensus upon which Roblin had built the progressive centre.

Just as Roblin used the 1958 election to shift the centre to the Keynesian
Left, Lyon spent the 1977 campaign trying to slide the spectrum back to the
Right, using the nascent neoliberal movement as a pretext for bringing
Manitoba into what he portrayed as the new, mainstream mode of thinking
about government and the economy. Lyon's mark on Manitoba politics
was deeper than his brief four-year term in the Premier's Office suggests
(Wesley and Stewart 2010). His attempt to reconstruct the political spectrum around the politics of the New Right served to polarize the party system as never before. But while the strategy helped him win one of the largest
majorities in the province's history, the brevity of his tenure suggests the
longer-term perils of pursuing adversarial politics in a province whose code
discourages such an approach. Lyon has been the only Manitoba premier
since the Second World War to fail in a bid for re-election – a fact attributable, in large part, to his unsuccessful bid to redefine the provincial code and
the very nature of Manitoba politics.

Continuing a pattern begun thirty years earlier, the Conservatives chose
a member of their progressive wing to replace Lyon in 1983. In Gary Filmon
the party found a moderate leader firmly committed to Keynesian Toryism,
both in terms of forced growth and the preservation of the welfare state.
These convictions were challenged once the party reached office, however,
for Filmon gradually steered the party back along a New Right course. In the
process, he abandoned the moderate mode of campaign discourse that had
defined Manitoba politics for much of the previous century. Thus, Filmon's
nine years in office represented a condensed history of his party's evolution
from Roblin to Weir and Spivak to Lyon. He rose to power as a proponent of
cautious, progressive conservatism, drifting to the New Right and polarizing

the electorate before losing control of government. He started out speaking in code but eventually abandoned the core principles of moderation and conciliation entrenched in the province's political code and culture.

The conversion of the Manitoba Progressive Conservatives from moderate red toryism under Duff Roblin to a more doctrinaire and partisan brand of neoliberalism continued as the party entered the twenty-first century. As a result, progressive conservatism remains largely outside the province's dominant discourse.

Following Filmon's resignation as party leader in 2000, the Manitoba Conservatives shifted further to the Right under Stuart Murray. The new leader appeared to prefer Lyon's campaign strategy of redefining the provincial code rather than speaking within it. Indeed, the party's 2003 "Statement of Principles" represents the clearest definition of Manitoba Conservatism – and the clearest illustration of the party's right-wing orientation – since Lyon's manifestos in the 1970s (PC Manitoba 2003). In fact, a comparison of campaign documents suggests Stuart Murray shared more with Alberta premiers Ernest Manning and Ralph Klein than he did with Manitoba Progressive Conservative sage Duff Roblin.

Similar New Right values were reflected in the party's philosophy under Murray's successor, Hugh McFadyen (PC Manitoba 2006). Here, too, there is evidence of a more doctrinaire brand of conservatism – one grounded in individualism and self-reliance – than the one that characterized more moderate, Progressive Conservative platforms such as those of Roblin and Spivak. Some evidence suggests McFadyen is attempting to pull the party back to the progressive centre after eight years in opposition. His promises to increase immigration, "respect the goals of the Kelowna Accord," improve women's health services, and enhance Manitoba's environmental record, along with his commitment to not privatize Manitoba Hydro without first securing unanimous support in the legislature (the Legacy Act), balanced his New Right plans for tax relief, democratic reform, and crime reduction to some extent. Moreover, the Tories appeared to back off, at least somewhat, from hard-line partisan rhetoric during the 2007 campaign. His failure to mention the Doer government in his twenty-seven-page platform suggests McFadyen may be attempting to put a more transpartisan face on his party (PC Manitoba 2007). If he is, in fact, trying to speak in code, McFadyen faces challenges similar to those confronted by Sidney Spivak. Reduced to a rural rump in the legislature, progressive Manitoba Conservatives face an uphill battle to regain the progressive centre on behalf of their party.

In sum, since Roblin's exit, the Manitoba PCs have struggled to balance the forces of Left and Right within their own party. This, in turn, has hampered them in their efforts to recapture the progressive centre in the province more generally. Space does not permit a detailed account of these leaders' attempts to speak in code and – in some cases – to alter the province's dominant discourse altogether (see Wesley 2009b, 311-28). Their inability to do either on a consistent or lasting basis offers one explanation for why new democracy has eclipsed progressive conservatism as the primary carrier of the province's modest and temperate political culture.

Ed Schreyer, 1969-79

Like progressive conservatism, new democracy emerged as a potent political ideology in Manitoba in the second half of the twentieth century. Submerged by the popularity of the Liberal-Progressives and, later, the Conservatives, the CCF-NDP's brand of moderate social democracy remained a minor, but by no means marginal, element of the province's political spectrum until the late 1960s. Since rising to power in 1969 under Edward Schreyer, however, the party has been a leading player in Manitoba's two-party-plus system. Moreover, notwithstanding (1) a decade of experimentation with the Saskatchewan brand of new democracy under Howard Pawley and Gary Doer in the early part of his tenure and (2) the relative decline of transpartisanship as an element of campaign discourse, the NDP's ideology has been the primary carrier of the province's modest and temperate political culture.

The opportunity to supplant progressive conservatism presented itself with the exit of Duff Roblin from provincial politics in 1967. The rise of Walter Weir to the premiership, combined with the Liberals' choice of rural Conservative Bobby Bend as their leader, gave the New Democrats ample space in the new centre of the political spectrum. A decade of Keynesian modernization under Roblin had rendered this the fertile middle ground of Manitoba politics. Most importantly, the New Democrats chose a telegenic – yet moderate – new leader at the outset of the 1969 campaign: Edward Schreyer.

Schreyer's rhetorical strategy was threefold and substantially in code. First, he sought to take hold of the progressive centre by portraying his party as the champion of progress versus inertia and as a moderate alternative to his dogmatic, conservative opponents. In doing so, he built an ideological coalition of left-leaning progressives; he linked social democrats and liberals under the NDP banner. Second, Schreyer sought to moderate his party's image by stressing pragmatism and his commitment to creating a better Manitoba. This included highlighting his own qualities as a competent manager of public affairs. And third, Schreyer took a distinctly populist approach to political competition. This meant downplaying any reference to opposition parties during campaigns and presenting the New Democrats as a government for the people. This populist touch was unique among Manitoba's most successful premiers but was in keeping – at least somewhat – with the province's code of transpartisanship.

Uniting Progressives

First and foremost, Schreyer's campaign style borrowed elements from Roblin's overall strategy. He eschewed debates that centred on Right versus Left in favour of discussions about progress versus idleness. This was particularly evident in the NDP leader's first campaign. In 1969, Schreyer implicitly likened the Tories' rightward turn to the Campbell government's inertia, highlighting what he saw as Manitoba's return to a dogmatic, laissez-faire style of government under Walter Weir. Schreyer proclaimed, "The age of gimmicks, excuses, and inaction is over ... An era of quality government is about to begin in Manitoba ... Ed Schreyer and the New Democrats will govern Manitoba with vigor and imagination ... [and] lead Manitoba into a new era of progress, an era of government for people" (Manitoba New Democratic Party 1969a). This was familiar rhetoric, considering Roblin's message just eleven years earlier. Further evoking the former Tory premier, Schreyer proposed to balance individualism with collectivism through a commitment to active government. "Our first priority must be to introduce a different set of values as the basis for government policy. The present government operates on the premise that it's every man for himself. Our government will base its policies on the principle that all resources, human, natural and industrial will be developed with the well-being of the individual at heart" (ibid.). That the progressive centre belonged to Roblin in the 1960s and Schreyer in the following decade should come as little surprise, considering these rhetorical parallels.

Throughout the 1970s, the Liberals and Conservatives shifted in and out of the dominant discourse as they switched leaders. Meanwhile, the New Democrats continued to steer a middle course with their moderate brand of social democracy – one that blended the traditional socialist concern for security and community with the liberal-democratic value of liberty and the individual. In this vein, Schreyer was a "New Dealer" at heart. The following quotation from Franklin Delano Roosevelt was placed prominently on the wall of the premier's office: "The test of our progress is not whether we add to the abundance of those who have much but in whether we provide for those who have little" (Marshall 1970). This combination of liberalism and socialism is evident in the following excerpt from Shreyer's 1977 platform, in which he attempts to blend concern for community solidarity with personal autonomy in his pledge

> to change our society from one based on competition and self-interest to one based on *cooperation* and a sense of responsibility to others. We believe that change in *society as a whole* comes about through the changes in the circumstances in which *individuals* live and thereby in individuals themselves ...
>
> We know that our economy must be planned, that the basic needs of the people must be seen as rights, and that truly creative and giving individuals exist only when the first two principles are fulfilled. (Manitoba NDP 1977c, emphasis added)

Further moderating his party's socialist image, Schreyer was also careful to arrest fears that his party was bent on drastic wealth redistribution. He noted that his vision was not "for the rich to give something to the poor, but for the whole population, acting collectively, to provide for its own needs" (Manitoba NDP 1973b). Moreover, in promising not to nationalize key industries in the province, Schreyer assured voters that "we do not feel inclined to impinge on private enterprise that is operating successfully" (Marshall 1970). Rather, by 1973, he reported:

> The Schreyer Government's commitment to develop industry throughout Manitoba has already helped create nearly 40,000 new jobs – mostly in private industry – in under 4 years, keeping unemployment down, and increasing provincial output by twice as much as in the previous decade.
>
> Small private industries are expanding with the help of new assistance programs, while limited public equity participation is ensuring Manitobans fair returns where their funds are backing business directly.
>
> Corporation taxes are being kept at competitive levels, but tax incentive "giveaways" have been rejected because they often end up increasing profits in eastern Canada or the U.S.A. (Chartier 1973)

Schreyer's definition of the progressive centre was captured in his government's *Guidelines for the Seventies,* published three months prior to the

1973 election. As a white paper (not unlike that released by Ernest Manning on Alberta's human resource development in 1967), the guidelines spelled out in greater detail Schreyer's attempts to balance liberalism and socialism. This document expressed his party's chief objective: to bring about "more equality of opportunity and eventually more equality of condition" (Manitoba 1973, 3).

This incrementalist approach was also in keeping with the second pillar of the Manitoba code, pragmatism. In his final campaign as leader, in 1977, Schreyer promised "to continue the kind of people's government we've enjoyed in eight years of progress" (Manitoba NDP 1977a). Although some observers agreed with this assessment, Schreyer's performance in government dispelled any notions that the 1969 election had ushered in an era of socialism in Manitoba. Many hard-line socialist supporters were disappointed. As Wiseman (1983, 125-26) and others note, "Little was done that had not been done elsewhere in Canada, and little at all of a controversial nature was done after the first few years in office. Over the years, the NDP had mellowed ideologically, and this process continued once it gained office." Schreyer conducted "little institutional experimentation," for instance, and "only marginally changed the role of the government in the economy" (Netherton 1992, 187). Indeed, to some, "the record of the NDP in Manitoba illustrates the limits of social democracy. The party, when in power, has never sought to go beyond the mild reform of capitalism" (Loxley 1990, 324).

This had been Schreyer's intention. Adopting Roblin's strategy and general Keynesian approach, Schreyer had succeeded the red tory as Manitoba's flag-bearer for progressivism. While angering elements of the party's left-wing base, he had successfully moved the New Democrats into the dominant discourse. In a very real sense, criticism from the Left only served to reinforce his message: Schreyer's NDP was a moderate party firmly positioned in the province's progressive centre.

"A Fairer Manitoba"
Schreyer's campaigns mirrored Roblin's in another sense. Both men cultivated a sense of "big change sweeping Manitoba." Schreyer suggested that "all across the province, people are talking about the New Democrats heading for government" (Manitoba New Democratic Party 1969c). A strong emphasis on the safeness of this change underpinned the boldness of these statements, however, as Schreyer repeatedly highlighted the pragmatic nature of his plans. In contrast to his opponents – who he accused of "offering

giveaways and vague schemes instead of genuine programs" (Manitoba NDP 1973c) – the NDP leader touted his party's platform as "a sensible, practical program certain to improve the quality of life for all Manitobans. The program is made up of reasonable objectives ... reasoned, practical and necessary to improvement of life for Manitobans ... They constitute a meaningful program, aimed at bringing to you at last Government Of, By and For the People. That's what democratic government should be all about. That's what the New Democratic Party is all about" (Manitoba New Democratic Party 1969c).

Thus, like Roblin, Schreyer criticized his opponents not for ideological wrong-headedness but for failing to develop adequate plans for the future. On the topic of sustainable development, for example, Schreyer argued:

> Our natural resources are, by law, the property of every citizen – so all Manitobans must be guaranteed a fairer share of development benefits.
>
> Until 1969, Manitobans were denied a proper share, because of short-sighted planning by previous governments.
>
> New resource policies must reverse this pattern by changing royalty and processing requirements – to encourage smelting and refining – and to create more jobs and increase incomes in Manitoba.
>
> Rational planning is essential to conserve both mineral and energy resources for future generations and to protect the environment – while encouraging economic expansion across the province. (Chartier 1973)

Planning was indeed a crucial element in Schreyer's pragmatic approach. In contrast to idealistic well-wishing, the NDP leader stated that "a party without a comprehensive program can never provide effective government. Just dealing with problems as they come up leads to stop-gap legislation and a haphazard approach to government. For Manitoba to reach its full economic and human potential, it must now chart a course which is fair to all and for which we can all work together" (Manitoba NDP 1973c).

True to code, Schreyer's plans were also noticeably incrementalist. "We recognize that fundamental change under our democratic system is a slow and laborious process," he stated in a party publication (Marlowe 1976, 1). Accordingly, the premier sought to build public confidence in his programs before expanding their principles into new domains. This was especially evident in his approach to public insurance and health care. As written in the party's pre-election newsletter in 1973: "The success of the provincial auto insurance program, Autopac, which has received praise from other provinces contemplating public insurance, will likely help the Premier in gaining support for NDP plans to enter the fire insurance field in direct competition with private companies. Plans to establish a provincially-run bank, plus an extension of health care services into the fields of dental health and prescription drugs are other plans that should benefit from the government's record of achievement" (Manitoba NDP 1973c; see also Chartier 1973).

Granted, Schreyer's rhetoric was not entirely devoid of ideological principle. As a social democrat, the premier did speak with a left-wing accent when he drew attention to inequalities in Manitoba society. According to his 1973 platform,

> The N.D.P. believes progress cannot be measured simply in terms of dollar totals. Overall qualitative effects on people's lives must be taken into account. The "growth at any cost" policies of other parties have been rejected because they concentrate benefits in the hands of a few – leaving most people no better off.
>
> The Schreyer Government is committed to development programming which balances social and economic goals – to increase benefits for the majority of citizens – those with average and lower incomes, pensioners, farmers and native people – to ensure real freedom for every Manitoban. (Manitoba NDP 1973a)

Yet, as a pragmatist, Schreyer was careful to balance his concern for fairness with his attention to efficiency. The two terms figure prominently throughout his campaign literature, including his promises to improve welfare, sustain public auto insurance, abolish medicare premiums, and readjust rural taxation.

The manner in which Schreyer framed urban poverty also reflected this balanced, pragmatic approach. Although he noted the human element, Schreyer was careful to emphasize the financial side of the issue. In a letter to all candidates, his campaign chairman wrote "*We all pay for slums!* An efficient government *cannot afford* slums. Slums cause increasing welfare costs, [increase] cost of police protection, [provide] fertile area for incidence of crime, [destroy] any chance of a decent family life (the right of any Canadian), [rob] young people of opportunity, etc" (Syms 1969; see also Manitoba New Democratic Party 1969b, 1969c).

The same was true of Schreyer's pitch for public automobile insurance. There, too, the focus was as much on frugality as it was on equality: "*Low cost government operated universal automobile insurance!* With the recent report of the B.C. Wooton Commission, what the NDP has been saying for years is now proved beyond any doubt. Full coverage for all motorists at a reasonable rate can only be achieved by a universal government-operated plan" (Syms 1969). Later, in 1977, Schreyer held the Crown corporation as "dramatic proof that this New Democratic government is the kind of *efficient, quality* government that Manitobans deserve" (Manitoba NDP 1977a, emphasis added).

Schreyer applied these same principles to the topic of health care. According to his campaign literature, "New Democrats believe government should be fair in assessing payment of government services. The NDP does not believe that a low income worker or farmer should have to pay the same amount for Medicare as the person earning $15,000 or more a year. That's why the New Democrats have said all along: adequate hospital and medical care based on your ability to pay" (Manitoba New Democratic Party 1969b). Yet, appealing to the frugal elements of Manitoba's political culture, Schreyer was quick to note the fiscal side of his health policy. "New Democrats say services to property should be paid via property taxes. But services to people should be paid from the provincial government revenue. That's fair. *And it's efficient*" (ibid., emphasis added).

Schreyer also promised a more balanced deal for farmers, arguing that Manitobans should not "expect a farmer to pay urban-based property tax while the land is being used for agricultural purposes" (Manitoba New Democratic Party 1969b). Rather, he proposed "an exemption of the difference on land and property tax based on productivity and sale value. When such land is sold, *then* collect the accrued exemption" (ibid.). "This NDP policy is *practical* and it is *fair*," Schreyer argued. "That's the basis of all NDP programs" (ibid.).

Overall, Schreyer's was a conscientiously pragmatic, balanced approach to securing both social justice and economic development. True to the Manitoba code, the NDP leader focused on comparing his party's managerial competence, fairness, and efficiency to what he portrayed as a history of mismanagement by Liberal and Conservative administrations. As Wiseman (1983, 109) puts it, the NDP's appeal was "more 'We can do things better' than 'We will do different things.'" Along these lines, Schreyer pledged to do more than the Weir and Campbell governments; he promised more investment in social services and education and faster economic development through better planning.

More than his policies, however, Ed Schreyer himself was the focal point of the NDP's campaigns in 1969, 1973, and 1977. Although it emphasized his "vigour and imagination," the party also played to the pragmatic component of the provincial code when it described their new leader. Drawing attention to precisely the same qualities possessed by Duff Roblin a decade earlier, the New Democrats' 1969 campaign literature framed Schreyer as "an experienced and vigorous Manitoban ... ready to take up the challenge of getting Manitoba moving again. Ready to work to improve the quality of life for all Manitobans ... [A] man who shuns phony gimmicks, a man who believes in *telling it like it is* ... He *gets things done*, quietly, but he does get them done, and the people of Manitoba know they can rely on him. His *ability, experience and cool head* will make him a winner" (Manitoba New Democratic Party 1969a, emphasis added).

Ultimately, like Roblin and Bracken, Schreyer wanted to be judged on his progress in creating a better Manitoba rather than more immodest claims such as creating the best of all societies. One of Schreyer's slogans for the 1977 campaign – "Manitoba Is Eight Years Better" – illustrates that he, like other premiers before him, wished to be measured against his predecessors rather than against his contemporaries (see Manitoba NDP 1977b).

A Touch of Prairie Populism

Of the three elements of the Manitoba code, Schreyer's rhetoric conformed least to the notion of transpartisanship. In some ways, the NDP leader's approach drew upon the tradition of great premiers before him. Like Bracken, Schreyer viewed himself as "premier of all Manitobans rather than as the party's agent" (Wiseman 1992a, 148). Accordingly, he tended to consider policy developed by the party's grassroots as "'guidelines' rather than as edicts, and he used the annual party convention to endorse and promote government policy" (Dyck 1996, 384).

At the same time, Schreyer considered himself congenial around the caucus table, allowing debate and dissent over even the most controversial policy issues. At the height of pitched debates about Bill 56 – legislation to establish public automobile insurance that sharply divided the legislature and his own caucus – Schreyer said of his flexible approach: "Normally, as far as party discipline goes, I'm quite lax. I don't believe a leader should operate like a little martinet" (Marshall 1970, 33).

On the campaign trail, Schreyer's platforms and published literature paid scant attention to partisan debates. Indeed, the Manitoba NDP leader avoided identifying his opponents by name, preferring to project his own vision and program rather than criticizing the alternatives. Schreyer's ground campaign differed markedly from his public speeches and published party literature, however. Like Roblin's "Talking Points," Schreyer's "Speakers' Notes" for NDP candidates contained scathing attacks on the Liberals and Conservatives and were designed – ostensibly – to polarize the party system in the NDP's favour (Manitoba NDP 1973a). On the issue of taxation, for instance,

> Our party's attitude ... is one of the main things which sets us apart from the Liberals and Conservatives.
>
> In answer to the ... question – Who should pay taxes? – we say most individuals, families, farmers, and small business people should pay *less,* as far as is possible – while the wealthy and big business should pay a fairer share than they have in the past – instead of earning big profits in Manitoba and transferring much of them out of the province.
>
> If you listen to the other parties, their answer to this question isn't the same. Sure, they talk about lower taxes for everybody – but when you really look at the details of their proposals, you find that they are really saying "slightly lower taxes for big corporations and people with high incomes." (Ibid.)

Schreyer's campaign manual also advised candidates to go on the offensive about public auto insurance:

> Autopac is one issue where the difference between the NDP government and the Conservative opposition is clear.
>
> The NDP was for it, the Conservatives were against it.
>
> The Conservatives said it wouldn't work. The NDP said it would work. The Conservatives would dismantle it at the first opportunity. The NDP will ensure that it continues to save money for Manitoba motorists.
>
> The Conservatives are wrong. Autopac works. Don't let them forget it. (Manitoba NDP 1973a)

In addition to these partisan jabs, there was also a strong element of populism in Schreyer's campaign rhetoric – a component that, while fitting within the general principles of transpartisanship, sat rather uneasily within the bounds of the province's code. Consider the following excerpt from his speech at the 1973 campaign launch. In it, we find constant reference to his government's populist roots:

We maintained that when we achieved power we would not forget where that power came from; that a government formed by us would not be a government of politicians, but a government for the people ...

Four years after our first election victory, I can say that that too was a promise we kept and in the long run it is probably the most important promise of all.

In 1969 we said to the family farmer, this is your government – and it has been.

We said to the northerners who have been ignored for so long, this is your government – and it has been.

We said to the pensioner, this is your government – and it has been.

We said to all those who are in the middle and low income group and who have had trouble meeting their tax bills, meeting their medical costs, paying for their auto insurance and keeping their jobs, this is your government – and it has been.

Schreyer's 1973 campaign slogan – "Keep Your Government Yours" likewise reflected this peculiar populist streak.

On the surface, Schreyer's rhetoric appears to be out of step with Manitoba's dominant narrative. Populism is central to Alberta's code, not Manitoba's. Yet, like William Aberhart and Ralph Klein, Ed Schreyer's rhetoric made constant reference to the importance of keeping government in the hands of the people. One way to interpret this discrepancy is to argue that Schreyer broke the mould of discourse in Manitoba – that his populist tendencies were out of code and constitute an anomaly in the province's political history. A second explanation is that Schreyer's appeals were a component of transpartisanship. Instead of appealing to partisan interests, he cited the people as the source of his authority and the public good as his main objective. From this perspective, Schreyer used populism the same way Bracken used wartime solidarity and Roblin used the need for modernization: as a means of placing province above party. Both of these interpretations are worthy of consideration. Both point to the fact that Schreyer paid less attention to Manitoba's code of flexible partisanship than he paid to progressive centrism and pragmatism during his campaigns.

In their 1977 platform, the New Democrats tied all three elements of the Manitoba code together, touting

Ed Schreyer's leadership. Manitoba needs it now, to continue the kind of people's government we've enjoyed in eight years of progress.

Since 1969 all Manitoba has benefited from some of the most innovative and effective legislation in all of Canada. Ed Schreyer and his New Democratic team have kept taxes down and provided the services and programs that all Manitobans need.

Ed Schreyer is an outspoken man, yet he's also a good listener. He's listened to Manitobans for eight years. And he's shared with the people of Manitoba a strong desire to make this province a better place to live. Ed Schreyer and the New Democratic government have acted on what they believe. As a result, Manitobans now have leadership they can trust. They've learned to trust Ed Schreyer, and your continued trust in this man, and in the New Democratic team, will ensure that Manitobans continue to enjoy the benefits of the most able, most progressive government in Canada. (Manitoba NDP 1977a)

The 1977 campaign left little doubt: Schreyer was the public face of the Manitoba NDP. The party's defeat that year, at the hands of Lyon's New Right Conservatives, sent shockwaves through the party and the province. Thus, when Schreyer left the leadership in 1979 to become Canada's first Manitoba-born governor general, the NDP faced the prospect of renewal.

In the meantime, Schreyer had helped to sustain at least two pillars of the Manitoba code, perpetuating the province's modest and temperate political culture in the process. The New Democrats' victory in 1969 marked the culmination of the Manitoba Left's conversion from radicalism to moderation, and the party's message played a key role in its success. On the fiftieth anniversary of the Winnipeg General Strike, the CCF-NDP had shed enough of its radical image to become one of Manitoba's leading progressive parties. By the end of Schreyer's premiership, new democracy had become a primary carrier of the province's moderate political culture.

Like the Conservatives after Roblin, the New Democrats had difficulty replicating Schreyer's electoral success. And they, too, abandoned key elements of Manitoba's political code. While Lyon pulled the Tories to the Right, Schreyer's successor, Howard Pawley, pulled the NDP out of the progressive centre, engaging the party in some of the most heated partisan and ideological competition in the province's history. Indeed, Pawley's adoption of Old and New Left rhetoric, and his embrace of the politics of polarization, made him more akin to Saskatchewan NDP leader Allan Blakeney than to his own provincial predecessor. Ironically, just as Lyon was importing a conservative style of rhetoric that resembled the Alberta code of individualism, Pawley was turning his party to the Saskatchewan Left. Together, the two Manitoba leaders engaged in relatively heated, ideological, and partisan conflict that included charged rhetoric that distinguishes the early-1980s dialogue from Manitoba's otherwise moderate brand of discourse.

This trend continued through the late 1990s, before Gary Doer gradually – if incompletely – eased "today's NDP" back into the moderate middle. Although Doer campaigned from the centre and emphasized the realistic nature of his programs, his rhetoric contained flashes of partisanship that appear to contradict the province's decades-old dominant discourse. This suggests that, although progressive centrism and pragmatism remain prominent, transpartisanship has become an unreliable – perhaps recessive – strain in Manitoba's political code.

Doer's Third Way

After seven years in office, Howard Pawley's majority government became the first in Canadian history to be defeated by a vote of one of its own members (Stewart 2009). Pawley's fall from favour was so precipitous that internal party polls revealed, on the day of the government's budget defeat, that the NDP was unsure of winning a single seat in the ensuing election (Netherton 1992, 199). No doubt trying to replicate Schreyer's dramatic victory two decades earlier, Pawley resigned as party leader just as the writs were dropped for the 1988 election. As in 1969, the ensuing NDP leadership race coincided with the general election. This time, however, new leader Gary Doer was unable to resurrect his party's fortunes. The New Democrats went down to their greatest defeat since 1966, dropping to 23.6 percent of the popular vote and just twelve seats. Given Pawley's abandonment of the politics of moderation, the NDP's grasp on the Manitoba code was equally imperilled (Wesley 2011).

The months following the 1988 election were grim times for the New Democrats. According to their newly minted leader, "We had a little work to do. Angus Reid's polls showed support for the NDP at 12 percent at the highest, and his comment was, 'Jesus Christ couldn't win if he was leader of the NDP.' Perhaps he was correct. But at the time I probably said that pollsters do not use accurate samples" (Doer 2000, 5). From these humble beginnings, Doer rebuilt his party's electoral strength while, at the same time, bringing new democracy back in line with the province's moderate political discourse. The New Democrat's path to power was by no means short. And Doer did not always speak in code.

It took eleven years in opposition for Gary Doer to hone his party's political message. Gradually, over three unsuccessful campaigns, the NDP leader adapted his party's social democratic ideology to the prevailing neo-liberal paradigm. By 1999, this pragmatic, at times transpartisan, Third Way approach had helped redefine the progressive centre along post-Keynesian lines, and it helped Doer become Manitoba's longest-serving premier since John Bracken. In the process, Manitoba's political culture of modesty and temperance was carried into the twenty-first century. The story of Doer's redefinition of "today's NDP" along Third Way lines is best told chronologically.

The term *Third Way* is used as a heuristic device to describe the movement of social democratic thinking away from "the bureaucratic, top-down government favoured by the old left" and "the aspiration of the right to dismantle government altogether" (Giddens 2000, 2). As its two most famous proponents, Tony Blair and Gerhard Schroeder, characterize it, the Third Way strives to meet traditional goals such as social justice through new means, including economic dynamism (Blair and Schroder 1999, 1).

Although the term *Third Way* is useful as an analytical tool or label, its applicability to ground-level politics in the Doer era should be assessed with caution. Although they adopted the general approach and strategies employed by New Labour, few in today's NDP would use the term *Third Way* to describe their approach to governance. According to Doer,

> We didn't borrow the "third way." It became an analysis of the Blair government, and then it became an analysis of our government. We didn't borrow that, because we were moving towards that long before this kind of analysis. The analysis always followed the policies, sometimes a year, sometimes five years behind what Blair did and what allegedly that meant for us. But being a party believing in economic growth, we weren't shy about saying it. We believed in economic growth, we practiced economic growth, and we got economic growth ... In our first year in office, we had a huge Immigration Forum, with labour and business, to try to move from 2,000 immigrants a year to 10,000. That was all based on economic growth and population growth. It was not based on redistributing the status quo. We never believed that that was doable and useful. So, before Blair's election, we were proposing ideas to be symbolic of what we thought would be an economic growth strategy as well as a social inclusion strategy. (Doer 2010)

In short, Doer argues, "The media spends more time on how you do things, and what people say, than the real products. And the pundits' analysis is usually long after what you've done. They put it in a sort of analytical box. So, 'third way'? We were doing some of these things long before we even knew the term existed" (ibid.).

Indeed, as one of his first acts as leader, Doer struck an informal pact with Filmon to sustain the Tory minority government for two years. Some suggest the deal was based on Doer's desire to buy time to rebuild the party (Carstairs 1993, 129-30). From this perspective, the move resembled the transpartisan approach of S.J. Farmer and Lloyd Stinson decades earlier. Others argue that Doer's support of Filmon's first budget was evidence of the New Democrat's acceptance of the tenets of neoliberalism (on the revenue, if not the expenditure, side) and the party's noticeable step to the political centre (Hull and Silver 1990, 336). Either way, Doer's decision to co-operate with the Tories was quintessentially in code and narrowed the poles of the Manitoba party system considerably between 1988 and 1990. As a result, the Liberals were squeezed out of the centre, and the NDP resumed its place as Manitoba's second-place party following the 1990 election.

Rejuvenated after regaining his party's position as official opposition, Doer changed the party's course by abandoning this spirit of transpartisanship. In a Schreyer-like effort to recapture votes from the flagging Liberals, New Democratic campaigns in the early 1990s focused chiefly on portraying the two old-line parties as one in the same. "In reality," according to Doer's 1990 platform, "the only important difference between the Liberals and the Tories is their names. They have the same big-business connections and the same corporate interests at heart ... Let's not kid ourselves. With Liberals like these, who needs Conservatives" (Manitoba NDP 1990b). Thus, despite its own collaboration with the Filmon government, the New Democratic Party emphasized the Liberals' co-operation with the minority Tories in their cuts to social services.[6]

The NDP drew other elements from its old CCF strategy, including portraying Manitoba as being on the verge of economic crisis. The Liberals and Tories were portrayed as chiefly responsible for the downturn, and the NDP were held up as the "one real choice for working people" (Manitoba NDP 1990a). "All signs point[ed] to a major economic recession," according to the 1990 NDP platform.

> Free trade, high interest rates, and the GST – all Tory creations – threaten our jobs, social services and communities. This is no time for the work-out policies of the Tories and Liberals. Indeed, these cheerleaders for corporate

Manitoba are part of the problem. The New Democrats offer real solutions. Instead of tax breaks for Filmon and Carstairs' corporate buddies, we stand for fair taxes for working people. Corporations must pay more. Instead of caving in on the federal Tory GST, New Democrats would refuse to collect it. Instead of cuts to health and social services, New Democrats stand for a universal, community-based health care system. We stand for tough plant closure laws to defend workers' jobs. We demand pay equity so that women no longer have to live on 65 per cent of what men are paid. We want improved health and safety laws to protect the lives and health of working people. For working people, Liberal and Tory governments mean fewer jobs. Social service cuts. A health care system in crisis. Working people deserve a strong voice. The clear choice is to vote New Democrat ...

[Furthermore] the federal Tories have cut health, education, and economic development funding to Manitoba, a policy started by the federal Liberals. Instead of solving problems, they create new ones like the GST. Provincial Liberals and Tories represent the same big business agenda. They oppose pay equity for women, tough workplace safety laws, and security for workers when plants are closed. Manitoba needs a strong voice, one which can represent our interests honestly. That strong voice belongs to Gary Doer. (Manitoba NDP 1990a)

By attacking both Filmon and Mulroney, Doer's early campaigns resembled those run by Howard Pawley in the mid-1980s. They also cast serious doubt on the persistence of transpartisanship as part of the Manitoba code.

Doer's rhetorical approach earned him even lower electoral returns than Pawley, however, while Filmon's majorities grew. With these results in mind, Doer's 1995 Platform – "Rebuilding Manitoba Together" – marked a minor turning point in his strategy and the beginning of the New Democrats' return to the provincial code. Although it focused on restoring the province's social services after seven years of Conservative government, his rhetoric was noticeably less partisan and confrontational. Instead, Doer appealed to Manitoba's traditions of accommodation and compromise:

Manitoba is a province rich in its diversity. In addition to our First Nations we have come from all parts of the globe ... Manitoba is a province built on the hopes and dreams of our people. We are all proud of the pioneering spirit that turned our prairie into Canada's bread basket, our individual and collective achievements that built a province-wide telephone network and a vital hydro electric company that will meet our energy needs today and into the 21st century. Our social fabric is built on that same spirit. We have come to see public, non-profit health care for all regardless of their circumstance as a right, not a privilege ... We have evolved world class universities and training colleges and a public education system that is open to all ... When we have succeeded, as we have done so often in the past, we did so because we worked together. Business, working people, farmers and others worked for a common goal. Government too has played an active part ... For Manitobans our province is like a family. We work hard, share each others' joys and in tough times we come together to overcome our problems. Lending a helping hand to a family member who needs help is part of our traditions. (Manitoba NDP 1995).

Granted, the anti-Conservative elements of Doer's rhetoric remained. However – like John Bracken, Duff Roblin, and Ed Schreyer – the NDP leader portrayed himself as placing conciliation and progress above partisan considerations; it was his opponents who were placing party before province. The preamble to his 1995 platform continued,

Today some of that spirit of success is gone. For seven years we have seen a government that only fosters confrontation. This is not in keeping with our traditions of cooperation and working together. Instead of building together for the future we have seen a government that sets one group against another – trying to create winners and losers. A government that sees high numbers of unemployed and record levels of poverty as unfortunate by-products of the marketplace ... Regrettably we have had a government guided not by a sense of compassion or care but by a blinding need to reduce expenditures at any cost. The results for Manitobans have been traumatic. (Manitoba NDP 1995)

Above all, 1995 marked the election in which Doer began to restake his party's claim to the progressive centre. This did not mean returning to the old, fertile middle ground cultivated by Duff Roblin and Ed Schreyer. Just as the global pivot point had shifted in the late 1950s – away from the laissez-faire paradigm of classic liberalism toward a new set of values hinging on Keynes's definition of the role of the state – the political spectrum had been transformed once more in the late twentieth century. Recognizing this, Doer acknowledged the deficiencies of Keynesianism in the neoliberal era

FIGURE 6

Doer's campaign platforms

"Five Good Reasons" (1999)	"Five Priorities for the Next Four Years" (2003)	"Forward with Gary Doer" (2007)
1 End hallway medicine and rescue health care	1 We will continue to improve our health care system	1 More improvements to health care for you and your family
2 Renew hope for young people	2 We will make it easier for young people to stay in Manitoba	2 Ensure a cleaner, healthier environment
3 Keep Manitoba Hydro and build a new partnership between business and labour for new and better jobs	3 We will continue to strengthen and diversify our economy	3 More skills and education opportunities for young people here at home
4 Make our communities safer	4 We will make our communities safer and more secure	4 Safer communities
5 Keep balanced budget legislation and lower property taxes.	5 We will make Manitoba an even more affordable place to live.	5 Building Manitoba for all of us
		6 Affordable Manitoba, affordable government
		7 Protect Manitoba Hydro for the benefit of all.

Sources: Manitoba NDP (1999, 2003b, 2007a).

and embraced the principles of Third Way social democracy (see Figure 6). His subsequent redefinition of new democracy in Manitoba constituted a redefinition of the progressive centre.

As Doer put it in his 1995 platform, times had changed, and so too must Manitoba politics.

> The days of ever-increasing government revenues are gone. Governments must reallocate resources to pay for new programs and we need to take the utmost care in determining the positive and negative impact of any and all new government programs on government revenues ... We'd like to tell you we can control all aspects of Manitoba's economy right here in Manitoba. But we can't. Changing world economics can and do have an impact right here at home ...
>
> Here in Manitoba New Democrats pledge not to raise any of the major personal tax rates. We also promise not to lower taxes for business. As a result of the cuts to federal funding of health and education Manitoba's finances do not allow for any major reductions in taxes. (Manitoba NDP 1995)

Doer's new, more moderate message appeared to boost his party's share of the popular vote by four percentage points, earning the NDP three additional seats. This was enough to reduce the Liberals to just three seats in the legislature. Yet the Filmon government actually increased its majority.

Few politicians survive three elections as leader of an opposition party, but Gary Doer did. Sensing momentum, the NDP leader maintained his party's new course after the 1995 campaign. He used the next four years to rebrand the Manitoba New Democrats as "today's NDP" – a new brand that reflected Doer's wholehearted adoption of the Third Way.[7]

Just as Schreyer had blended socialism with Left-liberalism in the 1970s, so too did Doer steer the New Democrats along the Third Way in an attempt to unite moderate Manitobans in the progressive centre (Grace 2003, 11; Wesley 2011). Here, cross-provincial parallels once again present themselves. Just as Roblin's brand of red toryism had resembled that of Peter Lougheed in Alberta, Doer's version of the Third Way resembled that of Roy Romanow in Saskatchewan (see Chapter 4). But, again, the reasons underlying the two premiers' success were starkly different. Doer's version fit well with the Manitoba code because of its middle-of-the-road qualities; it was a moderate, progressive platform that also happened to be left-of-centre. Romanow's worked in Saskatchewan because it stressed the value of community in the face of neoliberal individualism; it was a collectivist platform that was moderate out of necessity. In this sense, Doer's recipe for success borrowed as many ingredients from Schreyer as it did from Romanow, Broadbent, or Blair.

Thus, Doer's post-1995 platforms were "framed around pragmatic idealism" (Grace 2003, 4). His proposals were modest, in keeping with the provincial code and culture. "*Manitobans* know how great our province is," Doer stated in a 2003 campaign press release. "This is an affordable place to live with a healthy environment, great quality of life, good schools, an improving health care system and a strong economy" (Manitoba NDP 2003b, emphasis added). The humility in his rhetoric suggests the premier considered Manitoba's qualities to be a well-kept secret.

Doer's abandonment of Pawley's more aggressive brand of social democracy can be seen most clearly in his balanced approach to tax relief and the maintenance of social services. Reflecting on his party's victory in 1999,

We have found that when simple language is used, like one-half of one percent in income tax translates into a 10 percent reduction in university tuition, people will understand and accept an alternative to tax cuts, tax cuts, and more tax cuts. So long as people understand both the costs for alternative programs and the need for a *balance* between health care, education and training, and affordable government, they will accept the balanced vision. We found that by using this approach in our province – and I think Manitoba is very similar to Canada – we were able to win the constituencies that allowed us to win the election. (Doer 2000, 4)

This pragmatic approach was also evident in Doer's new campaign style. Whereas his early platforms were lengthy policy documents that contained a number of familiar NDP pledges across a wide variety of issues (see, Manitoba NDP 1990a, 1990b, 1995), his 1999 platform was dramatically different. Applying Schreyer's old adage that "pamphlets, not novels" win campaigns (Syms 1969), Doer explained: "In the past we used to have huge NDP policy weekends and would produce these fat books dedicated to policy. But this time we took a simpler approach, fearing that if we produced another 600-page document then we would almost certainly lose the election. In its place we produced five pledges and we made sure that each one, and this is perhaps a novel idea, could actually be implemented once we became the government" (Doer 2000, 5).

The decision to shift strategy reflected Doer's pragmatic approach to campaigning – his belief in "promising only what we know we can deliver." "Manitobans are tired of hearing a long string of promises from political parties that are broken almost immediately after election. Today's NDP believes Manitobans deserve a fresh start ... No one expects governments to perform miracles. But there are doable and achievable things a government can do to make a real difference for Manitoba families. Together we can do better for your family and your future" (Manitoba NDP 1999). Reflecting this change in campaign strategy, Doer's 1999 platform included only five core commitments (ibid.). In 2003, he set five priorities for the next four years, all of which he considered to be realistic and achievable (Manitoba NDP 2003a). "Building on Manitoba's success," Doer's 2007 platform contained many of the same pledges (see Figure 6).

Again, there remained an element of partisanship in Doer's message, particularly when he implored Manitoba to adopt his own brand of progress rather than returning "to the days of reckless Conservative cuts and privatization that hurt families so much" (Manitoba NDP 2007a). In a particularly aggressive move, the NDP also launched a parallel campaign website – whoishugh.ca – aimed at discrediting the Conservatives and their leader.

These moves suggest Doer retained Pawley's partisan impulse. They also point to significant parallels between his own 2007 campaign and Lorne Calvert's attempt to polarize the Saskatchewan electorate in the same year (see Chapter 4). These comparisons are certainly valid, and they may imply that transpartisanship is a recessive element in Manitoba's political ethos.

Yet, just as many of his predecessors had done, Doer frequently asked voters to join with him in a spirit of conciliation, to rise above brash partisan interests in the pursuit of provincial progress. "Together we've changed Manitoba a lot over the last seven years," he argued in 2007. "Now we're looking forward – with confidence and pride in our province's future ... Let's move forward together" (Manitoba NDP 2007a). Indeed, like Roblin's before him, Doer's campaign rhetoric is replete with references to the need to place the premiership and progress above partisanship (see Figure 6). "Everyday in government, *I have worked hard to be a premier for all Manitobans* and I will work hard to continue being a premier for all Manitobans," he wrote in 2003." At the outset of the 2003 campaign, he stated, "I believe that together Manitobans have accomplished a lot during the last four years ... Now is the time to put forward our vision and our plan to take Manitoba to the next level" (Manitoba NDP 2003b, emphasis added).

Doer's progressiveness was most evident in his 2007 slogan, "Forward with Gary Doer." According to a statement released at the outset of the campaign, "Doer said there is a lot at stake in this election. The NDP has made a lot of progress in key areas such as rebuilding health care, providing new opportunities for youth and ensuring Manitoba Hydro remains publicly owned for the benefit of all Manitobans. Doer said it is important to keep the momentum going and build on this progress as Manitoba moves forward" (Manitoba NDP 2007b).

All told, Gary Doer is among the most recent in a long line of party leaders to speak in Manitoba's political code of moderation. This was not always the case. Doer's early rhetoric drew more from Howard Pawley than from the traditions laid down by Bracken, Roblin, and Schreyer. Yet his conversion to the values of progressive centrism, pragmatism, and a more flexible brand of partisanship in the mid-1990s – together with his redefinition of Manitoba's moderate middle – has helped "today's NDP" regain its status as the primary carrier of Manitoba's modest and temperate political culture. In his reflections on his decade in power, Doer continues to eschew the type of ideological thinking that pervades politics elsewhere on the Prairies. "I think some of these terms, like left and right, are so out of date":

I mean, if you invest in universities and colleges, is that "left-wing" because it's inclusive, or is it "right-wing" because it improves productivity and innovation? ... When we invested in a climate change strategy, we not only had the benefits of cleaner air and water, which is a long-term objective, but we also had the economic growth of, say, buses. And in Washington, here, I'm watching Flyer buses go by me every day ... So is this a right-wing item because it's good for the economy, or a left-wing item because it's good for the environment? I think these terms are so outdated. The public is so much further ahead than the 1950s political science analysis that flows from most punditry in Canada. And the public has moved beyond the old definitions. (Doer 2010)

The party faced the challenge of maintaining its positive momentum after Gary Doer's departure from provincial politics in September 2009. With a fixed election date set for October 2011, new Premier Greg Selinger will have two years to develop his own brand of campaign rhetoric (Wesley 2010c).

Conclusion

This chapter began by asking how the values imported by Manitoba's founding fragment – a group of nineteenth-century British Canadian settlers from Ontario – have continued to influence Manitoba politics to this day. How have the progressive yet Tory-touched principles of modesty and temperance been transmitted over time? How has this political culture survived a full century of economic, social, and political development? And why does it continue to differ from the conservative values driving politics in Alberta and the social democratic principles guiding Saskatchewan?

A detailed examination of campaign literature reveals that Manitoba's most successful political parties have served a crucial function in this process. Their rhetoric contains constant references to the values of progressive centrism, pragmatism, and transpartisanship that have helped sustain Manitoba' broader political culture. John Bracken, Duff Roblin, and Ed Schreyer certainly fit this mould (although the latter's attachment to populism was somewhat out of place). In doing so, each of these premiers helped to redefine the progressive centre in Manitoba – Bracken around the paradigm of laissez-faire liberalism, Roblin around Keynesian red toryism, and Schreyer around a moderate brand of social democracy. Gary Doer's conversion to the Third Way in the mid-1990s constitutes the most recent of these redefinitions, one that moved the code into the neoliberal paradigm of the twentieth century.

These findings are verified by a recent study of Manitoba's political tradition. After completing a series of in-depth discussions with provincial political elites, past and present, Gerald Friesen (2010, 33-34) has concluded that Manitoba's political culture is primarily accommodationist:

> The interviewees suggested that Manitoba was a society of conscious conciliation, driven by a keen sense of what was fair and unfair. They saw the community as remarkably stable and its citizens as committed to collective well-being. They regarded it as a place of intersection because its central location in nation and continent enabled its representatives to act as mediators ...
>
> The first theme that stood out in the observations of this diverse group was a surprising insistence upon the degree of consensus in Manitoba's public sphere, at least in the last half-century. Despite their experiences in vigorous and heart-felt disputes over a wide range of public policies, they did not see government as a forum of profound disagreements. Though they acknowledged the litany of conflicts that has preoccupied historians and political scientists, many of the interviewees were at pains to emphasize the paramountcy of "conscious accommodation" in provincial political life. Duff Roblin, former premier, said: "I'm not sure that we are less extreme than other places, but one thing I would say is that there's less political bitterness here, less acrimony between the parties. My experience is mainly with D.L. Campbell. And my policies were as different from his as they could possibly be, but we never exchanged a harsh word. We gave the other fellow credit for good intentions and we didn't make disagreements into personal quarrels. We stuck to policy." The present premier of the province, Gary Doer, pointed to specific occasions when leaders of labour and business were able to meet informally to discuss their differences before they became serious ruptures.

Not all dominant party leaders have spoken in this code of moderation, of course. Walter Weir's connection with rural conservatism and the New Right appeals of Sterling Lyon, Gary Filmon, Stewart Murray, and (to a lesser extent) Hugh McFadyen demonstrate how several Tory leaders have spoken off script when it comes to Manitoba's dominant discourse. Likewise, early CCF-NDP leaders, plus Howard Pawley, have elected to speak with a more left-leaning – in many ways Saskatchewanian – accent than the Manitoba tradition prescribes. Yet the relatively lower rate of prolonged success enjoyed by these leaders only serves to reinforce the power of the

Manitoba code. Those party leaders who have found a way to speak from the progressive centre, while drawing on the values of pragmatism and trans-partisanship, have enjoyed more prolonged periods of achievement.

Conclusion
Decoding Prairie Cultures

This study began by positing the Prairie paradox – how could three such similar political communities have developed three such dissimilar political cultures? Given that the three Prairie provinces are separated by artificial boundaries, how did Alberta become Canada's cradle of conservatism; Saskatchewan, its bastion of social democracy; and Manitoba, the epitome of Canadian moderation? There is no "silver bullet" solution to these questions. The processes of cultural development and transmission are far from parsimonious, as the existing literature suggests. Conventional accounts, such as Nelson Wiseman's (1983, 1988, 1996, 2001, 2006, 2007), have stressed the historical importance of settlement patterns, transformative events, and political economies in explaining these disparities (see Chapter 1). *Code Politics* challenges such theories, finding them valid but incomplete.

To supplement these explanations, analysts must break open the "black box" of cultural transmission and ask how dominant values are conveyed over time. Processes of socialization and institutionalization clearly play a role (see Chapter 2). Dominant political values are cultivated in households, classrooms, history books, newspapers, and popular culture, and they are entrenched in the programs, policies, and agencies of the state. But the function of political elites is often overlooked in most analyses of cultural transmission. In particular, analysts have underestimated the role dominant political parties and their leaders play in carrying a society's core values from generation to generation and in conveying them from natives to new-comers. By emphasizing the principles embedded in their community's ethos, the rhetoric of parties and leaders during election campaigns has served as a quadrennial renewal of a province's political culture. These distinct narratives have served as stable, albeit mutable, institutions in the evolution of Prairie politics. Following a method of qualitative content analysis outlined in the Appendix, this examination of leading party platforms reveals that Prairie politics have been governed by three distinct political codes – dominant modes of discourse that have helped to sustain the values embedded in each province's unique political culture. As is detailed in Chapter 3, Alberta's campaigns have highlighted the importance of preserving freedom. Leaders from William Aberhart and Ernest Manning to Peter Lougheed and Ralph Klein have used events such as the Depression, the discovery of oil at Leduc, the federal government's National Energy Policy, and the 1980s recession, along with the province's American liberal political culture and resource-based economy, to create a dominant discourse based on the concepts of individualism, populism, and autonomy. According to this code, the Alberta government – and, by extension, the party in power – serves as the defender of provincial interests against external, oppressive forces, be they the federal government, a socialist menace, or any other Big Shot foe of the Alberta community.

By contrast, Saskatchewan's natural governing party – the CCF-NDP – has helped foster a political code based on security (see Chapter 4). Its platforms emphasize dirigisme, collectivism, and polarization, all of which serve to reinforce the state's position as a pioneer in Confederation, a provider of social services, and a director of the provincial economy. Leaders such as Tommy Douglas, Allan Blakeney, and Roy Romanow have crafted this image out of the province's Fabian-agricultural roots and boom-bust economy, portraying the Saskatchewan state as the caretaker of society and as an agent of social justice.

Meanwhile, dominant party leaders of various stripes in Manitoba have preached the importance of moderation by promoting progressive centrism, transpartisanship, and pragmatism throughout their campaigns (see Chapter 5). Taken together, these concepts have defined the provincial state's role as broker in federal-provincial relations, moderator of internal social issues, and participant in the provincial economy. Drawing on experiences such as the 1919 Winnipeg General Strike, the Depression, and historical floods as their basis, Manitoba elites have translated their province's

FIGURE 7

Toward solving the Prairie paradox

	Alberta	Saskatchewan	Manitoba
Transformative events	First World War Depression Leduc oil discovery Cold War	Depression Second World War	Riel rebellions Winnipeg General Strike
Political economy	Free enterprise (petroleum-based)	Strong public and co-operative sector (agriculture and natural resources)	Diversified, mixed economy
Founding fragment	American liberals	British Fabians	Ontario Tory-touched liberals
Political code	*Freedom*	*Security*	*Moderation*
Pillars	individualism populism autonomy	dirigisme collectivism polarization	progressive centrism transpartisanship pragmatism
Dominant parties	Social Credit (1935-71) Progressive Conservatives (1971-present)	Liberals (1905-44) CCF-NDP (1944-present)	Liberal-Progressives (1922-58) PCs and NDP (1958-present)

economic stability and Tory-touched, progressive heritage into a unique mode of campaign discourse.

By transmitting distinct, age-old value systems through a series of unique campaign narratives, and by perpetuating these codes over time, dominant party leaders have helped sustain the three different political cultures that now characterize the Canadian prairies (see Figure 7).

There are obvious disjunctions between what has been portrayed by these elites in their campaign rhetoric and the actual performance of these states. At various times, Saskatchewan governments have reduced their state's role as pioneer, provider, and director. Likewise, Manitoba elites have, from time to time, abandoned their code of moderation by choosing sides at the federal-provincial table during debates about private or public development or in domestic social disputes. The contradictions between rhetoric and reality are clearest in Alberta. For instance, the province has for decades produced one of the lowest rates of voter turnout in the country, raising doubts about the province's populist character (Pickup et al. 2004). By the same token, Alberta maintains one of the highest levels of per capita welfare spending in Canada, contradicting the individualist rhetoric of major party leaders (Tupper and Gibbins 1992, xv). And although western alienation remains barely below the surface of Alberta's political discourse, the provincial government (by most standards the wealthiest in the country) faces challenges in portraying itself as a hinterland victim of eastern Canada (Dyck 1996, 514; Norrie 1979). Yet the stereotype of Alberta's redneck political culture persists (Pal 1992, 1-2; Wiseman 2007, 248).

As in Manitoba and Saskatchewan, the portrayal of the state's role in Alberta has been as important as its actual performance. As Gibbins (1979, 143) suggests, "a strong belief in the spirit if not necessarily the practice of free enterprise, [and] a concomitant belief in the desirability if not the actuality of small, fiscally conservative governments" are both widely acknowledged components of the Alberta political ethos. According to some, part of the reason behind the survival of the province's political culture lies in the success of provincial elites in cultivating a series of myths about Alberta in their campaign rhetoric (Lisac 2004a, 2-3; Barrie 2006). Similar criticisms have been levelled at Saskatchewan's reputation for social democracy, which appears to be at odds with the conservative elements of its society (Eager 1980; Barrie 2006; Ornstein 1986). Likewise, Manitoba's creed of moderation, tolerance, and accommodation sits uneasily amid the tensions of a modern, multicultural, stratified society (Wesley 2010a; Friesen 2009).

Although the topic is certainly worthy of further investigation, the goal of the present study is not to challenge but rather to explain the persistence of these popular images. Addressing the question of whether Alberta is actually a populist, conservative, alienated society; whether Saskatchewan is an isolated, communitarian, and polarized province; or whether Manitoba is a modest and temperate community would require a separate research design. This book explains why the conventionally accepted definitions of these political cultures have survived, despite the contradictions and in the face of decades of political change.

Codes and Critical Junctures

By adapting their political codes to changing circumstances, dominant elites have helped transmit their communities' core values through otherwise critical junctures in each province's history. Consider how party leaders responded to three common historical pressures: the Great Depression, the emergence of medicare in the mid-twentieth century, and the economic downturn of the early 1990s. Elites in the various provinces framed these events quite differently, invoking the unique values embedded in their distinct political cultures and codes.

Alberta's William Aberhart, for instance, framed the economic crisis of the 1930s as a perversion of free-market capitalism. His response was to break the grip of central Canadian political and financial monopolists and restore power to the individual citizens of Alberta. This objective was in keeping with the province's culture of frontier liberalism, populism, and western alienation. Further east, William Patterson, the Liberal premier of Saskatchewan, portrayed the Great Depression as yet another instance of the province's fundamental isolation and vulnerability. Instead of focusing on returning power to individuals, Patterson emphasized providing security through state relief programs and community solidarity. Meanwhile in Manitoba, John Bracken viewed the Depression as a temporary, if drastic, downturn in an otherwise sound economy. Throughout the crisis – indeed, throughout his entire tenure, which included much of the Second World War – Bracken held firm to his classic liberal convictions and steered Manitoba along a steady, semi-partisan, middling course between right-leaning Social Credit and left-leaning socialism. In other words, the Depression was framed in terms of freedom in Alberta, security in Saskatchewan, and moderation in Manitoba.

The same framing devices were applied during the medicare debates of the 1950s and 1960s. Alberta's Ernest Manning saw universal health care as a threat to individual liberties, whereas Saskatchewan's Tommy Douglas saw it as a crucial element of social justice and security. Duff Roblin assumed a centrist position, viewing medicare as a means of attaining both economic and social progress for Manitobans. Considering these differences, the rhetoric of the three leaders bears repeating. According to Manning (1965, 3-4):

What is meant by "universal" is that the plan arbitrarily includes everybody, whether they need the benefits and whether they wish to be included or not. It is a compulsory program in which participation is compelled by the state and not left to the voluntary choice of the citizen himself.

This feature of the plan violates a fundamental principle of free society, namely, the right of each citizen to exercise freedom of choice in matters relating to his own and his family's welfare. Welfare state advocates will scream that this is not so but no man can truthfully say he has freedom of choice if he is forced to participate in a compulsory state scheme for his medical services, whether he wishes it or not.

Douglas disagreed. For him, health care was

a primary need of every individual. Therefore, the highest standard of health care that medical science can provide must be recognized as a fundamental right of every person.

But it is no longer possible for individuals – with limited financial resources – to pay the bills resulting from serious or prolonged illness. Medical science has made great advances. But most health services are costly and beyond the grasp of many of us.

Because of this, it must become the responsibility of society, of all of us together, to organize health resources for the benefit of all and with barriers to none. (CCF [Saskatchewan Section] 1960b)

Roblin, in contrast, adopted a moderate, balanced approach to medicare:

Health is fundamental to the well being of the community. No prosperous and modern community such as Manitoba can justify policies that fail to guard the health of the public ...

For any community good health is good business. The Roblin Government, recognizing this as well as the human values involved, has invested heavily in the health of the people of the province. (Progressive Conservative Party of Manitoba 1962c)

As these quotations reveal, Alberta and Saskatchewan assumed the right and left poles in the medicare debate, respectively, while Manitoba found the moderate middle between economic and social concerns. Each province's code was adapted to the circumstances at hand.

If their response to the health care issue illustrates how each community operated under the Keynesian paradigm, the recession of the late 1980s and early 1990s demonstrated how elites in Alberta, Saskatchewan, and Manitoba responded to the onset of neoliberalism. Alberta's code began the transition during Don Getty's premiership and ended with the rise of Ralph Klein. In Alberta, government restructuring took place under a familiar rubric when Klein drew on laissez-faire liberal values inculcated by the early

Socreds to conduct his revolution. Meanwhile, in Saskatchewan, neoliberalism was filtered through a social democratic political culture and code of security. The result was Romanow's Third Way, which redefined, but nonetheless retained, the dirigiste character of the Saskatchewan code. If Klein focused on the expenditure side of the equation (cutting government services and program spending), and Romanow on the revenue side (increasing fees and taxes), Gary Filmon and Gary Doer produced more balanced plans of action for Manitoba (de Clercy 2005; Denis 1995). True to the neoliberal paradigm of his time, the latter later shifted his party to the new progressive centre, accepting the tenets of balanced budget legislation, for instance, while promising to protect the province's social services and Crown corporations.

In all three instances – the Great Depression, the health care debate, and the late-twentieth-century recession – elites in each province developed similar policies. Each developed a system of social security, each signed onto national medicare, and each undertook massive programs of government restructuring. However, by following and adapting the values enshrined in their community's unique political ethos, leaders in each province were motivated by different ideological considerations. Their means might have been similar, but their visions and rhetoric differed. This is the very essence of code politics.

Once established (and continuously adapted), these dominant modes of discourse have helped keep politics in the Prairie provinces along three separate, seemingly paradoxical paths. The causal arrow runs both ways, of course: each political culture reinforces the code upon which it is based. One factor remains clear, however: dominant parties and their leaders have played a more critical role in defining and distinguishing the three political worlds of the Canadian prairies than conventional accounts suggest.

The Contours of Code Politics

Yet code politics are not entirely tidy. Caveats abound, for not all leaders have spoken in exactly the same way over the past seventy years. Different leaders have offered unique spins and placed different emphases on various pillars of each code (see Figures 2, 3, and 4). For instance, Ralph Klein's laissez-faire definition of freedom was more akin to that of Ernest Manning than it was to Peter Lougheed's brand of toryism. In Saskatchewan, Roy Romanow's Third Way definition of dirigisme conflicted in many ways with the orthodox version of social democracy promoted by his predecessor,

Allan Blakeney. And – although all paid homage to it – classic liberal John Bracken, province builder Duff Roblin, and social democrat Ed Schreyer all defined the progressive centre differently. Codes are open to interpretation, given the different conditions experienced by and the different predispositions of each leader.

Moreover, not all elements of each code have remained consistent over time. Individualism and populism received less attention in Peter Lougheed's rhetoric than it did in the rhetoric of his predecessors and successors. Dirigisme was constrained under Romanow's neoliberal vision for the Saskatchewan state. And, in a steady fashion since the mid-1970s, transpartisanship appears to have become a recessive strain in Manitoba's political code. Although closely linked, the various components of each code have varied in terms of their salience.

What is more, not all dominant party leaders have engaged in code politics. Neither Don Getty nor Ed Stelmach made much reference to the principles of freedom in their campaign rhetoric, just as Walter Weir, Sterling Lyon, Howard Pawley, and Gary Filmon eschewed the politics of moderation in Manitoba. Decades earlier, William Patterson abandoned the Saskatchewan code that he and his Liberal counterparts had spent nearly a generation constructing. The decision to speak in code is just that – a choice – and not all leaders have stayed within the confines of their province's dominant narrative.

Complicating matters further, party leaders have had notable rhetorical similarities across provincial lines. Although their definitions of each term differed, William Aberhart and Ernest Manning both spoke of security in Alberta, just as Tommy Douglas stressed the need for freedom in Saskatchewan. Likewise, Ed Schreyer's populist rhetoric was in keeping with Albertan traditions but appeared foreign to Manitoban politics. And while progress was a defining characteristic of Manitoba's code, the term figured in rhetoric throughout the region. These similarities are understandable, considering that all three provinces are modern liberal democracies.

These caveats are important to note because code politics is by no means a simple or comprehensive theory. It is a mid-level model that, when applied to the Prairie context, cannot account for various anomalies. Nonetheless, although they add nuance to our understanding of the distinct modes of discourse that exist in Alberta, Saskatchewan, and Manitoba, these outliers do not negate the general trend. Most dominant leaders in each province have spoken in code. This is not to say that they have spoken with exactly the same vocabulary. Nor does it mean they have spoken a completely different language than their counterparts in other provinces. Rather, party leaders in each province have shared a common accent that has both distinguished their political discourse and sustained their unique political culture.

The Limits of Code Politics

The scope and intent of this study must be kept in mind when interpreting and extrapolating from its findings. *Code Politics* reveals that an examination of dominant party campaign literature can help researchers understand the persistence of distinct political cultures in Alberta, Saskatchewan, and Manitoba. It does not provide a comprehensive solution to this paradox on the Canadian prairies. Rather, by focusing on agency, dynamics, and campaign discourses, this study supplements conventional wisdom that, to this point, has tended to focus on primordial, static, and structural factors. By explaining how original demographic, experiential, and economic differences have been translated into the dominant electoral discourses of each province and then cultivated and adapted over dozens of election campaigns, this model of code politics does not suggest that agency is the only explanation for the evolution of three different worlds in the region. As is emphasized throughout this study, structure provides the demand for certain political outcomes while agents provide the supply. Both are crucial to our understanding of political cultural development.

These limitations create important parameters around the use of the code politics model. The model cannot explain the electoral success of specific parties or the results of particular elections. Granted, within each province there are obvious parallels between the prominence of one set of political ideas on the one hand and the success of one type of political party on the other. The final case study on Manitoba politics offers an illustration. In that province, the party that promotes a moderate, progressive vision of the province is also the one that controls the legislature. Conservative fortunes have been highest when the party's program has been tempered by a Tory touch. By the same token, when the NDP's platform leans too much toward a more orthodox brand of social democracy, the party's electoral success is more limited. Although under different modes of discourse, the same tendencies exist in Alberta and Saskatchewan, provinces where parties and leaders who speak in code tend to fare better than those who do not.

These observations raise an obvious question. In addition to sustaining each province's distinct political ethos, is it possible that political codes have helped to sustain the very dominance of the parties that constructed them? Without further research and theoretical elaboration, this question will remain unanswered. The relationship between rhetoric and electoral success must remain speculative, not causal (for a discussion of this relationship, see Wesley 2009c). For example, the code politics model cannot explain why certain renditions of a province's political ethos were more popular than others. To do so would require a close examination of individual attitudes – a task that is both outside the scope of this book's explicitly supply-side focus and beyond the scope of data compiled on provincial politics in Canada. Nor is the code politics model designed to explain individual election outcomes. Code politics, on its own, cannot account for Sidney Spivak's loss to Ed Schreyer in 1973, Roy Romanow's triumph over Grant Devine in 1991, or Harry Strom's defeat at the hands of Peter Lougheed in 1971. As is suggested throughout this study and the existing literature, campaign rhetoric is believed to have played a crucial role in these outcomes. Yet, given that each dominant party leader spoke in code during these various elections, it was certainly not the only deciding factor. Comprehensive explanations of these individual election outcomes would require research on mobilization tactics, electoral redistributions, media framing, public opinion, and any number of other variables.

By the same token, using the lessons derived from this analysis as a foundation for future campaign strategies is no guarantee of success. Simply speaking in code will not be enough to return the New Democrats to power in Saskatchewan or the Conservatives to government in Manitoba, and it is certainly not the only key to success for opposition parties in Alberta. The code politics model is neither an all-in-one tool for explaining previous elections nor an instrument for predicting the future. Like all models and theories in political science, it is but one instrument among many available to help researchers make sense of the political world.

These limitations should not be viewed as shortcomings, however, for the aim of the analysis was never to account for the success of certain parties or the results of individual campaigns. Rather, *Code Politics* seeks to explain one mechanism through which political cultures are transmitted from generation to generation and from natives to newcomers. Therein lies the purpose, and the strength, of the code politics model. Furthermore, not even the structured agency outlined in this analysis conveys the whole story of why the three Prairie political cultures differ to such a great extent. A comprehensive account would include the many contingencies and microforces at play in each community and address the effect of formal institutional changes implemented by dominant parties while in office, not simply their activities during campaigns.

There are shortcomings involved in any path-dependent analysis. In particular, historical institutionalists have encountered three key criticisms related to infinite regress, ergodicity, and determinism (Pierson 2004; Putnam 1993). First, it is possible that the most critical branching points in Prairie party history occurred outside the scope of this study. An argument could be made that the three distinct biases established by provincial farmers during the Progressive era help explain why conservatism came to dominate Alberta; social democracy, Saskatchewan; and moderation, Manitoba (Morton 1967a). Tracing these roots even further, one could argue that the original branching point came with the formation of the federal government's immigration policy in the late nineteenth century. At that time, decisions were made to recruit and settle specific immigrant groups in certain areas of the Canadian west, helping to establish the unique patterns of settlement that form the foundation of most political culture accounts.

Second, the events described in historical institutional explanations are subject to an infinite number of contingencies. Seemingly small events or decisions can have an enormous impact on political outcomes, according to the principles of path dependency. As with questions of infinite regress, determining precisely which events matter, and which do not, is an inherently subjective exercise. The course of Prairie history was altered by huge events such as the Great Depression and the Second World War, and Prairie politics would have turned out differently without the contributions of the dominant leaders discussed throughout this study. However, smaller events – events in the pre-political lives of these leaders, for example – have played just as critical a role. If William Aberhart had not read Major Douglas's writings on social credit monetary theory in the summer of 1932, if Ernest Manning had not tuned into Aberhart's radio broadcasts as a youth, if Peter Lougheed had not witnessed first-hand the collapse of Tulsa's oil economy in the summer of 1952, Alberta politics would look quite different than it does today.

Analysts must not overlook the micro-level forces at play, just as they cannot afford to ignore earlier events in the histories of their cases. Instead, as with practitioners of any methodology, historical institutionalists must defend how they chose the most important or significant events in their analysis. Sometimes, as with the current study, data availability limits their capacity to examine earlier events or micro-level forces. In such cases, the analyst should acknowledge the importance of these additional factors and support his or her decision to focus on the specific elements contained in the analysis.

Taking these considerations into account, the concept of code politics does not offer a comprehensive solution to the Prairie paradox. As has been noted throughout this study, an examination of dominant elite discourses supplements existing, structural accounts in order to better explain how three such distinct political cultures developed in Manitoba, Saskatchewan, and Alberta. Future research will shed even more light on this research problem.

Third, analysts cannot neglect the threat of determinism that accompanies many path-dependent explanations. Berman (2001, 237) refers to this as a council of despair, in that many historical institutionalists imply that certain institutions are embedded so fully in a given polity that it is impossible to dislodge them. When applied to political codes, the implication is that Alberta politics will forever be dominated by the discourse of freedom, Saskatchewan by security, and Manitoba by moderation (see Wesley 2009c).

Given the entrenchment of these codes in laws, government programs, agencies, and other formal institutions, the challenges facing would-be code breakers are daunting. In Saskatchewan and Manitoba, for instance, the institutionalization of public utilities – in auto insurance, energy, electricity, and other areas – has created a series of "sacred cow" Crown corporations that have proven difficult for conservatives such as Ross Thatcher, Sterling Lyon, Grant Devine, Gary Filmon, and others to dislodge. By contrast, the absence of Crown corporations in Alberta and the presence of private-sector competition in these industries has created its own set of barriers to opposition forces on the Left. All told, under the confines of code politics, left-leaning visionaries in Alberta, right-wing idealists in Saskatchewan, and utopians in Manitoba face not only cultural barriers to their success, they also face real rhetorical and ideational barriers. In short, codes and cultures are imposing institutions.

Yet codes and cultures are not entirely immutable. Codes can be rewritten under certain circumstances, that is, when political actors are able to create or exploit an opportunity during a period of intense uncertainty to establish a new way of conceptualizing the state's role in society, the economy, or Confederation. Exogenous events may introduce uncertainty into the political system, thus creating opportunities for new political ideas (and the actors carrying them) to rise to prominence. Such events – including wars or depressions – are few and far between; moreover, as witnessed on the Canadian prairies, they do not always produce dramatic changes to the political status quo. Although they may create the prerequisite demand for change, political entrepreneurs must supply a popular and acceptable vehicle if major transformations are to take place. More often, leaders must first learn to play by the rules of the game before they can convert them to their own advantage; they must speak in code before altering the political language of their societies. As Pal (1992, 5) argues, to succeed in party politics "requires leadership, a capacity to sense instinctively the patterns of accepted discourse and the creative, even artistic ways in which they may be modified to suit different interests and agendas."

To break down the dominant discourses in their provinces, for instance, Duff Roblin and Peter Lougheed first adopted, then adapted, the political codes of Manitoba and Alberta, respectively. The Manitoba Tory leader "had to exorcise the province from the ideology and conventions of the Liberal-Progressives – not an easy task considering the degree to which the former paradigm [had] been institutionalized" (Netherton 1992, 182). To accomplish this, Roblin accepted the Liberal-Progressives' creed of moderation, progressive centrism, pragmatism, and transpartisanship, just as Lougheed drew upon the Socreds' principles of freedom, individualism, populism, and autonomy. The two leaders' strategy, however, was to point out the disjunctions between these ideals and the perceived realities of the worlds around them. Roblin suggested not that the idea of progress was outdated but that its definition by the Liberal-Progressives was outmoded. Lougheed did not suggest abandoning Alberta's quest for autonomy; rather, he suggested that this independence would be better preserved through engagement with the federal government rather than isolationism. Roblin and Lougheed were able to alter, then champion, their provinces' codes by pointing out these disjunctions.

Politics, therefore, is rarely a matter of opposing sides presenting conflicting values or paradigms. Rather, it is more often a contest between conflicting interpretations of those ideals. The most successful opposition parties seek to highlight not the anomalies left unsolved by the dominant narrative but rather the disjunction between the realities of political life and the promise contained in the existing code. These ideals constitute the community's creed – a relatively unsystematic conglomeration of symbols, values, and beliefs that serves as the guiding principles of a society and its political actors (Huntington 1981). In this sense, ideas guide political development in that the nonrealization of a society's creed may empower an opposition group to challenge the prevailing order by restating (or often reinterpreting) the basis of that original creed. Huntington (ibid., 32) argues that political competition seldom "takes the form of idea versus idea ... but rather of idea versus fact. The conflict is between ... groups who believe in the same political principles: those who find it in their interest to change existing institutions immediately so as to make them comply with those principles, and those who accept the validity of the principles but who perceive existing institutions as being in accord with the principles insofar as this is feasible."

Wright (1984, 112) uses this approach to explain the evolution of Alberta politics. In his assessment of the effect of the 1970s oil boom on the future of Alberta political life, he effectively forecasts the decline of Toryism under Don Getty and the rise of Ralph Klein's brand of neoliberalism. The accuracy of his prediction warrants a detailed quotation:

> [The] juxtaposition of forces over the past decade has been such that Albertans developed the illusion that they were responsible for their own good fortune. This view became embedded in the belief that their free enterprise ideology had led to efficiency, economic growth and a reduction of anxiety levels. The illusion persists into the eighties, and it is interesting to speculate about its durability should market forces lead to a situation in which economic growth continues to diminish in spite of local attempts to be efficient. It is likely that slow growth will cause anxiety because Albertans will carry a residue of addiction to the favorable circumstances which have existed in more prosperous times. There will thus be pressure on the provincial government to preserve the illusion by embarking on programs which force growth. Should such programs falter, one can anticipate that a reactionary political force will emerge to urge the return to the principles of classic capitalism. This would be the ultimate irony: that in order to preserve the illusion which made it so powerful, the provincial government might sow the seeds of its own downfall.

Thus, there is considerable room for contestation under the confines of any culture or code. The persistence of values such as conservatism and freedom in Alberta, social democracy and security in Saskatchewan, and modesty and moderation in Manitoba does not necessarily lead to closed systems of political competition. The rise of new forces – such as Lougheed's red toryism or Klein's neoliberalism, Douglas's moderate brand of socialism or Romanow's Third Way, Roblin's progressive conservatism or Schreyer's new democracy – suggests that these core value systems are malleable enough to accommodate a wide range of ideologies. The periodic, if limited and fleeting, success of opposition parties with their own unique worldviews offers further evidence. None of these provinces constitutes a hegemonic system.

The enduring nature of political codes need not give way to deterministic accounts of these communities.

Final Thoughts

As a research community, we are still far from uncovering all of the mysteries of ideational politics (Gerring 1998, 273-75; Hanson 2003; Campbell 2002; Blyth 1997). As Berman (2001, 236-37) notes, political scientists still struggle

> to find ways to identify in advance the conditions under which change is likely to occur. When has the process of delegitimization, for example, proceeded to appoint where ideational or cultural change is likely or even necessary? When are exogenous shocks likely to force leaders and publics to reconsider long held beliefs? What characteristics enable some carriers to convince people to abandon old beliefs and adopt new ones? The long-term goal in this area should be to develop a framework to predict when the "formative moments" in history will occur, to understand when political spaces will open up and the possibilities for ideational or cultural shifts will arise.

Ultimately, a major obstacle to our understanding of the development and diversity of political cultures lies in the fact that, even when the potential exists for divergence, analysts are still confronted with fundamentally human sets of behaviours. This means that potential divergences can be thwarted – openings closed – by political actors capable of reshaping the playing field. After all, parties and their leaders are not simply structured by history – they are agents of it. As a result, the fundamental sources of political ideas, codes, and cultures are far from parsimonious (Gerring 1998, 273-75).

Yet a key starting point must be to recognize the importance of both structure and agency, of demand and supply, in shaping the different political cultures of the Canadian prairies and elsewhere. Code politics is by no means the only solution to the Prairie paradox, but it takes us one step closer to understanding why and how western Canadians continue to live in such different political worlds.

Appendix
Deciphering Codes: The Study of Ideas in Political Documents

Despite its importance and growing acceptance, the study of ideas in documents remains a contested element of political science research (Jacobsen 1995, 283). To some detractors, ideas are too fluid to submit to the rigours of scientific analysis. For them, "Ideas and ideals are hard to quantify, to explain or even to classify, and they are usually rooted in particular times, places and people. For the theory-building enterprise of social science, ideology has been soggy ground" (Gerring 1998, 290). Others contend that ideas are residual, secondary factors in political life – that is, they are products of fundamental phenomena that are more deserving of our primary attention (see Hall 1989a, 361; Blyth 1997, 229; Lane 1992). Still other critics contend that ideologies are "just hooks: competing elites seize on popular ideas to propagate and to legitimize their interests, but the ideas themselves do not play a causal role" (Goldstein and Keohane 1993a, 4). Apter (1964, 16) refers to this criticism as one in which ideology is "viewed as a cloak for shabby motives and appearances." In truth, all of these criticisms have some merit (Berman 2006, 9-16). Ideas are inherently difficult variables to operationalize, and they are closely related to other factors, including political institutions, cultures and economies, and interests.

These critiques are not unique to ideas, however. The definition of key concepts is a perennial concern for political scientists examining a wide range of topics, from globalization and governance to postmodernism and social capital (Blakely and Bryson 2002). This concern challenges scholars to operationalize their terms rigorously, not abandon their pursuit entirely. Indeed, the investigation of these concepts only serves to further elucidate their meaning.

Notwithstanding these critiques, the importance of ideas to our understanding of politics remains unquestioned (see Popper 1972, 153-90). As Berman (2006, 9) suggests, "It would be impossible to discuss twentieth century history without using terms such as 'fascist', 'communist', or 'liberal', and one would be laughed at if one tried ... Even a cursory reading of history shows that ideologies have played an important role in driving events down paths they would otherwise not have taken. They link people who would not otherwise have been linked and motivate them to pursue political goals they would not otherwise have pursued." Thus, the question becomes one of how best to conceptualize ideas, not whether to study them (Blyth 1997).

This thinking is reflected in recent trends in the discipline, particularly in the areas of process tracing (e.g., Bates et al. 1998), political economy (Hall 1989b), international relations (Goldstein and Keohane 1993b), and historical institutionalism (e.g., Sikkink 1991; Blyth 2003), all of which have placed ideas under the microscope of political science. Several of these approaches have examined the role of ideas at the micro level, that is, their effect on individual decision making (e.g., Hall 1986). *Code Politics* takes a macro-level approach toward the role of ideas as values, examining their transmission throughout societies and over time rather than their precise impact on individuals' cognitive processes. This level of analysis corresponds with the treatment of political culture in the holistic sense.

Selecting a Methodology

Although political scientists are turning increasingly to ideas for explanations, the discipline has struggled to keep pace methodologically. This is particularly true in the area of qualitative content analysis, where scholars have yet to develop a proven, coherent system of methods for the study of the values embedded in political texts (Altheide 1996, 3; George 2006, 135; Manning and Cullum-Swan 1994, 463; Platt 2006, 83; May 2001, 176). Hence, the nature of the field offers both challenges and opportunities for the present study – an ideational examination of Prairie politics, conducted through a qualitative analysis of party platforms and other campaign materials.

Why the Prairies?

The Prairie provinces are appropriate for a study of political cultures, political parties, and political diversity in general. For over a century, Manitoba, Saskatchewan, and Alberta have played host to some of the most "concerted and diverse attempts to reconstitute the democratic experience within the Canadian polity" (Laycock 1990, 3). In each province and throughout the region, politics has featured a unique and persistent yet ever-changing struggle between the forces and parties of the Left and the Right. Whether pitting liberals against socialists, conservatives against social democrats, or followers of the New Right against those of the New Left, the history of Prairie campaigns parallels the very evolution of political ideology in Canada and elsewhere (Friesen 1996, 39-41). All told, the region has been a bastion of the country's co-operative, Social Gospel, populist, Progressive, neoliberal, and Third Way movements. As a result, between them, the three Prairie provinces have nurtured the world's first Social Credit government, North America's first social-democratic administration, and Canada's first genuine coalition government. In sum, the Prairies, "more than any other region ... [propose] new political institutions, new philosophies, new political parties and innovative public policies," making them compelling case studies in the role of political parties in the development of political culture (Wiseman 1992b, 283).

Why Platforms?

Given that the purpose of this study is to assess the relationship between widely held conceptions about political culture at the mass level on the one hand and elite-level codes of discourse on the other, the question arises as to how to measure the ideological content of the latter. As is discussed in Chapter 2, dominant political parties are only one set of elite actors contributing to the development of political culture on the Canadian prairies. Minor parties – not to mention parents, teachers, the media, and other actors – also play a significant role. Notwithstanding these contributions, however, dominant political parties are often the most visible and vocal exponents of political ideology in the region. Because their rhetoric reaches its highest volume and largest audience in the periods surrounding elections, analysis of their campaign materials is a particularly fruitful exercise. In short, if codes of elite discourse exist, and if researchers wish to obtain a valid indication of their ideological content, they will be found in the platforms, speeches, and other campaign artifacts produced by the leading parties in each province.

This brand of analysis is well established in the political science discipline (see Budge and Farlie 1983; Budge, Robertson, and Hearl 1987; Janda et al. 1995; Smith and Smith 2000; Budge et al. 2001; Petry and Landry 2001; Warwick 2002; Franzmann and Kaiser 2006; Sides 2006; Klingemann et al. 2007). Campbell and Christian (1996) examine campaign literature in their study of the ideological orientations of Canadian political parties (see also Ball et al. 2006; Christian and Campbell 1974, 1983, 1989, 1990). Internationally, the Comparative Manifestos Project (CMP) – the largest study of its kind – has grown over time to include a systematic content analysis of party platforms in fifty-two countries (including Canada) from 1945 to present. Its methodology provided the initial inspiration for the present study.

Robertson (1976, 72), a pioneer of platform-based research, summarizes the CMP's technique and urges analysts to "treat the party manifestos more as the best available indicators of what voters ought to believe about the parties, rather than what they actually believe. It is not part of our effort here to analyze what voters actually know, or how this affects democracy – that has been exhaustively researched elsewhere. We are investigating the activities of the parties themselves, to see, basically, how they would meet the requirements of competitive democracy given the best of voters." Following this lead, political party platforms and other forms of campaign literature constitute the primary data for this study. They reveal the parties' visions of the ideal provincial society as they are embodied in their rhetoric, principles, policies, and proposed programs. In the absence of survey data, election platforms serve as one of the few available historical sources of party ideology, and they exist for most political parties for most campaigns in Western democracies, including Canada (Laver and Garry 2000, 620; Volkens 2001, 34; Finegold and Swift 2001, 103). Formal platforms are not the only source for this information, of course (Gerring 1998, 294n21); where available, stump speeches, diaries, and internal party correspondence have also been incorporated.

Numerous analysts have pointed out the pitfalls involved in locating party platforms, especially in North America (Riker 1993, 83), Canada (Irvine 1987, 74; DeLong 1988), and her provinces (Imbeau et al. 2000, 796). As Carrigan (1968, vii) noted four decades ago, "The raw materials of history are frequently overlooked when readily available and impossible to find when the passage of time has given them greater historical significance. This is especially true of the platform and policy pronouncements of political parties. Even the party headquarters of contemporary political organizations do not maintain complete records of past campaigns. The result of such neglect is a noticeable gap in the source material on Canadian politics."

Other unfortunate events have also influenced the availability of these records. For example, massive floods in Manitoba destroyed entire archival collections in 1950 (Wiseman 1983, ii) and again in 1997. In more recent times, two factors – the advent of electronic data management and the organizational decline of many parties – have raised additional concerns. First, public archives are struggling both financially and technologically to keep up with the collection and storage of historical artifacts. In some instances, as in the case of party platforms and other website materials, documents are deleted soon after being placed online, making it difficult for archivists to amass a comprehensive collection of public documents. The problem has reached almost crisis proportions, prompting officials to warn that – if more resources are not devoted to the task – the 1990s and 2000s could be "lost information decades" (Huber 2007). Second, the financial and human resource strains facing many political parties – particularly the Prairie Liberals – have forced many to scale down or even abandon their party headquarters in favour of smaller offices. In the interests of saving space, and in the process of moving, many of these parties have been forced to destroy massive amounts of historical material. As well, the leader-dominated nature of modern parties has meant that once one leader's team vacates the party's office, many of their working archives are culled.

Despite these challenges, extensive research in libraries, archives, museums, and personal collections has produced a comprehensive collection of all major party platforms for every Prairie provincial election since 1932. Many thanks are owed to numerous people who assisted in the Prairie Manifesto Project. With over eight hundred individual pieces of literature (and growing), the collection is among the largest of its kind in North America. These files have been digitally recorded as part of the Poltext Project, allowing for the verification of the findings presented here, while also facilitating original research by independent scholars.[1]

Platforms were collected from many different sources, including party collections and websites; personal, academic, and government archives; newspapers and other media outlets; and other secondary sources. The documents collected under the Prairie Manifesto Project therefore assume many different forms, ranging from what might be termed classic manifestos – with lengthy and detailed statements of party aims – to simple lists of policy planks. Depending on the party and time period in question, platforms were published in pamphlets, study booklets, newspaper advertisements, candidates' manuals, convention proceedings, government publications, webpages, official press releases, Speeches from the Throne,[2] campaign addresses, and correspondence. Some were released prior to writs being dropped, others in the heat of the campaign. Each document included in this analysis was deemed appropriate if it represented an authentic statement of principle or programs and had "the backing of the leadership as the authoritative definition of party policy for that election" (Budge 1987, 18). A complete catalogue of these documents is available from the author; those specifically cited in this analysis are listed (by party) in the References.

Why Qualitative Analysis?

The sheer volume of data raises the question of whether to approach the material from a quantitative or qualitative perspective. As much as any other factor, this decision depends upon the research question at hand, for "different theoretical problems will always demand different types of data" (Laver 2001, 9). In simple terms, quantitative analyses are appropriate for investigations into issues of how often? or how many? whereas conditions, norms, and values are better suited to qualitative inquiry (Tashakkori and Teddlie 2003, 317). As King, Keohane, and Verba (1993, 4-5, emphasis added) put it, "trends in social, political, or economic behavior are more readily addressed by quantitative analysis than is the *flow of ideas among people* or the difference made by exceptional individual leadership." In other words, while "all social science requires comparison," quantitative research is best equipped for "judgments of which phenomena are 'more' or 'less' alike *in degree*," and qualitative research is best suited to examine differences *"in kind"* (ibid., 5). The present research problem, which focuses on the transmission of values and ideas over time, clearly fits into the latter category.

In no uncertain terms, to understand the relationship between political culture and political party rhetoric, one must examine the quality of political discourse, not its quantity. A qualitative approach is necessary because, to make sense of ideas in politics, "one must involve oneself in the meat and gristle of political life, which is to say in language. Language connotes the raw data of most studies of how people think about politics, for it is through language that politics is experienced" (Gerring 1998, 298). Galbraith (1976, 62) was correct in this regard: "The study of political culture is fundamentally the study of political rhetoric – the verbal and symbolic terms in which people discuss, define, and describe their political life."

Yet quantitative content analysis is by far the most popular choice among political scientists when it comes to dissecting political texts (see Ginsberg 1972; Paddock 1992, 1998; Royed 1996; Royed and Borrelli 1999; Mellos 1970; Janda 1968, 1980, 1982; Janda et al. 1995). Members of the Comparative Manifestos Project have developed the most widely used method in this subfield. Originally designed and refined by the Manifesto Research Group (MRG) of the European Consortium for Political Research, this technique has been employed, tested, and critiqued for over two decades and continues to serve as one of the discipline's standard measures of political competition (see Laver and Garry 2000). The CMP emerged out of the desire among political scientists to answer two key questions: "(a) what political issues divided post-war political parties and (b) were they converging or diverging in ideological or policy terms?" (Klingemann et al. 2007, xvii). The difference between these two objectives on the one hand and the purpose of the present study on the other is an important one.

The CMP's coding scheme uses specific statements – or quasi-sentences – as its unit of analysis and codes specific issue or policy "mentions" into one of over sixty issue areas. Each specific statement in each platform is coded into one (and only one) policy area. These statements range from general references to the quality of democracy or social justice to specific proposals about foreign relations, tax relief, or education. When combined, these coded statements create a sort of fingerprint that is unique to each political platform in terms of the issues and positions it contains.

The CMP method has been applied to Canadian platforms in several contexts, from the study of election and leadership campaigns to the public opinion–public policy nexus and mandate fulfillment (Landry 1991; Petry and Mendelsohn 2004; Imbeau et al. 2000; Crête, Imbeau, and Lachapelle 1994). Indeed, a specially designed, quantitative CMP-inspired coding scheme has been developed for future analysis of the Prairie Manifestos Project collection (Wesley 2007b). In this sense, as raw materials, the texts found in party platforms do lend themselves to quantitative analysis.

The coding of each platform into a series of distinct policy pledges was, however, ill-suited for the present research question. John Gerring, whose *Party Ideologies in America* (1998) served as a model for the present study, explains why: "To begin with, one would be forced to scale back the quantity of evidence examined in a fairly dramatic fashion." This may seem counterintuitive to those who assume that the quantitative tradition is better suited to reducing massive collections of data into more manageable amounts. The quantification of texts is a highly time-consuming process, however, particularly without the aid of a large research team or computerized coding. As one group of researchers puts it, "the manual coding of text into policy categories is time consuming, boring and potentially unreliable" (Kleinnijenhuis and Pennings 2001, 164). Indeed, many of the texts consulted for this book would have gone unanalyzed in pursuit of a quantitative methodology, to the detriment of the scope of evidence.

Although important, resource considerations did not drive the decision to pursue qualitative textual analysis. (Nor did the fear of boredom.) "Second, and perhaps more significantly," according to Gerring (1998, 297), "[quantitative] content analysis is somewhat less scientific than it appears. Since the meaning of terms is not static or univocal, words do not fall automatically within content analysis categories." These different meanings are often ignored, neglected, or (worse) misinterpreted in quantitative analyses of political texts that focus solely on the salience of certain policy themes. Consider the following two examples. For decades, Canadian policy-makers of all political persuasions – Left, Centre, and right, New Democrat, Liberal, and Conservative – have advocated the growth or preservation of the welfare state. Yet they do so for very different reasons. As Blake (1988, 32) suggests, "similar policies may be justifiable from what appear to be different ideological perspectives. For example, support for social welfare programs may reflect the desire for social order associated with Toryism, equality of opportunity linked to liberalism, and the emphasis on equality of condition in socialism." Coding advocacy of social welfare spending as a simple policy pledge (e.g., "support for unemployment insurance") misses these niceties.

Second, even the use of similar terms can evoke very different meanings. Consider the competing themes emphasized by Ernest Manning in Alberta and Tommy Douglas in Saskatchewan during election campaigns in 1948. To paraphrase, the former told Albertans, "You cannot have security without freedom," whereas the latter told Saskatchewan voters, "You cannot have freedom without security." The first statement clearly promotes a right-wing vision of the political community, whereas the second invokes a left-leaning ethos. Again, many quantitative approaches to content analysis – particularly automated techniques that use word counts or dictionaries – may gloss over the significant distinctions between such messages.

Hence, when using texts to assess the ideational impulses behind specific policies, analysts must examine the reasoning and motivation behind those promises and programs rather than making inferences from their existence

(Christian and Campbell 1990, 116). Instead of relying on counts or scores, analysts must "get inside" the documents to examine both their manifest and latent content (Dittrich 1983, 266; Boyatzis 1998, 16-28). To accomplish this, a thicker, more qualitative approach is required, one that shifts the focus from a quantitative analysis of specific policy content to a narrative analysis of the rhetoric found in the various texts.

Given these drawbacks, Gerring (1998, 297) argues that it is "unrealistic to expect [quantitative] content analysis to bear the entire burden of analysis on a subject as vast and complex as party ideology." Indeed, it is obviously inappropriate to assume that the full meaning and value of political texts can be reduced to a set of numbers (Frankenberg 2006). To discern rhetorical themes and narratives, then, platforms must be viewed as more than the sum of specific policy pledges. Rather, they are communication devices with iconic structures that contain "rhetorical constructions of political realities" (Smith and Smith 2000, 457).

For these reasons, *Code Politics* employs a thicker approach to content analysis. Although its resumé is dwarfed by that of the quantitatively oriented CMP school, qualitative platform analysis is not without its adherents, whether in Canada (Belkhodja 1999; Jenson 1976; Meisel 1960; Weinroth 2004), the United States (Bell 2006; Holian 2004; Pomper 1968; Gerring 1998), or Europe (Chhibber and Torcal 1997; Phillips 1998; Smith and Smith 2000). Like these studies, the present analysis approaches election materials as whole texts, as components of broader campaign discourses and, broader still, as part of an ongoing historical narrative (Abbott 1992). This approach required complete immersion in the data to dissect and synthesize dominant party platforms and discern the main themes of discourse that have characterized each party system. Specific attention was paid to the rhetoric presented by these dominant parties: the visions they presented to their communities, the rationales they offered for specific policy proposals, and the motivations for pursuing particular courses of action. Prominent words, phrases, and themes were highlighted. These were then compared across time, across parties, and across provinces in an effort to discern patterns of discourse.

Some analysts conducting qualitative textual analysis have referred to the process as one of "soaking and poking" (Putnam 1993, 12; King, Keohane, and Verba 1993, 36-43). This phrase certainly captures the style of inquiry involved – I did immerse myself in the data for over twelve months, in a process that, at times, involved as much osmosis as marination. Yet the imagery understates the level of methodological rigour involved in qualitative content analysis (Wesley 2010b). In fact, this inquiry employs a three-stage procedure that is well established in the social scientific community: (1) open coding, (2) axial coding, and (3) selective coding (see Neuman and Robson 2007, 336-40; Creswell 1998, 139-46; Hesse-Biber, Nagy, and Leavy 2006, 279-91; Boyatzis 1998; Marshall and Rossman 2006, 151-76; Richards 2005, 85-103).

Preliminary data analysis began during the first read through of the source materials. Once all of the documents were compiled, a single, principal platform was identified for each dominant party in each provincial election. These documents were then compared in terms of their core ideological tenor and rhetoric, *within and across* both party lines and provincial borders. Using the components of each province's political culture as a guide, broad themes were recorded using an established "memoing" technique, whereby notes were taken to identify core ideas as expressed by each party over time.

A remarkable level of rhetorical consistency emerged during this first stage of open coding. First, regardless of the specific party in power, and despite significant external events such as wars and depressions, leading political figures in each province appeared to "speak the same language" – that is, use the same style of rhetoric and terminology. Moreover, each of these so-called languages was unique to a province: successful party leaders in Manitoba spoke differently from their counterparts in Saskatchewan and Alberta. Lastly, each of these codes of party discourse was strongly associated with the political culture of the province in which it was dominant. The values embedded in the community's broader, mass-level ethos were clearly reflected in the campaign rhetoric of its leading politicians. For instance, Alberta's dominant parties appeared to speak with a liberty-based accent that distinguished them not only from their provincial rivals but also from dominant parties in Saskatchewan and Manitoba, where notions of togetherness and accommodation prevailed, respectively. The presence of these distinct narrative themes, and their strong correlation to each province's political culture, formed the working hypotheses for the remainder of the study: that unique codes of discourse existed in each of the provinces and that – by containing similar themes to those found in each province's broader value structure – these codes could help to explain the persistence of three separate political cultures on the Prairies.

Following a search for theoretical support for the code politics model (see, especially, Huntington 1981; Myrdal 1969; Hofstadter 1957 [1947]; Laitin 1986; Edelman 1964), this hypothesis was tested and refined through an expanded examination of the data. During this second stage of axial coding, all primary documents for all dominant parties were reviewed and formally coded using the tools of qualitative textual analysis. As Neuman and Robson (2007, 337) explain, this process differs from that employed by quantitative content analysts:

> A quantitative researcher codes after all the data have been collected. He or she arranges measures of variables, which are in the form of numbers, into a machine-readable form for statistical analysis. Coding data has a different meaning in qualitative research. A researcher codes by organizing the raw data into conceptual categories and creates themes or concepts. Instead of a simple clerical task, coding is an integral part of data analysis guided by the research question. Coding encourages higher-level thinking about the data and moves a researcher toward theoretical generalizations.

For the present study, relevant statements were highlighted in each platform and then labelled (or tagged) as expressions of one of several key concepts. In Alberta, these labels included terms such as *independence, province rights, liberty, power to the people,* and *protectionism,* whereas in Saskatchewan prominent tags included *togetherness, strong state, stability, partisanship, safety, co-operation,* and *collaboration.* Once again, broad but distinct rhetorical consistencies were found within provinces, regardless of the temporal context.

Examining the dominant party platforms, these various tags were then condensed into a series of discrete pillars that underpinned each provincial code. Freedom in Alberta was found to involve elements of populism, individualism, and autonomy as various dominant party leaders emphasized different pillars at different times. An expanded review of Saskatchewan CCF-NDP platforms revealed similarly stark rhetorical contours: security was grounded in collectivism, dirigisme, and polarization. And moderation in Manitoba consisted of progressive centrism, pragmatism, and transpartisanship. In some cases – including the use of *autonomy, security,* and the *progressive centre* – these tags were drawn directly from the texts themselves. In other cases, terms were chosen as a means of synthesis.

In a third and final stage of primary research, the data was mined through a process of selective coding. As Jones and McEwen (2002, 167) reveal, this involved examining the "saturation of categories ... which means that further analysis produces no new information or need for additional categories. In short, all the data are captured and described by key categories, and a core category emerges that tells the central story." In this sense, selective coding is a form of intra-coder reliability testing that ensures that all of the data fit into the assigned categories by adding, modifying, or deleting tags as necessary. This process was completed over several months and was re-inforced during the revision stage of completing this book.

Although the platforms of all major parties in each province were col-lected, space constraints meant that attention was devoted primarily to the longest-serving, most successful governing parties in each system: Social Credit and the Progressive Conservatives in Alberta; the CCF-NDP in Sas-katchewan; and the Liberal-Progressives, PCs, and New Democrats in Manitoba. A comprehensive treatment of all major opposition parties in each province would fill three entire books. Indeed, this is a goal of future research. This book, however, is confined to a discussion of the various codes in each province, and the primary focus is placed on the discourse as dominated by the most successful provincial parties on the Prairies. If codes exist, they are most likely to be found in dominant party platforms. By virtue of their success, it is reasonable to assume that their ideals most closely matched those of the general public and that their rhetoric served to set the tone of public debate during election campaigns. In sum, the research for this book followed what Bates and associates (1998, 10-14) refer to as the soak and poke method: it focused on "stories, accounts and context," while "extract[ing] formal lines of reasoning [that] facilitate both exposition and explanation."

Regardless of its rigour, however, there is an element of subjectivity in-herent in qualitative textual analysis. As Gerring (1998, 298) says of his own similar approach, "Try as one might, one cannot escape the interpretive na-ture of any study of ideology. Judgments about an ideology's coherence, dif-ferentiation, and stability are necessarily judgments of degree" (see also Laitin 1986, 13). All political scientists, be they of a quantitative or qualita-tive bent, are subject to such critiques. The difference, as Manheim, Rich, and Willnat (2002, 317) point out, is a follows:

Quantitative researchers are usually able to employ some well-established rules of analysis in deciding what is valid evidence for or against their theory. These include such tools as measures of statistical significance and statistical tests of validity, as well as formal logic. Qualitative researchers generally lack this type of commonly agreed to and "objective" tool. Rath-er, they must rely on their ability to present a clear description, offer a convincing analysis, and make a strong argument for their interpretation to establish the value of their conclusions. Advocates of qualitative methods argue that this is an inevitable result of seeking to deal with the richness of complex realities rather than abstracting artificially constructed pieces of those realities for quantitative analysis. Critics of their approach contend that the vagueness and situational nature of their standards of evidence make it difficult (if not impossible) to achieve scientific consensus and, therefore, to make progress through cumulative knowledge.

One particularly stinging critique holds that the findings of most qualitative analyses tend to be "conjectural, non-verifiable, non-cumulative, 'meanings' ... arrived at by sheer intuition and individual guesswork" (Cohen 1974, 5). In short, researchers who employ qualitative methods are subject to the criticism that they leave their readers with little choice but to trust that their interpretations of the data are accurate and legitimate.

To guard against these criticisms, disciplinary standards require social scientists to adhere to certain rules when it comes to treating texts as data. As Scott (2006, 3) suggests, "the general principles involved in handling documents are no different from those involved in any other area of social research." Texts only become scientific evidence when treated systematically. And certain standards apply to quantitative and qualitative scholars alike, for although textual data can be either counted (as a series of words, phrases, policies, or promises) or rendered as texts with symbolic, rhetorical, or iconic meaning, each approach must be trustworthy in its treatment of these documents. In particular, content analysts must establish the legitimacy of their research by protecting its authenticity, portability, precision, and impartiality.

Although it is beyond the scope of this Appendix, a complete discussion of the nature of trustworthiness in qualitative content analysis is available elsewhere (Wesley 2010b). This treatment explores various techniques to ensure that content analysts protect the authenticity, portability, precision, and impartiality of their research. Several of these tools, including the following, are applied to the present analysis:

- triangulation with other data sources and secondary literature to lend credibility and dependability to the analysis
- the presentation of detailed notes on methodology and findings to allow for scrutiny of both process and conclusions
- the in-depth study and use of established techniques, including a proven three-stage coding method

- the presentation of contrary evidence to place proper limitations on the findings
- the publication of raw materials for verification and external auditing[3]
- intense exposure to these raw materials to ensure authentic analysis
- reliability testing, in the form of selective coding
- the pursuit of peer assessment in the form of publications and conference papers on both findings (Wesley 2008a, 2008b, 2009b, 2010a, 2011) and method (Wesley 2009a, 2010b).

Ultimately, all students of social life must provide two key assurances of the trustworthiness of their analyses: (1) they must explicitly describe the process by which they interpreted their evidence, and (2) they must provide access to their data so that their findings can be verified (Guba and Lincoln 1994). In the case of qualitative textual analysis, this means findings must be "grounded, as much as possible, in copious quotations from the principals. At times, this may seem laborious. However the inclusion of actual language in a rhetoric-centred study should be seen as equivalent to the inclusion of raw data in a qualitative study; both allow the reader to evaluate the evidence without relying entirely on the author's own authority. It also provides a depth otherwise lacking in discussions of abstract concepts and content-analysis statistics" (Gerring 1998, 298).

Even with the inclusion of this evidence, qualitative analysts are still vulnerable to charges that they have been selective in incorporating data to suit their hypotheses. That is, they might have purposefully misrepresented, omitted, or downplayed evidence to bolster their arguments. In this sense, the student of rhetoric is not unlike the quantitative scholar: both face the temptation to massage data or falsify results. In this vein, beyond assurances of academic integrity, both qualitative and quantitative analysts must make every effort to offer access to their data for verification and further exploration. In the end, "As the saying goes, the proof is in the eating, or in this case the reading" (Lipset 1990, 18). Whether the evidence presented in this study confirms the presence and persistence of political cultural values in the campaign rhetoric of dominant parties is for the reader to decide.

Notes

1 A community's political culture is akin to its guiding ethos or psyche – the spirit of a society that informs its political customs and practices (Eisler 2004, 260). This definition is consistent with Myrdal's (1969, 3) contention that members of a society – regardless of "origins, classes, regions, creeds, and colors" – "have something in common: a social *ethos*"; Lipset's (1990, xiii) observation that most polities "vary in their organizing principles, in their basic beliefs about the sources of authority and values, and in their conceptions about the nature of their societies"; Inglehart's (1990, 423) contention that "prevailing worldviews differ from society to society, reflecting different historical experiences of different peoples"; and Elkins's (1985, 53) suggestion that "political cultures differ, among other ways, in the range of actions deemed appropriate, possible, plausible, or decent."

2 This divergence has led some analysts to refer to societal level tendencies as ethnic or mass political culture to distinguish them from elite political culture (Putnam 1971; Pye and Verba 1965; Formisano 2001, 397).

3 The term *code politics* should not be confused with the similar but distinct concept of operational codes. Whereas the former refers to a collective series of assumptions about politics shared by elites in a given community, the latter refers to the set of instrumental and philosophical beliefs guiding the behaviour of individual elites (Leites 1951; Holsti 1970; George 1969; McLellan 1971).

4 For critiques of Hofstadter's work and the Consensus School that it spawned, see Kendall and Carey (1970) and Friesen (2010).

CHAPTER 1: THE PRAIRIE PARADOX

1 This list of features resembles, but is not identical to, that offered by Dunn and Laycock (1992, 208), who argue that "Saskatchewan has four important aspects to its

political culture which must be examined in any analysis of its political development: populism, bipolarity, alienation, and the cult of modernity."
2 Large portions of this section are drawn from a lengthier discussion of Manitoba's
political culture (Wesley 2010a).
3 Wiseman's examinations have included not only the Prairies but also all ten Canadian provinces (see Wiseman 2007).
4 In conversations with Wiseman, he is reluctant to draw the dialectical conclusion
that early Toryism gave rise to later socialism in Manitoba.

CHAPTER 2: POLITICS OVER TIME

1 For a similar discussion of the freezing of political cleavages and party systems, see
Lipset and Rokkan (1967).
2 In a recent review, Sapiro (2004, 3-4) notes that "the discipline of political science is
not providing its next generation of scholars with an opportunity for sustained study
of political socialization." As a consequence, many political scientists are forced to
draw lessons from other disciplines.
3 One should not forget the role of the state in sponsoring many of these cultural activities (see Melnyk 1995).
4 Notwithstanding one known example, this is a fairly safe assumption in the Prairie
context. Former leader Lynda Haverstock (2001, 233-34) notes that she did not have
input into the drafting of the 1995 Saskatchewan Liberal platform. It was handed to
her by party advisers just prior to her first campaign appearance.

CHAPTER 3: CAMPAIGNS IN ALBERTA

1 Also included in this list are Aberhart's plans to fix prices (Aberhart 1935, 21, 35) and
control wages (ibid., 41, 55).
2 Of all the pieces of campaign literature collected for the Prairie Manifestos Project,
this is the only document that contains extensive private-sector advertising.
3 For more on the theorem and its divergence from Major Douglas's original plan, see
Macpherson (1977, 107-12) and Bell (1993b, 36-85).
4 This discussion does not address the perceived connection between Social Credit
and anti-Semitism. Although prevalent in the media, particularly in the early years
of the Aberhart government, allegations that the Alberta Social Credit movement
was entirely motivated by fear of a global Jewish financial conspiracy have never
been proven. More germane to this study, "anti-Semitism was never a feature of any
Alberta Social Credit electoral platform" (Bell 1993b, 72). Stingel (2000) provides an
excellent account of the perceived anti-Semitic nature of Alberta Social Credit.
5 To compare Manning's approach to health care with that of Saskatchewan CCF premier Tommy Douglas, see CCF (Saskatchewan Section) (1960b).
6 The electorate proved to be thoroughly divided on the plebiscite question. Option A
("Are you in favour of the generation and distribution of electricity being continued
by the Power Companies?") garnered 50.03 percent (139,991 votes) of the province-
wide vote. Option B ("Are you in favour of the generation and distribution of electricity being made a publicly owned utility administered by the Alberta Government
Power Commission?") won the support of 139,840 Albertans (49.97 percent).

7 Numerous analysts were proven incorrect in their prediction that the Conservatives would be defeated in 1993 (see, for example, Smith 1992; Tupper 1991; Archer 1992).

8 In addition to factors discussed in the main text, explanations abound for how Klein was able to orchestrate the so-called miracle on the Prairie (see Bruce, Kneebone, and McKenzie 1997; Barrie 2004, 269-75; Archer and Gibbins 1997; de Clercy 2005; Smith 2001, 300; Harrison and Laxer 1995b, 2-3; Taras and Tupper 1994, 75-77).

9 These issues included hiring more health professionals; building and renovating schools, hospitals, recreation complexes, and long-term care and seniors' facilities; improving transportation infrastructure (including highways, roads, and public transit); expanding treatment programs for addiction and mental illness; launching "a made-in-Alberta immigration strategy to deal with labour shortages"; introducing "the only realistic and achievable greenhouse gas reduction plan in Canada"; promoting rural development; phasing out the Alberta Health Care premium; capping post-secondary tuition increases to inflation and enhancing financial assistance programs for university and college students; investing in arts and culture; developing value-added industries; and conserving land, water, and air (PC Alberta 2008).

CHAPTER 4: CAMPAIGNS IN SASKATCHEWAN

1 Polarization was also a strategy employed by early Liberal Party leaders (including Jimmy Gardiner), whose attacks on the Anderson Conservatives were also particularly forceful (see Saskatchewan Liberal Party 1933, 17, 19-20).

2 Patterson also attacked Social Credit in 1938. Although it helped to stave off a Socred victory as in Alberta, the move had longer-term consequences because it allowed the CCF to build a valuable base of support and credibility as the only viable opposition party (Courtney and Smith 1972, 303; Lipset 1968a, 145-52).

3 Although the term *socialism* might have been downplayed, the 1944 CCF platform retained its socialistic commitment to "replace the present capitalist system with its inherent injustice and inhumanity [with] a social order from which the domination and exploitation of one class by another will be eliminated; in which economic planning will supersede unregulated private enterprise and competition; and in which genuine democratic self-government based on economic equality will be possible" (Co-operative Commonwealth Federation [Sask. Section] 1944d). Furthermore, while promising not to "confiscate anyone's property," the CCF maintained its pledge to socialize all financial machinery so that money, banking, and investment funds could be "made an instrument in a total war against poverty, insecurity and fear" (CCF [Saskatchewan Section] 1944). "It is absolutely essential to recognize that in CCF policy socialization of finance and socialization of industry go together. You cannot have one without the other ... Socialization of finance is not a cure-all; but it is a necessary part of the prescription" (ibid.).

4 According to the platform, "While no aspect of the program can be rigidly separated from other aspects, and while all are equally important, the above is the order in which a C.C.F. Government in Saskatchewan might be expected to introduce its program" (Co-operative Commonwealth Federation [Sask. Section] 1944d).

5 Importantly, farm security was not to be provided through the FLP's controversial use-lease program. Douglas was unequivocal when it came to his party's land tenure

policy: "The public is continually told that the C.C.F. intends to take ownership of the farms away from the farmers. This is absolutely untrue, always was untrue and always will be untrue" (Co-operative Commonwealth Federation [Sask. Section] 1944c). In highlighting his party's policies, Douglas asked voters, "Is there anything in these proposals that looks to you like an attempt to take away your farm? Does it not seem to you that, for the first time since Saskatchewan became a Province, the farmer will have security on his farm if these pieces of legislation are put into effect?" (ibid.). Just as with Patterson's Liberals, there were limits to Douglas's dirigiste vision of the state.

6   "Imported Social Credit speakers now invading Saskatchewan are trying to fool and mislead Saskatchewan citizens about conditions in Alberta ... Ask your Social Credit speakers to tell you the real truth about Alberta and how the people of that province are paying through the nose for needed services for which you pay much less in Saskatchewan ... On June 8th [1960], let us tell these Social Credit carpetbaggers to go back to Alberta and work in their own back yard ... Yes, We're Proud of Saskatchewan. We will Keep Saskatchewan in the Lead!" (CCF Saskatchewan Section 1960c).

7   The Saskatchewan CCF adopted the New Democratic Party brand following the 1967 election.

8   In particular, Blakeney refused to repay $500 million in collected potash revenue, as demanded by the Trudeau government and the Supreme Court (Gruending 2004, 304-5; Wilson 1980, 146-47).

9   Indeed, some suggest Romanow promoted "a profoundly organic and conservative approach to politics, tempered by a genuine concern for social needs. Far from being a neo-conservative or neo-liberal, as some have charged, he is closer to what Horowitz defined in the 1960s as a 'red tory'" (Leeson 2001, 9).

10 Blakeney actually coined the phrase *the Saskatchewan way* as part of his 1982 campaign (see Saskatchewan New Democratic Party 1982a).

11 The measure to end strikes was invoked twice in response to strikes by SaskPower workers in 1998 and nurses in 1999. Romanow's hard-line approach to negotiations with public sector employees was similar to that of Douglas and Lloyd (who stood firm against doctors in the 1960s), Blakeney (who broke a strike by hospital workers), and Calvert (who refused to relent in the face of a Saskatchewan Government and General Employees' Union strike in 2006).

CHAPTER 5: CAMPAIGNS IN MANITOBA

1   The term *stewardship* is borrowed, in part, from Morton's (1967a, 459-60) description of the liberal or liberal-progressive approach toward public ownership of hydroelectricity.

2   Roblin notes in his memoirs that the CCF's influence was felt most strongly in the areas of education, penal reform, and labour (Roblin 1999, 77-79). He also refers to his "own reading during World War II of the U.K. Beveridge Report" (ibid., 148).

3   The results of the 1958 election produced a hung Parliament, with the CCF holding the balance of power. In the end, the party rejected Campbell's offer of coalition and accepted Roblin's promises to work with the CCF on labour, social services, and economic development policy (Wiseman 1983, 70-71). "In 1955, for example, [Roblin]

supported virtually every CCF resolution introduced in the legislature," including nationalizing Winnipeg's natural gas and increasing welfare-state expenditures (ibid., 69).

4 Weir assumed the premiership on 27 November 1967 and lost the general election on 25 June 1969. His premiership was the third briefest in Manitoba history next to Hugh John Macdonald (who retired voluntarily after nine months in office in 1900) and David H. Harrison (who lost the 1888 election just twenty-four days after inheriting Norquay's position in December 1887). All three were Conservatives.

5 The following discussion addresses Lyon's public persona during campaigns. Others challenge this interpretation as being overly one-sided (Roblin 1999, 102; Dyck 1996, 412).

6 Liberal leader Sharon Carstairs responded, "Here were the PCs and the NDP, avowed public enemies, cutting deals together, not because they had any ideology in common – both are closer to the Liberals, in the middle of the political spectrum – but because it was the only way one could keep power and the other the hope to rebuild. Power is the name of this game. Public policy issues are irrelevant, and so too are the wishes of the electorate, apparently. Power alone is the altar at which politicians worship" (Carstairs 1993, 130; see also Gerrard 2006, 134).

7 When speaking at party events, particularly after 1997, Doer mentioned the influence of Tony Blair and New Labour on his own governing ideology (Lett 1997).

APPENDIX

1 Independent researchers will have access to this data, provided they receive approval from the sources from which the originals were obtained. For more on the Poltext Project, see http:www.poltext.capp.ulaval.ca.

2 Under Ralph Klein, the Alberta Progressive Conservatives used Speeches from the Throne (and Budget Addresses) as party platforms. According to Klein, "I think the budget and the throne speech are really the essence of an election platform" (Johnsrude 1997).

3 The electronic conversion of campaign literature is taking place in two stages. At the time of writing, all primary sources were stored in Adobe Acrobat (pdf) format. Over the course of the next two years, many of these documents will be converted into full-text files as part of the Poltext Project. The author is one of the project's researchers, joining an international consortium of academics working toward the collection and public distribution of political texts, including party platforms. For more information, see the Poltext website.

References

Abbott, Andrew. 1992. "What Do Cases Do? Some Notes on Activity in Sociological Analysis." In *What Is a Case? Exploring the Foundations of Social Inquiry*, edited by Charles C. Ragin and Howard S. Becker, 53-82. Cambridge: Cambridge University Press.

Aberhart, William. 1935. *Social Credit Manual: Social Credit as Applied to the Province of Alberta – Puzzling Questions and Their Answers*. Calgary: Western Printing and Litho.

Ajzenstat, Janet, and Peter J. Smith. 1998. "The 'Tory Touch' Thesis: Bad History, Poor Political Science." In *Crosscurrents*, edited by Mark Charlton and Paul Barker, 68-77. 5th ed. Scarborough: Nelson.

Alberta. 1944a. *This Is Social Credit!* Edmonton: Bureau of Information and News.

–. 1944b. *Progress in Alberta: 1935-1943, A Record of Achievement*. Edmonton: Alberta Publicity and Travel Bureau, King's Printer.

–. 1948a. *Electrifying Alberta*. Edmonton: King's Printer.

–. 1948b. *These Are the Facts*. Edmonton: Alberta Publicity Bureau, King's Printer.

–. 1952. *The Alberta Story: An Authentic Report on Alberta's Progress, 1935-1952*. Edmonton: The Publicity Bureau, Queen's Printer.

–. 1967. *A White Paper on Human Resources Development*. Edmonton: Queen's Printer.

Alberta NDP. 2008. "Our 4 Priorities." http:albertandp.ca.

Alberta Progressive Conservative Association. 1971. *Break-through for Alberta!* Calgary: Commercial Printers.

Alberta Progressive Conservative Party. 1971. *NOW: New Directions for Alberta in the Seventies – The Platform of the Alberta Progressive Conservative Party and Its Candidates, Alberta Provincial Election, 1971*. N.p.: n.p. Alberta Agriculture Library.

Alberta Social Credit Board. 1945. *Questions and Answers on Social Credit and Related Subjects.* Edmonton: Alberta Social Credit Board.

Alberta Social Credit League. 1955a. *A Personal Message to the People of Alberta by the Honourable Ernest C. Manning.* Edmonton: Bradburn Printers.

–. 1955b. "Compare Alberta with the Rest of Canada Then Vote Social Credit: Let's Carry On Together." *Edmonton Journal,* 28 June, 15.

–. 1963. *The Look of Leadership: In Every Field of Endeavour Alberta Leads.* Edmonton: Bradburn Printers.

–. 1967. *Your Future Has New "Horizons Unlimited" with Social Credit.* Edmonton: North Hill News.

–. 1971a. "Something We Believe Albertans Should Read." Edmonton: Bulletin Commercial Printers.

–. 1971b. "Thirty-Six Years of Growth." Edmonton: Bulletin Commercial Printers.

Alberta Social Credit Party. 1993. "Today's Social Credit: Principle Centred Leadership." Calgary: Alberta Social Credit Party.

–. 2008. "Social Credit Principles, Purposes and Objectives." http:www.socialcredit. com.

Allen, Richard, ed. 1973. *A Region of the Mind: Interpreting the Western Canadian Plains.* Regina: Canadian Plains Research Center.

Almond, Gabriel. 1956. "Comparative Political Systems." *Journal of Politics* 18, 3: 391-409.

Almond, Gabriel A., and G. Bingham Powell Jr. 1966. *Comparative Politics: A Developmental Approach.* Boston: Little, Brown.

Almond, Gabriel, and Sidney Verba. 1963. *The Civic Culture: Political Attitudes and Democracy in Five Nations.* Princeton, NJ: Princeton University Press.

–. 1980. *The Civic Culture Revisited.* Boston: Little, Brown.

Altheide, David L. 1996. *Qualitative Media Analysis.* Thousand Oaks: Sage.

Anderson, Benedict. 1983. *Imagined Communities: Reflections on the Origin and Spread of Nationalism.* New Haven: Verso.

Andrew, Caroline, John Biles, Myer Siemiatycki, and Erin Tolley, eds. 2008. *Electing a Diverse Canada: The Representation of Immigrants, Minorities, and Women.* Vancouver: UBC Press.

Andrews, Ken. 1982. "'Progressive' Counterparts of the CCF: Social Credit and the Conservative Party in Saskatchewan, 1935-1938." *Journal of Canadian Studies* 17, 3: 58-74.

Apter, David E. 1964. "Ideology and Discontent." In *Ideology and Discontent,* edited by David E. Apter, 1-46. New York: Free Press.

Archer, John H. 1980. "Some Reflections on the History of Saskatchewan: 1905-1980." In *The New Provinces: Alberta and Saskatchewan, 1905-1980,* edited by Howard Palmer and Donald B. Smith, 9-22. Vancouver: Tantalus Research.

Archer, Keith. 1992. "Voting Behaviour and Political Dominance in Alberta, 1971-1991." In *Government and Politics in Alberta,* edited by Allan Tupper and Roger Gibbins, 109-36. Edmonton: University of Alberta Press.

Archer, Keith, and Roger Gibbins. 1997. "What Do Albertans Think? The Klein Agenda on the Public Opinion Landscape." In *A Government Reinvented: A*

Study of Alberta's Deficit Elimination Program, edited by Christopher Bruce, Ronald Kneebone, and Kenneth McKenzie, 462-89. Toronto: Oxford University Press.

Archer, Keith, and Margaret Hunziker. 1992. "Leadership Selection in Alberta: The 1985 Progressive Conservative Leadership Convention." In *Leaders and Parties in Canadian Politics: Experiences of the Provinces,* edited by R. Kenneth Carty, Lynda Erickson, and Donald E. Blake, 80-100. Toronto: Harcourt Brace Jovanovich Canada.

Ball, Terence, Richard Dagger, William Christian, and Colin Campbell. 2006. *Political Ideologies and the Democratic Ideal: Canadian Edition.* Toronto: Pearson.

Bara, Judith, and Ian Budge. 2001. "Party Policy and Ideology: Still New Labour?" *Parliamentary Affairs* 54, 4: 590-606.

Barney, Darin. 2007. "The Internet and Political Communication in Canadian Politics: The View from 2004." In *Canadian Parties in Transition,* edited by Alain-G. Gagnon and A. Brian Tanguay, 371-84. 3rd ed. Scarborough, ON: Nelson.

Barnhart, Gordon L. 2004. "Walter Scott." In *Saskatchewan Premiers of the Twentieth Century,* edited by Gordon L. Barnhart, 1-38. Regina: Canadian Plains Research Center.

Baron, Don, and Paul Jackson. 1991. *Battleground: The Socialist Assault on Grant Devine's Canadian Dream.* Toronto: Bedford House Publishing.

Barr, John J. 1974. *The Dynasty: The Rise and Fall of Social Credit in Alberta.* Toronto: McClelland and Stewart.

–. 1984. "The Impact of Oil on Alberta: Retrospect and Prospect." In *The Making of the Modern West: Western Canada since 1945,* edited by A.W. Rasporich, 97-103. Calgary: University of Calgary Press.

–. 2004. "Harry Strom." In *Alberta Premiers of the Twentieth Century,* edited by Bradford J. Rennie, 183-202. Regina: Canadian Plains Research Center.

Barrie, Doreen. 2004. "Ralph Klein." In *Alberta Premiers of the Twentieth Century,* edited by Bradford J. Rennie, 255-79. Regina: Canadian Plains Research Center.

–. 2006. *The Other Alberta: Decoding a Political Enigma.* Regina: Canadian Plains Research Center.

Bates, Robert H., Anver Grief, Margaret Levi, Jean-Laurent Rosenthal, and Barry R. Weingast. 1998. *Analytic Narratives.* Princeton, NJ: Princeton University Press.

Belkhodja, Chedly. 1999. "La dimension populiste de l'emergence et du succes electoral du Parti Confederation of Regions au Nouveau-Brunswick." *Revue Canadienne de Science Politique* 32, 2: 293-315.

Bell, David V.J. 2000. "Political Culture in Canada." In *Canadian Politics in the 21st Century,* edited by Michael Whittington and Glen Williams, 317-46. Scarborough, ON: Nelson.

Bell, David V.J., and Lorne Tepperman. 1979. *The Roots of Disunity: A Look at Canadian Political Culture.* Toronto: McClelland and Stewart.

Bell, Edward. 1992. "Reconsidering *Democracy in Alberta.*" In *Government and Politics in Alberta,* edited by Allan Tupper and Roger Gibbins, 84-108. Edmonton: University of Alberta Press.

–. 1993a. "The Rise of the Lougheed Conservatives and the Demise of Social Credit in Alberta: A Reconsideration." *Canadian Journal of Political Science* 26, 3: 455-75.

–. 1993b. *Social Classes and Social Credit in Alberta.* Montreal/Kingston: McGill-Queen's University Press.

–. 2004. "Ernest Manning." In *Alberta Premiers of the Twentieth Century,* edited by Bradford J. Rennie, 147-82. Regina: Canadian Plains Research Center.

Bell, Edward, Harold Jansen, and Lisa Young. 2007. "Sustaining a Dynasty in Alberta: The 2004 Provincial Election." *Canadian Political Science Review* 1, 2: 27-49.

Bell, Jonathan. 2006. "Social Democracy and the Rise of the Democratic Party in California, 1950-1964." *Historical Journal* 49, 2: 497-524.

Benjamin, Les. 1964. "Attack – Attack – Attack – Attack." Personal correspondence with all candidates, campaign managers, and to all concerned. Saskatchewan Archives Board, Tommy Douglas Collection.

Berman, Sheri. 2001. "Ideas, Norms, and Culture in Political Analysis: Review Article." *Comparative Politics* 33, 2: 231-50.

–. 2006. *The Primacy of Politics: Social Democracy and the Making of Europe's Twentieth Century.* Cambridge: Cambridge University Press.

Bilson, Beth. 2004. "William J. Patterson." In *Saskatchewan Premiers of the Twentieth Century,* edited by Gordon L. Barnhart, 139-60. Regina: Canadian Plains Research Center.

Blair, R.S., and J.T. McLeod, eds. 1987. *The Canadian Political Tradition: Basic Readings.* Toronto: Methuen.

–, eds. 1993. *The Canadian Political Tradition: Basic Readings.* 2nd ed. Scarborough, ON: Nelson.

Blair, Tony, and Berhard Schroder. 1999. *Europe: The Third Way – Eie neue Mitte.* London: Labour Party and SPD.

Blais, André, Elisabeth Gidengil, Richard Nadeau, and Neil Nevitte. 2002. *Anatomy of a Liberal Victory: Making Sense of the 2000 Canadian Election.* Peterborough, ON: Broadview Press.

Blake, Donald E. 1988. "Division and Cohesion: The Major Parties." In *Party Democracy in Canada: The Politics of National Party Conventions,* edited by George Perlin, 32-53. Scarborough: Prentice-Hall.

Blake, Raymond B. 2008. "The Saskatchewan Party and the Politics of Branding." In *Saskatchewan Politics: Crowding the Centre,* edited by Howard Leeson, 165-88. Regina: Canadian Plains Research Center.

Blakely, Georgina, and Valerie Bryson. 2002. *Contemporary Political Concepts: A Critical Introduction.* London: Plato Press.

Blyth, Mark M. 1997. "'Any More Bright Ideas?' The Ideational Turn of Comparative Political Economy." *Comparative Politics* 29, 2: 229-50.

–. 2003. *Great Transformations.* Cambridge: Cambridge University Press.

Boyatzis, Richard E. 1998. *Transforming Qualitative Information: Thematic Analysis and Code Development.* Thousand Oaks, CA: Sage Publications.

Bracken, John. 1940. Personal correspondence with S.J. Farmer, 25 October, Archives of Manitoba, John Bracken Collection.

Broadbent, Edward. 1999. "Social Democracy or Liberalism in the New Millennium." In *The Future of Social Democracy: Views of Leaders from Around the World*, edited by Peter Russell, 73-93. Toronto: University of Toronto Press.

Bruce, Christopher, Ronald Kneebone, and Kenneth McKenzie. 1997. *A Government Reinvented? A Study of the Alberta Deficit Elimination Program*. Toronto: Oxford University Press.

Budge, Ian. 1987. "The Internal Analysis of Election Programmes." In *Ideology, Strategy and Party Change: Spatial Analyses of Post-War Election Programmes in 19 Democracies*, edited by Ian Budge, David Robertson, and Derek Hearl, 15-38. Cambridge: Cambridge University Press.

–. 1994. "A New Spatial Theory of Party Competition: Uncertainty, Ideology and Policy Equilibria Viewed Comparatively and Temporally." *British Journal of Political Science* 24, 4: 443-67.

Budge, Ian, and Judith Bara. 2001. "Content Analysis and Political Texts." In *Mapping Policy Preferences: Estimates for Parties, Electors, and Governments, 1945-1998*, edited by Ian Budge, Hans-Dieter Klingemann, Andrea Volkens, Judith Bara, and Eric Tanenbaum, 1-18. New York: Oxford University Press.

Budge, Ian, and Dennis Farlie. 1983. *Explaining and Predicting Elections: Issue Effects and Party Strategies in Twenty-Three Democracies*. London: George Allen and Unwin.

Budge, Ian, Hans-Dieter Klingemann, Andrea Volkens, Judith Bara, and Eric Tanenbaum, eds. 2001. *Mapping Policy Preferences: Estimates for Parties, Electors, and Governments, 1945-1998*. Oxford: Oxford University Press.

Budge, Ian, David Robertson, and Derek Hearl, eds. 1987. *Ideology, Strategy and Party Change: Spatial Analyses of Post-War Election Programmes in 19 Democracies*. Cambridge: Cambridge University Press.

Caldarola, Carlo. 1979. "The Social Credit in Alberta." In *Society and Politics in Alberta: Research Papers*, edited by Carlo Caldarola, 33-48. Toronto: Methuen.

Campbell, Colin, and William Christian. 1996. *Parties, Leaders and Ideologies in Canada*. Toronto: McGraw-Hill Ryerson.

Campbell, John L. 2002. "Ideas, Politics and Public Policy." *Annual Review of Sociology* 28: 21-38.

Carrigan, D. Owen. 1968. *Canadian Party Platforms, 1867-1968*. Toronto: Copp Clark.

Carstairs, Sharon. 1993. *Not One of the Boys*. Toronto: Macmillan Canada.

Carty, R. Kenneth. 2002. "Canada's Nineteenth-Century Cadre Parties at the Millennium." In *Political Parties in Advanced Industrial Democracies*, edited by Paul Webb, David Farrell, and Ian Holliday, 345-79. Oxford: Oxford University Press.

Carty, R. Kenneth, William Cross, and Lisa Young. 2000. *Rebuilding Canadian Party Politics*. Vancouver: UBC Press.

Carty, R. Kenneth, Lynda Erickson, and Donald E. Blake. 1992. *Leaders and Parties in Canadian Politics: Experiences of the Provinces*. Toronto: Harcourt Brace Jovanovich.

CCF Provincial Office (Saskatchewan). 1952. *Yours for Humanity, Security and Progress*. Regina: Service Printing.

–. 1954. *Ten Years of Progress: Ten Years of Achievement*. N.p.: n.p. Provincial Archives of Alberta, William Irvine Collection.

–. 1956a. *The Bunk! In Liberal Speeches*. Regina: Service Printing.

–. 1956b. *Farm Power in Politics*. Regina: Service Printing.

–. 1956c. *In Power Development Saskatchewan Leads with the CCF!* Regina: Service Printing.

CCF Saskatchewan. 1967a. *Education: Are We Missing the Boat?* Regina: Service Printing Co.

–. 1967b. *Resources and Development: Beware of the 'Quick Buck Philosophy'.* Regina: Service Printing Co.

–. 1967c. *Survival of the Fittest?* Regina: Service Printing Co.

CCF (Saskatchewan Section). 1944. *The C.C.F. Policy on Money*. Regina: Service Printing Co.

–. 1948a. *A Short But Important Story about Agriculture*. Regina: Service Printing Co.

–. 1948b. *A Short But Important Story about Labour*. Regina: Service Printing Co.

–. 1948c. *The Social Credit Hoax*. Regina: Service Printing Co.

–. 1948d. *Social Welfare and Health under a CCF Government*. Regina: Service Printing Co.

–. 1948e. *Things You Should Know about Taxes*. Regina: Service Printing Co.

–. 1949. *The Sensational Record of a CCF Government: 83 Facts about Saskatchewan*. Regina: Service Printing Co.

–. 1952a. *The Future Belongs to Saskatchewan*. Regina: Service Printing Co.

–. 1952b. *Progress in Power*. Regina: Service Printing Co.

–. 1952c. *Why Farmers Support the CCF*. Regina: Service Printing Co.

–. 1956a. *Quick Facts for Saskatchewan Voters!* Regina: Service Printers.

–. 1956b. *Yours for Humanity, Security and Progress*. Regina: Service Printers.

–. 1960a. *Facts about Saskatchewan Growth*. Regina: Service Printers.

–. 1960b. *Your Right To Health: What Will the Medical Care Plan Mean to You?* Regina: Service Printers.

CCF Saskatchewan Section. 1960a. *1960 CCF Program for More Abundant Living*. Regina: Service Printing Co.

–. 1960b. *The CCF Record in Saskatchewan*. Regina: Service Printing Co.

–. 1960c. *The Facts to Keep the Record Straight*. Assiniboia: Assiniboia Times.

–. 1960d. *More Abundant Living: CCF Program for 1960*. Regina: Central Press.

–. 1964. *1964 CCF Program: Keep Saskatchewan Ahead*. Regina: Service Printing Co.

CCF Saskatchewan Section of the New Democratic Party. 1964a. *Billion Dollar Province*. Regina: Service Printing Co.

–. 1964b. *Facts About Saskatchewan: No. 5 Medicare (1)*. Regina: Service Printing Co.

–. 1964c. *Regina South-West News*. Regina: Service Printing Co.

Chartier, Rene. 1973. Personal correspondence with G. Haslam, Archives of Manitoba, New Democratic Party Collection.

Chhibber, Pradeep, and Mariano Torcal. 1997. "Elite Strategy, Social Cleavages, and Party Systems in a New Democracy, Spain." *Comparative Political Studies* 30, 1: 27-54.

Chilton, Stephen. 1988. "Defining Political Culture." *Western Political Quarterly* 41, 3: 419-45.

Christian, William, and Colin Campbell. 1974. *Political Parties and Ideologies in Canada: Liberals, Conservatives, Socialists, Nationalists.* Toronto: McGraw-Hill Ryerson.

–. 1983. *Political Parties and Ideologies in Canada: Liberals, Conservatives, Socialists, Nationalists.* 2nd ed. Toronto: McGraw-Hill Ryerson.

–. 1989. "Political Parties and Ideologies in Canada." In *Canadian Parties in Transition: Discourse, Organization, Representation,* edited by Alain-G. Gagnon and A. Brian Tanguay, 45-63. Scarborough: Nelson.

–. 1990. *Political Parties and Ideologies in Canada.* 3rd ed. Toronto: McGraw-Hill Ryerson.

Clark, S.D. 1962. *The Developing Canadian Community.* 2nd ed. Toronto: University of Toronto Press.

Co-operative Commonwealth Federation (CCF). 1933. *Regina Manifesto (Programme of the Co-operative Commonwealth Federation, adopted at the First National Convention held at Regina, Sask., July, 1933).* Regina: Service Printing Co.

Co-operative Commonwealth Federation (Sask. Section). 1938a. *A Handbook to the Sask. C.C.F. Platform and Policy.* Regina: McInnis Brothers.

–. 1938b. *The Saskatchewan Co-operative Commonwealth Federation (C.C.F.) Provincial Platform.* Regina: McInnis Brothers.

–. 1944a. *The C.C.F. and Social Ownership.* Regina: McInnis Brothers.

–. 1944b. *The C.C.F. and Social Services.* Regina: McInnis Brothers.

–. 1944c. *C.C.F. Land Policy.* Regina: Central Press.

–. 1944d. *CCF Program for Saskatchewan.* Regina: Central Press.

–. 1944e. *Labor and Urban Security.* Regina: McInnis Brothers.

–. 1944f. *Sensational Legislation! by the C.C.F. Government in Saskatchewan.* Regina: Business Printers.

–. 1944g. *Socialism and Co-operatives.* Regina: McInnis Brothers.

–. 1944h. *What the Liberals Have Not Told You!* Regina: McInnis Brothers.

–. 1948a. *The CCF Election Platform: Plan for Plenty!* Regina: Service Printing Co.

–. 1948b. *This Thing Called Freedom (by Premier T.C. Douglas).* Regina: Service Printing Co.

–. 1948c. *Who Is Walter Tucker For?* Regina: Service Printing Co.

–. 1956. *As Different as Night and Day.* Regina: Service Printers.

Cohen, Abner. 1974. *Two-Dimensional Man: An Essay on the Anthropology of Power and Symbolism in Complex Society.* Berkeley: University of California Press.

Cooper, Barry. 2002. "Regionalism, Political Culture, and Canadian Political Myths." In *Regionalism and Party Politics in Canada,* edited by Lisa Young and Keith Archer, 92-112. New York: Oxford University Press.

Courtney, John C., and David E. Smith. 1972. "Saskatchewan: Parties in a Politically Competitive Province." In *Canadian Provincial Politics*, edited by Martin Robin, 290-318. Scarborough, ON: Prentice Hall.

Creswell, John W. 1998. *Qualitative Inquiry and Research Design: Choosing among Five Traditions*. Thousand Oaks, CA: Sage.

Crête, Jean, Louis M. Imbeau, and Guy Lachapelle, eds. 1994. *Politiques provinciales comparées*. Sainte-Foy: Les Presses de L'Université Laval.

Cross, William. 2004. *Political Parties*. Canadian Democratic Audit. Vancouver: UBC Press.

Dawson, Richard E., and Kenneth Prewitt. 1969. *Political Socialization*. Boston: Little, Brown and Company.

de Clercy, Christine. 2005. "Leadership and Uncertainty in Fiscal Restructuring: Ralph Klein and Roy Romanow." *Canadian Journal of Political Science* 38, 1: 175-202.

de Vlieger, Dan. 2001. "Drawing Boundaries: The Work of Saskatchewan's Provincial Constituency Boundaries Commission." In *Saskatchewan Politics: Into the Twenty-First Century*, edited by Howard Leeson, 133-40. Regina: Canadian Plains Research Center.

DeLong, Linwood R. 1988. "Preparing for Elections: A Library Perspective." *Canadian Library Journal* (December): 356-64.

Denis, Claude. 1995. "The New Normal: Capitalist Discipline in Alberta in the 1990s." In *The Trojan Horse: Alberta and the Future of Canada*, edited by Trevor Harrison and Gordon Laxer, 86-100. Montreal: Black Rose.

Dittrich, Karl. 1983. "Testing the Catch-All Thesis: Some Difficulties and Possibilities." In *Western European Party Systems: Continuity and Change*, edited by Hans Daalder and Peter Mair, 257-66. London: Sage.

Doer, Gary. 2000. "Policy Challenges for the New Century: The Manitoba Perspective." Paper presented at 2000 Donald Gow Lecture at Queen's University, Kingston, Ontario, 28 April.

–. 2010. Personal interview, 19 May.

Doern, Russell. 1981. *Wednesdays Are Cabinet Days: A Personal Account of the Schreyer Administration*. Winnipeg: Queenston House.

Dunn, Christopher, and David Laycock. 1992. "Saskatchewan: Innovation and Competition in the Agricultural Heartland." In *The Provincial State: Politics in Canada's Provinces and Territories*, edited by Keith Brownsey and Michael Howlett, 175-206. Mississauga: Copp Clark Pitman.

Durkheim, Emile. 1965 [1897]. *Suicide: A Study in Sociology*. New York: Free Press.

Dyck, Rand. 1996. *Provincial Politics in Canada*. Scarborough, ON: Prentice-Hall.

–. 2006. "Provincial Politics in the Modern Era." In *Provinces: Canadian Provincial Politics*, edited by Christopher Dunn, 57-96. 2nd ed. Peterborough, ON: Broadview.

Eager, Evelyn. 1980. *Saskatchewan Government: Politics and Pragmatism*. Saskatoon: Western Producer Prairie Books.

Eckstein, Harry. 1988. "A Culturalist Theory of Political Change." *American Political Science Review* 82, 3: 789-804.

Edelman, Murray. 1964. *The Symbolic Uses of Politics.* Urbana: University of Illinois Press.

Eisler, Dale. 2004. "Ross Thatcher." In *Saskatchewan Premiers of the Twentieth Century,* edited by Gordon L. Barnhart, 237-70. Regina: Canadian Plains Research Center.

–. 2006. *False Expectations: Politics and the Pursuit of the Saskatchewan Myth.* Regina: Canadian Plains Research Center.

Elazar, Daniel J. 1994. *The American Mosaic: The Impact of Space, Time, and Culture on American Politics.* Boulder, CO: Westview Press.

Elkins, David J. 1985. "British Columbia as a State of Mind." In *2 Political Worlds: Parties and Voting in British Columbia,* edited by Donald E. Blake, 49-73. Vancouver: UBC Press.

Elkins, David J., and Richard Simeon. 1979. "A Cause in Search of Its Effect, or What Does Political Culture Explain?" *Comparative Politics* 11, 2: 127-45.

Elliott, David R. 1980. "William Aberhart: Right or Left?" In *The Dirty Thirties in Canada,* edited by R.D. Francis and H. Ganzevoort, 11-31. Vancouver: Tantalus Research.

–. 2004. "William Aberhart." In *Alberta Premiers of the Twentieth Century,* edited by Bradford J. Rennie, 125-46. Regina: Canadian Plains Research Center.

Ellis, Richard J., and Dennis J. Coyle. 1994. "Introduction." In *Politics, Policy, and Culture,* edited by Dennis J. Coyle and Richard J. Ellis, 1-14. Boulder, CO: Westview Press.

Elton, David K., and Arthur M. Goddard. 1979. "The Conservative Takeover, 1971-." In *Society and Politics in Alberta: Research Papers,* edited by Carlo Caldarola, 49-72. Toronto: Methuen.

Engelmann, Frederick C. 1989. "Alberta: From One Overwhelming Majority to Another." In *Provincial and Territorial Legislatures in Canada,* edited by Gary Levy and Graham White, 110-25. Toronto: University of Toronto Press.

Fairbairn, Brett. 2009. "Canada's 'Co-operative Province': Individualism and Mutualism in a Settler Society, 1905 to 2005." In *Perspectives of Saskatchewan,* edited by Jene M. Porter, 149-74. Winnipeg: University of Manitoba Press.

Farrell, David M. 2006. "Political Parties in a Changing Campaign Environment." In *Handbook of Party Politics,* edited by R.S. Katz and W. Crotty, 122-33. Thousand Oaks, CA: Sage.

Farrell, David M., and Paul Webb. 2000. "Political Parties as Campaign Organizations." In *Parties without Partisans: Political Change in Advanced Industrial Democracies,* edited by Russell J. Dalton and Martin P. Wattenberg, 102-28. Oxford: Oxford University Press.

Finegold, Kenneth, and Elaine K. Swift. 2001. "What Works? Competitive Strategies of Major Parties Out of Power." *British Journal of Political Science* 31, 1: 95-120.

Fines, C.M. 1960. "Cost Estimates of So-Called Liberal and Conservative Platforms." Press release, Saskatchewan Archives Board, Pamphlet Collection.

Finkel, Alvin. 1989. *The Social Credit Phenomenon in Alberta.* Toronto: University of Toronto Press.

Fischer, James. 1986. "Liberals in Alberta: Studying the Lessons of History." Master's thesis, University of Alberta.

Flanagan, Thomas, and Martha Lee. 1992. "From Social Credit to Social Conservatism: The Evolution of an Ideology." In *Riel to Reform: A History of Protest in Western Canada*, edited by George Melnyk, 182-97. Saskatoon: Fifth House Publishers.

Flanagan, Tom. 2007. *Harper's Team: Behind the Scenes in the Conservative Rise to Power*. Montreal/Kingston: McGill-Queen's University Press.

Forbes, H.D. 1987. "Hartz-Horowitz at Twenty: Nationalism, Toryism, and Socialism in Canada and the United States." *Canadian Journal of Economics and Political Science* 20, 2: 287-315.

Formisano, Ronald P. 2001. "The Concept of Political Culture." *Journal of Interdisciplinary History* 31, 3: 393-426.

Fowke, Vernon. 1946. *The National Policy and the Wheat Economy*. Toronto: University of Toronto Press.

Francis, R. Douglas. 1989. *Images of the West: Responses to the Canadian Prairies*. Saskatoon: Western Producer Prairie Books.

–. 1992. "In Search of a Prairie Myth: A Survey of the Intellectual and Cultural Historiography of Prairie Canada." In *Riel to Reform: A History of Protest in Western Canada*, edited by George Melnyk, 20-42. Saskatoon: Fifth House Publishers.

Frankenberg, Gunter. 2006. "Comparing Constitutions: Ideas, Ideals, and Ideology: Toward a Layered Narrative." *International Journal of Constitutional Law* 4, 3: 439-59.

Franzmann, Simon, and Andre Kaiser. 2006. "Locating Political Parties in Policy Space: A Reanalysis of Party Manifesto Data." *Party Politics* 12, 2: 163-88.

Friesen, Gerald. 1984a. *The Canadian Prairies: A History*. Toronto: University of Toronto Press.

–. 1984b. "The Prairie West since 1945: An Historical Survey." In *The Making of the Modern West: Western Canada since 1945*, edited by A.W. Rasporich, 606-16. Calgary: University of Calgary Press.

–. 1996. *River Road: Essays on Manitoba and Prairie History*. Winnipeg: University of Manitoba Press.

–. 1999. *The West: Regional Ambitions, National Debates, Global Age*. Toronto: Penguin Books.

–. 2010. "The Manitoba Political Tradition." In *Manitoba Politics and Government: Issues, Institutions, and Traditions*, edited by Paul G. Thomas and Curtis Brown, 21-42. Winnipeg: University of Manitoba Press.

Galbraith, Gordon S. 1976. "British Columbia." In *The Provincial Political Systems: Comparative Essays*, edited by David J. Bellamy, Jon Pammett, and Donald C. Rowat, 62-75. Toronto: Methuen.

George, Alexander L. 1969. "The 'Operational Code': A Neglected Approach to the Study of Political Leaders and Decision-Making." *International Studies Quarterly* 13: 190-222.

–. 2006. "Quantitative and Qualitative Approaches to Content Analysis." In *Documentary Research*, Vol. 1., edited by John Scott, 135-60. Thousand Oaks, CA: Sage.

Gerrard, Jon. 2006. *Battling for a Better Manitoba: A History of the Provincial Liberal Party*. Winnipeg: Heartland Associates.

Gerring, John. 1998. *Party Ideologies in America, 1828-1996*. Cambridge: Cambridge University Press.

Gibbins, Roger. 1979. "Western Alienation and the Alberta Political Culture." In *Society and Politics in Alberta: Research Papers*, edited by Carlo Caldarola, 143-67. Toronto: Methuen.

–. 1980. *Prairie Politics and Society: Regionalism in Decline*. Scarborough, ON: Butterworth and Company.

–. 1984. "Political Change in the 'New West.'" In *The Making of the Modern West: Western Canada since 1945*, edited by A.W. Rasporich, 37-46. Calgary: University of Calgary Press.

–. 1998. "Alberta's Intergovernmental Relations Experience." In *Canada: The State of the Federation 1997 – Non-constitutional Renewal*, edited by Harvey Lazar, 247-70. Kingston: Institute of Intergovernmental Relations.

–. 2008. "Repositioning the New West in the New Canada." Paper presented at University of Calgary, Department of Political Science Speakers' Series, Calgary, Alberta, 19 March.

Giddens, Anthony. 2000. *The Third Way and Its Critics*. Cambridge: Polity Press.

Ginsberg, Benjamin. 1972. Critical Elections and the Substance of Party Conflict: 1844-1968. *Midwest Journal of Political Science* 16, 4: 603-25.

Goldstein, Judith, and Robert Keohane. 1993a. "Ideas and Foreign Policy: An Analytical Framework." In *Ideas and Foreign Policy: Beliefs, Institutions and Political Change*, edited by Judith Goldstein and Robert Keohane, 3-30. Ithaca, NY: Cornell University Press.

–, eds. 1993b. *Ideas and Foreign Policy: Beliefs, Institutions and Political Change*. Ithaca, NY: Cornell University Press.

Goodhand, Margo, ed. 2008. *The Greatest Manitobans: They Made a Better Province and a Better World*. Winnipeg: Winnipeg Free Press.

Grace, Joan. 2003. "Has the Manitoba NDP Been 'Good' for Women?" Paper presented at the annual meeting of the Canadian Political Science Association, Halifax, Nova Scotia, 1 June.

Green-Pedersen, Christoffer, and Kees van Kersbergen. 2002. "The Politics of the 'Third Way': The Transformation of Social Democracy in Denmark and the Netherlands." *Party Politics* 8, 5: 507-24.

Groh, Dennis G. 1970. "The Political Thought of Ernest Manning." Master's thesis, University of Calgary.

Gruending, Dennis. 1990. *Promises to Keep*. Saskatoon: Western Producer Prairie Books.

–. 2004. "Allan E. Blakeney." In *Saskatchewan Premiers of the Twentieth Century*, edited by Gordon L. Barnhart, 271-316. Regina: Canadian Plains Research Center.

Guba, Egon G., and Yvonna S. Lincoln. 1994. "Competing Paradigms in Qualitative Research." In *Handbook of Qualitative Research*, edited by N.K. Denzin and Y.S. Lincoln, 105-17. Thousand Oaks, CA: Sage.

Hackett, Robert A. 2001. "News Media's Influence on Canadian Party Politics: Perspectives on a Shifting Relationship." In *Party Politics in Canada,* edited by Hugh G. Thorburn and Alan Whitehorn, 381-97. 8th ed. Toronto: Prentice-Hall.

Hall, Peter A. 1986. *Governing the Economy: The Politics of State Intervention in Britain and France.* Cambridge: Polity Press.

–. 1989a. "The Politics of Keynesian Ideas." In *The Political Power of Economic Ideas,* edited by Peter A. Hall, 361-91. Princeton, NJ: Princeton University Press.

–, ed. 1989b. *The Political Power of Economic Ideas: Keynesianism across Nations.* Princeton, NJ: Princeton University Press.

Hanson, Stephen E. 2003. "From Culture to Ideology in Comparative Politics." *Comparative Politics* 35, 3: 355-76.

Hardwick, Walter G. 1984. "Transformation of the West from Industrial to Post-Industrial Society." In *The Making of the Modern West: Western Canada since 1945,* edited by A.W. Rasporich, 89-96. Calgary: University of Calgary Press.

Harrison, Lawrence E. 2000. "Introduction." In *Culture Matters: How Values Shape Human Progress,* edited by Lawrence E. Harrison and Samuel P. Huntington, vii-xxxiv. New York: Basic Books.

Harrison, Trevor. 1995. "The Reform-Ation of Alberta Politics." In *The Trojan Horse: Alberta and the Future of Canada,* edited by Trevor Harrison and Gordon Laxer, 47-60. Montreal: Black Rose.

Harrison, Trevor, and Gordon Laxer. 1995a. "Introduction." In *The Trojan Horse: Alberta and the Future of Canada,* edited by Trevor Harrison and Gordon Laxer, 1-19. Montreal: Black Rose.

–, eds. 1995b. *The Trojan Horse: Alberta and the Future of Canada.* Montreal: Black Rose.

Hartz, Louis. 1955. *The Liberal Tradition in America.* New York: Harcourt, Brace and World.

–. 1964. *The Founding of New Societies.* New York: Harcourt, Brace and World.

Haverstock, Lynda. 2001. "The Saskatchewan Liberal Party." In *Saskatchewan Politics: Into the Twenty-First Century,* edited by Howard Leeson, 199-250. Regina: Canadian Plains Research Center.

Henderson, Ailsa. 2004. "Regional Political Cultures." *Canadian Journal of Political Science* 37, 3: 595-615.

Hesse-Biber, Sharlene Nagy, and Patricia Leavy. 2006. *The Practice of Qualitative Research.* Thousand Oaks, CA: Sage.

Hoffman, George. 1983. "The 1934 Saskatchewan Provincial Election Campaign." *Saskatchewan History* 36, 2: 42-57.

Hofstadter, Richard. 1957 [1947]. *The American Political Tradition and the Men Who Made It.* New York: Alfred A. Knopf.

–. 1966. *The Paranoid Style in American Politics and Other Essays.* New York: Alfred A. Knopf.

Holian, David B. 2004. "He's Stealing My Issues! Clinton's Crime Rhetoric and the Dynamics of Issue Ownership." *Political Behavior* 26, 2: 95-124.

Holsti, Ole. 1970. "The 'Operational Code' Approach to the Study of Political Leaders: John Foster Dulles' Philosophical and Instrumental Beliefs." *Canadian Journal of Political Science* 3, 1: 123-57.

Horowitz, Gad. 1966. "Conservatism, Liberalism and Socialism in Canada: An Interpretation." *Canadian Journal of Economics and Political Science* 32, 2: 143-71.

Howlett, Michael. 2006. "De-mythologizing Provincial Political Economies: The Development of the Service Sectors in the Provinces 1911-2001." In *Provinces: Canadian Provincial Politics,* edited by Christopher Dunn, 353-72. 2nd ed. Peterborough, ON: Broadview Press.

Huber, Jordana. 2007. "Electronic Files a Strain on Archives." *Calgary Herald,* December 26, A3.

Hull, Jeremy, and Jim Silver. 1990. "Conclusion: Toward the Future." In *The Political Economy of Manitoba,* edited by Jim Silver and Jeremy Hull, 334-38. Regina: Canadian Plains Research Center.

Hum, Derek, and Wayne Simpson. 2009. "Manitoba in the Middle: A Mutual Fund Balanced for Steady Income." In *Manitoba Politics and Government: Issues, Institutions, and Traditions,* edited by Paul G. Thomas and Curtis Brown, 293-305. Winnipeg: University of Manitoba Press.

Huntington, Samuel P. 1981. *American Politics: The Promise of Disharmony.* Cambridge: Belknap Press.

Imbeau, Louis M., Rejean Landry, Henry Milner, François Petry, Jean Crête, Pierre-Gerlier Forest, and Vincent Lemieux. 2000. "Comparative Provincial Policy Analysis: A Research Agenda." *Canadian Journal of Political Science* 33, 4: 779-804.

Inglehart, Ronald. 1990. *Culture Shift in Advanced Industrial Society.* Princeton: Princeton University Press.

Innis, Harold A. 1956. *Essays in Canadian Economic History.* Toronto: University of Toronto Press.

Irvine, William. 1987. "Canada, 1945-1980: Party Platforms and Campaign Strategies." In *Ideology, Strategy and Party Change: Spatial Analyses of Post-War Election Programmes in 19 Democracies,* edited by Ian Budge, David Robertson, and Derek Hearl, 73-94. Cambridge: Cambridge University Press.

Irving, John A. 1959. *The Social Credit Movement in Alberta.* Toronto: University of Toronto Press.

Jacobsen, John Kurt. 1995. "Much Ado about Ideas: The Cognitive Factor in Economic Policy." *World Politics* 47, 2: 283-310.

Janda, Kenneth. 1968. "Retrieving Information for a Comparative Study of Political Parties." In *Approaches to the Study of Party Organization,* edited by William J. Crotty, 159-215. Boston: Allyn and Bacon.

–. 1980. *Political Parties: A Cross-National Survey.* New York: Free Press.

–. 1982. "Managing Qualitative Information and Quantitative Data on Political Parties." *Social Science Information Studies* 2: 113-29.

Janda, Kenneth, Robert Harmel, Christine Edens, and Patricia Goff. 1995. "Changes in Party Identity: Evidence from Party Manifestos." *Party Politics* 1, 2: 171-96.

Jenson, Jane. 1976. "Party Strategy and Party Identification: Some Patterns of Partisan Allegiance." *Canadian Journal of Political Science* 9, 1: 27-48.

–. 1987. "Changing Discourse, Changing Agenda: Political Rights and Reproductive Policies in France." In *The Women's Movement of the United States and Western Europe: Consciousness, Political Opportunity and Public Policy,* edited by Mary

F. Katzenstein and Carol Mueller, 64-88. Philadelphia: Temple University Press.

Johnson, James. 2003. "Conceptual Problems as Obstacles to Progress in Political Science: Four Decades of Political Culture Research." *Journal of Theoretical Politics* 15, 1: 87-115.

Johnson, Myron. 1979. "The Failure of the CCF in Alberta: An Accident of History." In *Society and Politics in Alberta: Research Papers,* edited by Carlo Caldarola, 87-107. Toronto: Methuen.

Johnsrude, Larry. 1997. "Klein Clears the Deck for Election Call." *Edmonton Journal,* February 11, A1.

Jones, David C. 1980. "The *Zeitgeist* of Western Settlement: Education and the Myth of the Land." In *Schooling and Society in 20th-Century British Columbia,* edited by J.D. Wilson and David C. Jones, 71-89. Calgary: Detselig.

Jones, Susan R., and Marylu K. McEwen. 2002. "A Conceptual Model of Multiple Dimensions of Identity." In *Qualitative Research in Practice,* edited by Sharan B. Merriam, 405-14. San Francisco: Jossey-Bass.

Kendall, Willmoore, and George W. Carey. 1970. *The Basic Symbols of the American Political Tradition.* Baton Rouge: Louisiana State University Press.

Key, V.O. 1964. *Politics, Parties, and Pressure Groups.* 5th ed. New York: Thomas Y. Crowell.

King, Gary, Robert Keohane, and Sidney Verba. 1993. *Designing Social Inquiry: Scientific Inference in Qualitative Research.* Princeton: Princeton University Press.

Kinsella, Warren. 2007. *The War Room: Political Strategies for Business, NGOs, and Anyone Who Wants to Win.* Toronto: Dundurn Press.

Kirchheimer, Otto. 1966. "The Transformation of West European Party Systems." In *Political Parties and Political Development,* edited by Joseph LaPalombara and Myron Weiner, 177-200. Princeton, NJ: Princeton University Press.

Kiss, Simon. 2009. "The Public Relations State in Alberta: Participatory or Post-Democracy." Paper presented at the annual meeting of the Canadian Political Science Association, 27 May, Carleton University, Ottawa.

Kitschelt, Herbert. 1994. *The Transformation of European Social Democracy.* Cambridge: Cambridge University Press.

Kleinnijenhuis, Jan, and Paul Pennings. 2001. "Measurement of Party Positions on the Basis of Party Programmes, Media Coverage and Voter Perceptions." In *Estimating the Policy Positions of Political Actors,* edited by Michael Laver, 162-82. London: Routledge.

Klingemann, Hans-Dieter, Andrea Volkens, Judith Bara, Ian Budge, and Michael D. McDonald, eds. 2007. *Mapping Policy Preferences II: Estimates for Parties, Electors, and Governments in Eastern Europe, European Union, and OECD, 1990-2003.* Oxford: Oxford University Press.

Kornberg, Allan, William Mishler, and Harold D. Clarke. 1982. *Representative Democracy in the Canadian Provinces.* Scarborough, ON: Prentice-Hall Canada.

Laitin, David D. 1986. *Hegemony and Culture: Politics and Religious Change among the Yoruba.* Chicago: University of Chicago Press.

Landry, Rejean. 1991. "Party Competition in Quebec: Direct Confrontation or Selective Emphasis." In *Party Politics in Canada,* edited by Hugh G. Thorburn, 401-13. 6th ed. Scarborough: Prentice-Hall.

Lane, Ruth. 1992. "Political Culture: Residual Category or General Theory?" *Comparative Political Studies* 25, 3: 362-87.

Lang, Timothy O.E. 1991. "Liberals in Manitoba: Provincial Decline and Resurgence." Master's thesis, University of Manitoba.

Laver, Michael. 2001. "Why Should We Estimate the Policy Position of Political Actors?" In *Estimating the Policy Positions of Political Actors,* edited by Michael Laver, 3-9. London: Routledge.

Laver, Michael, and John Garry. 2000. "Estimating Policy Positions from Political Texts." *American Journal of Political Science* 44, 3: 619-34.

Laxer, Gordon. 1995. "The Privatization of Public Life." In *The Trojan Horse: Alberta and the Future of Canada,* edited by Trevor Harrison and Gordon Laxer, 101-17. Montreal: Black Rose.

Laycock, David. 1990. *Populism and Democratic Thought in the Canadian Prairies, 1910 to 1945.* Toronto: University of Toronto Press.

Leadbeater, David, ed. 1984. *Essays on the Political Economy of Alberta.* Toronto: New Hogtown Press.

LeDuc, Lawrence. 1994. "Leaders and Voters: The Public Images of Canadian Political Leaders." In *Leaders and Leadership in Canada,* edited by Maureen Mancuso, Richard G. Price, and Ronald Wagenberg, 53-74. Toronto: Oxford University Press.

Leeson, Howard. 2001. "The Rich Soil of Saskatchewan Politics." In *Saskatchewan Politics: Into the Twenty-First Century,* edited by Howard Leeson, 3-13. Regina: Canadian Plains Research Center.

Leites, Nathan. 1951. *The Operational Code of the Politburo.* New York: McGraw-Hill.

Lett, Dan. 1997. "Doer Closes in On the Do-It Stage of His Leadership." *Winnipeg Free Press,* November 16, A4.

Lieutenant-Governor of Alberta. 1997. "Speech from the Throne." *Hansard,* 10 February.

–. 2001. "Speech from the Throne." *Hansard,* 12 February.

Lipset, Seymour Martin. 1968a. *Agrarian Socialism: The Cooperative Commonwealth Federation in Saskatchewan.* Garden City, NY: Doubleday.

–. 1968b. *Revolution and Counterrevolution.* New York: Basic Books.

–. 1990. *Continental Divide: The Values and Institutions of the United States and Canada.* New York: Routledge.

Lipset, Seymour Martin, and Stein Rokkan. 1967. "Cleavage Structures, Party Systems, and Voter Alignments: An Introduction." In *Party Systems and Voter Realignments: Cross-National Perspectives,* edited by Seymour Martin Lipset and Stein Rokkan, 1-64. New York: Free Press.

Lisac, Mark. 2004a. *Alberta Politics Uncovered: Taking Back Our Province.* Edmonton: NeWest Press.

–. 2004b. "Don Getty." In *Alberta Premiers of the Twentieth Century*, edited by Bradford J. Rennie, 229-54. Regina: Canadian Plains Research Center.

Long, J.A., and F.Q. Quo. 1972. "Alberta: One Party Dominance." In *Canadian Provincial Politics*, edited by Martin Robin, 1-26. Scarborough, ON: Prentice Hall.

Loxley, John. 1990. "Economic Planning under Social Democracy." In *The Political Economy of Manitoba*, edited by Jim Silver and Jeremy Hull, 318-30. Regina: Canadian Plains Research Center.

Macpherson, C.B. 1953. *Democracy in Alberta: The Theory and Practice of a Quasi-Party System*. Toronto: University of Toronto Press.

–. 1977. *Democracy in Alberta: Social Credit and the Party System*. 2nd ed. Toronto: University of Toronto Press.

Mallory, J.R. 1954. *Social Credit and the Federal Power in Canada*. Toronto: University of Toronto Press.

Manheim, Jarol B., Richard C. Rich, and Lars Willnat, eds. 2002. *Empirical Political Analysis: Research Methods in Political Science*. 5th ed. Toronto: Longman.

Manitoba. 1973. *Guidelines for the Seventies*. Vol. 1, *Introduction and Economic Analysis*. Winnipeg: Government of Manitoba.

Manitoba Liberal and Progressive Provincial Committee. 1932. "A Programme of Reconstruction and Readjustment." Manitoba Legislative Library.

–. 1936. "Manitoba Liberal and Progressive Election Manifesto."

Manitoba NDP. 1973a. "Election '73 Speakers' Notes." Archives of Manitoba, Co-operative Commonwealth Federation and New Democratic Party collection.

–. 1973b. News release, 4 June, Archives of Manitoba, Co-operative Commonwealth Federation and New Democratic Party Collection.

–. 1973c. "Record Good, More to Come: Schreyer." *Manitoba New Democrat* 3, 5: 1.

–. 1977a. *Leadership You Can Trust*. Winnipeg: Empire Printers.

–. 1977b. "Manitoba Is Eight Years Better." Pamphlet, Brandon University Archives, V. Gamey Papers.

–. 1977c. "Statement of Principles." Archives of Manitoba, Co-operative Commonwealth Federation and New Democratic Party Collection.

–. 1990a. "Gary Doer and the New Democrats: There Is Only One Choice on September 11." Manitoba Legislative Library.

–. 1990b. "Strong Voice, Clear Choice." Press release, Manitoba Legislative Library.

–. 1995. "Gary Doer – NDP – Rebuilding Manitoba Together." Manitoba Legislative Library.

–. 1999. "5 Good Reasons: Towards a Brighter Future – Gary Doer and Today's NDP." Prairie Manifesto Project Collection.

–. 2003a. "Five Priorities for the Next Four Years." http:www.todaysNDP.mb.ca.

–. 2003b. "Much Accomplished: More to Do." http:www.todaysNDP.mb.ca.

–. 2007a. "Forward with Gary Doer." http:www.todaysNDP.mb.ca.

–. 2007b. "Forward with Gary Doer: Building on Progress and Leadership for Manitoba's Future." http:www.todaysNDP.mb.ca.

Manitoba New Democratic Party. 1969a. *The Age of Gimmicks, Excuses, and Inaction Is Over ... An Era of Quality Government Is about to Begin in Manitoba.* Winnipeg: Wallingford Press.

–. 1969b. "The Big Change Sweeping Manitoba." Archives of Manitoba, New Democratic Party Collection.

–. 1969c. "Manitoba New Democrats Heading for Government." Archives of Manitoba, Liberal Party in Manitoba Collection.

Manitoba Progressive Conservative Association. 1962. *The Record of the Roblin Government*. Winnipeg: Manitoba Progressive Conservative Association.

Mann, William E. 1955. *Sect, Cult and Church in Alberta*. Toronto: University of Toronto Press.

Manning, Ernest. 1965. *National Medicare: Let's Look before We Leap*. Edmonton: Tele-Facts Publications.

–. 1967. *Political Realignment: A Challenge to Thoughtful Canadians*. Toronto: McClelland and Stewart.

Manning, Peter K., and Betsy Cullum-Swan. 1994. "Narrative, Content and Semiotic Analysis." In *Handbook of Qualitative Research*, edited by Norman K. Denzin and Yvonna S. Lincoln, 463-43. Thousand Oaks: Sage.

Manning, Preston. 1992. *The New Canada*. Toronto: Macmillan Canada.

Mansell, Robert. 1997. "Fiscal Restructuring in Alberta: An Overview." In *A Government Reinvented: A Study of Alberta's Deficit Elimination Program*, edited by Christopher Bruce, Ronald Kneebone, and Kenneth McKenzie, 16-76. Toronto: Oxford University Press.

Marchildon, Gregory P. 2004. "Roy Romanow." In *Saskatchewan Premiers of the Twentieth Century*, edited by Gordon L. Barnhart, 353-96. Regina: Canadian Plains Research Center.

–. 2005a. The Great Divide. In *The Heavy Hand of History: Interpreting Saskatchewan's Past*, edited by Gregory P. Marchildon. Regina: Canadian Plains Research Centre.

–, ed. 2005b. *The Heavy Hand of History: Interpreting Saskatchewan's Past*. Regina: Canadian Plains Research Centre.

–. 2005c. Why the Heavy Hand of History? In *The Heavy Hand of History: Interpreting Saskatchewan's Past*, edited by Gregory P. Marchildon. Regina: Canadian Plains Research Centre.

Marlowe, Paul. 1976. *History of Democratic Socialism on the Move in Canada*. Winnipeg: Kildonan New Democratic Party Association.

Marshall, Catherine, and Gretchen B. Rossman. 2006. *Designing Qualitative Research*. 4th ed. Thousand Oaks: Sage.

Marshall, Douglas. 1970. "How Manitoba Turned 100 by Standing On Its Head." *Maclean's*, December.

May, Tim. 2001. *Social Research: Issues, Methods and Process*. 3rd ed. Philadelphia: Open University Press.

McAllister, James A. 1984. *The Government of Edward Schreyer*. Montreal/Kingston: McGill-Queen's University Press.

McDevitt, Michael. 2005. "The Partisan Child: Developmental Provocation as a Model of Political Socialization." *International Journal of Public Opinion Research* 18, 1: 67-88.

McDevitt, Michael, and Steven Chaffee. 2002. "From Top-Down to Trickle-Up Influence: Revisiting Assumptions about the Family in Political Socialization."
Political Communication 19: 281-391.

McGrane, David. 2005. "Social Democracy and Western Alienation in Saskatch-
ewan Politics, 1900 to 2000." Paper presented at the annual meeting of the
Canadian Political Science Association, 2 June, University of Western Ontario,
London.

–. 2006. "Explaining the Saskatchewan NDP's Shift to Third Way Social Democracy."
Paper presented at the annual meeting of the Canadian Political Science Association, 3 June, York University, Toronto.

McLellan, David S. 1971. "The 'Operational Code' Approach to the Study of Political
Leaders: Dean Acheson's Philosophical and Instrumental Beliefs. *Canadian
Journal of Political Science* 4, 1: 52-75.

McLeod, Thomas H., and Ian McLeod. 2004. "T.C. Douglas." In *Saskatchewan Premiers of the Twentieth Century,* edited by Gordon L. Barnhart, 161-212. Regina:
Canadian Plains Research Center.

Meisel, John. 1960. "The Formulation of Liberal and Conservative Programmes in
the 1957 Canadian General Election." *Canadian Journal of Economics and Political Science* 26, 4: 565-74.

Meisel, John, and Matthew Mendelsohn. 2001. "Meteor? Phoenix? Chameleon? The
Decline and Transformation of Party Politics in Canada." In *Party Politics in
Canada,* edited by Hugh G. Thorburn and Alan Whitehorn, 163-78. 8th ed.
Toronto: Prentice-Hall.

Mellos, Koula. 1970. "Quantitative Comparison of Party Ideology." *Canadian Journal of Political Science* 3, 4: 540-58.

Melnyk, George. 1992. "The West as Protest: The Cycles of Regional Discontent." In
Riel to Reform: A History of Protest in Western Canada, edited by George Melnyk, 1-11. Saskatoon: Fifth House Publishers.

–. 1995. "Culture and the State in Alberta, 1971-1995." In *The Trojan Horse: Alberta
and the Future of Canada,* edited by Trevor Harrison and Gordon Laxer, 254-
67. Montreal: Black Rose.

Merelman, Richard M. 1991. *Partial Visions: Culture and Politics in Britain, Canada, and the United States.* Madison: University of Wisconsin Press.

Morton, W.L. 1957. *Manitoba: A History.* Toronto: University of Toronto Press.

–. 1967a. *Manitoba: A History.* Toronto: University of Toronto Press.

–. 1967b. *The Progressive Party in Canada.* Toronto: University of Toronto Press.

–. 1992a. "The Bias of Prairie Politics." In *Riel to Reform: A History of Protest in
Western Canada,* edited by George Melnyk, 12-19. Saskatoon: Fifth House
Publishers.

–. 1992b. "The Western Progressive Movement, 1911-1921." In *Riel to Reform: A History of Protest in Western Canada,* edited by George Melnyk, 149-61. Saskatoon: Fifth House Publishers.

Myrdal, Gunnar. 1969. *An American Dilemma: The Negro Problem in America.* Vol.
1. New York: Harper and Row.

Naylor, R.T., and G. Teeple. 1972. "The Ideological Foundations of Social Democracy and Social Credit." In *Capitalism and the National Question in Canada,* edited by Gary Teeple, 251-66. Toronto: University of Toronto Press.

Netherton, Alex. 1992. "The Shifting Points of Politics: A Neo-Institutional Analysis." In *The Provincial State: Politics in Canada's Provinces and Territories,* edited by Keith Brownsey and Michael Howlett, 175-206. Mississauga: Copp Clark Pitman.

–. 2001. "Paradigm and Shift: A Sketch of Manitoba Politics." In *The Provincial State in Canada,* edited by K. Brownsey and M. Howlett, 203-40 Peterborough, ON: Broadview Press.

Neuman, W. Lawrence, and Karen Robson. 2007. *Basics of Social Research: Qualitative and Quantitative Approaches.* Canadian ed. Toronto: Pearson.

New Democratic Party of Saskatchewan. 1980. *A Strong Party – A Strong Saskatchewan – A Strong Canada.* Regina: Merit Printing.

–. 1982. "For as Long as the Sun Shines: Working Together for Progress." Saskatchewan Archives Board, W.G. Knight Collection.

New Democratic Party of Saskatchewan and the Liberal Party of Saskatchewan. 1999. "An Agreement for a Coalition between the New Democratic Party of Saskatchewan and the Liberal Party of Saskatchewan." Manitoba Legislative Library, Saskatchewan SPR 1999 Coalition Government.

Nichols, H.E. 1963. *Alberta's Fight for Freedom.* Edmonton: Alberta Social Credit League.

Noel, Sid. 2007. "Leaders' Entourages, Parties, and Patronage." In *Canadian Parties in Transition,* edited by Alain-G. Gagnon and A. Brian Tanguay, 197-214. 3rd ed. Scarborough, ON: Nelson.

Norrie, Kenneth H. 1979. "Some Comments on Prairie Economic Alienation." In *Society and Politics in Alberta: Research Papers,* edited by Carlo Caldarola, 131-42. Toronto: Methuen.

–. 1984. "A Regional Economic Overview of the West since 1945." In *The Making of the Modern West: Western Canada since 1945,* edited by A.W. Rasporich, 63-77. Calgary: University of Calgary Press.

Norton, Diane Lloyd. 2004. "Woodrow S. Lloyd." In *Saskatchewan Premiers of the Twentieth Century,* edited by Gordon L. Barnhart, 213-36. Regina: Canadian Plains Research Center.

O'Neill, Brenda. 2002. "Sugar and Spice? Political Culture and the Political Behaviour of Canadian Women." In *Citizen Politics: Research and Theory in Canadian Political Behaviour,* edited by Joanna Everitt and Brenda O'Neill, 40-55. Oxford: Oxford University Press.

Ornstein, Michael D. 1986. "Regionalism and Canadian Political Ideology." In *Regionalism in Canada,* edited by Robert J. Brym, 47-88. Toronto: Irwin.

Paddock, Joel. 1992. "Inter-Party Ideological Differences in Eleven State Parties, 1956-1980." *Western Political Quarterly* 45, 3: 751-60.

–. 1998. "Explaining State Variation in Interparty Ideological Differences." *Political Research Quarterly* 51, 3: 765-80.

Pal, Leslie A. 1992. "The Political Executive and Political Leadership in Alberta." In *Government and Politics in Alberta,* edited by Allan Tupper and Roger Gibbins, 1-30. Edmonton: University of Alberta Press.

Palmer, Howard, and Tamara Palmer. 1976. "The 1971 Election and the Fall of Social Credit in Alberta." *Prairie Forum* 1, 2: 123-34.

Paltiel, Khayyam Zev. 1996. "Political Marketing: Party Finance, and the Decline of Canadian Parties." In *Canadian Parties in Transition,* edited by A. Brian Tanguay and Alain-G. Gagnon, 403-22. 2nd ed. Scarborough, ON: Nelson.

Pammett, Jon H., and Michael S. Whittington. 1976. "Political Culture and Political Socialization." In *Foundations of Political Culture: Political Socialization in Canada,* edited by Jon H. Pammett and Michael S. Whittington, 1-11. Toronto: Macmillan Company of Canada.

Panebianco, Angelo. 1988. *Political Parties: Organization and Power.* Cambridge: Cambridge University Press.

Pateman, Carole. 1980. "The Civic Culture: A Philosophic Critique." In *The Civic Culture Revisited,* edited by Gabriel Almond and Sidney Verba, 57-102. Newbury Park, CA: Sage.

Patten, Steve. 2001. "'Toryism' and the Conservative Party in a Neo-Liberal Era." In *Party Politics in Canada,* edited by Hugh G. Thorburn and Alan Whitehorn, 134-47. 8th ed. Toronto: Prentice Hall.

PC Alberta. 2004. "Building Alberta's Future." http:buildingalbertasfuture.com.

–. 2008. "Ed Stelmach." http:www.albertapc.ab.ca.

PC Manitoba. 2003. "Party Philosophy." http:www.pcmanitoba.com.

–. 2006. "Our Philosophy." http:www.pcmanitoba.com.

–. 2007. "Five for the Future: Hugh McFadyen's Five Key Priorities for the Future." http:www.pcmanitoba.ca.

Pelletier, Rejean. 1996. "The Structures of Canadian Political Parties." In *Canadian Parties in Transition,* edited by A. Brian Tanguay and Alain-G. Gagnon, 136-59. 2nd ed. Scarborough: Nelson.

Peterson, T. 1972. "Ethnic and Class Politics in Manitoba." In *Canadian Provincial Politics,* edited by Martin Robin, 69-115. Scarborough, ON: Prentice Hall.

Petry, François, and Rejean Landry. 2001. "Estimating Interparty Policy Distances from Election Programmes in Quebec, 1970-89." In *Estimating the Policy Positions of Political Actors,* edited by Michael Laver, 133-46. London: Routledge.

Petry, François, and Matthew Mendelsohn. 2004. "Public Opinion and Policy Making in Canada 1994-2001." *Canadian Journal of Political Science* 37, 3: 505-29.

Phillips, Louse. 1998. "Hegemony and Political Discourse: The Lasting Impact of Thatcherism." *Sociology* 32, 4: 847-67.

Pickup, Mark, Anthony Sayers, Rainer Knopff, and Keith Archer. 2004. "Social Capital and Civic Community in Alberta." *Canadian Journal of Political Science* 37, 3: 617-45.

Pierson, Paul. 2004. *Politics in Time: History, Institutions, and Social Analysis.* Princeton, NJ: Princeton University Press.

Pitsula, James M. 2004. "Grant Devine." In *Saskatchewan Premiers of the Twentieth Century*, edited by Gordon L. Barnhart, 317-52. Regina: Canadian Plains Research Center.

Pitsula, James M., and Ken Rasmussen. 1990. *Privatizing a Province: The New Right in Saskatchewan*. Vancouver: New Star.

Platt, Jennifer. 2006. "Evidence and Proof in Documentary Research: Part I, Some Specific Problems of Documentary Research." In *Documentary Research*, Vol. 1, edited by John Scott, 83-104. Thousand Oaks, CA: Sage.

Pomper, Gerald M. 1968. *Elections in America: Control and Influence in Democratic Politics*. New York: Dodd, Mead and Company.

Popper, Karl. 1972. *Objective Knowledge*. Oxford: Clarendon Press.

Praud, Jocelyne, and Sarah McQuarrie. 2001. "The Saskatchewan CCF-NDP from the *Regina Manifesto* to the Romanow Years." In *Saskatchewan Politics: Into the Twenty-First Century*, edited by Howard Leeson, 143-68. Regina: Canadian Plains Research Center.

Preece, Rod. 1977. "The Myth of the Red Tory." *Canadian Journal of Political and Social Theory* 1, 2: 3-28.

Progressive Conservative Association of Alberta. 1967. *Guideposts of the Progressive Conservative Party of Alberta*. Calgary: Burnand Printing Company.

–. 1971. *Progressive Conservatism in Alberta: The Rebuilding of a Political Party*. Calgary: Marshall and Donlevy Printing.

–. 1979a. *Election '79: Alberta Leadership ... The Time to Look Ahead*. Edmonton: Edmonton Journal Printing.

–. 1979b. "Pledge and Progress." Pamphlet, Glenbow Archives, John Kushner Collection.

–. 1980. *History of the Progressive Conservative Party of Alberta*. Edmonton: Progressive Conservative Association of Alberta.

–. 1982a. *For Alberta! A Proud Record of Positive Action ... in Programs for People*. Edmonton: Progressive Conservative Association of Alberta.

–. 1982b. *For Alberta! Vote Progressive Conservative*. Edmonton: Edmonton Journal Printing.

–. 1982c. "On November 2 There's a Lot at Stake for Alberta!" *Calgary Herald*, November 1, A16.

–. 1986. "Committed to the Future." *Calgary Herald*, 7 May, B9.

–. 1989a. "Leadership with Integrity." Pamphlet, Glenbow Archives, Sheldon Chumir Collection.

–. 1989b. "Strength and Community." Pamphlet, Alberta Legislative Library, Progressive Conservative Association of Alberta Pamphlet Collection.

–. 1993. "Ralph's Team *Will* Get the Job Done: Our Plan for a Better Alberta." Pamphlet, Alberta Legislative Library, Progressive Conservative Association of Alberta Pamphlet Collection.

–. 1997. "You and Ralph's Team: Building Alberta Together." Pamphlet, Alberta Legislative Library, Progressive Conservative Association of Alberta Pamphlet Collection.

Progressive Conservative Association of Manitoba. 1973. "Spivak." *Winnipeg Tribune,* June 15.

Progressive Conservative Party of Manitoba. 1958a. "36 Years Is Too Long for Any Government: Manitoba Cannot Afford a Continuance of Costly Blunders." *Winnipeg Tribune,* 10 May, 10.

–. 1958b. "Could There Be Any Greater Difference?" *Winnipeg Tribune,* 13 June, 9.

–. 1958c. "An Open Letter to All Electors." *Winnipeg Free Press,* 3 May, 7.

–. 1958d. "Talking Points for PC Speakers and Workers – Provincial Election 1958." Cards, Archives of Manitoba, Sterling Lyon Collection.

–. 1959a. "Let Us Get On with the Business of Manitoba!" Pamphlet, City of Winnipeg Archives, Magnus Eliason Collection.

–. 1959b. "Talking Points for PC Speakers and Workers – Provincial Election 1959." Cards, Archives of Manitoba, Sterling Lyon Collection.

–. 1960. "Resume Government Activities – Private and Confidential." Archives of Manitoba, Executive Council Collection.

–. 1962a. *Building a New Manitoba.* Winnipeg: SES Printers.

–. 1962b. "Progressive Conservative Party Platform." Archives of Manitoba, Sterling Lyon Collection.

–. 1962c. "Talking Points for PC Speakers and Workers – Provincial Election 1962." Cards, Archives of Manitoba, Executive Council Collection.

–. 1966a. "Leadership Means Good Government: Manitoba Moves Ahead with Roblin." Pamphlet, Glenbow Archives, Progressive Conservative Association of Alberta Collection.

–. 1966b. "Roblin Government Policies for a Greater Manitoba." Archives of Manitoba, Executive Council Collection.

–. 1966c. "Talking Points for PC Speakers and Workers – Provincial Election 1966." Cards, Archives of Manitoba, Sterling Lyon Collection.

Putnam, Robert. 1993. *Making Democracy Work: Civic Traditions in Modern Italy.* Princeton, NJ: Princeton University Press.

–. 2000. *Bowling Alone: The Collapse and Revival of American Community.* New York: Simon and Schuster.

Putnam, Robert D. 1971. "Studying Elite Political Culture: The Case of 'Ideology.'" *American Political Science Review* 65, 3: 651-81.

Pye, Lucian. 1973. "Culture and Political Science: Problems in the Evaluation of the Concept of Political Culture." In *The Idea of Culture in the Social Sciences,* edited by Louis Schneider and Charles M. Bonjean, 65-76. Cambridge: Cambridge University Press.

Pye, Lucian, and Sidney Verba, eds. 1965. *Political Culture and Political Development.* Princeton, NJ: Princeton University Press.

Rasmussen, Ken. 2001. "Saskatchewan: From Entrepreneurial to Embedded State." In *The Provincial State in Canada,* edited by Keith Brownsey and Michael Howlett, 241-76. Peterborough, ON: Broadview Press.

Rayner, Jeremy, and Tina Beaudry-Mellor. 2009. "Hope and Fear Revisited: Did the Provincial Election of 2007 Mark the Transition to a Stable Two-Party System in Saskatchewan?" *Canadian Political Science Review* 3, 1: 17-33.

Rea, J.E. 1970. "The Roots of Prairie Society." In *Prairie Perspectives*, edited by David P. Gagan, 46-57. Toronto: Holt, Rinehart and Winston.

Read, Chris. 2008. "From Scranton to Winnipeg: The Office Goes North." CBC News Online, 23 October. http:www.cbc.ca.

Regehr, Ted. 2004. "William M. Martin." In *Saskatchewan Premiers of the Twentieth Century*, edited by Gordon L. Barnhart, 39-68. Regina: Canadian Plains Research Center.

Regina and Area New Democrats. 1978. *A Record of Success: Great Promise for Tomorrow*. Regina: Service Printers.

Regina CCF Council. 1934. *Farmer-Labor Declaration of Policy*. Regina: The Corson Printing Company.

Regina Elphinstone New Democrats. 1986a. *Our Commitment to Saskatchewan*. Regina: Centax.

–. 1986b. *Together We Can Do It!* Regina: Centax

Regina Liberal Association. 1944a. *What Can Socialism Give You?* Regina: Commercial Printers.

–. 1944b. *Would They Follow Sweden's Example?* Regina: Commercial Printers.

Rennie, Bradford J. 2004. "Introduction." In *Alberta Premiers of the Twentieth Century*, edited by Bradford J. Rennie, vii-xiii. Regina: Canadian Plains Research Center.

Richards, Lyn. 2005. *Handling Qualitative Data: A Practical Guide*. Thousand Oaks, CA: Sage.

Riker, William H. 1993. "Rhetorical Interaction in the Ratification Campaigns." In *Agenda Formation*, edited by Willam H. Riker, 81-123. Ann Arbor: University of Michigan Press.

Roberts, David. 2001. "Canada Faces Potential Danger, Romanow Says." *Globe and Mail*, 24 January, A5.

Robertson, David. 1976. *A Theory of Party Competition*. London: Wiley.

Roblin, Duff. 1999. *Speaking for Myself: Politics and Other Pursuits*. Winnipeg: Great Plains Publications.

Roome, Patricia. 2004. "Alexander C. Rutherford." In *Alberta Premiers of the Twentieth Century*, edited by Bradford J. Rennie, 3-18. Regina: Canadian Plains Research Center.

Rosenbaum, Walter A. 1975. *Political Culture*. New York: Praeger Publishers.

Royed, Terry J. 1996. "Testing the Mandate Model in Britain and the United States: Evidence from the Reagan and Thatcher Eras." *British Journal of Political Science* 26, 1: 45-80.

Royed, Terry J., and Stephen A. Borrelli. 1999. "Parties and Economic Policy in the USA: Pledges and Performance, 1976-1992." *Party Politics* 5, 1: 115-27.

Russell, Frances. 2010. "The Evolution of Political Journalism in Manitoba." In *Manitoba Politics and Government: Issues, Institutions, and Traditions*, edited by Paul G. Thomas and Curtis Brown, 218-26. Winnipeg: University of Manitoba Press.

Sampert, Shannon. 2008. "More than Just Cowboys with White Hats: A Demographic Profile of Edmonton and Calgary." In *Electing a Diverse Canada: The*

Representation of Immigrants, Minorities, and Women, edited by Caroline Andrew, John Biles, Myer Siemiatycki, and Erin Tolley, 92-110. Vancouver: UBC Press.

Sapiro, Virginia. 2004. "Not Your Parents' Political Socialization: Introduction for a New Generation." *Annual Review of Political Science* 7, 1: 1-23.

Saskatchewan Federation of Labour. 1956a. *10,000 Government Employees Have a Great Stake in the Saskatchewan Election June 20.* Regina: Service Printers.

–. 1956b. *Vote for Continued Progress for Labour.* Regina: Service Printers.

–. 1960. Saskatchewan Election 1960: Read the Facts – Organize Action – Get Out the Vote. Regina: Service Printing Co.

–. 1964. *Election Special: Keep Saskatchewan Ahead.* Regina: Saskatchewan Federation of Labour Education Committee.

Saskatchewan Liberal Association. 1938. *Election Manifesto by the Government of Saskatchewan.* Regina: Commercial Printers.

–. 1944a. *Don't Let This Happen Here!* Regina: Commercial Printers.

–. 1944b. *Election Manifesto by the Government of Saskatchewan.* Regina: Commercial Printers.

–. 1944c. *Facts: A Record which Is a Challenge.* Regina: Commercial Printers.

Saskatchewan Liberal Party. 1933. *Platform Resolutions of the Saskatchewan Liberal Party.* Regina: Commercial Printers.

Saskatchewan NDP. 1971a. *New Deal for People.* Regina: Service Printing.

–. 1971b. *New Deal for People: New Democratic Party Northern Development Program 1971.* Regina: Service Printing.

–. 1975a. *The Blakeney Team ... Keeping Saskatchewan Ahead.* Regina: Service Printers.

–. 1975b. *NDP ... Keeping Saskatchewan Ahead.* Regina: Service Printers.

–. 1975c. *New Deal '75.* Regina: Service Printing Company.

–. 1978. *NDP Saskatchewan: A Solid Success ...* Regina: Service Printing Company.

–. 1982a. "Allan Blakeney and the NDP – Tested ... and Trusted." Pamphlet, Saskatchewan Archives Board, William Knight Collection.

–. 1982b. *NDP Saskatchewan: Keeping the Promise.* Regina: Centax.

–. 1982c. "Working with Everyone in the 80's." Pamphlet, Saskatchewan Archives Board, William Knight Collection.

–. 2003a. "Forward Together: Building the Future for Saskatchewan Families." Pamphlet, University of Regina Library, Pamphlet Collection.

–. 2003b. "There's a Lot to Be Proud of in Saskatchewan." Pamphlet, Saskatchewan Legislative Library, Pamphlet Collection.

Saskatchewan New Democratic Party. 1971. *This Booklet Is About Saskatchewan ...* Regina: Service Printing.

–. 1978. *New Decade of Progress: A Program for the 80's.* Regina: Service Printers.

–. 1982a. *The People Who Care ... about Keeping a Good Thing Going for Saskatchewan.* Regina: Centax of Canada.

–. 1982b. *We Care! NDP – We've Been Tested ... We Can Be Trusted.* Regina: Centax of Canada.

–. 1991a. *Let's Do It ... The Saskatchewan Way.* Regina: Midwest Litho.

–. 1991b. *Renewing the Saskatchewan Community: A New Democratic Vision for the 90s.* Regina: Saskatchewan New Democratic Party.

–. 1991c. *The Saskatchewan Way.* Regina: Midwest Litho.

–. 1995. *The Saskatchewan Way: It's Working.* Regina: PrintWest Communications.

–. 1999. *Platform: Building A Bright Future Together – The Saskatchewan Way!* Regina: PrintWest.

Saskatchewan New Democrats. 2003. "Forward Together." Pamphlet, University of Regina Library, Pamphlet Collection.

–. 2007. "Moving Forward Together: Making Life Better for Saskatchewan Families." http:saskndp.ca.

Saskatchewan Party. 2004. *Signal: The Newsletter of the Saskatchewan Party* 3, 1.

–. 2007. "Securing the Future: New Ideas for Saskatchewan." http:saskparty.com.

Saul, John Ralston. 2008. *A Fair Country.* New York: Viking Press.

Sayers, Anthony. 2002. "The Study of Political Leaders and Activists." In *Citizen Politics,* edited by Joanna Everitt and Brenda O'Neill, 301-20. Don Mills, ON: Oxford University Press.

Saywell, John T. 2002. *The Lawmakers: Judicial Power and the Shaping of Canadian Federalism.* Toronto: University of Toronto Press.

Scarrow, Susan E., Paul Webb, and David M. Farrell. 2000. "From Social Integration to Electoral Contestation: The Changing Distribution of Power within Political Parties." In *Parties without Partisans: Political Change in Advanced Industrial Democracies,* edited by Russell J. Dalton and Michael P. Wattenberg, 129-56. Oxford: Oxford University Press.

Scheuch, Erwin K. 1968. "The Cross-Cultural Use of Sample Surveys: Problems of Comparability." In *Comparative Research across Nations and Cultures,* edited by Stein Rokkan, 176-209. The Hague: Houton.

Scott, John. 2006. "Social Research and Documentary Sources." In *Documentary Research,* Vol. 1, edited by John Scott, 3-22. Thousand Oaks, CA: Sage Publications.

Scown, Dennis R. 1973. "A History and Analysis of the 1971 Alberta General Election." Master's thesis, University of Calgary.

Sears, David O., and Nicholas A. Valentino. 1997. "Politics Matters: Political Events as Catalysts for Preadult Socialization." *American Political Science Review* 91, 1: 46-65.

Shilliday, Jim. 1962. "Duff's Plan: Research, Loans and a Big Push for Industry." *Winnipeg Tribune,* 24 November.

Shiry, John. 1978. "Mass Values and System Outputs." In *Approaches to Canadian Politics,* edited by John H. Redekop, 36-58. Scarborough, ON: Prentice-Hall.

Sides, John. 2006. "The Origins of Campaign Agendas." *British Journal of Political Science* 36, 3: 407-30.

Sikkink, Kathryn. 1991. *Ideas and Institutions: Developmentalism in Argentina and Brazil.* Ithaca, NY: Cornell University Press.

Smith, Craig Allen, and Kathy B. Smith. 2000. "A Rhetorical Perspective on the 1997 British Party Manifestos." *Political Communication* 17: 457-73.

Smith, David E. 1969. "A Comparison of Prairie Political Development in Saskatchewan and Alberta." *Journal of Canadian Studies* 4, 1: 17-26.

–. 1976. "The Prairie Provinces." In *The Provincial Political Systems: Comparative Essays*, edited by David J. Bellamy, Jon Pammett, and Donald C. Rowat, 46-61. Toronto: Methuen.

–. 1981. *The Regional Decline of a National Party: Liberals on the Prairies.* Toronto: University of Toronto Press.

–. 1991. "Grits and Tories on the Prairies." In *Party Politics in Canada,* edited by Hugh G. Thorburn, 273-89. 6th ed. Scarborough: Prentice-Hall Canada.

–, ed. 2007. *Lipset's Agrarian Socialism: A Re-examination.* Regina: Saskatchewan Institute of Public Policy.

–. 2009. "Saskatchewan: A Distinct Political Culture." In *Perspectives of Saskatchewan,* edited by Jene M. Porter, 37-56. Winnipeg: University of Manitoba Press.

Smith, Peter J. 1984. "Urban Development Trends in the Prairie Provinces." In *The Making of the Modern West: Western Canada since 1945,* edited by A.W. Rasporich, 133-43. Calgary: University of Calgary Press.

–. 1992. "Alberta: A Province Just Like Any Other?" In *The Provincial State: Politics in Canada's Provinces and Territories,* edited by Keith Brownsey and Michael Howlett, 243-64. Mississauga, ON: Copp Clark Pitman.

–. 2001. "Experiments in Governance – From Social Credit to the Klein Revolution." In *The Provincial State in Canada,* edited by Keith Brownsey and Michael Howlett, 277-308. Peterborough, ON: Broadview Press.

Social Credit League of Alberta. 1940. *Let's All Pull Together and Keep Alberta in the Lead.* Edmonton: Armstrong-Cosans.

–. 1944. *Alberta Social Credit Platform: A Democratic Platform Advocating the Principles of True Democracy.* Edmonton: Armstrong-Cosans.

–. 1948. *The Next Five Years Can Be the Best: Vote Social Credit for Progress – Freedom – Security.* Edmonton: Modern Press.

–. 1952. *We've Come a Long Way Together since 1935.* Edmonton: Modern Press.

–. 1955. *Did You Know? The Accomplishments of a Social Credit Government.* Edmonton: Reliable Printing Co.

–. 1957. *Did You Know? The Accomplishments of a Social Credit Government.* Edmonton: Reliable Printing Co.

–. 1958. *Did You Know? The Accomplishments of a Social Credit Government.* Edmonton: Reliable Printing Co.

–. 1959. *Did You Know? The Accomplishments of a Social Credit Government.* Edmonton: Reliable Printing Co.

–. 1960. *Did You Know? An Authentic Report of Alberta's Progress with Social Credit Government.* Edmonton: Reliable Printing Co.

Spivak, Sidney. 1973. "Freedom and Opportunity: A Real Alternative – A Statement of Principles by the Progressive Conservative Party of Manitoba." Archives of Manitoba, Sterling Lyon Collection.

Stelmach, Ed. 2006. "Policy Platform." http:www.stelmach.ca.

Stewart, David. 1995. "Klein's Makeover of the Alberta Conservatives." In *The Trojan Horse: Alberta and the Future of Canada,* edited by Trevor Harrison and Gordon Laxer, 24-47. Montreal: Black Rose.

Stewart, David, and Keith Archer. 2000. *Quasi-Democracy? Parties and Leadership Selection in Alberta.* Vancouver: UBC Press.

Stewart, David K., and Anthony M. Sayers. 2008. "Leadership Change in a Governing Party: The Alberta Progressive Conservatives, 2006." Paper presented at the annual meeting of the Canadian Political Science Association, 1 June, University of British Columbia, Vancouver.

Stewart, Gordon. 2007. "The Beginning of Politics in Canada." In *Canadian Parties in Transition,* edited by Alain-G. Gagnon and A. Brian Tanguay, 17-32. 3rd ed. Scarborough, ON: Nelson.

Stewart, Ian. 1994a. "All the King's Horses: The Study of Canadian Political Culture." In *Canadian Politics,* edited by James P. Bickerton and Alain-G. Gagnon, 75-92. 2nd ed. Peterborough, ON: Broadview Press.

–. 1994b. *Roasting Chestnuts: The Mythology of Maritime Political Culture.* Vancouver: UBC Press.

–. 2002. "Vanishing Points: Three Paradoxes of Political Culture Research." In *Citizen Politics: Research and Theory in Canadian Political Behaviour,* edited by Joanna Everitt and Brenda O'Neill, 21-39. Oxford: Oxford University Press.

–. 2009. *Just One Vote: From Jim Walding's Nomination to Constitutional Defeat.* Winnipeg: University of Manitoba Press.

Stingel, Janine. 2000. *Social Discredit: Anti-Semitism, Social Credit, and the Jewish Response.* Montreal/Kingston: McGill-Queen's University Press.

Stokes, Janice Claire. 1993. "The Leftist and Provincialist Characteristics of Protest Party Politics in Alberta: Social Credit in Perspective." Master's thesis, Dalhousie University.

Street, John. 1997. *Politics and Popular Culture.* Philadelphia: Temple University Press.

Swainson, Donald. 1973. "Manitoba's Election: Patterns Confirmed." *Canadian Forum* (September): 4-7.

Swann, F. Richard. 1971. "Progressive Social Credit in Alberta, 1935-1940." PhD diss., University of Cincinnati.

Syms, Frank. 1969. Personal correspondence to candidate, campaign manager, and constituency president or secretary, n.d., University of Manitoba Archives, Edward R. Schreyer Collection.

Taras, David, and Allan Tupper. 1994. "Politics and Deficits: Alberta's Challenge to the Canadian Political Agenda." In *Canada: The State of the Federation 1994,* edited by Harvey Lazar, 61-84. Kingston: Institute of Intergovernmental Relations.

Taras, David, and Robert Weyant. 1988. "Dreamers of the Day: A Guide to Roles, Character and Performance on the Political Stage." In *Prime Ministers and Premiers: Political Leadership and Public Policy in Canada,* edited by Leslie A. Pal and David Taras, 2-15. Scarborough, ON: Prentice-Hall.

Tashakkori, Abbas, and Charles Teddlie, eds. 2003. *Handbook of Mixed Methods in Social and Behavioural Research.* Thousand Oaks, CA: Sage.

Taylor, K.W., and Nelson Wiseman. 1977. "Class and Ethnic Voting in Winnipeg: The case of 1941." *Canadian Review of Sociology and Anthropology* 14, 2: 174-87.

Thomas, David. 1997. *Whistling Past the Graveyard: Constitutional Abeyances, Quebec, and the Future of Canada*. Don Mills, ON: Oxford University Press.

Thomas, Lewis G. 1980. "Alberta, 1905-1980: The Uneasy Society." In *The New Provinces: Alberta and Saskatchewan, 1905-1980*, edited by Howard Palmer and Donald Smith, 23-41. Vancouver: Tantalus Research.

Thomas, Paul G. 1989. "Manitoba: Stuck in the Middle." In *Canada: The State of the Federation 1989*, edited by Ronald L. Watts and Douglas M. Brown, 75-104. Kingston: Institute of Intergovernmental Relations.

–. 2008. "Leading from the Middle: Manitoba's Role in the Intergovernmental Arena." *Canadian Political Science Review* 2, 3: 29-51.

Tocqueville, Alexis. 1988 [1848]. *Democracy in America*. New York: Harper and Row.

Torney-Purta, Judith. 2000. "Comparative Perspectives on Political Socialization." *Comparative Education Review* 44, 1: 88-95.

Trimble, Linda. 1997. "Comments on Chapter 13." In *A Government Reinvented: A Study of Alberta's Deficit Elimination Program*, edited by Christopher Bruce, Ronald Kneebone, and Kenneth McKenzie, 486-89. Toronto: Oxford University Press.

Tupper, Allan. 1991. "Alberta Politics: The Collapse of Consensus." In *Party Politics in Canada*, edited by Hugh G. Thorburn, 451-67. 6th ed. Scarborough, ON: Prentice-Hall Canada.

–. 2004. "Peter Lougheed." In *Alberta Premiers of the Twentieth Century*, edited by Bradford J. Rennie, 203-28. Regina: Canadian Plains Research Center.

Tupper, Allan, and Roger Gibbins, eds. 1992. *Government and Politics in Alberta*. Edmonton: University of Alberta Press.

Verba, Sidney. 1965. "Conclusion." In *Political Culture and Political Development*, edited by Lucian W. Pye and Sidney Verba, 512-60. Princeton, NJ: Princeton University Press.

–. 1980. "On Revisiting the Civic Culture: A Personal Postscript." In *The Civic Culture Revisited*, edited by Gabriel Almond and Sidney Verba, 394-410. Newbury Park, CA: Sage.

Verney, Douglas V. 1978. "Has There Been a Distinctive Canadian Political Tradition?" *Journal of Commonwealth and Comparative Politics* 26, 3: 231-56.

Volkens, Andrea. 2001. "Manifesto Research since 1979: From Reliability to Validity." In *Estimating the Policy Positions of Political Actors*, edited by Michael Laver, 33-49. London: Routledge.

Waiser, Bill. 2009. "The Myth of Multiculturalism in Early Saskatchewan." In *Perspectives of Saskatchewan*, edited by Jene M. Porter, 57-74. Winnipeg: University of Manitoba Press.

Walters, Ronald W. 1990. "Party Platforms as Political Process." *PS: Political Science and Politics* 23, 3: 436-38.

Ward, Norman. 1975. "Hon. James Gardiner and the Liberal Party of Alberta, 1935-40." *Canadian Historical Review* 61, 3: 303-22.

Warwick, Paul V. 2002. "Toward a Common Dimensionality in West European Policy Spaces." *Party Politics* 8, 1: 101-22.

Weinroth, Michelle. 2004. "Rituals of Rhetoric and Nationhood: The Liberal Anti-Deficit Campaign, 1994-1998." *Journal of Canadian Studies* 38, 2: 44-79.

Wesley, Jared J. 2006. "The Collective Centre: Social Democracy and Red Tory Politics in Manitoba." Paper presented at the annual meeting of the Canadian Political Science Association, 2 June, York University, Toronto, Ontario.

–. 2007a. "Canadian Provincial Party Systems: Toward a New Comparative Framework." Paper presented at the annual meeting of the Canadian Political Science Association, 1 June, University of Saskatchewan, Saskatoon, Saskatchewan.

–. 2007b. "Choice or Consensus? The 2006 Federal Liberal and Alberta Conservative Leadership Campaigns." Paper presented at the annual meeting of the Canadian Political Science Association, 30 May, University of Saskatchewan, Saskatoon.

–. 2008a. "Code Politics and the Prairie Paradox: Party Competition in Alberta, Saskatchewan and Manitoba." Paper presented at the annual meeting of the Prairie Provinces Political Science Association, 27 September, University of Regina, Saskatchewan.

–. 2008b. "Solving the Prairie Paradox: Myths and Party Politics in Alberta, Saskatchewan and Manitoba." Paper presented at the annual conference of the Midwest Political Science Association, 3 April, Chicago.

–. 2009a. "Building Bridges: Content and Narrative Analysis of Political Texts." Paper presented at the annual meeting of the Canadian Political Science Association, 27 May, Carleton University, Ottawa.

–. 2009b. "Code Politics: Party System Development on the Canadian Prairies." Paper presented at the annual meeting of the Canadian Political Science Association, 27 May, Carleton University, Ottawa.

–. 2009c. "In Search of Brokerage and Responsibility: Party Politics in Manitoba." *Canadian Journal of Political Science* 42, 1: 211-36.

–. 2009d. "Solving the Prairie Paradox: Codes and Party Politics in Alberta, Saskatchewan and Manitoba." PhD diss., University of Calgary.

–. 2010a. "Political Culture in Manitoba." In *Manitoba Politics and Government: Issues, Institutions, and Traditions,* edited by P.G. Thomas and C. Brown, 42-72. Winnipeg: University of Manitoba Press.

–. 2010b. "Qualitative Document Analysis in Political Science." Paper presented at "From Texts to Political Positions Workshop," 9 April, Vrije Universiteit Amsterdam.

–. 2010c. "Selecting Selinger: The 2009 Leadership Race and the Future of NDP Conventions in Manitoba." *Prairie Forum* 35, 1.

–. 2011. "Staking the Progressive Centre: An Ideational Analysis of Manitoba Party Politics." *Journal of Canadian Studies* 45, 1.

Wesley, Jared J., and David K. Stewart. 2010. "Sterling Lyon." In *The Premiers of Manitoba: 1870-2000,* edited by Barry Ferguson, 307-29. Regina: Great Plains Research Center.

Whitehorn, Alan. 1992. *Canadian Socialism: Essays on the CCF-NDP.* Toronto: Oxford University Press.

Whittington, Michael S. 1978. "Political Culture: The Attitudinal Matrix of Politics." In *Approaches to Canadian Politics*, edited by John H. Redekop, 138-53. Scarborough, ON: Prentice-Hall.

Wildrose Alliance Party of Alberta. 2008. "Our Vision for Alberta." http:www.wild rosealliance.ca.

Wilson, Barry. 1980. *Politics of Defeat: The Decline of the Liberal Party in Saskatchewan*. Saskatoon: Western Producer Prairie Books.

Wilson, John. 1974. "The Canadian Political Cultures: Towards a Redefinition of the Nature of the Canadian Political System." *Canadian Journal of Political Science* 7, 3: 438-83.

Wilson, Richard V. 1992. *Compliance Ideologies: Rethinking Political Culture*. Cambridge: Cambridge University Press.

Wilton, Carol. 2000. *Popular Politics and Political Culture in Upper Canada, 1800-1850*. Montreal/Kingston: McGill-Queen's University Press.

Wiseman, Nelson. 1983. *Social Democracy in Manitoba: A History of the CCF-NDP*. Winnipeg: University of Manitoba Press.

–. 1986. "The Use, Misuse, and Abuse of the National Election Studies." *Journal of Canadian Studies* 21, 1: 21-37.

–. 1988. "The Pattern of Prairie Leadership." In *Prime Ministers and Premiers: Political Leadership and Public Policy in Canada*, edited by Leslie A. Pal and David Taras, 178-91. Scarborough: Prentice-Hall.

–. 1992a. "From Jail Cell to the Crown: Social Democratic Leadership in Manitoba." In *Leaders and Parties in Canadian Politics: Experiences of the Provinces*, edited by R. Kenneth Carty, Lynda Erickson, and Donald E. Blake, 148-69. Toronto: Harcourt Brace Jovanovich Canada.

–. 1992b. "The West as a Political Region." In *Riel to Reform: A History of Protest in Western Canada*, edited by George Melnyk, 278-91. Saskatoon: Fifth House Publishers.

–. 1996. "Provincial Political Cultures." In *Provinces: Canadian Provincial Politics*, edited by Christopher Dunn, 21-62. Peterborough, ON: Broadview Press.

–. 1998. "Tory-Touched Liberalism: Political Culture in Canada." In *Crosscurrents*, edited by Mark Charlton and Paul Barker, 56-67. 5th ed. Scarborough, ON: Nelson.

–. 2001. "The Pattern of Prairie Politics." In *Party Politics in Canada*, edited by Hugh G. Thorburn and A. Whitehorn, 351-68. 8th ed. Toronto: Prentice-Hall.

–. 2002. "Social Democracy in a Neo-Conservative Age: The Politics of Manitoba and Saskatchewan." In *Canada: The State of the Federation 2001: Canadian Political Culture(s) in Transition*, edited by Hamish Telford and Harvey Lazar, 217-39. Kingston: Institute of Intergovernmental Relations.

–. 2006. "Provincial Political Cultures." In *Provinces: Canadian Provincial Politics*, edited by Christopher Dunn, 21-56. 2nd ed. Peterborough, ON: Broadview Press.

–. 2007. *In Search of Canadian Political Culture*. Vancouver: UBC Press.

Wiseman, Nelson, and K. Wayne Taylor. 1979. "Class and Ethnic Voting in Winnipeg during the Cold War." *Canadian Review of Sociology and Anthropology* 16, 1: 60-76.

Wishlow, Kevin. 2001. "Rethinking the Polarization Thesis: The Formation and Growth of the Saskatchewan Party, 1997-2001." In *Saskatchewan Politics: Into the Twenty-First Century,* edited by Howard Leeson, 169-98. Regina: Canadian Plains Research Center.

Women's Auxiliaries of the Social Credit League. 1968. "Women's Auxiliaries of the Social Credit League." Pamphlet, Glenbow Archives, Joe and Roberta Seargent's Social Credit Collection.

Wright, R.W. 1984. "The Irony of Oil: The Alberta Case." In *The Making of the Modern West: Western Canada since 1945,* edited by A.W. Rasporich, 105-14. Calgary: University of Calgary Press.

Young, Walter D. 1978. *Democracy and Discontent.* 2nd ed. Toronto: McGraw-Hill Ryerson.

Index